BECKETT AND PROUST

BECKETT AND PROUST

Nicholas Zurbrugg

COLIN SMYTHE
Gerrards Cross, Bucks
BARNES AND NOBLE BOOKS
Totowa, New Jersey
1988

Copyright © 1988 by Nicholas Zurbrugg

All rights reserved
First published in 1988 by Colin Smythe Limited
Gerrards Cross, Buckinghamshire

British Library Cataloguing in Publication Data

Zurbrugg, Nicholas
 Beckett and Proust.
  1. Beckett, Samuel——Criticism and interpretation
  2. Proust, Marcel——Influence——Beckett
  I. Title
  843'.914   PQ2603.E378Z/

ISBN 0-86140-047-X

First published in the United States of America in 1988 by
Barnes and Noble Books, Totowa, N.J. 07512

ISBN 0-389-20784-5

Set by Action Typesetting Limited, Gloucester
Printed and bound in Great Britain by
Billing & Sons Ltd, Worcester

CONTENTS

ACKNOWLEDGEMENTS

According to Proust, there are few reasons for repeatedly rewriting a book in order to bring it to its fruition. According to Beckett, there are few reasons for writing a book in the first place. Perhaps both Proust and Beckett overlook the catalyst of encouragement.

For too many years, too many travels and too many typewriter ribbons, this book has been sustained by more kindness and encouragement than I can probably remember. Precipitated by my reading of Beckett and Proust in the mid-seventies in Rouen and Norwich, and first forced into what Beckett would call the 'vulgarity of a plausible concatenation' in the late seventies at Oxford, these chapters gradually found their final form in the eighties, during the humid summers of Brisbane, and away from the humid summers of Brisbane, during fellowships at Canberra, Dunedin and Iowa City.

Will Moore, Vera Daniel, Keith Gore, Rosemary Pountney, Anthony Pilkington, James Knowlson, Teresa Francis, Paul Tickell and Francis Warner all guided this book through its early stages. John Fletcher, Stanley Gontarski, Peter Norrish, Nola Leov, Anthony Thorlby and Michael Hollington all encouraged and looked over the later stages of this book in their turn. To all these friends and colleagues, my considerable thanks. In addition, I must also thank James Acheson, John Pilling, Deirdre Bair, James Grauerholz, Phillip Kraeger, Mr. J.A. Edwards of the Reading University Library Beckett Archive, and M. Jérôme Lindon of Les Éditions de Minuit; all of whom facilitated my access to research materials.

Let me additionally express my very sincere thanks to all the institutions whose generosity made my research possible; to St. John's College, Oxford, for the Senior Scholarship that allowed me to prolong my days in the 'home of lost causes'; to the Zaharoff Foundation, for a grant permitting research in Paris; to the Humanities Research Centre, Canberra, for a Summer Fellowship; to the French department of the University of Otago, for offering me a William Davis Visiting Fellowship; to the department of Fine Art, the University of Iowa City, for a Visiting Fellowship, and to the unfailing generosity of the School of Humanities, Griffith University, Brisbane.

Earlier and variant versions of portions of this book have appeared in the following publications. A version of chapter eight was published in *AUMLA*, No.55 (May 1981); earlier sections of chapter nine were published in the *Journal of Beckett Studies*, No.9 (1984) and in *Sub-Stance*, No.48 (1986); and a variant of my argument in the Conclusion appears in *Beckett's Later Fiction and Drama: Texts for Company* (ed. James Acheson and Kateryna Arthur) (London: Macmillan, 1987). My thanks to the editors of these publications for permission to use these materials.

It also gives me particular pleasure to thank all those friends who have helped this book along its way: Joan Camilleri; the poets Henri Chopin and Robert Lax; the artists Lourdes Castro (who drew the silhouettes of Beckett and Proust for the cover of this book), Barry McCallion and Marjorie Jenkins; my research assistant, Susan Lovelock; my publisher, Colin Smythe, for his confidence in this book, and his patience during its completion; and more distantly, Raoul Hausmann, William Burroughs, Brion Gysin, John Cage, Roland Barthes, Jean Baudrillard and Jonathan Culler: *auteurs* extraordinaires, whose pages remain alive with insight and inspiration.

I hope this book proves testimony to my lasting admiration and respect for the writings of Proust and Beckett. Like all scholars, I must add my profound thanks to Samuel Beckett for permission to quote from his unpublished writings, and for all his attention and assistance.

Finally, to my mother and father, who have given me so much and helped me in so many ways, I dedicate this book, long awaited, but possibly, worth the waiting.

Nicholas Zurbrugg
Kersey, 1 October 1987

PREFACE

To read the writings of Marcel Proust or Samuel Beckett is to embark upon the discovery of two of the most complex and most rewarding authors of our century. To embark upon a comparative study of Proust and Beckett is to undertake a critical odyssey which may well flounder, over and over again.

The purpose of this book is to re-evaluate the fiction of Proust and Beckett by comparing and contrasting the different existential visions which arise from their respective responses to the problems of perception and communication; problems which lie at the very heart of Proust's and Beckett's fiction, and which in turn, perhaps, might be said to animate the very heart of 'Modernist' and 'Post-Modernist' fiction.

The general dilemma of Modernist Fiction is succinctly defined by Virginia Woolf, in her famous essay on 'Modern Fiction' of 1919. Woolf argues that if only writers abandoned literary conventions for a fiction of 'feeling', then a new mode of writing might evolve in which there would be 'no plot, no comedy, no tragedy, no love interest or catastrophe in the accepted style'.[1] In the place of realism and its rationalized universe, Woolf proposes a 'varying ... unknown ... uncircumscribed' order of things, commensurate with her conviction that 'Life is not a series of gig lamps symmetrically arranged; life is a luminous halo, a semi-transparent envelope surrounding us from the beginning of consciousness to the end'.[2] The entire radical tradition in Modernist and Post-Modernist literature might be envisaged as a series of alternatives to such 'symmetrically arranged' reality; or in Beckett's memorable formulation, as alternatives to 'the grotesque fallacy of a realistic art — "the miserable statement of line and surface", and the penny-a-line vulgarity of a literature of notations'.[3]

These words from Beckett's early essay *Proust* (1931), both translate and elaborate the passage from Proust's *A la recherche du temps perdu* (published in eight parts between 1913 and 1927) in which the hero, Marcel, vehemently derides realistic literature

1

as: 'la littérature qui se contente de "décrire les choses", d'en
donner seulement un misérable relevé de lignes et de surfaces'
(the literature that contents itself with "describing things", with
merely offering a miserable statement of line and surface).[4] As is
so often the case in Beckett's *Proust*, his argument, and the pithy
jargon with which he presents and ornaments it, are so close in
spirit to Proust's sentiments that it seems obvious that both
writers responded identically towards the limitations of the
'symmetrically arranged' 'literature of notations'.

Yet, as this book will attempt to demonstrate, any similarity
between the conclusions of Proust's fiction and the conclusions
of Beckett's fiction is at best extremely superficial. Indeed,
viewed in a very general perspective, Proust and Beckett might
be differentiated as key figures in the two quite distinct phases of
twentieth-century literature known as Modernism and Post-
Modernism, which, for the sake of convenience, might be
associated respectively with the cultural epochs between 1890
and 1935, and between 1935 and the present day.[5] While both
Modernist and Post-Modern novelists appear hypersensitive to
the problems arising from the relativity of perception, their
solutions to these problems, and their concomitant existential
credos, are frequently as different as chalk and cheese.

For Modernist novelists such as Marcel Proust, reality
remained puzzlingly 'varying', 'unknown' and 'uncircumscribed' until those magic moments of revelation (common to the
final pages of works by such giants of Modernism as Joyce,
Lawrence, Mann, Musil and Woolf),[6] in which the confusions of
habitual perception became resolved in the light of some instant
of transcendental insight. In Proust's case, this insight takes the
form of the 'luminous halo' of involuntary memory. But for the
many Post-Modern novelists such as Samuel Beckett (and here
one might refer to such Post-Modern writers as Burroughs,
Grass and Robbe-Grillet),[7] the cloudy confusions of relative
perception admit of no silver lining or 'luminous halo'. Far from
sharing the Modernist hero's final sense of deliverance *from*
perceptual confusion, the Post-Modern hero frequently experiences unrelieved deliverance *to* perceptual confusion. Thus
Beckett, for example, tellingly caricatures his own work as
evocations of distress for which readers must 'provide their own
aspirin'.[8]

Similarly, whereas the Modernist hero is apt to break out
without warning into ecstatic eulogies of art and literature,
deeming them to be the very embodiment of transcendental

values, the Post-Modern hero (or anti-hero) tends to consecrate his failing energies to the thankless task of delineating the illusions and the poverty of his every utterance. Helpfully illustrating this distinction by comparing his own fiction with that of Joyce, Beckett has poignantly observed:

Joyce is a superb manipulator of material . . . He was making words do the absolute maximum of work . . . The kind of work I do is one in which I'm not master of my material . . . I'm working with impotence, ignorance.[9]

These statements are of course well known, and this distinction between the confident, positive relativism of the Modernist novelist and the pessimistic, negative relativism of the Post-Modern novelist might well appear self-evident. Paradoxically, though, almost all of Beckett's critics effortlessly *equate* the conclusions of Proust and Beckett when discussing Beckett's ideas in *Proust*. This essay is certainly enthralling as a record of Beckett's early responses to Proust's solutions to the relativity of language and perception, but it is certainly not the paragon of critical objectivity that Beckett's admirers believe it to be. Far from offering an accurate account of Proust's values, and thereby revealing the 'law' that many Beckettian critics would identify within both writers' work,[10] Beckett's *Proust* is alarmingly ambiguous.

Sometimes Beckett's essay affords accurate summaries of Proust's ideas, and also indicates certain elementary correspondences between basic assumptions of the two writers. But elsewhere, it perversely conflates the values of its author with those of its subject by attributing Beckett's own distinctively 'anti-Proustian' priorities to the Proustian vision. Slow to distinguish these crucial differences between Proust's and Beckett's ideas, Beckett's critics are over-hasty to assert that both writers share the Proustian virtue that Beckett's *Proust* eloquently defines as: 'spiritual development in the sense of depth', resulting from the act of 'shrinking from the nullity of extracircumferential phenomena' (*PTD*, 64-5).

Neglecting the differences between the two writers' manifestations of 'spiritual development', and exaggerating the superficial similarity between Proustian and Beckettian virtues, most analyses of Beckett's work successively misrepresent Beckett's vision, Proust's vision, and the complex relationship between their respective visions, abundantly substantiating

Beckett's warning in the first sentence of his essay 'Dante . . . Bruno. Vico . . Joyce' (1929), that 'The danger is in the neatness of identifications'.[11] By contrast, analysis of the differences between Proust's and Beckett's responses to the relativity of language and perception allows both their individual visions, and the relationship between them, to be re-evaluated according to the comparative approach that Beckett himself advocated in 'Papini's Dante', an early book review of 1934, in which he suggests that 'Analysis of what a man is not may conduce to an understanding of what he is'.[12]

Seen in terms of Beckett's discussion of the painters Bram and Geer van Velde, in his article 'La Peinture des Van Velde ou le monde et le pantalon' (1945), Proust's and Beckett's fictional responses to their shared preoccupation with the limits of language and perception might be thought of as 'deux oeuvres . . . qui semblent se réfuter, mais qui en fait se rejoignent au coeur du dilemme' (two works . . . which seem to contradict one another, but which in fact overlap at the heart of the problem).[13] Beckett concluded that 'L'analyse de cette divergence . . . aidera peut-être à situer les deux oeuvres, l'un vis-à-vis de l'autre' (The analysis of this divergence . . . might perhaps help to situate the two works, one in terms of the other). So too is it hoped that this book's comparative analysis of the convergences and divergences between Proust's and Beckett's fiction may similarly redefine their individual visions, and clarify the relationship between their works.

The first part of this book will re-evaluate Proust's vision in *A la recherche du temps perdu*, proposing an alternative analysis of this novel to that most frequently elaborated in previous critical studies of Proust. The second part will analyse and re-evaluate Beckett's idiosyncratic account of Proust's vision in his essay *Proust*, indicating the ways in which his argument fluctuates between accurate insights and the wayward interpolation of his own emergent ideas.

Finally, the third section of this book will attempt to re-evaluate Beckett's vision by tracing the ways in which he consistently reverses (and complements) Proustian values throughout his major fictional works, from the unpublished *Dream of Fair to Middling Women* of the early thirties, to *Ill seen ill said*, *Worstward Ho* and other ghostly narratives of the early eighties. Over and over again, Beckett's writings compulsively investigate, appropriate, elaborate, distillate, denigrate, negate and generally illuminate the implications of Proust's most provocative images, themes and motifs. And over and over again, Becket proves himself to be both Proust's opposite and Proust's equal as an explorer of 'Thoughts, no, not thoughts. Profounds of mind'.[14]

Beckett's work could, of course, be discussed in many other comparative contexts, and from time to time this book will consider Beckett's vision in terms of that other giant of Modernism, James Joyce, and in terms of two of the most interesting of Beckett's fellow Post-Moderns, William Burroughs and Roland Barthes.[15] Hopefully, such comparative and contrastive analysis and interpretation casts some light upon its subject. As Beckett himself hints, 'Comparison of texts should give the answer'.[16]

Taking Beckett's hint to heart, this book would attempt to identify the advantages of reassessing the quality of Beckett's and Proust's visions by considering these two remarkable writers in tandem, one in terms of the other. For better or worse, its pages now await the reader. Like Beckett's 'Arsene', the lines below may only add:[17]

What I could say, or at least a part, and I trust not the least diverting, I think I have said ... Now for what I have said ill and for what I have said well and for what I have not said, I ask you to forgive me.

1
PROUST AND CRITICAL PERSPECTIVES

As literary theorists such as Roland Barthes and Michel Foucault
have had occasion to observe, literary criticism has long been
restricted by its compulsion to explain texts in terms of the lives
of their authors. [1] Critical responses to Marcel Proust's *A la
recherche du temps perdu* offer no exception to this rule. For
Proust's life and death offer such a moving example of the way in
which the Modernist writer sacrificed health and wealth to the
'religion' of art that one feels obliged to read his masterpiece as
a thinly veiled autobiographical account of its author's
pilgrimage towards artistic salvation.

Moreover, such a reading appears perfectly consistent with the
plot and the narrative point of view of this novel, which is, after
all, the literary autobiography of a writer named Marcel, who
gradually recounts the way in which he discovered his artistic
vocation. Finally, Marcel affirms that art alone reveals the
meaning of life, confidently proclaiming such maxims as: 'La
vraie vie...c'est la littérature' (III.895) (True life...is literature),
and: 'la vérité suprême de la vie est dans l'art' (III.902) (the
supreme truths of life lie in art). Not surprisingly, Proust's critics
have emphasized that *A la recherche du temps perdu* is primarily a
novel depicting the difficulties of the artistic vocation and
celebrating the transcendant value of art.

Unfortunately, this kind of approach to *A la recherche du temps
perdu* oversimplifies the complexity of Proust's vision by
equating it with the restricted paradigm of his life and with the
restricted perspective of the novel's narrator, rather than
considering the 'implied vision' of *A la recherche du temps perdu* as
a whole, by giving attention to the implications of *all* the points
of view in the novel. [2] Proust might well have written a
conventional, three-hundred page novel simply tracing the
portrait of the artist as a young, middle-aged and elderly man.
But as the three thousand or so pages of *A la recherche du temps*

perdu exhaustingly testify, this extraordinary novel panoramic-
ally juxtaposes the portraits of innumerable young, middle-aged
and elderly artists and non-artists, in a fictional cosmos wherein
Marcel's point of view is but one among many. It is important,
then, to keep Marcel's 'truths' within some sort of perspective,
as Proust himself indicated in a letter to Jacques Rivière.

Writing about the opinions of his immature narrator-hero,
Proust emphasized that Marcel's judgments are frequently
erroneous in the early phases of the novel, and ruefully reflected
that the inattentive reader might well take these judgments
literally and misconstrue the overall, 'implied' values of the
novel. Proust concludes:

Je suis donc forcé de peindre les erreurs, sans croire devoir dire que je les
tiens pour des erreurs; tant pis pour moi si le lecteur croit que je les tiens
pour la vérité. [3]
(I am thus obliged to depict errors, without bothering to admit that I
consider them to be errors; too bad for me if the reader believes that I
consider them to be the truth.)

Significantly, Marcel's mature revelations are not the only
'truths' in *A la recherche du temps perdu*. As has been suggested,
the novel entertains both artistic and non-artistic modes of self-
realization and both artistic and non-artistic truths. Accordingly,
Marcel's final insights are themselves relative rather than
absolute, and require evaluation within the dualistic perspective
of great 'life' and great 'art' that Proust adumbrated in his earlier
novel *Jean Santeuil*, in which the narrator specifies that: 'un grand
homme, une belle oeuvre nous redonnent confiance dans la vie
et dans la pensée' (a great man or a beautiful work of art restore
our confidence in life and in the intellect). [4] By responding over-
literally to Marcel's seductively simplistic suggestion that
authentic existence is attainable *only* through art, Proust's critics
have consistently overlooked the more subtle, dualistic quality of
his vision.

In his early writings, such as his essay 'La Personne
d'Alphonse Daudet "Oeuvre d'Art"' (1897), [5] Proust optimistically intimates that the exceptional individual may embody
both artistic *and* non-artistic values. Hence the very title of this
essay proposes that the writer Alphonse Daudet is himself a
living work of art, insofar as his ebbing life combines both
humane and artistic virtues. Not only does this dying writer
continue to think, compose, dictate and write (*CSB*, 401), but he
also comfortingly radiates the generous and inspiring presence

that Proust qualifies as: 'une véritable grâce royale' (*CSB*, 400) (a truly regal grace). This concept of 'grace' is particularly revealing in Proust's works, since it is the term that he invariably uses to denote exemplary states of being, such as the serenity that his early writings discern in trees and flowers, and such as the elegance and the harmony that his later writings discern in certain exemplary physical and verbal gestures and in certain exemplary musical, literary and artistic compositions.

While the vegetal grace of trees and flowers appears to be a purely 'natural', spontaneous quality, Proust suggests that different manifestations of human grace are the consequence of different kinds of selfless sacrifice and moral effort. Thus, his essay on Alphonse Daudet observes that Daudet is 'détaché de lui-même et tout à nous' (detached from himself, and entirely given to us), and still more tellingly observes that Daudet 'semblait sortir d'une lutte, mais il respirait le calme de la victoire' (*CSB*, 401) (seemed to emerge from a struggle, but breathed with the calm breath of victory). This ethical notion of a 'struggle' for existential 'victory' is fundamental to Proust's ideals in *A la recherche du temps perdu*, where it is given even more explicit formulation during the key episode in which the artist Elstir explains to the young Marcel that:

On ne reçoit pas la sagesse, il faut la découvrir soi-même après un trajet que personne ne peut faire pour nous. .... Les vies que vous admirez, les attitudes que vous trouvez nobles n'ont pas été disposées par le père de famille ou par le précepteur ... Elles représentent un combat et une victoire. (I.864)
(One does not receive wisdom, one has to find it for oneself after a journey that nobody else can make in our place. .... The lives that you admire, the attitudes that you consider to be noble, have not been handed down by the father of the family or by the family tutor. .... They represent a battle and a victory.)

Despite Marcel's claims to the contrary, these sentences contain the key to Proust's existential priorities in *A la recherche du temps perdu*. Repeatedly, the novel suggests that the victories and the defeats of its artistic and non-artistic characters derive from the subtle ethical 'battles' in which they variously determine their destinies. Yet, upon reading Proust's critics, one might well conclude that his vision has no more subtlety than the slogan 'Four legs good, two legs bad', voiced by the pigs in George Orwell's *Animal Farm*. For according to most studies of *A la recherche du temps perdu*, Proust's vision might well be summarized as 'artists good, others bad', since the authors of these studies doggedly decree that while Proust's artists (such as the composer Vinteuil, the painter Elstir, the writer Bergotte, and the would-be writer Marcel) are saved, all of the non-artists in the novel (such as Marcel's grandmother, his mother, and such of his friends as Swann and Saint-Loup) are unequivocally damned. It is perhaps instructive to consider the way in which Proust's critics monotonously oversimplify his vision. A paragraph of examples should suffice to indicate the prevailing temper of almost all studies of *A la recherche du temps perdu*. The recurrent use of the word 'only' betrays their authors' disregard for the fundamental relativism of Proust's vision.

Far from conceding that Proust juxtaposes modes of artistic and non-artistic salvation, and modes of artistic and non-artistic damnation, Michel Raimond argues that 'only . . . great artists . . . have access to authentic existence'; Georges Cattui likewise claims that 'only artists and poets . . . are saved and justified'; Leo Bersani confirms that 'only art . . . is able to fulfill'; and George Stambolian similarly concludes that for Proust 'the only true path to success and salvation . . . is art'.[6] Jean Pommier, Germaine Brée and E.F.N. Jephcott more elaborately insist that: 'Neither the world of society . . . nor love introduce authentic existence. Art alone has the key'; that '(Proust) does not admit that there are several roads that lead to heaven; he only admits one, his, and Bergotte, Vinteuil, Elstir, and the narrator all . . . support his position'; and that as a result of this single-minded concept of authentic existence 'all the other characters have lived in vain . . . salvation can be realised only by artists'.[7] Extending this argument, critics such as Roger Shattuck, Henri Peyre and Jean Rousset conclude that Proust's novel is concerned above all with the transition from 'the provisional nature of life' to 'the straight and narrow path of art'; from 'the plane of existence' to 'that of creation'; and from 'the level of life to its level of artistic creation'.[8] Overawed by the omnipresent Marcel, almost all of Proust's critics share Roger Shattuck's conviction that *A la recherche du temps perdu* is quite simply 'a monument to the artistic vocation'.[9]

A small number of critics tentatively dissent from this dogmatic, 'orthodox' approach to Proust's vision. For example, Ernst Curtius's pioneering study not only concludes that 'artistic creation represents the most perfect mode of experience',[10] but also very interestingly reflects that, although art offers the ideal manifestation of spiritual truth, it is not the only manifestation of such truth. According to Curtius's argument:[11]

Art is ... not the only path leading to the sphere of eternal truth.
Perhaps the laws of spiritual reality are most clearly reflected in art, but
the same laws may be observed in all the other domains of the spirit.

Unfortunately, Curtius's book does not elaborate this
hypothesis. In much the same way, Harry Levin intriguingly
speculates that there may be some equivalence between artistic
and non-artistic instances of selflessness in Proust's novel, since
Proust 'interlinks ... the disinterested imperatives of Vinteuil
and Bergotte with the unselfish motives of Marcel's mother and
grandmother', [12] but, like Curtius, Levin fails to substantiate this
insight. Angus Wilson also fleetingly hints that the ideals of art
may find their counterpart in what he describes as the 'hallowed
ground' of Marcel's relationship with his grandmother; [13] and his
namesake, Edmund Wilson, likewise toys with the possibility
that Proust entertains two sets of standards, 'supplied, on the
one hand, by ... artists ... but on the other hand, by Swann and
by the narrator's mother and grandmother'. [14] But, once again,
Wilson merely outlines his theory, and never elaborates it
comprehensively. At most, he rather plaintively questions the
assumptions of orthodox Proustian criticism, wondering: 'Is it
really true ... that literature and art are the only forms of creative
activity which can enable us to meet and master reality?'. [15]
    The confusions of Edmund Wilson — and, one suspects, of
many other of Proust's critics — appear to be caused by Marcel's
confession that his artistic vocation surpasses all moral
obligations. In Marcel's terms: 'le devoir de mon oeuvre primait
celui d'être poli ou même bon' (III.986) (the demands of my work
had priority over the need to be polite, or indeed to be good).
With either this statement or one of its counterparts in mind,
Wilson speculates that Marcel is 'too selfish to live for others as
his grandmother had done'; [16] a notion which coexists very
uneasily with his previous suggestion that both Marcel and his
grandmother exemplify Proustian standards, and which
patently contradicts Harry Levin's speculation that Proust's
artists and non-artists display similarly 'unselfish motives'.
    In a sense, both Wilson and Levin are partially correct. Wilson
accurately surmises that Marcel's vocation prevents him from
living 'for others as his grandmother had done', and yet Levin
also convincingly argues that Marcel and his grandmother both
pursue their respective vocations most successfully when
obeying 'disinterested imperatives' and 'unselfish motives'. For
here, as in Proust's early essay on Daudet, exemplary actions

seem to occur when the artist or non-artist is 'détaché de lui-même' (*CSB*, 401) (detached from himself), and free from selfish, egotistical desires. However, while the essay on Daudet implies that artistic and non-artistic virtues might be embodied simultaneously by one exemplary living work of art, Proust's mature vision in *A la recherche du temps perdu* suggests that artistic and non-artistic virtues pertain to the mutually exclusive vocations of those artists who create works of art, and of those non-artists who accomplish good deeds. In this respect, Marcel's avowal that his artistic responsibilities take priority over any obligation to be polite or good is not so much a confession of incurable selfishness or amorality (as Wilson supposes it to be), as a statement distinguishing between the artistic quality of his vocation and the benevolent quality of the vocation of non-artists such as his grandmother. If Marcel cannot be 'good', then this is because he cannot simultaneously create works of art *and* accomplish good deeds.

Marcel's distinction does not imply that the exemplary artist is in any way more 'selfish' than the exemplary non-artist. Both necessarily undergo a 'battle' to detach themselves from the selfish motivations of the ego, and therefore both exhibit the same disinterested imperatives discussed by Levin. Yet, at the same time, their analogous sacrifices culminate in different modes of exemplary self-realization, and in this respect Wilson quite accurately specifies that Marcel cannot live for others as his grandmother does. For Marcel can no more devote his life to good deeds than his grandmother can consecrate her life to music, art or literature. Quite simply, their respective talents and their respective vocations are incompatible. Nevertheless, as Marcel reflects in his crucial meditations upon the death of the writer Bergotte, both exemplary works of art and exemplary good deeds are realized only by those who cultivate the three cardinal virtues in *A la recherche du temps perdu*: goodness, scrupulousness, and the unselfishness that Marcel associates with self-sacrifice. Pondering upon the unexpected quality of such great works of art and of such good deeds, he memorably concludes:

il n'y a aucune raison dans nos conditions sur cette terre pour que nous nous croyions obligés à faire le bien, à être délicats, même à être polis, ni pour l'artiste athée à ce qu'il se croie obligé de recommencer vingt fois un morceau ... Toutes ces obligations, qui n'ont pas leur sanction dans la vie présente, semblent appartenir à un monde différent, fondé sur

la bonté, le scrupule, le sacrifice ... ces lois dont tout travail profond de
l'intelligence nous rapproche et qui sont invisibles seulement — et
encore! — pour les sots. (III.187–8)
(there is no earthly reason why we should feel obliged to do good, to be
considerate, or even to be polite, nor indeed why the aetheist artist
should feel obliged to begin a work twenty times in succession ... All of
these obligations, which certainly find no justification in our present
way of life, seem to belong to another world, founded upon goodness,
scrupulousness and sacrifice ... those laws towards which all profound
works of the intelligence draw us, and which are only invisible — and
which only remain invisible! — for fools.)

One could not ask for a clearer statement of Proust's existential
priorities. Looking, for once, beyond the specific obligations of
his own artistic vocation, Marcel unambiguously outlines the
way in which the ethical obligations — or 'laws' — of goodness,
scrupulousness and sacrifice inform both the artistic ideal of
unexpectedly dedicated creativity, and the non-artistic ideal of
unexpectedly dedicated benevolence. Yet, as Beckett cogently
comments in the very first sentence of his essay on Proust, 'The
Proustian equation is never simple' (*PTD*, 11). For, as the reader
discovers, Proust further complicates his existential vision by
suggesting that these two ethically identical ideals are mutually
exclusive. Their incompatibility is best introduced with reference
to another key passage in *A la recherche du temps perdu*, in which
Marcel once again looks beyond the local priorities of his own
vocation, and objectively distinguishes between the prerequisites of this mode of self-realization and the prerequisites of
the antithetical, non-artistic vocation of his friend Robert de
Saint-Loup.

Although Marcel sometimes has mixed feelings about Saint-
Loup, and occasionally argues that friendship is devoid of value,
his thoughts in the following passage perspicaciously concede
that, at their best, Saint-Loup's friendship and good deeds are
informed by the very qualities of benevolence, scruple and
sacrifice that his own meditations upon the death of Bergotte
associate with all kinds of exemplary action. In a very interesting
coda to these reflections upon Saint-Loup, Marcel additionally
explains that if Saint-Loup happens to realize himself through
acts of benevolence and friendship, it is because Saint-Loup is
not an artist, and thus must necessarily realize his best potential
in an 'external' way, in society, in relation to other people. By
contrast, the artist, or those whom Marcel defines elsewhere as
'ceux d'entre nous dont la loi de développement est purement

interne' (I.907) (those among us who must realize themselves according to purely internal laws), must necessarily realize his best potential in an 'internal' way, away from society, in solitude, by creating works of art.

Just as Marcel gradually discovers that the successful artist must avoid the temptation to create derivative or vulgar works, and like Daudet, must 'detach' himself from egotistical concerns, so too does he remark that Saint-Loup avoids vulgar forms of social intercourse, such as the infatuations of the romantic love that he derides as the illusion of the ego. With such subtle distinctions between these two adequate modes of self-realization in mind, Marcel's reflections upon Saint-Loup conclude:

Or, la sincérité et le désintéressement de Saint-Loup étaient ... absolus et c'était cette grande pureté morale qui, ne pouvant se satisfaire entièrement dans un sentiment égoïste comme l'amour, ne rencontrant pas d'autre part en lui l'impossibilité qui existait par exemple en moi de trouver sa nourriture spirituelle autre part qu'en soi-même, le rendait vraiment capable, autant que moi incapable, d'amitié. (I.779)
(However, the sincerity and selflessness of Saint-Loup were ... absolute, and it was this great moral purity, which neither found complete satisfaction in an egotistical emotion such as romantic love, nor felt constrained, as I did, to obtain its spiritual nourishment from within, that made him as truly capable, as I was incapable, of friendship.)

One might well argue that this is at once one of the most important and one of the most neglected passages in *A la recherche du temps perdu*. For despite the fact that these observations clearly attribute the same ethical qualities to 'true' friendship that Marcel subsequently attributes to exemplary art (and thus designate such art and friendship as incompatible but complementary manifestations of analogous spiritual reality), Proust's critics invariably reduce the relativity of this perspective to the inflexibility of Marcel's most prejudiced subjective utterances.

Marcel is particularly prone to contrast the advantages of creative solitude with the disadvantages of social intercourse in such sweeping asides as: 'l'amitié n'est pas seulement dénuée de vertu comme la conversation, elle est de plus funeste' (I.907) (friendship is not simply worthless like conversation, but is downright dangerous). And Proust's critics are in turn irrepressibly prone to equate such partial, 'artistic' truths with the entirety of his existential vision. Responding over-literally and under-critically to such assertions, battalions of books have concluded with André Maurois and Harold March that Proust judged friendship to be 'dangerous' and 'a sheer waste of time'.[17] Even such prudent critics as Gilles Deleuze and George Stambolian suggest that 'friendship never offers anything other than false communications', and that 'Proust associates ... friendship with the superficial self whose "egoism" prevents communication with another'.[18] Yet, as Marcel intimates in the passage above, Saint-Loup communicates authentic benevolence precisely because his actions transcend the superficial egoism of 'un sentiment égoïste comme l'amour'.

This ill-founded negative appraisal of friendship in Proust's novel leads critics to assume that all forms of human relationship in *A la recherche du temps perdu* are equally 'dangerous', and thus confirms the critical cliché that Proust envisaged no other virtue and no other mode of salvation than those of the artist. But, as this book will attempt to indicate, a significant number of passages in *A la recherche du temps perdu* support the alternative thesis that Proust's existential vision is essentially dualistic in quality. Elstir and Marcel (who are both artists, as it happens) maintain that great art and noble lives, dedicated creativity and dedicated good deeds, and true manifestations of art and friendship, are all the consequences of similar existential 'battles', of the same three cardinal 'laws', and of identical self-lessness transcending the superficiality of egotistical satisfaction.

This dualistic perspective may be traced back to Proust's earliest writings. Indeed, the entirety of Proust's work seems to celebrate ideal modes of artistic and non-artistic existence predicated upon his youthful concept of ideal natural harmony. Just as Marcel confides at one point that 'La nature ... m'avait ... mis ... sur la voie de l'art' (III.889) (Nature placed me on the road to art), Proust might well have claimed that the conclusions of his early essays on exemplary natural phenomena placed him on the road towards his subsequent existential priorities.

These early examples of Proust's enthusiasm for natural harmony are best introduced with reference to his short essay 'Allégorie', initially, an uncollected fragment from the typescript of the subsection of *Les Plaisirs et les jours* (1896) entitled *Les Rêveries, regrets couleur du temps*. This self-conscious and somewhat sentimental parable tells the story of a verdant meadow, commonly known as 'the garden', which successively loses all its flowers, all its beauty and all its perfumes — 'tout ce qu'il aimait le mieux' (*PJ*, 177) (everything that it loved most) — in a series of savage storms that finally leave it completely flooded. Eventually though, 'le jardin sentit son eau calmée, devenue pure, parcourue d'une estase infinie' (*PJ*, 178) (the garden felt that its waters had become calm, pure and filled with an infinite ecstasy), since its waters now reflect the rest of nature, uniting it with the cosmos. That this state forms a paradigm for human happiness is made abundantly clear by Proust's conclusion: 'Heureux le coeur ainsi défleuri, ainsi saccagé, si maintenant plein de larmes il peut lui aussi refléter le ciel' (*PJ*, 178) (Happy the heart that has been racked and sacked in this way, if now, full of tears, it too may reflect the heavens).

Not surprisingly, Proust elaborates this ideal in *Jean Santeuil*, the early unfinished novel that he wrote more or less concurrently with his essays in *Les Plaisirs et les jours* during the late 1890s. Advancing from flower to flower and from tree to tree, this novel's youthful hero, Jean Santeuil, receives revelation after revelation from the harmony, the authenticity and the grace of natural phenomena, becoming ever-more 'avide de sympathiser avec toute la nature qui était en lui comme autour de lui' (*JS*, 531) (eager to become at one with all the traces of nature within him and around him). Unlike such Beckettian heroes as Molloy, who morosely comments, 'The glorious, the truly glorious weather would have gladdened any other heart than mine. But I have no reason to be gladdened by the sun and I take good care not to be',[19] Jean Santeuil is exceedingly gladdened by manifestations of sunlit nature. Indeed, as the narrator concludes in the passage below, such visions of harmonious nature offer Jean his first taste of 'perfect joy':

Les bois, les vignes, les pierres elles-mêmes s'étaient harmonisés avec la lumière du soleil et la pureté du ciel, et quand le ciel se voilait, comme par un changement de ton, la multitude des feuilles, la terre des chemins, les toits de la ville, tout restait uni dans un monde nouveau. Et chacun des sentiments de Jean semblait sans effort rester aussi à l'unisson (de) toutes choses, et il sentait cette jouissance parfaite qui résulte de l'harmonie. (*JS*, 492–3)

(The woods, the vines, the very stones, were united in harmony with the brightness of the sun and the purity of the sky, and when the sky became overcast, then, as though by a simple change of tone, the multitude of leaves, the very earth of the roads, the roofs of the town, everything remained united in a new world. And, almost effortlessly, Jean's every sensation seemed a part of this unity, and he knew the perfect joy that comes from harmony.)

Jean Santeuil's discovery of natural harmony prefigures his discovery of similar harmonious qualities in exemplary works of art and in exemplary non-artistic actions, and these in turn anticipate Proust's existential ideals in *A la recherche du temps perdu*. In much the same way, the highly individual, authentic quality of the ideal artistic and non-artistic actions of Proust's heroes is similarly prefigured by the unusual authenticity that Jean Santeuil attributes to certain flowers and trees, such as the solitary digitalis which evinces:

cet isolement, absolu, éternel, qui lui donnait pour la première fois le sentiment de cette chose qui n'en était pas une autre, qui était hors de toutes les autres. *(JS*, 471)
(that absolute, eternal sense of isolation which gave him for the first time the impression of something which had no counterpart, something that was beyond all counterparts.)

Despite his wish to pluck this flower and to take it with him, Jean dares not do so, for as the narrator explains, 'On craint de toucher à ce qui est à ce point soi-même' *(JS*, 471) (One fears to touch something which is so utterly itself). The whole of the existential dilemma in *A la recherche du temps perdu* arises from the difficulties of being utterly and authentically oneself.

Considered together, the harmony and the individuality of the flowers and trees that Jean Santeuil admires combine to form their grace, a quality that Jean repeatedly identifies in such observations as his reverent references to the 'grâce nonchalante' *(JS*, 280) (nonchalant grace) of lilacs, and the 'nonchalance gracieuse' *(JS*, 331) (gracious nonchalance) of a solitary, sunlit tree. Like the harmony and the individuality that Jean Santeuil first discerns in nature, this sense of grace is also identified in the exemplary artistic and non-artistic actions that Proust celebrates both in *Jean Santeuil* and in *Les Plaisirs et les jours*. His introduction to *Les Plaisirs et les jours* is particularly interesting in this respect, since it tentatively equates both of these human modes of grace by comparing the moral and spiritual grace of his late friend Willie Heath with the artistic grace of the paintings of Van Dyck and da Vinci.

Entitled 'A mon ami Willie Heath', this introductory essay dedicates *Les Plaisirs et les jours* to Willie Heath in homage to his 'élégance morale' *(PJ*, 6) (moral elegance), and then attempts to define this special quality with reference to Van Dyck and da Vinci, concluding:

Mais si la grâce de votre fierté appartient de droit à l'art d'un Van Dyck, vous releviez plutôt du Vinci par la mystérieuse intensité de votre vie spirituelle. (*PJ*, 6).
(But if your proud grace obviously belongs to the art of a painter like Van Dyck, you have more in common with da Vinci in terms of the mysterious intensity of your spiritual life.)

This comparison of non-artistic and artistic manifestations of grace is not a passing coincidence. Proust plays with the concept of 'grace' on five occasions in this text, and repeats this comparison elsewhere in *Les Plaisirs et les jours*, in 'Portrait de Madame ***', an essay in which he similarly refers to 'une grâce qui trouble à l'égal d'une émotion artistique' (*PJ*, 166) (a quality of grace that disturbs with the intensity of an artistic emotion). For the purposes of this survey of Proust's early existential priorities, the most revealing example of his concept of non-artistic grace is to be found in *Jean Santeuil*, in the description of the remarkable way in which Bertrand de Réveillon reveals and communicates his friendship for Jean. Significantly, Bertrand's affection is revealed by gestures which exemplify each of the ideals that Jean discovers in nature. They are harmonious, utterly authentic, and astonishingly graceful.

This outstanding display of friendship occurs as Bertrand climbs onto and races over the tables of a crowded café in order to greet Jean Santeuil as rapidly as possible. This gesture is, of course, an earlier variant of the identical episode in *A la recherche du temps perdu* (in which Robert de Saint-Loup similarly manifests his friendship for Marcel by leaping over a series of table tops in a crowded café), and is therefore doubly fascinating, both as a key incident in Proust's early writing, and as the precursor of an equally consequential episode in his mature writing.

A casual reading of this passage reveals that Bertrand de Réveillon's gesture has much in common with the heroic last days of Daudet. Just as Daudet is praised for his 'véritable grâce royale', Bertrand's movements are described as being 'impalpable et gracieuse' (*JS*, 447) (impalpable and graceful), and as exhibiting 'quelque chose d'un peu irréel, de gracieux et de charmant' (*JS*, 451) (something a little unreal, something graceful and charming). Just as Daudet's grace offers the calming influence of its 'grandeur réconfortante' (*CSB,*400) (comforting grandeur), Bertrand's graceful movements are similarly 'infiniment reposante' (*JS*, 454) (infinitely restful). Finally, just as Daudet gives his all to his visitors, being 'tout à nous', so too is

Bertrand praised as 'un hôte généreux qui donne tout ce qu'il possède' (*JS*, 453) (a generous host who gives away everything that he possesses). Further analysis reveals that this episode is still more interesting in terms of the way in which it attempts to define the preconditions of this generous, comforting and graceful gesture.

While Proust's essay on the dying Daudet is predominantly eulogistic in tone, rather than analytical, and at most suggests that Daudet's grace arises from his selflessness — or the fact that he is completely 'détaché de lui-même' — the description of Bertrand's grace in *Jean Santeuil* carefully identifies the factors contributing to this exemplary manifestation of friendship. In so doing, it implicitly or explicitly introduces a number of the crucial distinctions that subsequently inform Proust's vision in *A la recherche du temps perdu*. These distinctions are particularly important in terms of the way in which they distinguish between relative and absolute modes of perception and communication, by contrasting the habitual, voluntary, and self-conscious actions of everyday existence with the non-habitual, involuntary and 'unconscious' actions that pertain to a 'universal' mode of existence. It is suggested that while the former categories may at best express partial, relative, and counter-productively 'personal' truths, the latter categories permit the expression and the apprehension of authentic, absolute, and exemplarily 'impersonal' formulations of the highest artistic and non-artistic truths. Such truths appear to share both the 'absolute, eternal' quality that Jean Santeuil initially attributes to those perfectly realized flowers which are 'beyond all counterparts', and the capacity to communicate the 'perfect joy' that Jean first perceives in revelations of natural harmony.

Jean Santeuil commences his analysis of Bertrand's grace by examining its habitual qualities. To some extent, this grace derives from Bertrand's aristocratic upbringing, which pre-scribes the superficial gracefulness that Jean identifies with Bertrand's 'élégance aristocratique' (*JS*, 450) (aristocratic elegance). Secondly, and more significantly, Bertrand's grace also derives from the habitual moral scruples that might be defined in terms of Proust's concept of 'élégance morale' (*PJ*, 6) (moral elegance). These scruples consciously reject two distinct existential obstacles: 'la frivolité (qui) ... nous retire l'état de grâce' (*JS*, 522) (the frivolity which withdraws our sense of grace), and the narrow social values which inhibit authentic affection. In other words, if Bertrand's habitual exposure to aristocratic conventions prescribes his 'aristocratic elegance', the 'moral elegance' of his scruples leads him to reject the restrictions of these social conventions in order to manifest his benevolence as fully as possible. Reconstructing Bertrand's motivations, Jean Santeuil speculates that Bertrand must have reasoned: 'Ces convenances, je les écarte, je les réduis en cendres, j'en fais un trophée qu'avec ma grâce que j'ignore je dépose à tes pieds.' (*JS*, 452) (These social conventions, I'm brushing them aside, I'm reducing them to ashes, and, with a grace of which I'm unaware, I present them as a trophy, at your feet.) This speculation is tellingly paradoxical. Although Bertrand may consciously determine to reject social conventions, it is clearly beyond his capabilities to meditate upon grace of which he is unaware. With this paradox, Jean Santeuil's analysis introduces the non-habitual quality of Bertrand's grace.

While Bertrand's grace initially derives from the habitual influence of his upbringing and from the more active habitual influence of his premeditated scruples, it finally appears independent of his volition, appearing as 'une grâce qui s'ignorait' (*JS*, 454) (an unconscious grace). Jean Santeuil categorically insists that 'il n'y a grâce que si ... elle est inconsciente' (*JS*, 453) (grace cannot exist unless ... it is unconscious), and then explains that far from being a preordained, hereditary factor, this unconscious quality is symptomatic of the infinitely more prestigious universal factor that seems to inform man's most authentic modes of artistic and non-artistic communication.

This universal quality appears to be peculiar to ideal truths which are both manifested and perceived by 'universal' faculties which transcend the relativity of habitual experience and the superficiality of the ego. Accordingly, such universal actions are neither something in which the exemplary artist or non-artist may take pride, nor indeed something that can be consciously achieved, although it seems that they may be consciously facilitated by the existential scruples and battles which eliminate obstacles to successful self-realization. With such distinctions in mind, Jean Santeuil concludes his meditations upon the 'universal' significance of Bertrand's graceful benevolence by pondering upon the paradox that Bertrand's most authentic expression of his affection is ironically something of which Bertrand is unaware, something that he could not claim as his very own achievement, and, still more curiously, something that appears quite distinct from the habitual relationship that they associate with their friendship:

Car la beauté de cette signification est une vérité dont l'individu est porteur et symbole, et non auteur. De là vient que la perception d'un tel rapport, ne s'adressant en nous qu'a l'esprit universel, ne peut nous donner que de la joie. Pardon, Bertrand, d'avoir, ce soir-là, aimé en vous une beauté dont ne pouvait s'enorgueillir votre amour-propre, et qui ne pouvait entrer dans notre affection. (*JS*, 455).
(For the beauty of this significance resides in a mode of truth of which the individual is the bearer or the symbol, and not the author. From this it follows that the perception of such relations, which only address our universal faculties, can only bring us joy. Forgive me then, Bertrand, if, that evening, I loved in you a beauty which can no more flatter your self-esteem than it can claim to play a part within our friendship.)

Jean Santeuil's final musings are perhaps an overstatement. Strictly speaking, Bertrand's universal gestures are an aspect of their friendship, although Jean might well argue that the quality of these benevolent gestures is quite distinct from the quality of their habitual acts of friendship. Put another way, Bertrand's gestures introduce an alternative dimension of 'universal' friendship, revealing the kind of solicitude that Proust's *A la recherche du temps perdu* subsequently designates as 'la parfaite amitié' (II.415) (perfect friendship). Despite this minor ambiguity, this passage is particularly significant as one of the most detailed early formulations of Proust's concept of the 'universal' communication and apprehension of 'universal' truths, and indeed, of his concomitant notion that the exemplary, 'universal' truth is something of which the exemplary artist or non-artist is 'porteur ... et non auteur' (the bearer and not the author).

While this episode in *Jean Santeuil* elaborately exemplifies and analyses the advantages of a non-artistic mode of 'universal' communication, a number of Proust's other early essays discuss the parallel advantages of artistic and literary variants of this process. Closely following the suggestion that Bertrand de Réveillon's graceful, universal gestures offer an invaluable alternative to the social conventions that he brushes aside, Proust's essay entitled 'Chardin et Rembrandt' argues that such artists owe their greatness to the fact that they reveal 'le monde réel' (the real world) by helping mankind to:

sortir d'un faux idéal pour pénétrer largement dans la réalité, pour y retrouver partout la beauté, non plus prisonnière affaiblie d'une convention ou d'un faux goût, mais libre, forte, universelle. (*CSB*, 380) (leave a false ideal in order to enter reality more profoundly, and to discover all of its beauty, no longer the feeble prisoner of a convention or of a deceptive fashion, but free, strong, and universal.)

In much the same way, Proust's meditations upon 'Les Éblouissements par la comtesse de Noailles' distinguish between the enduring values of 'le moi profond' (*CSB*, 537) (the profound self), and the superficiality of 'le moi social, contingent' (*CSB*, 536) (the contingent, social self). Proust extends this distinction in his '*Notes sur la littérature et la critique*', which reflect upon the way in which these two aspects of the self attribute radically different values to great literature. Viewed from the habitual perspective of the social self, great literature merely appears to embody subjective or personal truths, and is thus of limited validity. But viewed from the non-habitual perspective of the profound or universal self, great literature may be defined as the objective and impersonal revelation of universal truths, and is therefore of considerable validity. Encapsulating these considerations in one of his interminable sentences, Proust concludes:

Les écrivains que nous admirons . . . nous montrent (que) ce qui a paru précieux et vrai à ce moi tout de même un peu subjectif qu'est notre moi oeuvrant, l'est aussi, d'une valeur plus universelle, pour les moi analogues, pour ce moi plus objectif, ce tout-le-monde cultivé que nous sommes quand nous lisons, l'est non seulement pour notre monade particulière mais aussi pour notre monade universelle. (*CSB*, 311) (The writers that we admire . . . show us that those things which appear precious and true to the predominantly subjective self that forms our everday working self, are also valuable, in a more universal way, to other analogous selves, that is to say, to that more objective self of the cultivated everyman that we all become when we are reading, and are thus of value not only for our individual monad, but also, for our universal monad.)

It follows that both the creation and the apprehension of great art necessitate the 'universal' capacity to look beyond habitual, subjective reality.

As one might well surmise after reading these early essays, the mature Proustian vision of *A la recherche du temps perdu* similarly advocates that the relativity of habitual experience be remedied by universal values, universal creativity, and universal modes of communication and perception. Upon reaching the final pages of this novel, it comes as no surprise to learn that his preceding

existential adventures have at long last led Marcel to determine
to reformulate his revelations within 'un langage universel'
(III.903) (a universal language), for the benefit of 'l'esprit
universel' (III.897) (the universal consciousness) of his readers.

Moreover, as one might also anticipate after considering both
Proust's early writings and the endless critical studies of his
work, *A la recherche du temps perdu* does not confirm the conclusions of its critics by neatly equating authentic existence with
artistic existence, but analyses the difficulties of successful self-
realization in terms of a vast hierarchy of artistic and non-artistic
actions. Indeed, rather than evaluating these dual modes of self-
realization in terms of the binary values that his early writings
associate with 'social' and 'universal' modes of reality — Proust's
A la recherche du temps perdu contemplates and evaluates the
actions of its artists and non-artists within a tripartite framework
of positive, negative and nihilistic modes of reality; a complex
and subtle perspective, that Beckett's imperfect essay on Proust
perfectly defines as 'dualism in multiplicity' (*PTD*, 11). The
following chapter will consider Proust's presentation of the
variously 'positive' modes of existence in *A la recherche du temps
perdu*.

2

POSITIVE MODES OF EXISTENCE IN *A LA RECHERCHE DU TEMPS PERDU*

As Beckett had occasion to observe in one of his early book reviews, it is by no means easy to evaluate Proust's characters. For far from helpfully incarnating the kind of permanent virtues and vices that Virginia Woolf might have likened to 'a series of ethical gig lamps symmetrically arranged', the wayward heroes of *A la recherche du temps perdu* bewilderingly exhibit the most disparate ethical impulses. At their simplest they evince the unusual ability to be what Beckett termed 'a saint and a snob in the one breath', while, at their most perplexing, their contradictions culminate in the confusions that Beckett enthusiastically associated with 'the stupifying antics of those two indeterminates, Charlus and Albertine'.[1]

Charlus and Albertine are certainly two of the most baffling offspring of Proust's imagination, and yet, with the single exception of Albertine's 'antics', the actions of all Proust's characters seem susceptible to classification within the positive, negative and nihilistic categories that we have attributed to his vision. Put another way, these categories appear to demarcate the different ethical zones within which Proust's characters successively rise and fall, and within which they fleetingly reveal the ethical 'gig lamps' of their most accomplished and most impoverished actions. Of all Proust's characters, Albertine offers the solitary substantial exception to this pattern. For she alone remains immature and ethically neutral, trapped, as it were, within a zone of habitual hedonism. By contrast, all her fellow characters break away from habitual existence whenever they follow the ethically potent directives of their positive, negative and nihilistic impulses. Considered in geometric terms, as parts of a sphere of existential possibilities, their variously positive and variously negative non-habitual actions might be represented respectively as upper and lower semi-circles of non-habitual action, subdivided by a horizontal diameter representing the habitual modes of action to which these two semi-circles of non-habitual action offer antithetical alternatives. Placed in diagrammatic summary, these two non-habitual alternatives to habitual existence might be represented by the following figure:[2]

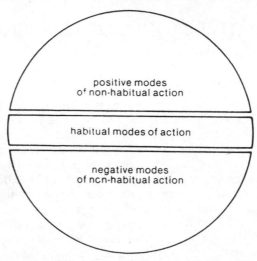

positive modes
of non-habitual action

habitual modes of action

negative modes
of ncn-habitual action

The characteristics of 'habitual' modes of existence are usually defined by the general maxims about 'people', or 'one' or 'we' that Marcel and other characters intermittently formulate throughout *A la recherche du temps perdu*. For example, Charlus scornfully comments: 'La vérité c'est que les gens voient tout par leur journal' (III.785) (The fact is that people see everything in terms of what they read in their newspapers); while Marcel similarly comments upon the limitations of habitual modes of perception in such asides as 'on prend toujours un nom dans son acceptation actuelle' (III.993) (one always responds to a name in terms of its current status), and 'le temps qui change les êtres ne modifie pas l'image que nous avons gardée d'eux' (III.987) (time, which modifies all beings, makes no impression upon the images of them that we remember).

Nevertheless, despite the fact that Proust considers the general consequences of habitual existence in such passing observations, and that he also exemplifies the specific consequences of habitual existence in his accounts of such varied characters as Albertine, Mme Verdurin, and Elstir, his abiding interest in *A la recherche du temps perdu* is not so much the quality and the consequences of habitual existence, as the quality and the consequences of his characters' alternatives to habitual reality. Although the limitations of habitual existence affect all of Proust's characters, their lives seem primarily significant in terms of the ways in which they elaborate positive and negative modes of non-habitual action. In this respect, Proust's fictional concerns share something of the unbridled passion for the extremes of human behaviour that Charlus amusingly reveals when declaring: 'Je déteste le genre moyen ... il me faut ou les princesses de la tragédie classique ou la grosse farce. Pas de milieu.' (III.830) (I hate anything average ... I must either have princesses from high tragedy or else low farce. Nothing middling).

Accordingly, the extremes of positive action in the novel are best introduced not so much by contrast with 'middling' habitual actions, as by contrast with its extremes of negative action. These negative actions are in turn best introduced as the manifestations of what Marcel terms: 'le monde inhumain du plaisir' (I.164) (the inhuman world of pleasure). This curious concept derives from Marcel's distinction between negative modes of existence characterized by their 'inhuman' appetite for the superficial and frequently cruel gratification of immediate 'pleasures', and positive modes of existence characterized by their patient attainment of the more profound and more benign satisfaction that Proust associates with 'joys' born of the sacrifice of such dehumanizing 'pleasures'.

Marcel introduces these distinctions between positive 'joys' and less positive 'pleasures', and between the positive and negative forms of sacrifice which precede them, in *Un Amour de Swann*. Reflecting upon the ironic way in which Swann impetuously sacrifices future 'joys' with his mistress Odette, in order to savour the superficial satisfaction of alleviating his jealous suspicion of her infidelity, Marcel grimly comments: 'Que de bonheurs possibles dont on sacrifie ainsi la réalisation à l'impatience d'un plaisir immédiat!' (I.274) (How frequently we sacrifice the realization of potential joys in our haste to attain immediate pleasure!).

Offering a splendid example of the baffling way in which Proust's characters may one minute embody existential folly, and the next minute denounce the folly of their behaviour, it is Swann himself who subsequently elaborates these distinctions by emphasizing the spiritual value of those generous souls who are willing to sacrifice such imperious pleasures for the well-being of their friends. According to Swann:

il y a des soirs où un être d'une essence un peu délicate doit savoir
renoncer à un plaisir, quand on le lui demande ... puisque c'est sur sa
réponse qu'on classera une fois pour toutes sa qualité d'âme. (I.289–90)
(there are certain evenings when any reasonably sensitive being should
know how to renounce a pleasure, when requested to do so ... since it
is upon the basis of their response that their spiritual quality will be
evaluated once and for all.)

Swann subsequently refines these distinctions still further when
didactically pleading with Odette to consider her spiritual
quality:[3]

Ce qu'il faut savoir, c'est si vraiment tu es cet être qui est au dernier rang
de l'esprit ... l'être méprisable qui n'est pas capable de renoncer à un
plaisir. Alors, si tu es cela, comment pourrait-on t'aimer, car tu n'es
même pas une personne, une créature définie, imparfaite, mais du
moins perfectible? Tu es une eau informe qui coule selon la pente qu'on
lui offre, un poisson sans mémoire et sans réflexion, qui, tant qu'il vivra
dans son aquarium, se heurtera cent fois par jour contre le vitrage qu'il
continuera à prendre pour de l'eau. (I.290)
(What I need to know, is whether or not you are really one of those
beings at the very lowest level of the spirit ... one of those despicable
beings who are incapable of renouncing a pleasure. For, if this is what
you are, then how could one love you, for you would not even be a
person, a definite being, imperfect, but at least perfectible? You would
simply be formless water, flowing with the lie of the land, a fish without
memory or mind, which, so long as it survives in its aquarium, hurtles
a hundred times each day against the glass that it continually confuses
with open water.)

While the severity of these confidences does little to substantiate
Swann's reputation as a sensitive and seductive lover, his
terminology offers the reader of *A la recherche du temps perdu* a
number of extremely helpful concepts.

Quite clearly addressing 'la valeur spirituelle d'Odette' (I.290)
(the spiritual value of Odette), rather than any merely intellectual
qualities, Swann's comments initially establish that Proust's
characters inhabit a hierarchy of spiritual values, in which the
lowest form of spiritual life is equated with those characters who
cannot sacrifice superficial pleasures. These suggestions appear
quite consistent with the substance of *A la recherche du temps
perdu*, which not only advocates the selfless sacrifice that Marcel
numbers among the three cardinal virtues in his meditations
upon the death of Bergotte (III.188), but explicitly contrasts the
spiritual profundity of those exemplary actions accomplished

when characters such as Saint-Loup define themselves as 'ces êtres qui savent se refuser un plaisir' (II.860) (those capable of refusing pleasure), with the spiritual poverty of those noxious actions which come about when characters such as Mme Verdurin 'n'avait pas eu le courage de renoncer à un plaisir' (III.239) (lacked the courage to renounce pleasure). In each of these instances, Saint-Loup and Mme Verdurin transcend the spiritual neutrality of habitual existence.

Bearing this distinction in mind, it would seem that Swann's conclusion confuses two distinct modes of existence by simultaneously accusing Odette of both the spiritual impoverishment of those who cannot refuse pleasures, and the spiritual neutrality of those who are not even imperfect beings, but 'formless'. While the latter concept nicely defines the inactive, unreflective, and ultimately amoral condition of habitual existence, it applies less happily to the active, reflective and ultimately immoral condition of those who consciously sacrifice their positive potential in order to attain superficial pleasures. In other words, Odette, like all of Proust's characters, save perhaps for the 'indeterminate' Albertine, is best defined as 'une créature définie, imparfaite, mais du moins perfectible'(I.290) (a definite being, imperfect, but at least perfectible). Nevertheless, despite the inaccuracy of Swann's general conclusions, his specific formulae prove to be particularly appropriate concepts for defining both the majority of Proust's characters, who are all 'imperfect, but ... perfectible', and for defining the inscrutable and amoral Albertine, who of all Proust's characters is most accurately conceived of as 'formless water' rather than as 'a definite being'.

Proust's critics are particularly fond of assuming that Marcel's vain attempts to define the unknown quantity of Albertine's character typify the difficulties of all human intercourse; indeed Beckett boldly asserts that 'The tragedy of the Marcel-Albertine liaison is the type-tragedy of the human relationship' (*PTD*, 18). Nevertheless, although the 'Marcel-Albertine liaison' exemplifies many of the perceptual errors that Proust attributes to all amorous relationships, Marcel's confusion before Albertine is as atypical of human relationships as a whole in *A la recherche du temps perdu*, as Albertine herself is atypical of the characters in this novel. For whereas almost all of her fellow characters are at least partially 'formed', or are certainly hard at work 'forming' or 'deforming' their potential according to their different existential decisions, Albertine offers the peculiar instance of a Proustian character who, in Swann's terms, is 'not even ... a person, a

definite being', but a 'formless' being. As such, she is not just an
unknown quantity, but is also an unknowable quantity, since
she quite literally has no specific identity. At most, she reflects
the hedonistic habits and whims of the inscrutable nymphets
among whom she leaps and bounds.

Upon first glimpsing Albertine and her friends, Marcel is
particularly attracted to the very formless and anonymous
quality of their 'beauté fluide, collective et mobile' (I.790) (fluid,
collective and mobile beauty), and before long he persuades himself that the soft plasticity of Albertine's mobile features shares
the mysterious quality of the sea. Elaborating this fancy in a
rapturous tirade offering every indication that Albertine's enigmatic physiognomy evinces the same 'universal' quality that
Proust eulogizes in such early essays as 'Allégorie' (*PJ*, 177-8),
Marcel contentedly concludes that her seductive physical
immaturity is infinitely superior to the unprepossessing maturity
that he associates with the 'complete solidification' of 'un visage
que les luttes de l'existence on durci' (I.906) (a face hardened by
life's struggles). According to his reasoning:

l'adolescence est antérieure à la solidification complète et de là vient
qu'on éprouve auprès des jeunes filles ce rafraîchissement que donne le
spectacle des formes sans cesse en train de changer, de jouer en une
instable opposition qui fait penser à cette perpétuelle recréation des
éléments primordiaux de la nature qu'on contemple devant la mer.
(I.906)
(adolescence is anterior to this complete solidification, and it is for this
reason that the company of young girls offers us the same refreshing
sensation that we encounter before the spectacle of all ceaselessly
changing forms evincing that unstable interplay of opposing forces
which reminds us of the perpetual re-creation of the primordial
elements of nature that we contemplate before the sea.)

The flaw in this argument is that it evinces the same ethical
naivety which informs both the amoral movements and the
amoral perceptions of Albertine and her friends. Indeed, as
Marcel subsequently discovers when reflecting more objectively
upon Albertine, her seductive physical immaturity is but the tip
of the infinitely disturbing ethical iceberg of her spiritual
immaturity. Unlike the mature face to which Marcel refers, and
unlike the flooded meadow described by Proust in 'Allegorie',
Albertine has no experience of 'life's struggles'. And quite unlike
the rest of the characters in *A la recherche du temps perdu*, who all
consciously respect or consciously reject moral standards in their

effort to attain 'joys' or 'pleasures', she and her friends are oblivious to standards of any kind, save for the amoral and hedonistic 'standard' of their own adolescent grace.

Accordingly, Albertine's 'refreshing' physical elegance exemplifies the most elementary manifestation of human grace, rather than a 'universal' quality. By the same token, Marcel's initial unreserved enthusiasm for her amoral physical grace exemplifies a correspondingly elementary mode of perception, rather than the kind of ideal 'universal' lucidity advocated by Proust's early essays. Briefly, Marcel's first impressions of Albertine are as superficial and as ethically 'incomplete' as she is herself. By contrast, Marcel's ensuing insights reveal that Albertine and her friends are not the 'nobles et calmes modèles de la beauté humaine' (I.791) (noble and calm models of human beauty) that he first imagines them to be, but rather a group of conceited and amoral adolescents who both pride themselves upon their habitual 'maîtrise de gestes' (I.789) (mastery of gestures), and judge other people according to the analogous 'virtue' of:

un certain mélange de grâce, de souplesse et d'élégance physique, seule forme sous laquelle elles pussent se représenter ... la promesse de bonnes heures à passer ensemble. (I.790)
(a certain mixture of grace, suppleness and physical elegance, the only form under which they could visualize ... the presence of someone offering them hours of fun.)

Marcel's ability to make such discriminations and to identify the way in which Albertine and her friends are 'incapables de subir un attrait d'ordre intellectuel ou moral' (I.790) (incapable of responding to an intellectual or moral quality) is doubly significant. Firstly, it exemplifies the more subtle quality of his own values and perceptions. Secondly, it also prepares the reader for his more ambitious analyses of more substantial manifestations of human grace then either Albertine's amoral 'grâce infantine' (III.115) (infantile grace), or the adult equivalent of this kind of studied, superficial grace that he derisively dismisses as: 'La simple gymnastique élémentaire de l'homme du monde' (I.202) (The simple, elementary gymnastics of high society). These substantial manifestations of human grace are best introduced with reference to the graceful leaping movements of Saint-Loup.

Like Bertrand de Réveillon before him, in *Jean Santeuil*, Saint-Loup realizes his benevolent potential most authentically when he races over the table-tops of a crowded restaurant in order to offer his unreserved attention to a friend — in this case, the ailing Marcel. As in *Jean Santeuil*, this graceful gesture is particularly important as an example of 'universal' non-artistic communication transcending the superficiality of those conventional gestures that Marcel derides as the 'elementary gymnastics' of the man of the world. Paradoxically, Proust's critics have consistently maintained that Saint-Loup's leaping movements reveal no more prestigious quality than the physical elegance of those who inherit the gift of aristocratic social graces.

This confusion is of crucial importance, for, as Jean Santeuil remarks, the elementary gymnastics of good manners and the exemplary actions that best realize man's spiritual values are mutually exclusive:

si l'on songe que l'automatisme appelé bonnes manières détruit toute spontanéité, toute exercise véritable de l'esprit, toute possibilité de poésie, on concevra aussi que le véritable exercice de l'esprit, la poésie, détruise tout automatisme et toutes bonnes manières. (*JS*, 525)
(if one recollects that the automatism known as good manners destroys all spontaneity, all true workings of the spirit, and all possibility of poetry, then one will also appreciate that all true workings of the spirit, all kinds of poetry, destroy all traces of automatism and good manners.)

It follows from this observation that if all non-artistic gestures simply reflect the superficial refinement of good manners, then all true workings of the spirit and all 'poetry' are peculiar to the artist. This is, of course, precisely the conclusion towards which Proust's critics canter after crudely typecasting Saint-Loup's movements as yet another of Proust's examples of spiritually impoverished social graces.

The shortcomings of this approach are best indicated by contrasting the surprising simplicity of most critical accounts of Saint-Loup's leaping movements with the complexity of Marcel's analysis of Saint-Loup's 'parfaite amitié' (II.415) (perfect friendship). As we shall see, Marcel stipulates that Saint-Loup's gestures share all the spiritual qualities that he also identifies in exemplary works of art, and that, like great art, his movements transcend the limitations of habitual reality and habitual modes of communication. But let us briefly consider the conclusions of those critics for whom all Proustian artists seem as superior as their non-artistic counterparts (such as Saint-Loup) appear irredeemably inferior.

Like Beckett, most of Proust's critics attribute Saint-Loup's grace to his 'excessively good birth and breeding' (*PTD*, 66). Henri Peyre refers to Saint-Loup's 'mechanical ... generosity', and Germaine Brée similarly argues that his movements are pre-destined, so that 'any apparent development in personality is a sham'.[4] Confirming this thesis, Howard Moss refers to his 'inherited grace'; Gaëtan Picon posits that Saint-Loup is admired because of 'the ancient race perceived beneath his apparent individuality'; and E.F.N Jephcott suggests that he pleases Marcel primarily as 'a manifestation of the law of heredity'; while Adele King speculates that 'Saint-Loup is so aristocratic in his bodily grace that there was no more aristocracy left in his hereditary make-up to give nobility to his mind'.[5]

Albert Feuillerat more perceptively discerns a degree of nobility in Saint-Loup's leap, suggesting that it functions as an alternative to the unscrupulous behaviour of his aristocratic friends; but he then oversimplifies the function of this nobility by triumphantly declaring it to be Proust's fictional monument to the nobility of his late friend Bertrand de Fénelon.[6] Challenging Feuillerat for reducing the complexity of *A la recherche du temps perdu* to the simplicity of a *roman à clef*, F.C. Green oversimplifies the significance of Saint-Loup's gestures in his turn by suggesting that they exemplify 'the result of the artist's *acte intellectuel*',[7] rather then any special degree of spiritual nobility. Nevertheless, for all its limitations, Green's conclusion has the distinction of deriving from an inspired misreading of Marcel's persistently neglected analysis of Saint-Loup's graceful movements.

Marcel initially compares Saint-Loup with a racehorse, describing his movements as an 'exercise de voltige' (II.411) (a jumping display), and the careless reader might well assume that Saint-Loup's movements share the triviality of Marcel's ter-minology. But as Green's conclusions indicate, Marcel explicitly dissociates the superiority of Saint-Loup's graceful gestures from the vulgar 'elementary gymnastics' of high society, by carefully explaining:

S'il n'avait pas ... aimé quelque chose de plus élevé que la souplesse innée de son corps, s'il n'avait pas été si longtemps détaché de l'orgeuil nobiliare, il y eût eu ... une vulgarité importante dans ses manières. (II.414)
(If he had not ... loved something more elevated than the innate suppleness of his body, and if he had not been long detached from aristocratic pride, there would have been ... a self-important vulgarity in his manners.)

Green associates this 'something more elevated' with the *'superior intelligence'* which, he claims, 'impels Saint-Loup to make friends outside his own class'.[8] This assumption overestimates the intellectual quality of Saint-Loup's graceful movements, and underestimates their far more significant spiritual and moral qualities.

Marcel certainly attributes Saint-Loup's remarkable movements to 'un choix que l'on ne peut faire que dans les hauteurs de l'intelligence' (II.415) (a choice that can only be made in the heights of the intelligence). But, as in his subsequent reference to the way in which the three 'laws' of goodness, scruple and sacrifice inform 'tout travail profond de l'intelligence' (III.188) (all profound works of the intelligence), his emphasis is upon the ethical heights and the ethical profundity of such choices and such works, rather than upon any purely cerebral or rational quality pertaining to the intelligence. Significantly, this ethical quality not only corresponds to the ethical quality that Marcel discerns in the work of the exemplary artists in *A la recherche du temps perdu*, but also elaborates the ethical principles that Proust attributes to exemplary artists and non-artists in his early essays, and in *Jean Santeuil*.

For example, just as the dying Daudet is 'détaché de lui-même' (*CSB*, 401), Saint-Loup is detached both from the naive love of physical elegance that Marcel first encounters in Albertine and her friends, and from the vulgar self-importance that betrays the analogous ethical immaturity of such graceful pillars of high society as the duc de Guermantes. And just as Bertrand de Réveillon brushes aside all social conventions and distinctions in order to offer Jean Santeuil his friendship (*JS*, 452), Saint-Loup likewise abandons his hereditary social advantages in order to leap over the class barrier that separates him from his friend, as Marcel repeatedly remarks when referring to 'la situation de naissance et de fortune qu'il inclinait devant moi . . . qu'il me sacrifiait' (II.415) (the family and fortune that he laid at my feet . . . that he sacrificed for me). Eventually, having transcended the limitations of personal pride and of social conventions, Saint-Loup manifests the supreme non-artistic virtue of '(une) grâce inconsciente' (II.415) (unconscious grace), just as Bertrand de Réveillon's movements evince 'une grâce qui s'ignorait' (*JS*, 454) (an unconscious grace).

Marcel also suggests that Saint-Loup's non-habitual grace might be described as 'quelque chose de bien plus général que moi-même' (II.414) (something much more general than myself), just as Bertrand de Réveillon's graceful gestures are described as being 'universal' rather than personal or habitual. But whereas Jean Santeuil implies that such non-habitual reality 'ne peut nous donner que de la joie' (*JS*, 455) (can only bring us joy), Marcel introduces a further distinction by suggesting that the vulgarity of habitual social grace is complemented by both positive and negative variants of non-habitual reality. As he reflects in the following rather convoluted meditation, both Saint-Loup's unambiguous virtue and Charlus's ambiguous vices offer exceptions to the vulgar social graces of the duc de Guermantes:

Ce que la familiarité d'un Guermantes — au lieu de la distinction qu'elle avait chez Robert, parce que le dédain héréditaire n'y était que le vêtement, devenu grâce inconsciente, d'une réelle humilité morale — eût décelé de morgue vulgaire, j'avais pu en prendre conscience, non en M. de Charlus chez lequel des défauts de caractère que jusqu'ici je comprenais mal s'étaient superposés aux habitudes aristocratiques, mais chez le duc de Guermantes. (II.415)
(The extent to which the familiarity of a member of the Guermantes family — far from evincing the distinction of Robert, whose hereditary air of disdain, now transformed into unconscious grace, was only the apparel of his real moral humility — might reveal their vulgar arrogance, was made plain to me, not by M. de Charlus, whose aristocratic habits had become obscured by certain weaknesses of character that I had not understood up to now, but by the duc de Guermantes.)

While this passage cannot be said to analyse the negative non-habitual behaviour that Marcel appears to have in mind, it valuably reiterates Marcel's extremely important suggestion that the involuntary, non-habitual quality of 'unconscious grace' not only transcends the vulgarity of self-important habitual behaviour, but also transcends both the amorality of habitual behaviour, and the immorality of negative non-habitual behaviour, by evincing the voluntary and conscious scruples of 'real moral humility'. These considerations discredit two of the most cherished misconceptions of orthodox Proustian criticism, and indeed of Beckett's *Proust*.

The first of these misconceptions is the peculiar conviction that 'Proust is completely detached from all moral considerations' and that, accordingly, 'There is no right and wrong in Proust nor in his world' (*PTD*, 66). The fallacy of this argument should be obvious. Marcel may now and then claim to be oblivious to moral considerations, but more often than not he assiduously exemplifies the workings of the moral code that he associates with the 'laws' of goodness, scruple and sacrifice (III.188).

Following on from the assumption that Proust depicts an amoral world, and entertaining the standard critical myth that the only truths within this world are the truths of art, the second of these misconceptions postulates that within such a world all intimations of artistic truth, and all manifestations of artistic truth, are necessarily involuntary. In Beckett's terms: 'There is only one real impression and one adequate evocation. Over neither have we the least control' (*PTD*, 14–15). Like so many of the conclusions of Proust's critics, this assertion is at best a half-truth. While Proust's characters lack 'the least control' over their initial, involuntary impressions of authentic existence, they appear to enjoy some measure of control over the process by which they subsequently consolidate this preliminary experience in their respective evocations of authentic existence.

In other words, Proust appears to conceive of an intermediary zone between the banality of habitual existence and the universality of the ideal non-habitual; a zone in which the artist accidently discovers those truths that his subsequent works consciously and carefully portray. For Marcel this preliminary revelation takes the form of the involuntary memories that he introduces with reference to the way in which the savour of a *madeleine* soaked in tea conjures up his past with an intensity unattainable by 'la mémoire volontaire, la mémoire de l'intelligence' (I.44) (voluntary memory, the memory of the intelligence). Pondering upon the arbitrary quality of this rediscovery of the past, he concludes:

C'est peine perdue que nous cherchions à l'évoquer, tous les efforts de notre intelligence sont inutiles. Il est caché hors de son domaine et de sa portée, en quelque objet matériel (en la sensation que nous donnerait cet objet matériel) que nous ne soupçonnons pas. Cet objet, il dépend du hasard que nous le rencontrions avant de mourir, ou que nous ne le recontrions pas. (I.44)
(It is a sheer waste of time trying to evoke it, all the efforts of the intelligence are useless. It is hidden beyond its domain and out of reach, in some material object (in the sensation offered by this material object) whose existence we least suspect. As for this object, it is a matter of pure chance whether we come across it before we die, or whether we never come across it all.)

At the same time, Marcel specifies that such unpredictable insights are subsequently refined by the intelligence, just as the experiments of scientists interact with the analyses of the intelligence, 'avec cette différence que chez le savant le travail de l'intelligence précède et chez l'écrivain vient après' (III.880) (with the difference that whereas the work of the intelligence comes first for the scientist, it comes second for the writer). Far from claiming that the artist cannot exert the least control over his evocations of such revelations, Marcel castigates all those who *will not* impose the least control over their insights, alluding contemptuously to the way in which '(ceux) qui n'extraient rien de leur impression, vieillissent inutiles et insatisfaits, comme des célibataires d l'Art!' (III.892) (those who have made nothing of their impressions, grow old, useless and unfulfilled, as if they were the old bachelors of Art!). Like the young Marcel, these old 'bachelors' lack the courage to control their destinies, yielding to 'la lâcheté qui nous détourne de toute tâche difficile, de toute oeuvre importante' (I.46) (the cowardice that turns us away from all difficult tasks, and from all important work).

It would seem, then, that Marcel's analyses of his own vocation, and of the vocation of his fellow artists, leads him to envisage this intermediary zone between habitual and universal modes of existence in terms of two successive phases. While the preliminary discovery of uncontrollable, involuntary memories permits the would-be artist to transcend the vulgarity of habitual existence, a subsequent period of voluntary and conscious discipline appears to prepare the artist for the possibility of creating exemplary works evincing the unconscious grace that Marcel associates with the universality of ideal, non-habitual experience. This voluntary and conscious application of the intelligence, and of the moral 'laws' that Marcel considers inseparable from great art, would seem to be a precondition, rather than a cause, of such unconscious grace (which by definition transcends all voluntary and conscious directives). Thus, the presence or absence of these measures of control serve to indicate the extent to which any one character has or has not rejected the vulgarity and indolence of habitual existence.

Marcel's initial bemused response to his involuntary memories is thus a clear index of the extent to which he is 'imperfect, but at least perfectible' (I.290), when categorized within Swann's terminology, while the finest works of art by Vinteuil, Elstir and Bergotte all testify to moments when their creators were 'perfect' rather than merely 'perfectible'. The same distinction operates among their non-artistic counterparts. While the artistic perfection of the finest compositions by Vinteuil, Elstir and of the finest compositions by Vinteuil, Elstir and Bergotte finds its counterpart in the 'perfect friendship' (II.415) of Saint-Loup (and within analogous evocations of benevolence evinced by Marcel's grandmother), Marcel's involuntary memories appear to find their counterpart within the curious phenomenon of Odette's transfiguration.

Although Odette is not given to generous impulses, her sudden 'transfiguration' unexpectedly releases her benign 'real self' from the confines and confusions of habitual existence, just as Marcel's involuntary memories unexpectedly remove him from the restrictions of habitual reality, and reveal his 'real self', by precipitating the process by which 'l'essence permanente et habituellement cachée des choses se trouve liberée, et notre vrai moi qui, parfois depuis longtemps, semblait mort ... s'éveille' (III.873) (the habitually hidden permanent essence of things is liberated, and our real self, which may long have appeared to be dead ... awakens). But whereas Marcel's escape from habitual existence instigates the *private* miracle by which the artist discovers self-knowledge, Odette's 'transfiguration' exemplifies the *public* miracle by which the non-artist awakens and discloses his or her habitually dormant benevolence.

Accordingly, the features of the transfigured Odette no longer advertize her disturbing appetite for mysterious pleasures. Her face is instead 'vidé pour un instant de la préoccupation fébrile et joyeuse des choses inconnues qui faisaient souffrir Swann' (I.314) (cleared for an instant of all signs of that restless, eager pursuit of those unknown things which caused Swann so much suffering), and radiates a certain elementary benevolence, rather than the 'agitation mauvaise' (I.314) (negative agitation, or more colloquially, 'bad vibrations') that Marcel associates with those suffering from unrest or harbouring malevolent machinations.

Marcel describes Odette's surprising serenity by comparing it with the kind of natural spectacle that Proust celebrates in his early writings:

alors, tout d'un coup, quelque pensée simplement humaine, quelque bon sentiment comme il en existe dans toutes les créatures, quand dans un moment de repos, ou de repliement elles sont livrées à elles-mêmes, jaillissait de ses yeux comme un rayon jaune. Et aussitôt tout son visage s'éclairait comme une campagne grise, couverte de nuages qui soudain s'écartent, pour sa transfiguration, au moment du soleil couchant. (I.314)

(then, all at once, some purely human thought, some generous impulse such as everyone feels during moments of relaxation or introspection, when they are restored to themselves, flashed from her eyes like a golden ray. And immediately, her face was illuminated like a grey, overcast horizon, which the clouds unveil, for its transfiguration, just as the sun is setting.)

Like Marcel's involuntary memories, Odette's 'transfiguration' restores her to her 'real self' by the miracle of 'un moment . . . de repliement': a concept that might variously be translated as a 'moment of introspection', 'a moment of withdrawal', or literally, 'a moment of enfolding'; and which seems to offer an accidental and fugitive variant of the process by which the fully realized work of art, and the fully realized manifestation of the non-artist's benevolence, constitute 'un . . . profond repli sur soi-même' (III.893) (a profound enfolding of the self).

As Elstir reminds Marcel, the profound distillation of the self which precipitates admirable art and admirable lives is neither accidental nor hereditary, but rather the consequence of the ethical 'battle . . . and victory' (I.864) by which man transforms involuntary manifestations of artistic and non-artistic truths into profound revelations of these truths. And as Marcel's speculations indicate, Saint-Loup's victorious attainment of 'real moral humility', and his subsequent display of 'perfect friendship', typify the existential 'battle' which Proust's characters must undertake in order to transcend the limitations of relative truth and relative communication. This 'battle' takes place several times in Marcel's narrative. Like Saint-Loup, Marcel's grandmother (who seems to be the only other 'victorious' non-artist in *A la recherche du temps perdu*), and Vinteuil, Elstir and Bergotte (who seem to create the most exemplary music, painting and literature in this novel), all appear to communicate their finest values after first cultivating the 'real moral humility' that Marcel deems inseparable from the most positive actions of his fellow beings.

Most of Proust's critics have little time and little sympathy for Marcel's grandmother. Roger Shattuck, for example, argues that, like all of the other 'gifted amateurs' among Marcel's acquaintances, she impoverishes his life, declaring: 'Swann, Charlus, even his grandmother . . . often lead him astray';[9] while Germaine Brée refuses point-blank to take any of Marcel's non-artistic acquaintances seriously, claiming that 'all human relationships even including the narrator's relationship with . . .

his grandmother, are in essence comedies'.[10] Indeed, according to Germaine Brée, Proust deliberately humiliates Marcel's grandmother, when, at the end of her life, 'He gives us a pitiless description of a human being who rapidly becomes physically and morally exhausted and dies'.[11]

Such judgments are as inappropriate as they are inaccurate. Proust's vision is essentially relative in quality, and it therefore makes little sense to impute any single, monolithic quality to any group of Proustian characters, as Shattuck and Brée do, when identifying those characters who 'lead Marcel astray', or those characters whose relationships are 'in essence comedies'. Considered very generally, it might be argued that *all* of Proust's characters are comic from time to time, just as all of his characters go 'astray' from time to time, and therefore might lead others astray in their wake. At the same time, all of Proust's characters necessarily enrich Marcel's appreciation of the vices and virtues of mankind (rather than impoverishing his understanding) since, in the formulation of Proust's early essay entitled 'Journées de lecture', 'leur échec est instructif' (*CSB*, 188) (their failure is instructive). Confirming this hypothesis, Marcel muses that even man's most unreasonable and most unrealizable dreams are of value since 'leur échec instruise' (III.183) (their failure instructs).

Considered more specifically, Shattuck's and Brée's conclusions seem curiously insensitive to Marcel's claim that far from leading him astray, or merely constituting a geriatric buffoon, his grandmother: 'me sauvait de la sécheresse de l'âme' (II.755) (saved me from spiritual aridity). This claim may be a trifle generous, but it merits serious consideration insofar as Marcel carefully describes at least two occasions when his grandmother manifests exemplary spiritual qualities while communicating her affection to him. In both of these instances (and perhaps on her deathbed too), Marcel's grandmother transcends habitual, conversational communication, by communicating with sonic gestures, somewhat as Saint-Loup transcends conversation by communicating with the physical gestures of his leaping movements.

The first of these extraordinary manifestations of affection occurs during Marcel's first visit to Balbec, when his grandmother comforts him by making the apparently inconsequential gesture of tapping upon the partition that separates their room. One might not imagine that this gesture would elicit much further comment. Nevertheless Marcel not only ponders upon the remarkable quality of the peculiar discourse that arises each morning when his grandmother responds to his own tentative tappings, but suggests that, like the finest compositions by Vinteuil, this tapping 'symphony' permits the miracle of 'la communication des âmes' (III.258) (the communication of souls). Elaborating this notion in lines brimful with his most evocative concepts, he refers to:

(cet) doux instant matinal qui s'ouvrait comme une symphonie par le dialogue rythmé de mes trois coups auquel la cloison, pénétrée de tendresse et de joie, devenue harmonieuse, immatérielle, chantant comme les anges, répondait par trois autres coups ... où elle savait transporter l'âme de ma grand'mère tout entière. (I.670)
(this perfect early morning moment which began like a symphony with the rhythmical dialogue of my three taps to which the partition, penetrated with tenderness and joy, and suddenly harmonious and immaterial, like the song of angels, replied with three other taps ... in which it somehow transported the entirety of my grandmother's soul.)

His references to the harmony and the immateriality of sounds akin to 'the song of angels', which somehow convey the entirety of a soul, are all pregnant with allusions to other key passages in Marcel's narrative and in Proust's earlier writings. The harmonious and immaterial quality of his grandmother's tapping noises both recalls the 'impalpable and graceful' (*JS*, 447) quality that Jean Santeuil and Marcel attribute to the leaping gestures that communicate the exemplary affection of Bertrand de Réveillion and Robert de Saint-Loup, and anticipates Marcel's admiration for the similarly harmonious and immaterial *septuor* of Vinteuil, establishing some kind of parity between these different alternatives to habitual modes of communication. Marcel's suggestion that his grandmother's tapping gestures resemble 'the song of angels' similarly anticipates his comparison of the sleeping Albertine's exhalations with 'le pur chant des Anges' (III.114) (the pure song of the Angels). But far from establishing any parity between these two kinds of 'angelic song', this superficial similarity points to the disparity between the exemplary sonic gestures of Marcel's grandmother and the vacuous sonic gestures of Albertine. Like the disparity between Saint-Loup's exemplary physical gestures and Albertine's vacuous physical gestures, this distinction illustrates Proust's thesis that ideal self-realization and ideal communication necessitate the exceptional selflessness that Saint-Loup and

Marcel's grandmother appear to attain when making their most eloquent gestures.

At best, Albertine's seductive sonic gestures offer the most elementary alternatives to habitual communication. In Marcel's terms, her breathing is 'apaisante' (III.116) (appeasing), because it shows no sign of her habitual 'expression de ruse ou de vulgarité' (III.114) (expression of cunning and vulgarity), and merely evinces the neutrality of 'la vie inconsciente des végétaux' (III.70) (the unconscious life of vegetables). By contrast, the sonic gestures of his grandmother express the plenitude of positive affection that he identifies with 'the entirety' of her soul. Admittedly, he does not specify that his grandmother's sonic gestures arise from the selflessness and moral humility that seem inseparable from exemplary communication in *A la recherche du temps perdu*, or at least, he does not allude to these qualities in this particular example of his grandmother's ability to communicate her benevolence. But Marcel's second account of his grandmother's occasional capacity to express such eloquent affection unambiguously attributes this feat to her equally unusual selflessness, and there seems no reason to doubt that the immaterial harmony of her tapping derives from identical virtue.

Marcel's grandmother's second exemplary manifestation of her affection occurs when she speaks to him by telephone from Paris, while he is staying at Doncières with Saint-Loup. Paying particular attention to the tone of his grandmother's voice (rather than to any specific utterance), Marcel is astonished by the way in which it appears to incarnate 'sa douceur même' (II.135) (her very affection), and reasons that this consummate communication of kindness arises both from her abandonment of the habitual principles which usually stifle her solicitude and, more significantly, from the unusual selflessness that permits the sonic gestures of her voice to express her affection with such purity. Marcel concludes:

ma grand'mère, me sentant loin et malheureux, croyait pouvoir s'abandonner à l'effusion d'une tendresse que, par "principes" d'éducatrice, elle contenait et cachait d'habitude. Elle était . . . presque décantée, plus que peu de voix humaines ont jamais dû l'être, de toute dureté, de tout élément de résistance aux autres, de tout égoïsme! (II.135)
(my grandmother, feeling that I was far away from home and unhappy, believed herself to be justified in giving way to a burst of affection which, for educational "principles", she would habitually have held

back and kept hidden. It was … almost completely decanted, more so than almost any other human voice can have been, of all harshness, of all traces of opposition to other people, of all egotism!)

It might additionally be argued that Marcel's grandmother also triumphantly offers yet another manifestation of her exemplary affection as she lies dying (rather than that she is being humiliated by her final illness, as Germaine Brée maintains). For although Marcel's description of the last days of his grandmother begins by dispassionately delineating both her cheerful stoicism and her suicidal nihilism, this unsentimental objectivity should not be confused with the satirical perspective that Germaine Brée attributes to Proust's vision. For, as Marcel intimates in his final reflections upon his dying grandmother, she not only appears to evince her indomitable solicitude with the gestural discourse of her very last breaths and her very last shudder, but also dies reflecting the very purity that he previously praised when remarking upon the way in which her voice is 'decanted … of all egotism!'

Gradually becoming aware that the unusual sonority of his grandmother's dying breath invokes the entirety of her habitually hidden benevolence, Marcel once again abumbrates his hypothesis that the most perfect modes of communication are both non-habitual and unconscious:

Qui sait si, sans même que ma grand'mère en eût conscience, tant d'états heureux et tendres comprimés par la souffrance ne s'échappaient pas d'elle maintenant …? On aurait dit que tout ce qu'elle avait à nous dire s'épanchait, que c'était à nous qu'elle s'adressait … cette effusion (II.344)
(Who knows, perhaps, even without my grandmother knowledge, all of the joyful and tender impulses which had hitherto been held down by her suffering now escaped from her …? One would have said that everything she had to tell flowed forth, and that it was to us that she addressed … this effusion.)

In much the same way, Marcel tentatively intimates that the physical gestures with which his grandmother responds to his last embrace are similarly an expression of her remarkable devotion.

Remarking that his grandmother's hands begin to flutter as his lips touch her for the last time, and that she subsequently shudders from top to toe, Marcel at first surmises that these movements are nothing more than a reflex action, before speculating that they might alternatively furnish further testimony to the peerless quality of her affection, over which death itself — or, more accurately, the unconsciousness preceding death — has no dominion. Suggesting that his grandmother's love somehow transcends the realm of 'the senses', he recounts:

Quand mes lèvres la touchèrent, les mains de ma grand'mère s'agitèrent, elle fut parcourue tout entière d'un long frisson, soit reflexe, soit que certains tendresses aient leur hyperesthésie qui reconnaît à travers le voile de l'inconscience ce qu'elles n'ont presque pas besoin des sens pour chérir. (II.344)
(When my lips touched her, my grandmother's hands began to flutter, and a long shudder ran all the way through her body, perhaps from a reflex action, or perhaps because certain kinds of affection have the hyperaesthetic capacity to see through the veil of unconsciousness, and to discern those things that they can virtually appreciate without recourse to the senses.)

Quite clearly, Marcel's grandmother offers him a number of striking examples of the ideal gestural communication that he associates with exemplary non-artistic self-realization. Far from leading him astray (as Albertine does by leading him to idolize her vacuous physical and sonorous gestures), Marcel's grandmother — like Saint-Loup — offers him the inspiring spectacle of 'perfect friendship'. And far from being humiliated by her death, Marcel's grandmother finally offers a picture of triumphant innocence: 'les traits délicatement tracés par la pureté et la soumission, les joues brillantes d'une chaste espérance' (II.345) (her features delicately tinged with purity and modesty, her cheeks glowing with chaste optimism).

Like Marcel's grandmother and like Saint-Loup, the exemplary artists in *A la recherche du temps perdu* manifest their most precious potential in an unconscious manner, after first forsaking all conventional values and all traces of egotistical desire. In this respect, their creativity not only conforms to the implicit 'laws' of non-artistic self-realization, which Marcel exemplifies in his descriptions of the finest hours of his grandmother and Saint-Loup, but also correspond to the parallel artistic 'laws' that he explicitly formulates at the end of his chronicle, and to the similarly explicit precepts that Proust elaborates in his early essays on the creative process.

Perhaps the most important of all Proust's early dictums is his assertion, in his essay 'John Ruskin', that: 'le premier devoir de l'artiste est de ne rien ajouter de son propre cru' (*CSB*, 111) (the artist's first duty is never to add anything from his own imagination). This commandment appears to precipitate Jean Santeuil's equally crucial proclamation that man is 'the bearer ... and not the author' (*JS*, 455) of his talents, and similarly anticipates Marcel's eventual discovery that 'nous ne sommes nullement libres devant l'oeuvre d'art ... nous ne la faisons pas à notre gré, mais ... nous devons ... la découvrir' (III.881) (we are not free to choose our works of art ... we cannot create them to our liking, but ... we must ... discover them).

It is in this sense that the composer Vinteuil is an 'explorateur de l'invisible' (I.351) (explorer of the invisible), since his works discover, and, as it were, uncover, the new creative possibilities that Marcel vividly evokes as 'un ordre de créatures surnaturelles ... que nous n'avons jamais vues' (I.351) (a supernatural species ... which we have never seen before). Swann has therefore every reason to suggest that rather than inventing his exquisite 'little phrase', Vinteuil 's'était contenté ... de la dévoiler, de la rendre visible' (I.351) (had been content ... to unveil it, to make it visible). As Marcel comments, had Vinteuil employed the powers of his imagination, rather than those special powers with which he unveils the forms of his 'invisible' subject-matter and makes them visible, then his work would be tainted by a certain air of deception. In Marcel's terms:

tout amateur un peu fin se fût tout de suite aperçu de l'imposture, si Vinteuil, ayant eu moins de puissance pour en voir et en rendre les formes, avait cherché à dissimuler, en ajoutant çà et là des traits de son cru. (I.351)
(any music-lover with the slightest sensitivity would have immediately noticed the deception, if Vinteuil, lacking sufficient powers to discern and describe these forms, had attempted to cheat by substituting the touches of his imagination.)

According to Marcel, all great art — and indeed all great wisdom — arises from the revelation of profound insights rather than from the inventions of man's imagination. It is thus the attainment of those who climb 'la pente abrupte de l'introspection' (the steep slope of introspection), rather than 'la pente aisée de l'imagination' (III.465) (the easy slope of the imagination). If Vinteuil's music appears to be original, then this orginality pertains to the rare profundity of his vision, and to the 'accent unique' (unique accent) which Marcel discerns in all of his musical explorations, and which he takes to be 'une preuve de l'existence irréductiblement individuelle de l'âme' (III.256) (a proof of the irreducibly individual existence of the soul). In other words, by unveiling what Jean Santeuil might term 'universal' truths, rather than the superficial individuality that Marcel associates with the idiosyncratic inventions of the imagination, Vinteuil finally reveals the far more profound individuality of his introspective powers. Or, as Proust commented in his early essay 'Contre l'Obscurité', authentic self-realization and the realization of universal values (or the 'universal soul') are the concomitant attainments of those who heed 'une autre loi de la vie qui est de réaliser l'universel' (another of life's laws, which is that one must realize the universal), and who are thus aware that:

les hommes ... doivent être fortement individuels ... et ... c'est quand ils sont le plus eux-mêmes qu'ils réalisent le plus largement l'âme universelle. (*CSB*, 394)
(men ... must be utterly individual ... and ... it is when they realize themselves most authentically that they offer the most authentic realization to universal values.)

Such stirring maxims obviously beg the question of defining the best way of realizing such utterly individual and utterly universal values. While Marcel intermittently insists that exemplary actions sacrifice the distractions of superficial pleasures in order to pursue profounder joys, and whilst his analysis of Vinteuil's music argues that profound creativity necessitates the sacrifice of the workings of the imagination, his meditations upon Elstir's painting additionally intimate that great art sacrifices the workings of the intelligence. At first sight, this suggestion confusingly contradicts Marcel's injunction that the artist should combine and refine his most valuable insights with the intelligence, somewhat as the scientist combines rational and experimental operations (III.880). But rather than conflicting with one another, these two proposals seem to refer to two successive phases in the creative process.

Marcel appears to postulate that the artist's intelligence initially accomplishes part of the creative process, if only by instigating its activity and by rejecting the superficiality of habitual assumptions; and that it then benevolently eliminates itself, upon reaching the intelligent conclusion that the final phases of the creative process require the intervention of some sort of extra-rational faculty. These unusually benign, self-sacrificing rational impulses might be defined by reference to Marcel's concept of 'l'intelligence positive' (I.236) (the positive intelligence), and by contrast with the 'negative' intelligence that he associates with the relativity of man's habitual delusions and which he evokes in such asides as: 'dès que l'intelligence raisonneuse veut se mettre à juger des oeuvres d'art, il n'y a plus rien de fixe, de certain: on peut démontrer ce qu'on veut' (III.893) (once the reasonings of the intelligence presume to evaluate art, everything becomes unstable and uncertain: one can prove whatever one wants).

Introducing the surprising virtues of this 'positive intelligence', and insisting that it offers a more substantial point of departure than a naive confidence in man's intuitions and instincts, Marcel explains:

Mais ... de ce que l'intelligence n'est pas l'instrument le plus subtil, le plus puissant, le plus approprié pour saisir le vrai, ce n'est qu'une raison de plus pour commencer par l'intelligence et non par un intuitivisme de l'inconscient, par une foi aux pressentiments toute faite. C'est la vie qui, peu à peu, cas par cas, nous permet de remarquer que ce qui est le plus important pour notre coeur, ou pour notre esprit, ne nous est pas appris par le raisonnement mais par des puissances autres. Et alors, c'est l'intelligence elle-même qui, se rendant compte de leur supériorité, abdique, par raisonnement, devant elles, et accepte de devenir leur collaboratrice et leur servante. (III.423)

(But ... the fact that the intelligence is not the most subtle, the most powerful and the most appropriate means of seizing the truth is but one further reason for beginning with the intelligence and not with the intuitions of the unconscious, or with faith in ready-made presentiments. Little by little, and day by day, life shows us that the things that are most important to our hearts, or to our minds, are revealed to us, not by our rational faculties, but by other forces. And thus it is, that our very intelligence, acknowledging their superiority, abdicates, rationally, before these forces, and accepts to be their collaborator and their servant.)

As our analyses of Beckett's *Proust* and early fiction will demonstrate, Beckett's refusal to concede that such 'positive intelligence' could 'be abolished in its own tension', [12] and could therefore facilitate extra-rational alternatives to habitual perception, contributes both to the idiosyncracies of his conclusions in this essay, and to the fascinating anti-Proustian quality of his own fictional world, in which positive variants of the intelligence — and positive variants of almost anything at all! — seem singularly few and far between.

Nevertheless, Proust's fictional horizons abound with both positive and negative manifestations of almost every aspect of existence. And if Marcel frequently mocks the perceptual limitations of habitual, 'negative' modes of the intelligence, he unambiguously celebrates the positive, self-sacrificing intelligence that facilitates the painting of Elstir, observing:

L'effort qu'Elstir faisait pour se dépouillir en présence de la réalité de toutes les notions de son intelligence était d'autant plus admirable que cet homme qui avant de peindre se faisait ignorant . . . avait justement une intelligence exceptionnellement cultivée. (I.840)
(The effort that Elstir made to strip himself in the presence of reality of all the assumptions of his intelligence was all the more admirable insofar as this man who made himself ignorant before he began to paint . . . was blessed with an exceptionally cultivated intelligence.)

As Elstir himself emphasizes in his reference to the importance of existential battles (I.864), such sacrifices precipitate the authentic and complete modes of self-realization that man attains only after first experiencing and embodying the inauthentic and incomplete attitudes of 'toutes les incarnations ridicules ou odieuses qui doivent précéder cette dernière incarnation-là' (I.864) (all of the ridiculous and odious incarnations that necessarily precede this final incarnation). Accordingly, those who feel ashamed of their former selves may at least feel confident that they have at last lived life to the full, since, in Elstir's terms, such retrospective shame is:

un témoignage que nous avons vraiment vécu, que c'est selon les lois de la vie et de l'esprit que nous avons des éléments communs de la vie . . . extrait quelque chose qui les dépasse. (I.864)
(evidence that we have really lived, and that by following the laws of life and of the spirit, we have made something quite uncommon . . . out of the common elements of existence.)

The profoundly Proustian ideal of having 'really lived' becomes particularly important in terms of the way in which it offers striking contrasts with the Beckettian ideal of living as little as possible. This distinction is best introduced with reference to Beckett's early play *Eleuthéria* (or 'Freedom') of 1947, in which the ironically named Victor describes his ideal way of life as one in which he might victoriously live, or more accurately, victoriously *unlive*:

En étant le moins possible. En ne pas bougeant, ne pas pensant, ne pas rêvant, ne pas parlant, ne pas écoutant, ne pas percevant, ne pas sachant, ne pas voulant, ne pas pouvant, et ainsi de suite.[13]

(By being as little as possible. By not moving, not thinking, not dreaming, not speaking, not hearing, not perceiving, not knowing, not wanting, not being able, and so on.)

The great virtue of Elstir's generalizations is that their open frame of reference respects the essential dualism of Proust's ideals, whereas Marcel's partisan formulations of identical insights misleadingly attribute successful self-realization and communication to art, and to art alone. In this respect, Marcel's predominantly perspicacious reflections upon the way in which Vinteuil and Elstir transcend the habitual reality that Elstir associates with the 'common elements of existence' are flawed by his failure to indicate that the non-habitual gestural discourse of exemplary non-artists, such as his grandmother and Saint-Loup, similarly transcends the limitations of habitual language. Elaborately pondering upon the difficulties of communicating the uncommon insights that seem inseparable from great art, Marcel concludes:

Mais alors, n'est-ce pas que ces éléments, tout ce résidu réel que nous sommes obligés de garder pour nous-mêmes, que la causerie ne peut transmettre même de l'ami à l'ami, du maître au disciple, de l'amant à la maîtresse, cet ineffable qui différencie qualitativement ce que chacun a senti et qu'il est obligé de laisser au seuil des phrases où il ne peut communiquer avec autrui qu'en se limitant à des points extérieurs communs à tous et sans intérêt, l'art, l'art d'un Vinteuil comme celui d'un Elstir, le fait apparaître, extériorisant dans les couleurs du spectre la composition intime de ces mondes que nous appelons les individus, et que sans l'art nous ne connaîtrions jamais. (III.257–8)

(But then, isn't it true that all of these elements, the entirety of this substratum of reality which we are obliged to keep to ourselves, and which conversation is powerless to convey even from friend to friend, from master to disciple, or from lover to mistress, this ineffable reality which distinguishes the quality of our perceptions, and which we are obliged to leave at the threshold of those phrases with which we communicate with others by limiting ourselves to exterior points of reference, shared by everyone, and therefore devoid of interest, all of these elements are made visible by art, by the art of a Vinteuil or of an Elstir, which reveals within the colours of its spectrum the intimate composition of those worlds which we describe as individual, and which without art we would never know.)

These thoughts lead in their turn to yet another beguiling half-truth:

Et ... je me demandais si la Musique n'était pas l'exemple unique de ce qu'aurait pu être — s'il n'y avait pas eu l'invention du langage, la formation des mots, l'analyse des idées — la communication des âmes. Elle est comme une possibilité qui n'a pas eu de suites; l'humanité s'est engagée dans d'autres voies, celle du langage parlé et écrit. (III.258) And ... I wondered if Music was not the unique example of what might have been — were it not for the invention of language, the formation of words, and the analysis of ideas — the communication of souls. It seems to be an issueless possibility; humanity followed other paths, those of spoken and written language.)

It is certainly very tempting to accept these eulogies of music and art at face value. Yet it should be obvious that although both this meditation and Marcel's preceding ruminations upon the art of Vinteuil and Elstir memorably convey his contempt for the inferiority of habitual, verbal communication (and his corresponding admiration for non-habitual, extra-verbal 'exteriorizations' of non-habitual reality such as Vinteuil's music and Elstir's painting), it does not follow, as Marcel claims, that such creativity affords the unique example of 'the communication of souls'. For, as we have seen, the sonorous gestural discourses of Marcel's grandmother communicate what he himself defines as: 'the entirety of my grandmother's soul' (I.670), 'her very affection' (II.315), and 'everything she had to tell us' (II.344); just as Saint-Loup's physical gestural discourse communicates the entirety of his benevolence. Far from being 'issueless', the exemplary extra-verbal communication of artists like Vinteuil and Elstir has evident counterparts in the exemplary extra-verbal communication of non-artists such as Marcel's grandmother and Saint-Loup.

At this point, one might well wonder how Marcel defends literature, which, after all, derives from the very 'invention of language' to which music, art, and non-artistic gestural communication all offer their respective alternatives. He appears to argue that just as the music of Vinteuil is identifiable in terms of its 'unique accent' (III.256), so too is great literature characterized by a qualitative accent which transcends the banality of 'exterior points of reference ... devoid of interest' (III.258), and which offers 'la preuve la plus authentique de génie, bien plus que le contenu de l'oeuvre elle-même' (III.375) (the most authentic proof of genius, more so even than the actual content of the work). Illustrating this hypothesis with reference to Bergotte's prose, he explains:

Cet accent n'est pas noté dans le texte, rien ne l'y indique et pourtant il s'ajoute de lui-même aux phrases, on ne peut pas les dire autrement, il est ce qu'il y avait de plus éphémère et pourtant de plus profond chez l'écrivain, et c'est cela qui portera témoignage sur sa nature.(I.553)
(This accent is not designated in the text, nothing indicates that it is there and yet it emerges of its own accord in the phrases, they cannot be read aloud in any other way, it is at once that which is most ephemeral and yet most profound in a writer's work, and it is this accent that bears witness to the quality of his personality.)

While he does not specify that this 'accent' arises from any particular ethical sacrifice (such as the sacrifices of social conventions, of egotistical desires, and of the workings of the imagination and of the intelligence, which appear to be prerequisites to the finest actions of Vinteuil, Elstir, Marcel's grandmother and Saint-Loup), Marcel stipulates that Bergotte's literary 'accent' appears only 'aux moments où dans ses livres Bergotte était entièrement naturel' (I.553) (in those parts of his books in which Bergotte was entirely natural). As Proust's early essays repeatedly indicate, the Proustian concept of the 'natural' — not to mention the 'entirely natural' — is pregnant with the ethical attributes that he imputes to all exemplary states of self-realization in which the 'natural' subject — be this man or flower or plant or tree — evinces the grace peculiar to utterly universal and utterly individual states of existence.

In this respect, the literary 'accent' of Bergotte appears to be just as much a symptom of those moments of ethical purity in which he attains exemplary self-realization, as the musical 'accent' of Vinteuil's finest compositions, the painterly 'accent' of Elstir's finest compositions, and the equally inimitable 'accents' of the finest sonorous and physical gestures of Marcel's grandmother and Saint-Loup are all symptoms of their most authentic moments of self-realization.[14] In terms of Proust's 'John Ruskin', the peculiarly individual moments of extra-verbal communication that arise during all of the exemplary actions in *A la recherche du temps perdu* share the quality of maximal self-realization that this essay defines as:

un état de grâce où toutes nos facultés, notre sens critique aussi bien que les autres, sont accrues. (*CSB*, 140)
(a state of grace in which all of our faculties, our critical faculties as well as all the others, are at their height.)

Like so many of Proust's formulations of his existential ideals, these lines beg comparison with Beckett's quite antithetical desideratum. Just as Elstir's suggestion that man should 'really live' awaits its negation in Victor's avowal in *Eleuthéria* that man should live 'as little as possible', this early essay's eulogy of those moments when 'all of our faculties ... are at their height' is subsequently subverted by Beckett's *Mercier et Camier* (1946), in the following exchange between the heroes of this early novel:

Or, le sommes-nous? dit Camier.
Sommes-nous quoi? dit Mercier.
En pleine possession de nos facultés, dit Camier.
J'espère que non, dit Mercier.
(Well, are we? said Camier.
Are we what? said Mercier.
In full possession of our faculties, said Camier.
I hope not, said Mercier.)[15]

Put more succinctly, and more crudely, in terms of Beckett's English translation of *Mercier et Camier* (1970), and in terms of one of the final statements in his recent play *Rockaby* (1981), the existential priorities of Beckett's characters might be summarized by the exasperated cry of 'Fuck life!', voiced initially in *Mercier and Camier* by Watt, and once again in *Rockaby* by 'V'.[16]

Proust's approach to existence is, it seems, more subtle: it is perhaps best characterized in terms of the conclusion to his early story entitled 'Sentiments filliaux d'un parricide', in which the titular parricide weighs the claims of 'l'horreur de sa vie' (the horror of his life) and of '(les) premiers rayons de la joie de vivre' (the first rays of the joys of existence), asking: 'quelle est vraie, quel est "le Vrai"?' (*CSB*, 159) (which one is true, which one is "the Truth"?). For, as one discovers, the remarkable relativity of Proust's vision in *A la recherche du temps perdu* derives from the peculiar zeal with which he analyses both the positive and the negative variants of all his characters' actions. In Beckett's terminology, Proust 'respects the dual significance of every condition and circumstance of life' (*PTD*, 69), rather than execrating existence with the four-letter imprecations favoured by Watt and by 'V'.

Clearly, then, the subtlety of Proust's analyses of positive modes of action in *A la recherche du temps perdu* exceeds the complexity that even such painstaking studies as Deleuze's *Proust et les signes* attribute to this novel. Proust does not simply associate ideal self-realization with the 'signs' of *one* supreme mode of existence, as Deleuze postulates when insisting upon 'la supériorité des signes de l'Art sur tous les autres' (the superiority of the signs of Art over all the others), [17] but evinces a plurality of superior signs (or superior 'accents'), within a sliding scale of actions, according to which, both artistic and non-artistic actions sporadically transcend the mediocrity of habitual existence. As Marcel indicates, the most positive modes of artistic and non-artistic action in *A la recherche du temps perdu* both sometimes gravitate, by way of involuntary revelations of artistic and non-artistic values, and by virtue of voluntary sacrifices of those social, egotistical, fanciful and rational impulses that seem inimical to these values, towards heightened states of being, or 'grace', in which they unconsciously contribute to 'the communication of souls' (III.258)

On other occasions, of course, the less positive actions of Proust's artistic and non-artistic characters both gravitate in the opposite direction, towards the pole of existential failure that Swann associates with 'le dernier cercle de Dante' (I.287) (the last of Dante's circles). The following chapter will now consider the ways in which Proust's analysis of the negative actions of his characters testifies still further to his unremitting respect for the 'dual significance of every condition and circumstance'.

3

NEGATIVE MODES OF EXISTENCE IN
A LA RECHERCHE DU TEMPS PERDU

'Imparfaite, mais du moins perfectible' (I.290) — imperfect, but at least perfectible: such is the condition of Proust's characters in *A la recherche du temps perdu*. While the masterpieces of such Proustian artists as Vinteuil and Elstir, and the most generous gestures of such non-artists as Marcel's grandmother and Saint-Loup, suggest the ways in which man's habitual imperfection may be successfully transcended, the trials and tribulations of such characters as Swann and Charlus constantly remind Marcel of man's capacity to degenerate from his habitual condition towards the very depths of imperfection.

The cliché 'trials and tribulations' is, of course, far too vague an evocation of Proust's concept of existential imperfection. For just as his analyses of exemplary actions attribute man's perfectibility to positive forms of self-sacrifice, which allow the artist and the non-artist alike to transcend the mediocrity of habitual, egotistical, rational and imaginary reality, and to attain authentic self-realization by employing their finest faculties to the full, his analyses of non-habitual modes of flawed self-realization similarly attribute these instances of exceptional imperfection to specific ethical factors. Proust seems to conceive of three main categories of exceptionally flawed behaviour, evoking the antitheses of exemplary affection and of exemplary creativity, and additionally introducing a mode of imperfection without any really substantial positive counterpart: the category of imperfect 'social' behaviour. These three categories of exceptional existential imperfection are perhaps best introduced with reference to the way in which Marcel, Swann and Charlus evince the very reverse of the exemplary affection manifested by Marcel's grandmother and Saint-Loup.

Marcel very significantly stipulates that his grandmother's love is 'decanted ... of all egotism' (II.315), and similarly distinguishes Saint-Loup's peerless affection from the self-indulgent passion that he deems to be 'an egotistical emotion' (I.779). In both instances, it is the selfless quality of their emotion that allows them to communicate their affection successfully to Marcel. With such distinctions in mind, it comes as no surprise to find that imperfect and unsuccessful modes of affection are flawed by their egotistical quality. For, far from being selflessly offered to the loved one, the flawed affection of Proust's passionate lovers is always offered to the preconceived and ill-conceived inventions of the lover's imagination.

As Beckett perspicaciously commented in his analysis of what he termed 'The tragedy of the Marcel-Albertine liaison' (*PTD*, 18), the person of Albertine 'counts for nothing' (*PTD*, 53) in Marcel's amorous vision. What seem to count are the idiosyncratic stereotypes of ideal love-objects that Marcel traces back to 'de vieilles rêveries qui dataient de mon enfance' (I.807) (old dreams dating from my childhood). Successively projecting these stereotypes upon Albertine, her friend Andrée, and upon various shopgirls, Venetian girls, and finally any young girls at all, Marcel — like all of Proust's passionate lovers — is not so much the victim of any particular loved one, as the victim of his past and present illusions and delusions. As he eventually discovers, 'ce qui est ... procréateur de souffrances dans l'amour ... ce n'est pas la femme, c'est l'habitude' (III.1022) (that which brings about the sufferings of the lover ... is not the loved one, but habit).

The passionate lovers in *A la recherche du temps perdu* are, however, not merely painfully dependent upon the gratification of their own idiosyncratic stereotypes, or upon what the American novelist, William Burroughs, appropriating the argot of drug addiction, has memorably defined as an 'image fix'.[1] For, while the sufferings of the passionate lover derive in part from the impossibility of satisfying 'addiction' to a particular preconceived image of the ideal love-object, they are also caused by Proust's law of repulsion which dictates that his characters always take flight from passionate attention. As Marcel explains in one of his many formulations of this 'law', 'Plus le désir avance, plus la possession véritable s'éloigne (III.450) (The more ardently one desires, the more remote the chance of true consummation becomes). Indeed, insofar as Proust's characters inhabit a world in which the passionate lover always vainly awaits 'la douceur, toujours refusée par le destin, d'être aimée' (II.919) (the joy, forever denied by destiny, of being loved), the imperfections of passionate love might appear axiomatic, rather than dependent upon any ethical considerations.

Nevertheless, even though requited love appears unattainable and utterly extinct in Proust's fictional cosmos, the extraordinary sufferings of such unrequited lovers as Marcel are very much the consequence of their ethical failings, or more precisely, of their perceptual indolence. For while Marcel is the inevitable victim of Albertine's indifference to his attentions, he is also continually prey to his own unfortunate tendency to misinterpret unfamiliar reality by confusing it with his 'old dreams', and with other careless impressions of unfamiliar reality. For example, rather than analysing the unfamiliar reality of Albertine and of the sea in their own right, Marcel tranforms both of these new realities into causes of suffering by conflating them and intermingling them with his most cherished amorous fantasies. This confusion proves doubly deleterious. First of all, it infects his general impressions of Albertine and the sea. Secondly, it obscures the potential advantages of his initial encounter with Albertine and Gilberte, when his passionate perspective blinds him to their rare sincerity on this occasion, and alarms them so much that they are never again 'aussi franches que dans la première minute' (III.694) (as frank as they had been during these first few moments).

Ultimately, Marcel knows very little more about Albertine at the end of his painful sentimental education than he initially apprehended when thinking of her as 'indifferente à tous, et marine, comme une mouette' (III.848) (indifferent to everyone, and a creature of the sea, like a seagull). As he finally confesses, the limits of his understanding of Albertine are very much the consequence of the limited — or 'clumsy' — categories with which he first attempted to define her. Accordingly, he concludes: 'Et c'était moi qui, n'ayant pas su le comprendre ... avais tout gâté par ma maladresse.' (III.694) (And it was I who, because of my misunderstandings ... had ruined everything with my clumsiness.) Marcel's dilemma, like that of the other passionate lovers in *A la recherche du temps perdu*, is that such perceptual 'clumsiness' goes from bad to worse, as he employs ever more self-indulgent perceptual categories, and becomes ever more removed from the half-glimpsed reality of Albertine's mysterious charm, and from the sea's ethereal beauty.

According to Beckett's masterly analysis of Marcel's successive illusions, Marcel's misinterpretations of Albertine constitute 'A series of subtractions, each ... being replaced by an infinitely less precious notion' (*PTD*, 46). According to Marcel, his successive enthusiasms for Albertine, Andrée, and any manifestation of 'la jeunesse' (III.628) (youth) provide ever-impoverished substitutes for his first 'precious' impressions of Albertine and the sea. 'Subtraction' or 'substitute': in both analyses the emphasis falls squarely upon the way in which Marcel undergoes a losing rather than a getting of wisdom. In Marcel's own terms:

Andrée, ces autres femmes, tout cela par rapport à Albertine — comme Albertine avait été elle-même par rapport à Balbec — étaient de ces substituts de plaisirs se remplaçant l'un l'autre en dégradation successive, qui ... font de notre vie comme une suite de zones concentriques ... et degradées, autour d'un désir premier. (III.552) (Andrée and these other girls were all, in relation to Albertine — just as Albertine had been, in relation to Balbec — examples of those substitute pleasures, replacing one another in an ever more degraded succession, which ... transform our lives into a series of concentric zones ... each one more degraded than the others ... encircling an original desire.)

As the reader might expect, these successive zones of 'substitute pleasures' offer the very antithesis of the profound 'joys' that Marcel associates with authentic self-realization. (I.274)

While exemplary modes of existence in *A la recherche du temps perdu* are associated with those moments in which characters are utterly themselves, like the utterly individual flowers admired by Jean Santeuil (*JS*, 471), Marcel's successive enthusiasms for his images of Albertine and her substitutes deprive him of what he terms '(les) joies de la solitude' (III.27) (the joys of solitude), and finally leave him 'trop absent de moi-même pour penser' (III.70) (too absent from myself to think). Eventually, he not only becomes sporadically 'absent' from himself (and thus unable to realize himself by profound, creative thought), but he abandons virtually the entirety of his attention to the mercies of his self-indulgent imagination. Rather than valiantly sacrificing his egotistical and imaginative desires, in the kind of 'battle and victory' advocated by Elstir (I.864), in order to dedicate himself to his artistic vocation and in order to facilitate positive self-realization, Marcel dedicates his energies to the satisfaction of his jealous suspicions, admitting:

Je sentais bien que ces curiosités étaient sans valeur en elles-mêmes ... Mais je continuais à tout sacrifier à la cruelle satisfaction de ces curiosités passagères. (III.511)

(I realized that these suspicions were absolutely worthless ... But I continued to sacrifice everything to the cruel satisfaction of these passing suspicions.)

In general terms, this sacrifice of 'everything' entails the subordination of all values to the priorities of Marcel's jealous imagination. All perceptions are evaluated in terms of their capacity to throw light upon Albertine's mysterious behaviour. But since his very image of Albertine is in many respects a figment of his imagination, fact rapidly becomes fiction, and fiction rapidly becomes fact, as he relentlessly confuses primary, secondary, and imaginary data in flights of fancy which finally bear almost no resemblance to Albertine's reality. As he intimates in the following meditation, the illusions of passionate love derive neither from the image of the loved one nor from the realm of profound, introspective, self-knowledge, but from the ever-accelerating errors of the lover's uncontrollable imagination. Carefully introducing this crucial distinction between the relatively egotistical quality of the imagination, and the more objective and, in consequence, more valuable domain of introspection, Marcel ponders:

Si ... un graphique avait pu représenter les images qui accompagnaient ma souffrance, on eût aperçu celles de la gare d'Orsay ... de Saint-Loup penché sur le pupitre incliné d'un bureau de télégraphe ... jamais l'image d'Albertine. De même que ... notre égoïsme voit tout le temps devant lui les buts précieux pour notre moi, mais ne regarde jamais ce *Je* lui-même qui ne cesse de les considérer, de même le désir qui dirige nos actes descend vers eux, mais ne remonte pas à soi, soit que, trop utilitaire, il se précipite dans l'action et dédaigne la connaissance, soit recherche de l'avenir pour corriger les déceptions du present, soit que la paresse de l'esprit le pousse à glisser sur la pente aisée de l'imagination plutôt qu'à remonter la pente abrupte de l'introspection. (III.465)

(If ... a chart had been able to record the images that accompanied my suffering, it would have shown those of Orsay station ... of Saint-Loup leaning over the sloping desk of a telegraph office ... but never the image of Albertine. Just as our ... egotism always looks ahead to those ends most valued by our self, but never looks at that particular *I* which ceaselessly considers them, so too does the desire which prompts our actions always descend to their level, without ever looking up to examine itself, perhaps, because being too utilitarian, it plunges into action and disdains knowledge, perhaps because it explores the future in order to repair present errors, or perhaps because its spiritual indolence leads it to slide down the easy slope of the imagination rather than ascend the steep slope of introspection.)

As is so frequently the case, Marcel's terminology is far from clear. Nevertheless, he appears to be suggesting that man's imaginative and introspective faculties share the same kind of relationship as man's voluntary and involuntary memories. Like man's voluntary memories, the images of the imagination seem to have little permanent value and seem limited by their subjective, egotistical quality. By contrast, man's introspective insights appear to partake of a more permanent and more objective reality pertaining to what Marcel defines as the observing 'I' (as opposed to the desiring 'self'), just as man's involuntary memories identify the permanent, universal qualities informing different sensations. Introspective knowledge, then, appears to pertain to the more profound dimension of the self from which Marcel is signally absent when juggling with his different images of Albertine (III.70). By contrast, the images of the imagination appear to be the volatile inventions of Marcel's egotistical, spiritually indolent self, and moreover, inventions which ultimately bear very little resemblance to any particular reality (and which are therefore potentially even more confusing, and even more devoid of value, than his habitual observations). In other words, far from celebrating the fertility of man's imagination, as one might well expect the Modernist narrator-hero to do, Marcel appears to conclude that the images of the imagination are as nefarious to authentic self-perception as those of introspection are conducive to this ideal.

Considered in very general terms, Marcel's scepticism before the images of the imagination seems to derive from his discovery that such images often contradict one another, rather than harmoniously coexisting in the kind of metaphorical vision with which he associates true enlightenment. In this respect, Marcel simply reiterates Proust's longstanding enthusiasm for the kind of metaphorical perceptions that his earliest writings celebrate as 'un lien profond entre deux idées, deux sensations' (*CSB*, 303) (a profound link between two ideas, two sensations), and which Proust associates with his ability to 'sentir entre deux impressions, entre deux idées, une harmonie très fine que tous ne sentent pas' (*CSB*, 304) (detect between two impressions, two ideas, a particularly subtle harmony that many fail to notice).

These ideas from Proust's early 'Notes sur la littérature et la critique'[2] find their mature counterpart towards the end of *A la recherche du temps perdu*, in the famous paragraph in which Marcel concludes:

Ce que nous appelons la réalité est un certain rapport entre ces
sensations et ces souvenirs qui nous entourent simultanément ... la
vérité ne commencera qu'au moment où l'écrivain prendra deux objets
différents, posera leur rapport ... et les enfermera ... dans une
métaphore. (III.889)
(That which we call reality is a certain relationship between those
sensations and memories that surround us simultaneously ... truth
only begins to be expressed when a writer takes two different objects,
reveals their relationship ... and encloses them ... in a metaphor.)

As Marcel gradually learns, these metaphorical revelations are
attained during voluntary and involuntary moments of introspection, when man reads between the lines of reality, and
perceives unexpected symptoms of the unity and harmony of
both his own existence and of existence as a whole. But as Marcel
also discovers during his prolonged infatuation for Albertine, the
different images of the passionate lover's imagination seldom
cohere in such pleasant configurations. On the contrary, their
conflicting connotations frequently afflict Marcel with the
violence that he eloquently associates with 'l'assaut des images'
(II.316) (the assault of images).

   This concept is peculiarly modern, or rather *Post-Modern*,
insofar as it prefigures such lines as the opening paragraph of
Alain Robbe-Grillet's *La Maison de rendez-vous*, in which the
narrator disarmingly confides:

La chair des femmes a toujours occupé, sans doute, une grande place
dans mes rêves. Même à l'état de veille, ses images ne cessent de
m'assaillir. [3]
(Female flesh has, I suppose, always occupied pride of place in my
dreams. Even upon awakening, its images incessantly beset me.)

So much has been written about the Modernist quality of
Proust's harmonious, metaphorical vision, and about its symbolist aesthetic, that it is easy to overlook Proust's analyses of
aggressive, contradictory images, which neither fall neatly into
Proustian metaphors, nor conveniently evince Baudelairian
'correspondances', but 'assault' and 'beset' the unfortunate
perceiver.

   In this respect, Proust intermittently anticipates the way in
which Post-Modern novelists such as Beckett, Burroughs and
Robbe-Grillet have paid far more attention to disconcerting,
unharmonious groups of images and perceptions, than to the
predominantly harmonious images and perceptions celebrated

by their Modernist predecessors. Thus, while Marcel's moments of involuntary introspection reveal the sublime coherence of 'a certain relationship' between the 'sensations and memories that surround us simultaneously' (III.889), the conflicting images of his imagination generate precisely the kind of perceptual anxiety to which William Burroughs characteristically alludes in an interview, when drily ruminating:

What anxiety is, is contradictory signals. That's what causes the feeling of shakiness and powerlessness; you are getting simultaneous signals that are contradictory. [4]

In Burroughs's terms, Marcel's anxiety begins when his cherished image of Albertine as a 'creature of the sea' (III.848) is contradicted by, and confused with, his recollection of Mlle Vinteuil's lesbian frolics at Montjouvain (I.159–65). Eventually this disturbing memory becomes intermingled with his maritime image of Albertine until, by a curious process of imaginative association and dissociation, these confused and contradictory 'signals' not only negate the pleasure that Marcel initially derived from his identification of Albertine and sea, but additionally inhibit, and indeed prohibit, the innocent joy that he first experienced before the sea itself. For as Marcel explains, his unwelcome memory of Mlle Vinteuil's perverse antics at Montjouvain not only disrupts his association of Albertine with 'the primordial elements of nature that we contemplate before the sea' (I.906), but somehow becomes associated in its turn with his concept of the sea, and thus prevents him from ever again enjoying the spectacle of the sea in its own right.

Describing this crisis, and alluding to the way in which the unruly associations of his memory become inseparable from the very prospect of the sea at Balbec, Marcel dejectedly relates:

C'est cette scène que je voyais derrière celle qui s'étendait dans la fenêtre et qui n'était sur l'autre qu'un voile morne, superposé comme un reflet. Elle semblait elle-même, en effet, presque irréelle, comme une vue peinte ... plus inconsistante encore que l'image horrible de Montjouvain qu'elle ne parvenait pas à annuler, à couvrir, à cacher — poétique et vaine image du souvenir et du songe. (II.1129–30)
(It was this scene that I discerned behind the one which was framed by the window, and which seemed a mere veil, sadly stretched out or superimposed in front of the former, like a reflection. As a matter of fact, this very vista seemed almost unreal, like a painted scene ... even more unsubstantial than the horrible image of Montjouvain that it could no

more cancel than it could cover it or hide it — a vain and poetic image born of my memories and my musings.)

The very antithesis of Marcel's final euphoria before the revelations of his involuntary memories at the Guermantes Hotel, these meditations upon the bankrupt and unreal quality of art, nature, memory and the imagination offer testimony to one of his most dispirited moments. If Marcel finally recovers, then it is because he painfully extricates himself from his long 'addiction' to his imagination's successive images of Albertine. Eventually he conquers the 'spiritual indolence' (III.465) that makes him vulnerable to such 'substitute pleasures' (III.552), and determines to enclose and record his involuntary revelations within a work sensitive to the way in which man's finest perceptions 'touchent simultanément ... à des époques si distantes ... dans le Temps' (III.1048) (simultaneously touch one another ... across such distant epochs ... in Time).

In other words Marcel's timely spiritual maturity finally permits him to transcend the perceptual chaos peculiar to the passionate lover's simultaneous perceptions, and to both entertain and explicate the higher reality of harmonious simultaneous perceptions. He is fortunate only to be temporarily 'addicted' to the images of the passionate imagination. Indeed, as he rather smugly reflects after his final involuntary revelations, the confusions of passionate love offer the budding writer a number of useful insights. Alluding to sufferings of all kinds, Marcel contentedly contemplates the consoling ways in which:

ces situations imprévues nous forcent à entrer plus profondément en contact avec nous-même, ces dilemmes douloureux que l'amour nous pose à tout instant, nous instruisent, nous découvrent successivement la matière dont nous sommes fait. (III.909)
(these unforeseen situations force us to become more profoundly aware of ourselves, these painful problems that love constantly presents, teach us, and successively show us what we are made of.)

Yet as he additionally intimates, this kind of consolation is reserved only for those who survive the afflictions of passionate love. For while Marcel is only temporarily afflicted by the confusion and the dejection resulting from his infatuation for Albertine (which at worst simply delays the realization of his literary vocation), other characters, such as Swann and Charlus, never really recover from their amorous illusions, and never fulfil their positive existential potential. In this respect the flawed affection of passionate love is far more destructive than Marcel's final musings might suggest; indeed, Swann's 'amour' for Odette offers Marcel an elaborate cautionary tale regarding the perils of self-indulgent idolatry and infatuation.

Like Marcel's intoxicating obsession for Albertine, Swann's 'love' — or infatuation — for Odette arises from his imagination's modification of an original perception — or the process that Marcel terms: 'un long oubli de l'image première' (I.382) (the long obliteration of an original image). And like Marcel's conflicting images of Albertine, Swann's indolent and egocentric images of Odette gradually remove him further and further from the woman with whom he assumes himself to be in love, by confusing her with his favourite reveries and transforming her into a figment of his imagination. Significantly, Swann's first impression of Odette is far from favourable.

Reflecting upon his response to her physical appearance, Swann initially finds that:

elle était . . . non pas sans beauté, mais d'un genre de beauté qui lui était indifférent, qui ne lui inspirait aucun désir, lui causait même une sorte de répulsion physique. (I.195)
(she was . . . certainly not without beauty, but had a kind of beauty which left him indifferent, which inspired no physical desire in him, and which even caused a kind of physical repulsion in him.)

And in much the same way, many years later, when his ardour for Odette has subsided and he once again considers her relatively objectively, Swann reaffirms that she is nothing more nor less than 'une femme qui ne me plaisait pas, qui n'était pas mon genre!' (I.382) (a woman who never really pleased me, who was not even my type!). If Swann falls in love with Odette, this unlikely infatuation is very much his own paradoxical creation. As Marcel observes, Swann precipitates his love for Odette by associating her, and then identifying her, with the image of the women of his dreams, somewhat as he himself associates Albertine with 'old dreams dating from (his) childhood' (I.807). Carefully analysing this metamorphosis of Odette's image, Marcel concludes:

Et sans doute . . . en pensant ainsi à elle quand il était seul, il faisait seulement jouer son image entre beaucoup d'autres images de femmes dans des rêveries romanesques; mais si, grâce à une circonstance quelconque . . . l'image d'Odette de Crécy venait à absorber toutes ces

rêveries, si celles-ci n'étaient plus séparables de son souvenir, alors
l'imperfection de son corps ne garderait plus aucune importance . . .
puisque, devenu le corps de celle qu'il aimait, il serait désormais le seul
qui fût capable de lui causer des joies et des tourments. (I.199)
(And no doubt . . . as he thought about her in this way when he was
alone, he merely played her image between many other images of
women in his romantic dreams; but if, thanks to some circumstance or
other . . . the image of Odette de Crécy chanced to absorb all of these
other dreams, if these other dreams became inseparable from her
memory, then the imperfection of her body lost all importance . . . since,
having become the body of the one whom he loved, it was henceforth
the only one capable of causing him pleasure or pain.)

Having incorporated Odette's image into the world of his
'romantic dreams', Swann's over-active imagination additionally integrates Odette's image into the aesthetic domain of his
artistic dreams. Associating and then identifying Odette's
features with those of Botticelli's 'Zipporah', Swann finally
congratulates himself for demonstrating the qualitative parity
between the two, and for discovering that 'le plaisir qu'il avait à
voir Odette trouvât une justification dans sa propre culture
esthétique' (I.224) (the pleasure with which he contemplated
Odette found its justification in his own aesthetic principles).
Wryly commenting upon the curious way in which Swann's
exercise of imaginative mind over mediocre matter transforms
Odette's physical imperfections into a living 'masterpiece',
Marcel explains that

Le mot d'"'oeuvre florentine" rendait un grand service à Swann. Il lui
permit . . . de faire pénétrer l'image d'Odette dans un monde de rêves
où elle n'avait pas eu accès jusqu'ici et où elle s'imprégna de noblesse.
(I.224)
(The formula of "Florentine work" did Swann a great service. It enabled
him to infiltrate Odette's image into a world of dreams to which she had
hitherto had no access, and in which she now became filled with
prestige.)

But as Marcel's subsequent comments indicate, this fanciful
formula also does a great disservice to Swann's introspective
faculties, since it prevents him from appreciating either Odette's
physiognomy or Botticelli's originality in their own right (just as
his similarly self-indulgent indentification and conflation of his
intoxicating infatuation for Odette with the ethereal beauty of
Vinteuil's music, obscures both his own self-knowledge and his
appreciation of the orginality of Vinteuil's art). Addressing this

problem, and alluding to the way in which Swann's and Odette's response to the 'little phrase' which they fondly think of as 'l'air national de leur amour' (I.219) (the national anthem of their love) finally prevents Swann from ever listening to the entirety of Vinteuil's sonata, Marcel explains:

Il la considérait moins en elle-même ... que comme un gage, un souvenir de son amour qui ... faisait penser à Odette en même temps qu'à lui, les unissait; c'était au point que, comme Odette, par caprice, l'en avait prié, il avait renoncé à son projet de se faire jouer par un artiste la sonate entière, dont il continua à ne connaître que ce passage. "Qu'avez-vous besoin du reste? lui avait-elle dit. C'est ça *notre* morceau". (I.218–19)
(He considered it not so much in its own terms ... but rather, as a pledge, as a memento of his love, which ... evoked Odette, and, at the same time, himself, uniting them; indeed it reached the point that when Odette, by a mere caprice, made the suggestion, he abandoned his plan to ask a musician to play the entire sonata for him, and continued to know no more of it than this passage. "What do you want with the rest of it? she had asked him. This, after all, is *our* part of it''.)

In this respect, both Swann and Odette inhibit Swann's potentially positive self-realization as a critic of the arts by reducing art and music to the triviality of his amorous illusions. His greatest error is his wilful confusion of the immateriality of art with the materiality of Odette,[5] while her greatest error is that by accident or design she distracts Swann's attention from profound, immaterial realities. In this instance, by a mere caprice, she leads him to sacrifice his plan to explore and analyse the entirety of Vinteuil's sonata. On other occasions, her very presence disturbs him and proves inimical to introspection. Just as Marcel becomes aware that Albertine's company leaves him 'absent' from himself (III.70), and eventually deprives him of all pleasure before the sea at Balbec, Swann finds that

l'agitation où le mettait la présence d'Odette ... le privait du calme et du bien-être qui sont le fond indispensable aux impressions que peut donner la nature. (I.271)
(the agitation which he felt in Odette's presence ... deprived him of that indispensible sense of calm and well-being which informs all our impressions before nature.)

Worse still, Swann's agitated adulation for Odette completely disorientates his sense of values. On the one hand, he overvalues Odette by equating her with the beauty of Vinteuil's music. On the other, he undervalues, and indeed gravely misjudges, the quality of Vinteuil's music by associating it with Odette's infidelity.

Introducing the strange process by which Swann's troubled imagination convinces him that Vinteuil's compositions, like the machinations of Mme Verdurin, are somehow or other responsible for Odette's new liaison with M. de Forcheville, Marcel explains how Swann denounces both Mme Verdurin and Vinteuil's sonata in identical terms, as literal or metaphorical pimps or procurers:

"Entremetteuse", c'était le nom qu'il donnait aussi à la musique qui les convierait à se taire, à rêver ensemble, à se regarder, à se prendre la main. Il trouvait du bon à la sévérité contre les arts. (I.287)
("Procuress", such too, was the name that he also gave to the music which had invited them to sit in silence, to dream together, to gaze at one another, and to hold each other's hands. He saw considerable merit in the view of those who sternly criticize the arts.)

At this point in his misadventures, Swann becomes completely detached from the reality of his own feelings, from the reality of Odette, and from the reality of the musical and artistic works which he confuses with what he takes to be Odette's virtues and vices, and enters well and truly into the condition that Marcel describes as being 'absent' from oneself (III.70). And just as Marcel's absence from himself leads him to 'sacrifice everything' (III.511) to the chimera of Albertine, so too do Swann's hapless confusions lead him to sacrifice all his values and all his aspirations in order to placate his addiction to Odette's increasingly dissatisfying presence. Eventually, Swann himself reflects with alarm upon the alacrity with which

il sacrifierait ses travaux, ses plaisirs, ses amis, finalement toute sa vie, à l'attente quotidienne d'un rendez-vous qui ne pouvait rien lui apporter d'heureux. (I.354)
(he would sacrifice his work, his pleasures, his friends, his whole life in fact, in order to await a weekly rendez-vous which could not really offer him an ounce of happiness.)

Such negative forms of self-sacrifice are, of course, the very reverse of the positive sacrifice of egotistical desires which informs Marcel's grandmother's distillation and communication of her quintessential benevolence on those occasions when, far from being 'absent' from herself, she realizes her finest potential with maximum intensity.

Nevertheless, however fatal Marcel's and Swann's passionate imaginings may prove to the realization of their better selves, their confusions are at least precipitated by misguided enthusiasm for two mysterious individuals, namely, Albertine and Odette. In this respect, their flawed affection results from their indolent and self-indulgent responses to the mystery of the human personality. As such, it may be distinguished from the second, even more flawed and even more degenerate travesty of affection that Marcel associates with the utterly impersonal, anonymous sexual relationships that he derides as 'la saisie d'un morceau de chair' (II.362) (the seizing of a piece of flesh).

Marcel's principal objection to such impersonal sexual relations is that they are 'anonymes, sans secret, sans prestige' (III.362) (anonymous, without secret, without prestige). Put another way, they lack the 'réalité immatérielle' (III.362) (immaterial reality) that the passionate lover both discerns in and attributes to the object of his passion, and therefore have no 'prestige'. Thus, Marcel reasons that he could never fall in love with a girl encountered in a brothel, since the very accessibility and predictability of her presence would deprive her of the immaterial, secretive 'prestige' that he senses when glimpsing the mysterious Albertine from afar. In other words, what he seeks, and what other passionate lovers such as Swann seek, is not so much 'a piece of flesh', as 'ce charme de l'inconnu qui ne serait pas ajouté . . . à une jolie fille trouvée dans ces maisons où elles vous attendent' (III.141) (this charm of the unknown which would not surround . . . a pretty girl found in one of those houses where they await you). To some extent, then, the passionate lover's sentimental wild-goose chase has the superficial virtue of pursuing an unknown, immaterial, or metaphysical reality: a saving grace to which the pursuit of anonymous and purely material, or physical, sexual gratification can make no claim.

Marcel's disdain for such anonymous sexual gratification is anticipated by a number of Proust's earlier writings, such as the minor episode in *Jean Santeuil* entitled 'Daltozzi suivant les femmes', in which the narrator evokes the partially pathetic and partially comic way in which the workings of impersonal sexual pleasure are invariably thwarted by the spanner of disastrously personal outbursts of conversation. Having described the gestural communication, or 'muet consentement' (mute agreement), by which Daltozzi and one of his anonymous partners rather impressively 'échangaient en une seconde électriquement, sous ... l'aveu de l'envie la plus basse, le secret inexprimable et doux de leur être, le rêve vague et vain de leur vie' (*JS*, 846–7) (exchanged instantaneously and electrically, via ... this avowal of the basest desire, the sweet and inexpressible secret of their being, the vague and vain dream of their existence), Jean Santeuil adds that the moment that they speak to one another their 'electric' erotic idyll becomes abruptly short-circuited,

la voix suggérant aussitôt l'idée d'une personne semblable à nous qui peut nous causer des plaisirs et des peines, mais des plaisirs et des peines humaines. (*JS*, 847)
(their voices immediately evoking the idea of a person like themselves who could cause them pleasures and pains, and moreover, human pleasures and pains.)

Such erotic communication is, then, quite literally impersonal and inhuman, since its very possibility depends upon the neutralization of all traces of human and personal discourse, and upon the absence of all signs of individuality save for the promiscuity that Marcel defines as man's 'basest desire'. As such, this communication is utterly sensual rather than spiritual; utterly physical rather than metaphysical; and the very antithesis of the 'universal' communication that Marcel associates with the most authentic modes of artistic and non-artistic self-realization.

Jean Santeuil is, nevertheless, quite fascinated by the way in which the gestural codes and discourses of sexual desire appear to transcend the limitations of habitual verbal communication by communicating man's 'inexpressible' secrets. But at the same time, Jean Santeuil is also well aware that this erotic communication is sub-spiritual in quality, and that its very existence necessitates the negation of man's 'human' qualities. In much the same way, the narrator of *Jean Santeuil* muses that while corporeal communication seems relatively uncomplicated, insofar as that which 'est fait physiquement pour s'unir, s'unit sans une hésitation' (is made for physical coupling, couples without hesitation), 'les lois ne sont plus les mêmes quand on entre dans le monde des âmes' (*JS*, 509) (different laws apply when one enters into the world of souls).

As should now be quite apparent, Marcel's abiding pre-occupation in *A la recherche du temps perdu* is precisely the nature of those laws which inform 'the world of souls', and which in turn permit 'the communication of souls' (III.258). Accordingly, although he is initially entranced by his discovery of the gestural language of erotic desire, and attempts to analyse its conventions with all the enthusiasm of Roland Barthes's analysis of such 'mythologies' as the discursive conventions of strip-tease,[6] Marcel subsequently suggests that as a force which utterly destroys man's capacity to enter into the communication of 'souls', such impersonal erotic desire is even more nefarious to authentic affection and authentic self-realization than the illusions of passionate love.

Perhaps Marcel's most traumatic revelation of the gestural language of impersonal erotic desire is at the beginning of *Sodome et Gomorrhe* (II.601) when he spies upon the successive gestures with which M. de Charlus and Jupien exchange both the verbally and socially inexpressible sentiment of their homosexual desire for one another. Observing their ballet of gestures with the eyes of a sentimental naturalist, rather than with the eyes of an existentialist moralist, Marcel associates their fleeting movements with 'ce sentiment de la brièveté de toutes choses ... qui rend si emouvant le spectacle de tout amour' (this feeling for the brevity of all things ... which makes every manifestation of love so moving); delights in 'la beauté des regards de M. de Charlus et de Jupien' (II.605) (the beauty of M. de Charlus's and Jupien's glances); and finally persuades himself that these gestures partake of the same natural laws as 'la fécondation de la fleur par le bourdon' (II.632) (the fertilization of the blossom by the bumble bee).

While this biological analogy is not quite so self-indulgent as the fanciful metaphorical vision which previously prompts Marcel to equate Albertine with the sea and with its seagulls (III.848), it has much in common with Charlus's peculiarly rose-tinted vision of his liaison with Jupien. Somewhat as the late Maurice Chevalier crooned 'Every little breeze seems to whisper Louise', Marcel confides that initially, like Charlus, he finds Jupien's image to be inseparable from 'le soleil de l'après-midi et les fleurs de l'arbuste' (II.630) (the afternoon sunshine and the blossoming plants).

However, when reconsidering Charlus in a more sober frame of mind, Marcel denounces his subsequent sexual escapades in Jupien's brothel as 'la démence complète' (III.838) (complete insanity), asking:

comment un certain sentiment de dignité personelle et de respect de soi-même ne l'avait ... pas forcé à refuser à sa sensualité certaines satisfactions. (III.838)
(why a certain sense of dignity and of self-respect had not forced him to refuse certain sensual satisfactions.)

In a sense this question is merely rhetorical. For as Marcel explains earlier in his narrative, Charlus lacks all sense of dignity and self-respect for the simple reason that he has become completely alienated from his better self, and has degenerated into a caricature of his sensuality, or in Marcel's terms, a caricature of 'l'évolution de son mal' (the evolution of his disorder), and of 'la révolution de son vice' (III.763) (the revolution of his vice).

Musing yet again upon those existential conflicts in which man's finer potential struggles for ascendency with his worse potential, Marcel suggests that Charlus's greatest failing is his voluntary surrender to his vices. Rather than engaging in the kind of existential battle advocated by Elstir (I.864), Charlus, like his fellow customers in Jupien's brothel, exhibits 'quelque chose de répugnant ... la non-résistance à des plaisirs dégradants' (III.835) (something repugnant ... acquiescence to degrading pleasures), and accelerates his degeneration to the point at which 'ses qualités ancestrales (étaient) entièrement interceptées par le passage en face d'elles du défaut ou du mal générique dont ils sont accompagnés' (III.763) (his ancestral qualities were entirely intercepted and occluded by the hereditary faults or disorders which accompanied them). Finally, then, Charlus is not simply 'absent' from his better self, as Marcel is, when distracted and tormented by Albertine (III.70), but becomes completely divided from his better self. Pondering upon this transformation, Marcel reflects that:

M. de Charlus était arrivé aussi loin qu'il était possible de soi-même, ou plutôt il était lui-même si parfaitement masqué par ce qu'il était devenu et qui n'appartenait pas à lui seul mais à beaucoup d'autres invertis, qu'à la première minute je l'avais pris pour un autre d'entre eux ... qui n'était pas M. de Charlus, qui n'était pas un grand seigneur, qui n'était pas un homme d'imagination et d'esprit, et qui n'avait pour toute ressemblance avec le baron que cet air commun à tous, qui maintenant chez lui, au moins avant qu'on se fût appliqué à bien regarder, couvrait tout. (III.763–4)
(M. de Charlus had become as distant as he could be from himself, or rather, he was so perfectly masked by what he had become and by what belonged not only to him but to many other inverts, that at first sight, I took him to be just another of them ... someone who was not M. de Charlus, who was not a great aristocrat, was not a man of wit and imagination, and whose only resemblance to the baron lay in that common trait, shared by them all, which now, on first inspection at least, completely enveloped him.)

Eventually Charlus's very perceptions are likewise 'enveloped' by his sexual desire, so that both mentally and physically he embodies the decline that Edmund Wilson generously defines as 'the cruel paradox of a fine mind and a sensitive nature at the mercy of instincts which humiliate them'.[7] Just as Charlus's distinguished physiognomy becomes reduced to the 'common trait' of Jupien's clients, the subtleties and discriminations of his 'don spirituel' (II.953) (spiritual gifts) degenerate into the comic simplicity of the 'catégorie spéciale' (III.787) (special category) and the 'causes spéciales' (III.787) (special causes) with which Charlus evaluates and explicates all aspects of society. Charlus not only imagines himself to be surrounded by other members of his own 'special category', '(voyant) facilement partout des pareils à lui' (II.919) (effortlessly recognizing others such as himself everywhere), and needlessly spurns the company of such innoxious acquaintances as Cottard so as to preserve his heterosexual 'identity'; but still more imaginatively attributes the course of the first world war to the 'special causes' of a network of homosexual alliances between the crowned heads of Europe: a theory that Marcel impatiently dismisses as Charlus's 'explication stupide' (III.788) (stupid explanation).

In much the same way, Marcel's own perceptions are similarly — if rather less extravagantly — distorted during those moments of unrestrained sexual desire in which he completely fails to recognize various acquaintances save in terms of potential partners, confusing Gilberte with 'une cocotte' (III.574) (a tart), and reducing Rachel's identity to that of 'l'actrice qui le faisait de l'oeil' (III.1000) (the actress making eyes at him). Like the illusions of passionate love, the illusions of passionate lust are inimical to authentic perception.

As Marcel observes, Charlus's failure to maintain either his hereditary aristocratic dignity or his habitual perspicuity derives from his 'weakness of character' (II.415), or more specifically from his vice, 'le plus grand de tous, le manque de volonté' (III.836) (the worst of them all, a lack of will-power). Marcel has good reason to dub this vice 'the worst of all', since it accounts both for the flawed affection and the flawed creativity of Swann and Charlus. Just as Swann's passionate pursuit of Odette, and Charlus's dispassionate pursuit of anonymous sex, offer increasingly extreme antitheses of ideal affection (or ideal 'non-artistic' action), Swann's dilettantism and Charlus's enthusiasm for sadistic spectacles similarly subvert the ideal creativity (or ideal 'artistic' action) in this novel.

Although Swann's failings are usually less extreme than those of Charlus, their existential errors arise from the same ethical impoverishment. Both Swann and Charlus are chronically idle. Swann, for example, belongs to

cette catégorie d'hommes intelligents qui ont vécu dans l'oisiveté et qui cherchent une consolation et peut-être une excuse dans l'idée que cette oisiveté offre à leur intelligence des objets aussi dignes d'intérêt que pourrait faire l'art ou l'étude, que la "Vie" contient des situations plus intéressantes, plus romanesques que tous les romans. (I.193)
(that category of intelligent men who live indolently and who seek consolation, and perhaps, justification, in the idea that this indolence offers their intelligence objects quite as worthy of attention as art or study, and that "Life" contains situations that are more interesting and more strange than any works of fiction.)

Charlus shares Swann's confidence that 'life suffices', explaining to Marcel: 'Je ne travaille pas pour l'histoire . . . la vie me suffit, elle est bien assez intéressante, comme disait le pauvre Swann' (III.299) (I am not working for posterity . . . life is enough for me, it is quite interesting enough, as poor Swann used to say). Swann and Charlus never transform their fantasies into tangible works of art, unlike Marcel, who initially dissipates his creative energies by confusing Albertine with the fantasies that he poignantly describes as 'un roman que j'avais mis des millions de minutes à écrire' (III.350) (a novel that I had spent millions of minutes writing), but who finally decides to write a real novel. At most, Swann misguidedly weaves his misunderstandings about Odette into the comedy of errors that Marcel describes as 'tout un roman' (III.574) (a whole novel), just as Charlus perceives 'tout un roman' (II.1061) in the movements of Morel. But as Marcel specifies, when comparing the failings of the ailing Elstir with those of Swann, such fancies bear little relation to authentic creativity.

Swann's creative gifts are of course those of a critic rather than those of an artist. While the decline of Swann's career as a critic can be traced back to the time when he forsakes the study of Vermeer that Marcel speaks of as being 'abandonnée depuis des années' (I.198) (abandoned many years ago), this decline culminates when Swann finally transfers his attention from works of art to people who resemble works of art. Put another way, Swann turns from the immateriality of art to the materiality of 'life'; from the spiritual beauty of a figure by Botticelli to the physical charms of Odette, who not only resembles a 'Virgin' by

Botticelli, but also offers the less virginal advantages of being 'prête à être embrassée et possédée' (I.238) (ready to be embraced and possessed). It is, of course, precisely these 'éléments communs de la vie' (I.864) (common elements of life) that successful Proustian artists — such as Elstir — self-consciously reject, in order to create their finest works.

Nevertheless, as Elstir grows older his scruples relax, and he finds himself 'De plus en plus enclin à croire matérialistement qu'une part notable de la beauté réside dans les choses' (III.770) (More and more inclined toward the materialist belief that a significant portion of beauty is to be found in things). Finally, Elstir complacently conflates life with art, and devotes himself to 'l'adoration des modèles' (I.852) (the adoration of models), confusing the immateriality of his own paintings with the material beauty of those who posed for them. Identifying the indolence which leads Elstir — like Swann — to such inactive, perceptual plagiarism, and emphasizing that their confusions between art and life fall short of authentic creativity, Marcel concludes:

Et ainsi la beauté de la vie, mot en quelque sorte dépourvu de signification, stade situé en deçà de l'art et auquel j'avais vu s'arrêter Swann, était celui où, par relentissement du génie createur, idolâtrie des formes qui l'avaient favorisé, désir du moindre effort, devait un jour rétrograder peu à peu un Elstir. (I.852)
(And thus the beauty of life, a concept which in a sense has no meaning, and which signifies a state falling short of art and the point at which I had seen Swann come to a halt, was in turn the state to which, as a result of his declining creative genius, his idolatry of the forms which had favoured it, and his desire to make the least possible effort, an artist such as Elstir was gradually to fall.)

Towards the end of his narrative, Marcel once again distinguishes authentic creativity from all kinds of derivative thought and plagiarism, be these the fantasies of amorous dilettentes such as Swann, the narcissistic fancies of declining artists such as Elstir, or even the joy of those who study 'la belle pensée d'un maître' (the most sublime thoughts of a master). For such joy, however reverent and pure, 'les réduit tout de même à n'être que la pleine conscience d'un autre' (III.894) (reduces them, when all is said and done, to nothing more than complete awareness of another). Briefly, ideal creativity appears to necessitate the perceiver's complete awareness — and adequate expression — of his own most sublime insights.

If Swann's dilettantism confuses reality with the paintings

prompting 'his own aesthetic principles' (I.224), Charlus's dilettantism is predominantly literary. Accordingly, Charlus is described as acting 'par littérature' (III.242) (for literary motives), and as 'se livrant à son goût de littérature' (III.274) (giving way to his literary tastes). For example, while Swann seeks refuge and consolation in 'artistic' aspects of 'life', Charlus identifies himself with such literary figures as Balzac's princesse de Cadignan; an 'artistic' confusion which momentarily excites a measure of Marcel's admiration:

Mais le baron était fort artiste. . . . Et maintenant que depuis un instant il confondait sa situation avec celle décrite par Balzac, il se réfugiait en quelque sorte dans la nouvelle . . . et . . . il avait cette consolation de trouver dans sa propre anxiété . . . quelque chose de "très balzacien". (II.1058)
(But the baron was highly artistic. . . . And now that he had confused his situation for an instant with that described by Balzac, he more or less took refuge in the story . . . and . . . at least had the consolation of finding that his own anxiety . . . had a "very Balzacian" quality.)

Marcel's indulgence towards this literary fantasy is understandable, insofar as Charlus's 'transposition mentale' (II.1059) (mental transposition) is at once amusing, imaginative, and relatively harmless and undisturbing. At worst, it is primarily a private, escapist fantasy, which, like Swann's artistic fantasies, allows Charlus to 'laisser de côté le fond des choses' (I.210) (set deep realities aside). By contrast, Charlus's tendency to extend such fantasies into the more public, 'theatrical' dimension of sadistic spectacles and rituals proves infinitely more disturbing, and offers a second, more degenerate alternative to ideal creativity (just as Charlus's dispassionate lust extends the delusions of passionate love into a second, more degenerate alternative to ideal affection).

At first, this 'theatrical' phase of Charlus's dilettantism takes the form of quarrelsome tirades. Rather than silently indulging in private literary fantasies, Charlus appears driven to offer his imagination more public and more voluble expression. According to Marcel,

Il avait pris l'habitude de crier très fort en parlant, par nervosité, par recherche d'issues pour des impressions dont il fallait — n'ayant jamais cultivé aucun art — qu'il se débarrassât, comme un aviateur de ses bombes. (III.799)
(He had acquired the habit of shouting out loud in conversation, out of

nervousness, and in order to give vent to the feelings which — having never mastered any art — he had to unleash, somewhat as a pilot unloads his bombs.)

Far from constituting a heroic metaphor, Marcel's analogy between Charlus and a bomber pilot points to the alarmingly compulsive quality of Charlus's vociferous outbursts. Just as bombs are at times arbitrarily jettisoned far from their targets, 'en plein champ' (in the open country), Charlus's tirades similarly occur 'au hasard' (haphazardly), falling either upon an absence of ears, 'là où ses paroles n'atteignaient personne' (where there was no audience for his words), or else falling upon singularly reluctant ears 'dans le monde où . . . il était écouté par snobisme . . . et, tant il tyrannisait les auditeurs . . . par crainte' (III.799) (in society, where . . . people listened to him out of snobbery . . . and, so effectively did he tyrannize them . . . out of fear). At best, then, these outbursts offer Charlus's imagination a certain verbal relief, rather than any valid mode of expression or communication.

In this respect, Charlus's dilemma bears remarkable similarity to the plight of the indolent intellectuals in *Jean Santeuil*, whom Proust evokes in terms of their peculiarly restless enthusiasm, alluding to:

les assemblées où des hommes intelligents et ardents n'ont pas à leur activité un but intérieur et désintéressé, (et où) vous les voyez, avec une sorte d'acharnement maladif, comme s'ils avaient besoin absolument de dépenser leur intelligence et leur sensibilité pour qu'elles les laissent tranquilles. (*JS*, 630)
(those gatherings where intelligent and enthusiastic men cannot find disinterested and interior ends for their activities, (and where) you see them, with a kind of feverish eagerness, as though they were compelled to exhaust their intelligence and their sensitivity before they could rest in peace.)

Lacking any 'art' and any 'disinterested and interior' motivation, Charlus's tyrannical tirades exhibit precisely this 'feverish eagerness', and additionally anticipate the equally anguished logorrhoea of such Beckettian characters as 'Mouth' in *Not I*, or indeed of any number of other equally incurable victims of the affliction that the narrator of *Texts for Nothing* diagnoses as 'wordshit'.[8]

Somewhat as Beckett's characters seek refuge from mental torment in both verbal and physical rituals, engaging in the

consoling ceremonies that 'Man' (and more recently, Ruby
Cohn) have celebrated as 'just play',[9] Charlus transforms his
melodramatic monologues into melodramatic mini-dramas or
happenings, to be performed both by others and by himself.
Thus he becomes the producer of increasingly sadistic
'spectacles' and 'scenes'. Quite early on in *A la recherche du temps
perdu*, Charlus confides to Marcel that he is particularly fond of
'les spectacles exotiques' (exotic spectacles). He enthusiastically
suggests that Marcel should help him to organize 'des parties
pour faire rire' (some amusements), where guests might be
entertained by 'une luttre entre (Bloch) et son père où il le
blesserait comme David Goliath' (a fight between Bloch and his
father in which he would offer him the injury that David gave
Goliath), or by some other 'farce assez plaisante' (agreeable little
farce), such as the spectacle of seeing Bloch 'frapper à coups
redoublés . . . sa carogne de mère' (II.288) (thrash . . . his old hag
of a mother). Later, when Charlus unexpectedly harangues him
in his turn, Marcel concludes that this unmotivated scene is quite
literally a theatrical 'scene' rather than an expression of any
personal disagreement, and that like much of Charlus's
behaviour it is 'préparée et jouée . . . par amour du spectacle'
(II.559) (prepared and played . . . out of a love of drama).

Charlus's dilemma, of course, is that his 'love of drama'
becomes more and more degenerate, and more and more
destructive. Successively retrogressing from his private literary
fantasies, to his verbal chastisement of others, and to his plans to
spy upon Bloch's chastisement of his parents, Charlus finally
stage-manages his own chastisement in Jupien's brothel, where
he hopes that this ritual will afford '(le) plaisir sadique de se
mêler à une vie crapuleuse' (III.825) (the sadistic pleasure of
sharing a debauched existence). Ironically, Charlus is denied this
perverse pleasure because his partner in crime is at once insufficiently perverse and insufficiently criminal, and merely
offers Charlus '(un) effort factice vers la perversité' (III.827) (a
pale imitation of perversity).

At the same time, Charlus overestimates his own capacity for
evil, and is at most 'un faux méchant' (III.317) (a superficial
sinner), insofar as his neglected (but not entirely extinguished)
benevolent potential constantly thwarts his sadistic fantasies. In
this respect, Charlus has many similarities with the potentially
virtuous Mlle Vinteuil, who is also an 'artiste du mal' (I.164)
(artist in evil) rather than a wholly evil person, and whose
perverse experiments, like those of Charlus, merely afford 'une

simulation de méchanceté' (an illusion of wickedness) rather than 'la vraie et joyeuse méchanceté qu'elle aurait voulue' (III.262) (the genuine and joyful wickedness to which she aspired). Constantly failing to satisfy his 'soif de mal' (III.827) (thirst for evil), and equally consistently failing to realize his better self, Charlus becomes prey to the perceptual contradictions and agitations of the condition that Marcel describes as 'le même cercle vicieux' (III.827) (the same old vicious circle): an existential limbo which has much in common with the fate of Marcel's nihilistic tante Léonie, who is compared with a waterlily, trapped forever in the 'vicious circle' of a stream's conflicting currents (I.168–9).

While Swann's and Charlus's failings illustrate the ways in which flawed affection and flawed creativity render man evermore imperfect, and ever-more distant from his 'perfectible' potential, a third category of characters, exemplified primarily by the vindictive Verdurin couple, indicate the imperfection of a further category of actions, which, *faute de mieux*, might be defined as social actions. These actions offer positive and negative alternatives to habitual modes of 'social' or 'public' relations (as opposed to more 'private', interpersonal relationships, such as Marcel's relationship with his grandmother or Swann's relationship with Odette).

Marcel does not really describe any substantial example of exemplary 'social action', although this distinction might be attributed to the generosity of the golden-hearted millionaires named Larivière, who unselfishly look after a café belonging to their impoverished cousins 'sans vouloir toucher un sou' (III.845) (without asking for a sou). By contrast, Marcel offers extensive examples of the ways in which imperfections proliferate among man's more public, social relations. As in the domains of flawed affection and flawed creativity, he conceives of two kinds of flawed social interaction, the one more pernicious than the other. He associates the first, and least pernicious, of these phases with the cruel indifference of those infatuated with social conventions and the values of high society: an attitude anticipated by the vanity of Albertine and the *jeunes filles en fleurs*.

Like the *jeunes filles en fleurs*, such pillars of society as the Guermantes and the Verdurins tend to evaluate existence in terms of 'a certain mixture of grace, suppleness and physical elegance' (I.790), rather than according to any more sophisticated, ethical criteria. Indeed, they often owe their reputations to their 'correction presque enfantine des manières' (II.251) (almost childishly punctilious manners). For example, M. de Guermantes is renowned as an 'adorable modèle des grâces juvéniles' (III.721) (adorable model of childish grace), while the Verdurins's friend, the sculptor Ski, perfects gestures which, as Marcel scathingly remarks, 'eussent été gracieux s'il eût eu encore neuf ans' (II.874) (would have seemed graceful had he still been only nine years old).

As Marcel's comments suggest, he regards such elegance to be as 'essentiellement puérile' (I.909) (essentially puerile) as the childish grace of the *jeunes filles en fleurs*; and he dismisses it as 'le charme fallacieux des gens du monde' (II.567) (the fallacious charm of high society), accusing his aristocratic friends of lapsing into 'la stérilité' (sterility), rather than cultivating 'une activité sociale véritable' (II.470) (authentic social activity). In a sense, these remarks merely confirm his contempt for the sterility of all modes of habitual existence, rather than specifically condemning a negative mode of 'social action'. But as Marcel indicates on a number of occasions, his friends' obsession with social conventions frequently degenerates into the cruel indifference which seems to form the first phase of negative social action. This cruelty may best be introduced by contrast with the following account from *Monsieur Proust* (the memoirs of Proust's housekeeper, Céleste Albaret), in which Céleste Albaret gives some idea of Proust's own conception of 'positive social action'.

Referring to an occasion during one of Proust's illnesses when she confided to Proust that she had remained with him, rather than going to mass, Céleste Albaret tellingly recalls that Proust replied: 'Céleste, savez-vous que vous faites quelque chose de bien plus noble et de bien plus grande que d'aller à la messe? Vous donnez votre temps à soigner un malade. C'est infiniment plus beau' (Céleste, don't you realize that you are doing something far nobler and far greater than going to mass? You're giving up your time in order to take care of someone who is ill. That's infinitely more beautiful).[10] If the authenticity of this anecdote be accepted, then it would seem clear that Proust valued generous actions far more than pious conventions. Yet far from selflessly sacrificing their time in order to offer solicitude to their suffering friends, such socialites as the Guermantes and the Verdurins ruthlessly sacrifice the ties of friendship in order to remain faithful to the impious, and thoroughly hedonistic dictates of social conventions.

Perhaps the most striking example of this cruelty is the

occasion when M. de Guermantes refuses to acknowledge Swann's revelation of his fatal illness, for fear that any expression of sympathy might delay the delights of a dinner party, and excuses his departure on the pretext that both he and his wife are virtually 'dying' themselves, explaining: 'elle est déjà très fatiguée, elle arrivera au dîner morte. Et puis je vous avouerai franchement que moi je meurs de faim' (II.597) (she is already exhausted, and will be dead by the time she arrives at the dinner. And then, let me confess quite frankly that I'm personally dying of hunger). If the irony of these lines condemns M. de Guermantes, Marcel's commentary censures Mme de Guermantes even more explicitly for failing to 'témoigner de la pitié à un homme qui va mourir' (show pity to a dying man), and for heeding the social convention which decrees that she should 'aller dîner en ville' (dine in town), because it 'demandait . . . moins d'efforts' (II.595) (called for less effort). In other words, like all of Proust's other imperfect characters, Mme de Guermantes's failure arises from her refusal to sacrifice pleasures by engaging in the kind of existential struggle advocated by Elstir (I.864).

M. de Guermantes similarly manifests this kind of 'détermination de ne pas renoncer à un plaisir' (II.725) (determination not to give up a pleasure) when news of his cousin's death threatens to disrupt his departure to another fashionable *fête*. Callously protesting, 'Il est mort! Mais non, on exagère, on exagère!' (II.725) (Dead is he! No, no, no, they're exaggerating, exaggerating!) he anticipates the way in which M. Verdurin adamantly employs almost identical rhetoric, when the inconvenient announcement of princesse Sherbatoff's death moves him to remonstrate: 'Vous, vous exagérez toujours' (III.228) (You, you're always exaggerating).

Unlike this singularly impassive response to the afflictions of friends and relations, the second phase of negative 'social action' consists of the more *active* cruelty that Marcel defines as 'cette indifférence aux souffrances qu'on cause' (that indifference to the sufferings that one causes), and which he damns in the same breath as 'la forme terrible et permanente de la cruauté' (I.165) (the most terrible and permanent form of cruelty). Fleetingly exemplified in terms of Mme de Guermantes's appetite for what Marcel succinctly terms 'les satisfactions . . . de persécution' (III.577) (the pleasures . . . of persecution), and by the cruel 'distraction' (II.484) that she derives from the driving her servant Poullein to despair, by thwarting his every attempt to meet his

fiancée (II.484, II.597), this active cruelty is primarily the
province of the redoubtable Mme Verdurin.

Explaining that 'Mme Verdurin et son mari avaient contracté
dans l'oisiveté des instincts cruels à qui les grandes
circonstances, trops rares, ne suffisaient plus' (II.900) (In the
course of their indolent existence, Mme Verdurin and her
husband had developed cruel instincts which the paucity of
everyday events no longer satisfied), Marcel traces the way in
which the relatively benevolent 'besoin de s'engouer, de faire
aussi des rapprochements' (need to become besotted, and also to
bring people together), which initially prompts them to form
their salon, degenerates into their malevolent 'désir de brouiller,
d'éloigner' (III.229) (compulsion to quarrel, to drive people
apart).

Like Swann, who abandons his study of Vermeer (I.198), and
like Charlus, who similarly abandons his artistic vocation, the
Verdurins — or M. Verdurin at least — are examples of those
lapsed intellectuals whom Marcel describes as: 'les gens trop
intelligents pour la vie relativement oisive qu'ils mènent et où
leurs facultés ne se réalisent pas' (III.699) (those who are too
intelligent for the relatively indolent lifestyle that they lead, and
in which their faculties remain unrealized). As Marcel discovers,
M. Verdurin once worked as an art critic and wrote a book on
Whistler, until he abandoned such activity upon that 'renoncement à écrire' (III.709) (renunciation of writing) that coincided
with his marriage to Mme Verdurin and with his addiction to
morphine. The dilemma for all of these lapsed intellectuals is that
the superficiality of high society continually frustrates their
impatience for 'une satiété que les plaisirs sociaux sont
impuissants à donner' (III.287) (satisfactions which social
pleasures are powerless to provide).

Somewhat as Charlus's search for such satisfactions drives him
to seek fulfilment by organizing and participating in his sadistic
and masochistic 'spectacles', the Verdurins similarly turn to
sadistic satisfactions in order to enliven their existence, and
entertain themselves by sabotaging their friends' successive
romances. Thus, having 'bien pu brouiller Odette avec Swann'
(II.900) (well and truly led Odette to quarrel with Swann), Mme
Verdurin proudly reflects that she has equally successfully
severed Brichot's amorous liaisons, 'avec sa blanchisseuse
d'abord, Mme de Cambremer ensuite' (III.281) (firstly with his
laundry maid, and then with Mme de Cambremer): an
intervention which leaves poor Brichot 'presque complètement

aveugle et, disait-on, morphinomane' (III.281) (almost completely blind, and, according to rumour, addicted to morphine). In much the same way, Charlus is left 'à demi mourant' (III.323) (more dead than alive) after the Verdurins have carefully incited the quarrel between Morel and Charlus that Marcel grimly defines as 'l'exécution de Charlus' (III.309) (the execution of Charlus).

In this respect, since the enlivenment of the Verdurin's existence frequently culminates in the decline or the demise of their 'faithful', there is considerable irony in Mme Verdurin's claim: 'je n'assassine pas mes invités' (II.970) (I don't murder my guests). Nowhere is this more apparent than in a variant account of the fate of Saniette, who falls victim to one of M. Verdurin's characteristic outbreaks of rage, and is reported to have 'tombé d'une attaque dans la cour de l'hôtel' (fallen after a heart attack in the courtyard of the house), as he leaves the Verdurins' salon. While M. Verdurin quite predictably denies the gravity of this news, insisting 'ce ne sera rien' (everything will be all right), Marcel rather more soberly relates: 'Mort, du reste, Saniette ne l'était pas. Il vécut encore quelques semaines, mais sans reprendre que passagérement connaissance' (III.266) (As a matter of fact, Saniette was not dead. He lived on for several weeks more, without ever really regaining consciousness). Swann, it might be argued, is peculiarly fortunate to survive the machinations of the Verdurins and, for all his personal resentment against this dreadful duo, he certainly carries conviction when he associates their salon and their behaviour with: 'ce qu'il y a de plus bas dans l'échelle sociale, le dernier cercle de Dante' (the lowest point on the social scale, the last of Dante's circles). He adds for good measure: 'Nul doute que le texte auguste ne se réfère aux Verdurins!' (I.287) (Evidently this august text refers to the Verdurins!).

Paradoxically, the Verdurins serve both to exemplify the most culpable variant of the 'negative' or 'imperfect' modes of action in *A la recherche du temps perdu*, and to illustrate Proust's suggestion that even the most imperfect behaviour coexists with a capacity for perfectibility. Thus, in his alternative account of Saniette's death,[11] Marcel relates that the Verdurins unexpectedly pay Saniette's rent during the last few months of his life, when his losses on the stock-exchange simultaneously leave him the victim of bankruptcy and of a fatal heart-attack; an act of charity which leaves Marcel to speculate that:

il ne faut jamais en vouloir aux hommes, jamais les juger d'après tel souvenir d'une méchanceté, car nous ne savons pas tout ce qu'à d'autres moments leur âme a pu vouloir sincèrement et réaliser du bon. (III.326)
(we should never blame our fellow men, and never judge them according to this or that memory of their wrongs, since we never really know the extent to which their hearts may have sincerely desired and realised some good on other occasions.)

Upon reflection, Marcel concludes that this capacity for generosity does not make M. Verdurin a good man, but rather a man capable of 'Une bonté partielle' (III.327) (Partial goodness): a statement which helpfully indicates the way in which Marcel's relativistic perspective is nevertheless moralistic, rather than 'completely detached from all moral considerations' (*PTD*, 66), as Beckett and other critics have maintained. Finally, Marcel once again emphasizes the complexity of reality, and the concomitant complexity of all acts of perception and narration, alluding to:

la difficulté de présenter une image fixe aussi bien d'un caractère que des sociétés et des passions. (II.327)
(the difficulties of presenting a fixed image, be this of a character, of a society, or of the passions.)

This archetypal reference to the problem of the relativity of perception, and to the parallel problems of narration, both harks back to such earlier prefigurations of the Modernist dilemma as Walter Pater's eloquent evocation of 'impressions unstable, flickering, inconsistent, which burn and are extinguished with our consciousness of them',[12] and looks forward to such subsequent, Post-Modern, evocations of immobility as Alain Robbe-Grillet's mischievous decision to set *La Maison de rendez-vous* in the Far East, because 'les choses changent vite sous ces climats' (things change rapidly in those climes),[13] and Beckett's dramatization of conditions in which 'It's never the same pus from one second to the next' and in which 'Nothing is certain'.[14] Significantly, both Pater and Proust insist that the difficulties of attaining authentic 'fixed images' of reality are not insuperable, and that non-habitual clarity may arise from a world of habitual confusion.

In Pater's terms, man may have access to the 'irresistibly real' by employing his 'finest senses', in a state in which 'the greatest number of vital forces unite in their purest energy'.[15] Pater concludes:

To burn always with this hard gem-like flame, to maintain this ecstasy, is success in life. Failure is to form habits: for habit is relative to a stereotyped world.

Proust similarly argues that man may at times transcend both the 'stereotyped world' of habit, and the imperfect non-habitual world of flawed affection, flawed creativity, and flawed social relations, when in 'a state of grace in which all our faculties . . . are at their height' (*CSB*, 140), and thus in a state in which he is utterly himself, rather than 'absent' from himself (III.70), or worse still, 'as distant as he could be from himself' (III.763). In this respect, it is important to understand that although Marcel's experience of negative modes of existence frequently depresses him, and frequently culminates in highly pessimistic assertions, he finally argues — like Swann — that man both can and should successfully strive to perfect himself, rather than adopting the Beckettian assumption that there is 'Nothing to be done' (*WFG*, 9).

Marcel's mature existential vision is perhaps best exemplified by the following passage from *Le Côté de Guermantes*, in which he meditates upon a cluster of pear trees and cherry trees, finding them to be:

Gardiens des souvenirs de l'âge d'or, garants de la promesse que la réalité n'est pas ce qu'on croit, que la splendeur de la poésie, que l'éclat merveilleux de l'innocence peuvent y resplendir et pourront être la récompense que nous nous efforcerons de mériter. (II.160–61)
(Custodians of memories from the golden age, witnesses to the promise that reality is not what we suppose it to be, and that the splendour of poetry and the marvellous radiance of innocence may shine within it, and may be the reward that we should make every effort to merit.)

To the three cardinal virtues of 'goodness, scrupulousness and sacrifice' (III.188), Marcel thus adds the existential ideals of the 'splendour of poetry' and the 'radiance of innocence' (and elsewhere, more fleetingly, the ideal of 'authentic social activity' (II.470)), insisting, very significantly, that these are 'rewards' that man should 'merit'.

For reasons best known to himself, Beckett's analysis of Proust's *A la recherche du temps perdu* remained curiously indifferent to these virtues and ideals. What seems to have interested Beckett much more was the confusion resulting from the imperfect non-habitual actions reversing these ideals, and the plight of those few Proustian characters trapped within the third category of actions that we have defined as nihilistic actions: a realm of inactivity corresponding to Swann's concept of 'une fange d'où il ne sera plus possible à la meilleure volonté du monde de jamais (se) relever' (I.287) (a mire from which it would be impossible to extricate oneself even with the best will in the world). The following chapter will examine this third, peculiarly 'Beckettian' realm of Proust's *A la recherche du temps perdu*.

4

NIHILISTIC MODES OF EXISTENCE IN
A LA RECHERCHE DU TEMPS PERDU

According to Beckett's essay on Proust (1931), Proust's characters exhibit 'a grotesque predetermined activity, within the narrow limits of an impure world' (*PTD*, 89). Yet according to Beckett's early book review entitled 'Proust in Pieces', his characters are also 'baffling ... indeterminates', capable of proving 'a saint and a snob in the one breath'.[1] Beckett's confusion conveniently points to the curious way in which a minority of nihilistic characters in Proust's novel are not so much the highly volatile, self-determining beings that Swann describes as 'Imperfect, but at least perfectible' (I.290), and that Edmund Wilson eloquently evokes as 'phenomena whose moral values are always shifting', as relatively static beings whose moral value has degenerated to such an extent that it can no longer really 'shift', and who are thus 'grotesquely predetermined ... within the narrow limits of an impure world'.[2]

As we have seen, the variously positive achievements and the variously negative achievements of Proust's 'perfectible' characters derive from the extent to which these characters respect or neglect the three cardinal virtues of 'goodness', 'scruple' and 'sacrifice' (III.188). The decline of these virtues, and the degeneration of the 'perfectible' Proustian character into the nihilistic Proustian character, appears to be accelerated by the forces that might be thought of as the three exterminating angels in *A la recherche du temps perdu*: the nefarious influences of illness, grief, and old age. Marcel introduces these three catalysts of nihilism during his account of his delinquent behaviour during Swann's dinner at Combray, at the very beginning of *A la recherche du temps perdu*.

Describing his excessive demands for his mother's attention during this traumatic dinner party, Marcel speculates that his failure to control his anxiety finally provokes: 'une première

Beckett and Proust

concession ... une première abdication de sa part devant l'idéal qu'elle avait conçu pour moi' (a first concession ... a first abdication on her part from the ideal that she had conceived for me). As a result, for the first time his mother 's'avouait vaincue' (I.38) (admitted herself to be defeated). Indeed, by forcing his mother to give in to his self-indulgent behaviour, Marcel senses that he has somehow precipitated the same kind of spiritual defeat as that inaugurated and accelerated by illness, grief, and old age, and finally acknowledges that:

j'avais réussi, comme auraient pu faire la maladie, des chagrins, ou l'âge, à détendre sa volonté, à faire fléchir sa raison. (I.38)
(I had succeeded, just as illness, grief, or old age might have done, in weakening her will, and in bending her principles.)

Marcel's accusations against himself might be a little extreme, but as his experiences demonstrate, illness, grief, and old age frequently appear to activate the nihilism that seems the most irremediable condition in *A la recherche du temps perdu*.

In their most extreme form, these three forces lead to a complete renunciation of all positive action, and the attempt to immobilize the perceptual faculties; a condition best exemplified in terms of the voluntary 'inertie absolue' (I.50) (absolute inertia) of Marcel's tante Léonie. This deliberate 'ablation' of existential desire has little in common with the 'battle' advocated by Elstir (I.864). However, it has much in common both with the 'wisdom' that Beckett imputes to *A la recherche du temps perdu* (*PTD*, 18), and the anti-wisdom of such Beckettian anti-heroes as Murphy, of whom the reader learns, 'To die fighting was the perfect antithesis of his whole practice, faith, and intention'.[3]

At first sight, tante Léonie appears to be the helpless victim of grief. Chronicling the successive phases of her retreat from the world, to the point at which she appears to have 'renoncé à tout' (I.57) (given up everything), Marcel explains that

depuis la mort de son mari, mon oncle Octave, (elle) n'avait plus voulu quitter, d'abord Combray, puis à Combray sa maison, puis sa chambre, puis son lit et ne ''descendait'' plus, toujours couchée dans un état incertain de chagrin, de débilité physique, de maladie, d'idée fixe et de dévotion. (I.49)
(ever since the death of her husband, my uncle Octave, she refused to leave, first of all Combray, then her house in Combray, then her bedroom, then her bed, and finally no longer 'descended', remaining in bed in a bewildering state of grief, physical deterioration, illness, obstinacy and piety.)

His reference to the 'état incertain', or the 'bewildering' (more literally, 'uncertain') quality of tante Léonie's lifestyle offers a key phrase in this description, pointing to the peculiar mental agitation that her physical stasis and her solitude are powerless to assuage. Indeed, it is precisely this kind of mental agitation that appears to have caught Beckett's imagination as he read *A la recherche du temps perdu*,[4] prompting his energetic annotation of such subsequent passages as the occasion in *La Prisonnière* when Marcel muses that isolation is no guarantee against contradiction or uncertainty, since: 'On n'a pas besoin d'être deux, il suffit d'être seul dans sa chambre, à penser' (III.87) (It is not necessary for there to be two people, it is enough that one should be alone in one's room, and thinking).[5]

Like Beckett's characters, tante Léonie suffers because she is alone, in her room, thinking. At first, Marcel suggests that this mental agitation, with its verbal correlative, 'un perpétuel monologue qui était sa seule forme d'activité' (I.50) (a perpetual monologue that formed her sole activity), is predominantly comical in quality. For example, one learns that this eccentric geriatric 'prêtait à ses moindres sensations une importance extraordinaire' (I.50) (attributed the most extraordinary importance to her slightest sensations), and also extends equal attention to such trivial details of everyday life in Combray as the identity of 'un chien "qu'elle ne connaissait point"' (I.58) (a dog that "she did not know"). Somewhat similarly, Beckett's later characters, such as the narrator of *Company* (1980), muse upon the potential distraction of anonymous animals, offering such asides as: 'A dead rat. What an addition to company that would be.'[6] In other words, tante Léonie, like the narrator of *Company*, spends — or expends — much of her time by studying insignificant details from habitual existence.

As Marcel subsequently intimates, this preoccupation with the trivial and with the habitual arises partly from the fact that tante Léonie is incapable of more profound activity. Though she may *plan* an excursion, such as her wish to visit Tansonville once again, it would seem that the very act of envisaging such enterprises exhausts her. As Marcel observes: 'Elle eût aimé revoir ... Tansonville; mais le désir qu'elle en avait suffisait à ce qui lui restait de forces; sa réalisation les eût excédées' (I.143) (She would have liked to see ... Tansonville again; but her desire to do this employed all her remaining strength; its realization would have exceeded it). Yet, at the same time, tante Léonie does very slowly accumulate a certain amount of energy, and it is precisely this minimal energy which most troubles her, since it both transcends the habitual quality of everyday existence, and yet proves insufficient to effect any substantial and positive mode of non-habitual action. Somewhat as the drunken porter in Shakespeare's *Macbeth* finds that drink 'provokes the desire but . . . takes away the performance', tante Léonie's occasional bursts of energy simultaneously provoke and frustrate non-habitual action, and thus constitute the discomforting stimulus that Marcel describes as '(ce) léger tropplein . . . dont elle était incapable de savoir et de décider comment user' (I.116) (this little surplus . . . which she could never know or decide how to use). The unsatisfactory quality of tante Léonie's response to such bursts of energy both exemplifies and contributes to her existential decline.

Although tante Léonie's sheltered existence initially offers an antidote to the shock of losing her husband, this 'traintrain . . . (qui) ne subissait jamais aucune variation' (I.110) (routine which never admitted any variation) finally becomes an antidote against the shock of *any* kind of non-habitual activity. In other words, the combined forces of grief and of indolence accelerate tante Léonie's surrender to 'la douceur . . . du repos' (I.144) (the pleasures of passivity); and as a result of her collaboration with the exterminating angels of illness, grief, and old age, tante Léonie prematurely exhibits 'ce grand renoncement de la vieillesse qui se prépare à la mort' (I.143) (that great resignation of old age preparing itself for death).

The irony and the culpability of tante Léonie's existential surrender derives from the fact that it is excessively premature, or 'plus tôt . . . que cela n'arrive d'habitude' (I.143) (much earlier . . . than is usual). While none of the characters in *A la recherche du temps perdu* die with the effortless 'truly regal grace' (*CSB*, 400) that Proust previously eulogized in 'Alphonse Daudet "Oeuvre d'Art"', they are almost all intrinsically 'at least perfectible' (I.290), and capable, therefore, of putting up some kind of struggle against degeneration. Tante Léonie, however, appears to have allowed herself to degenerate to such a point that she is beyond redemption. Put another way, her final plight corresponds to Swann's reference to the way in which certain habits can degrade man 'jusqu'à une fange d'où il ne sera plus possible à la meilleure volonté du monde de jamais le relever' (I.287) (until he becomes caught in a mire from which it would be impossible to extract him, even with the best will in the world).

If tante Léonie's culpability resides in her voluntary inertia, the irony of her condition resides in the fact that this inertia is constantly agitated by her occasional bursts of energy. In this respect, she exemplifies the unfortunate condition that Marcel diagnoses elsewhere as 'agitation mauvaise' (I.314) or 'negative agitation'. He uses this term to define the antithesis of Odette's serenity during her 'transfiguration' (I.314), but the term also functions very eloquently as a description of the peculiar mental agitation common to both tante Léonie and the inhabitants of Beckett's fictional universe. Introducing this singular agitation, Marcel evokes tante Léonie's imperfect inertia in a number of telling comparisons, alluding first of all to the fate of certain plants,

comme tel nénufar à qui le courant au travers duquel il était placé d'une façon malheureuse laissait si peu de repos que, comme un bac actionné mécaniquement, il n'abordait une rive que pour retourner à celle d'où il était venu, refaisant éternellement la double traversée. Poussé vers la rive, son pédoncule se dépliait, s'allongeait, filait, atteignait l'extrême limite de sa tension jusqu'au bord où le courant le reprenait, le vert cordage se repliait sur lui-même et ramenait la pauvre plante à ce qu'on peut d'autant mieux appeler son point de départ qu'elle n'y restait pas une seconde sans en repartir par une répétition de la même manoeuvre. (I.168–9)
(such as a waterlily, which the current, in which it had the misfortune to find itself, left in so little peace, that like a mechanical ferry, it no sooner reached one bank than it returned to the one from which it had come, eternally repeating its return journey. Pushed towards the far bank, its stalk would unfold, stretch out, flow forwards, right to its breaking-point, until the current caught it up again, its green line once again folding upon itself, and dragging the poor plant back to what might with every reason be called its point of departure, since it scarcely rested there for more than an instant before departing once again to repeat the same manoeuvre.)

This botanical description offers a startling paradigm for the many and varied ways in which Beckett's characters relentlessly and compulsively 'come and go'. One thinks, for example, of Beckett's early novel *Murphy*, in which Neary enters Mooney's bar 'moving slowly from one stool to another until he had completed the circuit of the counters, when he would start all over again in the reverse direction' (*Murphy*, 42); in which Murphy himself is described 'walking round and round Pentonville Prison' or 'round and round cathedrals that it was too late to enter' (*Murphy*, 54); and in which Celia and Miss Carridge listen

to the 'soft padding to and fro' of the 'old boy' who is 'Never still'
(*Murphy*, 50), just as May, in Beckett's more recent *Footfalls*
(1976), is similarly compelled to pace to and fro, 'one two three
four five six seven wheel one two three four five six seven
wheel'.[7] More specifically, of course, this description is also
paradigmatic of the fate of tante Léonie! But whereas Beckett
does not usually explicitly analyse the reasons why his characters
must 'come and go', Marcel hazards that if tante Léonie's
agitation resembles this 'poor plant', then it is perhaps because
she is to be numbered among 'certains neurasthéniques' (certain
neurasthenics),

qui nous offrent sans changement au cours des années le spectacle des
habitudes bizarres qu'ils se croient chaque fois à la vieille de secouer et
qu'ils gardent toujours; pris dans l'engrenage de leurs malaises et de
leurs manies. (I.169)
(who over the years continually offer us the spectacle of the strange
habits which they forever believe themselves to be on the brink of
banishing, and which they always retain; caught up in the mesh of their
maladies and their manias.)

If these words complement Marcel's botanical analogy with a
medical explanation for tante Léonie's dilemma, he finally entertains a more literary and mythological concept of this condition,
finding the aforementioned waterlily to be:

pareil aussi à quelqu'un de ces malheureux dont le tourment singulier,
qui se répéte indefiniment durant l'éternité, excitait la curiosité de
Dante. (I.169)
(also rather like one of those poor souls whose peculiar torments,
repeated over and over again throughout eternity, excited the curiosity
of Dante.)

Once again Proust's terminology (or that of Marcel) anticipates
Beckett's terminology (or that of the Beckettian narrator). For
example, the torment of those inhabiting Beckett's *Le Dépeupleur*
(1970) prompts reference to 'l'attitude qui arracha à Dante un de
ses rares pâles sourires' (in Beckett's own translation, 'the
attitude which wrung from Dante one of his rare wan smiles),[8]
just as the narrator of Beckett's *Company* (1980) apparently likens
himself to 'the old lutest cause of Dante's first quarter-smile'
(*Company*, 85).

Significantly, though, Marcel's analysis of tante Léonie does
not content itself with the implied explication of such botanical,
medical and literary allusions. For as the reader might anticipate,

tante Léonie's actions are also evaluated in terms of the same moral priorities with which Marcel evaluates all the other characters in *A la recherche du temps perdu*. Having identified tante Léonie's apparent incapacity to employ her rare bursts of surplus energy, Marcel traces the ways in which her inability to offer this energy positive use, leads her to employ it negatively, on those occasions when she seeks distraction at any cost, desiring 'du nouveau, fût-ce du pire' (I.115) (something new, even if it were for the worst).

At first, tante Léonie appears to employ her sporadic energies by inventing mischievous stories about her maid, Françoise. Becoming dissatisfied with such silent, solipistic entertainment, she subsequently regales herself by narrating these stories out loud, in the privacy of her bedroom, whence Françoise (and the ever-eavesdropping Marcel) overhear:

de mordants sarcasmes qui s'adressaient à elle et dont l'invention n'eût pas soulagé suffisamment ma tante s'ils étaient restés à l'état purement immatériel et si en les murmurant à mi-voix elle ne leur eût donné plus de réalité. (I.117)
(biting sarcasms which were directed at her, and whose invention would not have sufficiently comforted my aunt if they had remained purely immaterial, and if the act of muttering them aloud under her breath had not allowed her to make them more realistic.)

Just as Charlus's fantasies about an 'agreeable little farce' (II.288) in which Bloch might thrash his aged mother seems to lead to Charlus's enactment of this kind of 'drama', when he pays to have himself beaten in Jupien's brothel (III.815), tante Léonie's fantastic stories about Françoise finally find similar enactment, as Marcel remarks when explaining:

Quelquefois, ce "spectacle dans un lit" ne suffissait même pas à ma tante, elle voulait faire jouer ses pièces. (I.117)
(Sometimes, these "bedroom spectacles" failed in their turn to satisfy my aunt, and she had to see her works performed.)

Accordingly, tante Léonie finally enacts her fictional accusations in Françoise's presence, offering herself the satisfactions that Marcel condemns as 'un divertissement cruel' (I.177) (a cruel diversion). The parity between this kind of cruelty and that of the Verdurins is made all the more explicit when Marcel specifies that tante Léonie's cruelty arises from 'une méchanceté née de l'oisiveté' (I.118) (a malice born from indolence), just as the

Verdurins 'avaient contracté dans l'oisiveté des instincts cruels' (II.900) (had developed cruel instincts in the course of their indolent existence). On occasion, then, both the Verdurins and tante Léonie exemplify the indifferent cruelty that Marcel deplores as 'cette indifférence aux souffrances qu'on cause et qui, quelques autres noms qu'on lui donne, est la forme terrible et permanente de la cruauté' (I.165) (that indifference to the sufferings which one causes, and which, whatever else one might call it, is the most terrible and the most permanent form of cruelty).

Nevertheless, tante Léonie is not simply just another example of a Proustian character whose indolence accelerates flagrant cruelty, but rather, the supreme example of a Proustian character who becomes helplessly entangled in 'absolute inertia' (I.50), or at least in near-absolute inertia. Paradoxically, it may well seem that tante Léonie is peculiarly active, in the sense that, as Jeffrey Mehlman has suggested, there is 'a touch of the novelist in this dreadful crank'.[9] But very significantly, tante Léonie's 'fictions' arise not so much from a desire to create the ideal, positive literature that Marcel associates with revelations of 'that which is most ... profound in a writer's work' (I.553), as from her need to create stories which expend her surplus energy, and which screen her from profound, introspective reality. Rather than exploring and excavating profound truths, in the manner of the finest works of Vinteuil, Bergotte, and Elstir, tante Léonie's fictions serve to obscure the bankrupt quality of her own profound reality, and thereby to console and comfort her. Put another way, they illustrate Marcel's thesis that 'nous avons le don d'inventer des contes pour bercer notre douleur' (III.464) (we have the gift of inventing stories to soothe our sufferings). In other words, tante Léonie invents fictional reality as an antidote to the pain of her own profound reality, somewhat as the narrator of Beckett's *Company* confesses to 'craving for company ... In which to escape his own' (*Company*, 77).

Tante Léonie's greatest moments of anguish are therefore those moments when she involuntarily moves beyond the comfortable confines of her 'traintrain' (I.110) and becomes vulnerable to variants of more profound perceptions, which, almost by definition, can only offer intolerable intimations of her Dantesque fate. The most momentous example of this kind of excruciating exposure to lucid self-perception occurs when tante Léonie has the celebrated nightmare witnessed by the ever-alert Marcel, who notices that her sleeping features seem absorbed by 'une sorte de terreur' (I.109) (a kind of terror), and then overhears her confess that this terror was caused by a dream in which 'mon pauvre Octave était ressucité et . . . il voulait me faire faire une promenade tous les jours!' (I.110) (my poor Octave was resurrected and . . . he wanted to make me go for a walk every day!). At first sight, this curious dream appears to be nothing more complicated than another illustration of tante Léonie's eccentricity. But, as Jeffrey Mehlman convincingly argues, this dream serves primarily as an index of the difference between the felicity informing the 'unified image' offered by Marcel's positive involuntary memories, and the infelicity of such 'connaissance paranoïaque' (paranoid perceptions) as those afforded by tante Léonie's negative insights into her helpless condition.[10] Tante Léonie's nightmare, or involuntary vision, offers a negative or 'paranoid' mode of self-knowledge insofar as it reminds her of the world of exterior, positive action (exemplified here by her husband's wish to take her for a walk), which she has been making every effort to deny and suppress. At the same time, it also proffers painful intimation of her existential impotence. Firstly, it reminds her of a whole realm of existence that she would prefer not to remember, and secondly, it reminds her of her inability to take any effective action within this world, even if she wanted to.

The obvious irony in tante Léonie's nightmare is, of course, that her sense of terror arises from her discomfort before the prospect of having to leave her cherished routines in the little world of her bedroom, in order to walk with her resurrected husband in the big world. Jeffrey Mehlman concludes that this nightmare demonstrates that 'we hate our dear, beloved men' and that 'her very existence . . . depends upon their denial'.[11] Tante Léonie certainly seems eager to deny the existence of her once beloved Octave. But this denial seems contingent not so much upon a hatred of others, or of 'our dear, beloved men', as upon a hatred of herself. It would appear, then, that tante Léonie's horror before the resurrection of her husband is prompted by her horror of any stimuli which might remind her of her own suppressed reality, or which threaten to force her to enter into contact with herself. To modify Mehlman's conclusions, her very existence depends upon her denial of *herself*. If there is indeed 'a touch of the novelist' about tante Léonie, then it is a touch of nihilistic, self-denying creativity that short-circuits and neutralizes all profound communication, rather than the positive, self-discovering creativity that Marcel associates with ideal art and with 'the communication of souls' (III.258).

While the sufferings of tante Léonie provide Marcel with his most vivid revelation of the perils of nihilism, two other characters amusingly afford additional examples of the destructive potential of nihilistic behaviour, although, as minor figures in Marcel's narrative, their mannerisms and motivations are described somewhat sparingly. In much the same way as tante Léonie progressively retreats from the bourgeois world of Combray, the bitter Mme de Citri abandons the trappings of Parisian social life in a series of ever more dashing and ever more devastating gestures. Finding 'tout le monde idiot' (everybody idiotic), and having 'renoncé au monde . . . (et) les soirées pour des séances de musique' (given up the social world . . . and its evenings for musical gatherings), she subsequently deems music to be boring, pronouncing: 'Ah! Beethoven, la barbe!' (II.688) (Ah! Beethoven, what a bore!). As Marcel explains, Mme de Citri finally declares everything to be boring, and no longer even bothers to use language to express her contempt for existence, but adopts a mode of gestural communication that seems to be the very antithesis of the triumphant gestural communication of Marcel's grandmother and Saint-Loup. As Marcel relates:

elle ne se donnait même pas la peine de dire ''la barbe'' mais se contentait de faire passer sa main, comme un barbier, sur son visage. Bientôt, ce qui fut ennuyeux, ce fut tout . . . Finalement ce fut la vie elle-même qu'elle vous déclara une chose rasante. (II.688)
(she did not even take the trouble to express her boredom by saying ''la barbe'' but contented herself with the gesture of passing her hand, with the movement of a barber, over her face. Soon, the thing that bored her, was everything . . . Finally it was life itself that she declared to be boring.)

Marcel does not attribute this consuming boredom, and its concomitant nihilism, to any one of the three debilitating forces of illness, grief, and old age, but very interestingly suggests that Mme de Citri's 'besoin de destruction' (II.688) (thirst for destruction), 'rage concentrée' (concentrated rage), and 'nihilisme' all seem to be more advanced symptoms of the vices that Mme de Guermantes occasionally displays, 'bien qu'à un état beaucoup moins avancé' (II.687) (albeit in a far less advanced state). In other words, Marcel emphasizes the way in which voluntary inertia accelerates the failings of those rather more moderately indolent aristocrats like Mme de Guermantes and

Mme Verdurin, and reduces exceedingly indolent characters, such as tante Léonie and Mme de Citri, to a semi-tragic and semi-comic condition in which they become the incurable victims of their own nihilism.

If Mme de Citri's 'caractère négateur' (II.687) (negative character) seems to be something of an accident of birth, Marcel's brief description of the equally gloomy concierge of Mme de Montmorency toys with the possibility that this character's misanthropic gestures might well result from grief, or illness, or the combination of both these and those other forces which have contributed to the curious way in which

la concierge, toujours les yeux rouges, soit chagrin, soit neurasthénie, soit migraine, soit rhume, ne vous répondait jamais, vous faisait un geste vague indiquant que la duchesse était là et laissait tomber de ses paupières quelques gouttes au-dessus d'un bol rempli de ''ne m'oubliez pas''. (II.750)

(the concierge, who was always red-eyed, be this from grief, or from neurasthenia, or from migraine, or from some cold, never answered you, but made you a vague gesture indicating that the duchess was there, and dropped a few tears from her eyes over a bowl filled with ''forget-me-nots''.)

If tante Léonie, Mme de Citri, and Mme de Montmorency's concierge all surrender to the temptations of nihilism, the moral victory of Marcel's grandmother arises precisely from the ways in which she struggles against the exterminating angels of illness and old age. Marcel himself employs the metaphor of the exterminating angel when he alludes to her 'lutte épuisante' (exhausting struggle) and to the ravages of 'l'ange invisible avec lequel elle avait lutté' (II.316) (the invisible angel with whom she had struggled). Marcel's grandmother, then, is most significant of all as an anti-nihilist.

Yet, initially, Marcel's grandmother manifests all the symptoms of the nihilistic renunciation which he has previously associated with tante Léonie. At first, '(elle) renonçait à prononcer un seul mot et restait immobile' (II.332) (she abandoned all conversation and remained motionless); next, 'Elle ne voulait plus penser' (II.333) (She no longer wanted to think); and finally, having lost all wish to live and having abortively attempted suicide by jumping out of a window, 'elle cessa de vouloir, de regretter' (II.333) (she ceased either to desire anything or to regret anything). After the death of Albertine, Marcel also very similarly undergoes the temptations of nihilism:

'J'essayais de ne penser à rien' (III.522), (I tried not to think of anything). And in much the same way, after his near-fatal fall at the end of the novel, Marcel once again finds himself to be 'indifférent à tout' (III.1041) (indifferent to everything); in a state in which: 'mes yeux préféraient se fermer' (III.1042) (my eyes preferred to remain closed); and in which: 'je n'aspirais plus qu'au repos, en attendant le grand repos qui finirait par venir' (III.1041) (I no longer aspired to anything other than rest, while awaiting the great rest that would at last come to me).

The crucial difference between the ways in which Marcel and his grandmother respond to the temptations of nihilism and the lure of 'the great rest that would at last come', and the ways in which tante Léonie, Mme de Citri, and Mme de Montmorency's concierge respond to these temptations, resides, of course, in the fact that Marcel and his grandmother finally resist their nihilistic impulses. In this respect, their final actions manifest a positive mode of serenity, rather than acquiescence to 'le grand repos' (III.1041) (the great rest), which presumably forms the apex of the indolent 'douceur ... du repos' (I.144) (pleasure ... of passivity) sought by tante Léonie (and, moreover, sought by such Beckettian prototypes as Belacqua, the hero of *Dream of Fair to Middling Women*, who desires nothing more than existence 'at the dead point, in a tranquil living at the neutral point' (*Dream*, 24)). With this difference in mind, Marcel nicely distinguishes the way in which his grandmother's last hours bespeak victory and optimism rather than defeat and pessimism, specifying that 'Son calme n'était plus la sagesse du désespoir mais de l'espérance' (II.334) (Her calm was no longer that of the wisdom of despair, but that of the wisdom of hope). [12] As if to underline the positive quality of his grandmother's death, Marcel not only records the ways in which her last breaths and last movements offer eloquent gestural communication to her enduring benevolence, but also insists that despite 'les désillusions de la vie' (the disillusionments of life), she dies evincing 'une chaste espérance' (a chaste optimism), 'un rêve de bonheur' (a dream of happiness), and 'une innocente gaité' (II.345) (an innocent gaiety).

This final 'happiness' resulting from 'the wisdom of hope', and following a certain existential plenitude during which Marcel's grandmother realizes her positive potential once again, by communicating 'everything she had to tell us' (II.344), stands in sharp contrast with the inarticulate anguish of tante Léonie's imperfect inertia, and additionally offers a striking alternative to the altogether antithetical happiness informing the last lines of Beckett's recent *Mal vu mal dit* (1981), in which the dying narrator impatiently anticipates the all-consuming void of non-existence:

Adieu adieux. Puis noir parfait avant-glas tout bas adorable son top départ de l'arrivée. Première dernière seconde. Pourvu qu'il en reste encore assez pour tout dévorer. Goulûment seconde par seconde. Ciel terre et tout le bataclan. Plus miette de charogne nulle part. Léchées babines baste. Non. Encore une seconde. Rien qu'une. Le temps d'aspirer ce vide. Connaître le bonheur.
Farewell to farewell. Then in that perfect dark foreknell darling sound pip for end begun. First last moment. Grant only enough remain to devour all. Moment by glutton moment. Sky earth the whole kit and boodle. Not another crumb of carrion left. Lick chops and basta. No. One moment more. One last. Grace to breathe that void. Know happiness. [13]

At the same time, Marcel's emphasis upon his grandmother's 'innocent gaiety' hark back to his earlier celebration of 'the marvellous radiance of innocence' and the 'splendour of poetry', which seem to be embodied by the beauty of the pear trees and cherry trees that he comes across while walking with Saint-Loup (II.160–61). Just as he finds natural counterparts to these two ideals of human behaviour, he also occasionally finds natural counterparts to the nihilism of tante Léonie, Mme de Citri and the concierge of Mme de Montmorency, and hints that such inarticulate, 'vegetal' nihilism is often the consequence of old age. This concept of 'nihilistic vegetation' is best introduced with reference to Marcel's description of the aged M. de Norpois and Mme de Villeparisis, a passage which is in turn best introduced with reference to a fleeting episode in Proust's earlier novel, *Jean Santeuil*, entitled 'Vieux époux'.

This episode in *Jean Santeuil* rather sentimentally sketches the way in which Jean Santeuil's aged parents help each other to overcome their infirmities, 'Les mouvements de chacun ... (étant) une série de précautions prises ... contre la faiblesse de l'autre' (The movements of each ... being a series of precautions taken ... to counter the weaknesses of the other). Jean Santeuil rapturously concludes:

Et maintenant il était beau de les voir ainsi rapprochés, mêlés, confondus, tordus ensemble et s'étayant l'un l'autre comme deux arbres enlacés. (*JS*, 869)
(And now it was pleasant to see them together in this way, mixed, confused, and twisted together, and supporting one another like two trees that had become entwined.)

Such comforting and harmonious imagery is entirely absent from Marcel's analogous evocation of M. de Norpois and his mistress, Mme de Villeparisis, whom he describes as trees smitten by the force that he deplores as: 'la vieillesse ... l'état le plus misérable pour les hommes' (III.1018) (old age ... the most miserable condition for mankind).

Once 'belle comme un ange' (as beautiful as an angel), Mme de Villeparisis has become 'une petite bossue, rougeade, affreuse' (III.634) (a little hunchback, red-faced, and frightful), while the formerly diplomatic M. de Norpois is similarly humiliated by the years, which transform 'son langage, jadis si plein de réserve' (his conversation, hitherto so full of reserve), into 'une véritable intempérance' (sheer intemperance), displaying 'cette violence sénile de certains octogénaires' (III.631) (that senile violence common to certain octogenarians). Far from being harmoniously intertwined like Jean Santeuil's parents, these elderly lovers scarcely bother to converse. Indeed, somewhat like Estragon and Vladimir in Beckett's *Waiting for Godot*, they allow prolonged silences to punctuate their utterances to one another; and considered very generally, they seem to epitomize the dilemma that Marcel diagnoses as 'ce grand renoncement de la vieillesse ... qu'on peut observer ... même entre les anciens amants' (I.143) (that great resignation of old age ... that one can discern ... even among old lovers).

Paradoxically, despite the fact that they appear 'indifférents l'un à l'autre' (III.1054) (indifferent to each other), Marcel suggests that Mme de Villeparisis is totally devoted to M. de Norpois, observing: 'On voyait qu'elle ne vivait plus guère que pour lui' (III.1052) (One could see that she virtually lived for him alone). The enigma of this 'indifferent' devotion becomes resolved when Marcel explains that it is the consequence of habit. Briefly, M. de Norpois and Mme de Villeparis are two more victims of habitual behaviour — in this instance, of habitual affection. Envisaging them as branches of trees which are doomed to follow one another, neither totally united nor capable of being totally apart (or as 'branches' which lack the harmony of Jean Santeuil's parents, but which share the uneasy relationship of such Beckettian couples as Estragon and Vladimir, or Lucky and Pozzo), Marcel finally describes them as:

courbés par le temps comme deux branches qui ont pris la même inclinaison, se touchent presque et que rien ne pourra plus ni redresser ni éloigner l'une de l'autre. (III.1054)

(curved by time, like two branches which have assumed the same slant, which almost touch one another, and which nothing can ever straighten out again, or separate from each other.)

This evocation of the way in which old age reduces passionate love to meaningless and inescapable habits only employs the image of equally 'nihilistic vegetation' metaphorically, as a counter-image to the 'positive vegetation' with which Jean Santeuil equates the harmony of his aged parents. But in *A la recherche du temps perdu*, Marcel ponders upon more literal examples of 'nihilistic nature'. These in turn offer counter-images to the literal examples of 'ideal nature' that both Marcel and Jean Santeuil celebrate. Significantly, though, Marcel's vision is far more sophisticated than that of Jean Santeuil. Whereas Jean Santeuil's vision frequently appears mediated by rose-tinted spectacles, Marcel appears sensitive to both positive and negative variants of reality. Still more significantly, the 'dualism in multiplicity' (*PTD*, 11) of Marcel's vision is consistently informed by moral criteria. Accordingly, his visions of nihilistic natural phenomena form yet another piece of the ethical jigsaw which collectively evinces the implied moral vision of *A la recherche du temps perdu*. In this respect, the most haunting image of nihilistic vegetation in this novel occurs during Marcel's contemplation of the trees at Hudimesnil: an incident — or 'jigsaw piece' — which is probably best explicated with reference to two extremely interesting episodes of *Jean Santeuil*.

In the first of these, 'Charmes de la mauvaise saison', Jean Santeuil contemplates a number of 'vieux arbres qui continuaient à se plaindre éternellement de leurs douleurs' (*JS*,513) (old trees which eternally complained of their miseries); characterizing them as 'les arbres stériles' (*JS*, 512) (sterile trees). A subsequent episode of the novel, 'L'Hiver', offers yet another version of this plaintive spectacle, when Jean Santeuil comes across another such group of 'sterile trees', observing: 'Les arbres se plaignaient, faisaient avec leurs bras décharnés des gestes impuissants' (*JS*, 518) (The trees bewailed their fate, making impotent gestures with their emaciated arms).

These images are extraordinarily evocative, and at once conjure up analogous gestures in key passages of both Proust's and Beckett's mature writing. In Proust's instance, these passages appear to anticipate Marcel's fascination before the trees at Hudimesnil, which similarly wave their emaciated branches, provoking Marcel's comment:

Je vis les arbres s'éloigner en agitant leurs bras désespérés, semblant me
dire: Ce que tu n'apprends pas de nous aujourd'hui, tu ne le saurais
jamais. (I.719)
(I watched the trees fade away as they waved their arms despairingly,
seeming to say to me: Unless you understand our lesson today, you will
never apprehend it.)

Marcel senses that he has not managed to decode their
deciduous discourse, and admits: 'je ne sus jamais ce qu'ils
avaient voulu m'apporter' (I.719) (I never found out what they
were trying to tell me). Yet, despite this avowal of incompre-
hension, his first impression of the trees seems perfectly lucid. In
other words, Marcel appears to grasp the basic significance of
these mysterious trees, although, at this particular moment, he
also seems unable to relate its significance to his own situation.
Contemplating their despairing gestures, he hints that they
resemble 'des fantômes du passé' (phantoms from the past), and
finally meditates:

Dans leur gesticulation naïve et passionnée, je reconnaissais le regret
impuissant d'un être aimé qui a perdu l'usage de la parole, sent qu'il ne
pourra nous dire ce qu'il veut et que nous ne savons pas deviner. (I.719)
(In their naive and passionate gestures, I recognized the impotent regret
of a loved one who has lost the use of speech, and realizes that he cannot
tell us what he wants to tell us, and that we cannot make out what this
is.)

Arguably, the primary significance of the Hudimesnil trees lies
precisely in their function as a vegetal image of verbal impotence.
In other words, it might not really matter if Marcel fails to
discover what it is they have not managed to say. Most important
of all is the fact that they exemplify the torment of inadequate
expression, or more specifically, the torment of those who have
grown old and (in the terms of *Jean Santeuil*) 'sterile', without
ever having taken the trouble to express themselves. It would
appear, then, that these trees attempt to warn Marcel of the
dangers of indolence, and of the perils of living life vacuously,
until it is too late to offer adequate expression to his most
important insights. In this respect, the frustrated and impotent
gestures of these trees seem to have much in common with the
equally agitated verbal gestures of dilettantes such as Charlus,
whose interminable and intemperate monologues similarly offer
'une réalisation imparfaite' (III.286) (an imperfect expression) to
whatever he has to say.

The fundamental difference between the issueless verbal gestures of Charlus, and the issueless, despairing gestures of the Hudimesnil trees, resides in the way in which the trees evince a far more enduring mode of suffering than the fleeting frustration arising from the inconsequential conversations that leave Charlus and his interlocutors 'inassouvis même après des heures passés ensemble' (III.287) (unsatisfied even after hours spent together). For, as Marcel suggests, when associating these trees with 'sorcières' (witches), 'nornes' (I.719) (Norns) and 'phantoms', there is something ghostly, magical and mythical about their torment. They seem to partake of the eternal anguish afflicting the trees observed by Jean Santeuil (*JS*, 513), or indeed the eternal, Dantesque condition that Marcel associates with the waterlily which reminds him of tante Léonie (I.169).

The 'impotent regret' of the 'despairing arms' of these trees also offers an uncanny prototype for the despairing gestures with which Beckett repeatedly exemplifies the impossibility of adequate communication in his novels and his plays, by evoking or by dramatizing what he variously terms 'the pathos of dangling arms', the equal pathos of arms 'waving in sad helpless love', or the corresponding pathos of 'gestures of helpless compassion'.[14] Such gestures all consolidate the hypothesis in Beckett's essay on Proust, that 'There is no communication because there are no vehicles of communication' (*PTD*, 64) — a hypothesis which Beckett repeatedly illustrates in his own subsequent writings.

Yet for all Beckett's insistence that Proust portrays 'the attempt to communicate where no communication is possible' (*PTD*, 63), and that his fiction therefore implies that 'We cannot know and we cannot be known' (*PTD*, 66), it remains evident that Proust's vision is far more complex. Sometimes he depicts such epitomes of inarticulate nihilism as tante Léonie and the Hudemesnil trees, but on other occasions he depicts equally emphatic instances of successful communication and successful self-realization.

In other words, Beckett's incomparable sensitivity to the negative and nihilistic dimensions of *A la recherche du temps perdu* is consistently flawed by his inexplicable indifference to the positive dimensions of this novel. Ultimately, Beckett imposes his own 'negative relativism' (*PTD*, 85) upon Proust's novel; an error to which Beckett himself alluded, many years later, in the curiously understated confession: 'Perhaps I overstated Proust's pessimism a little'.[15]

Reconsidered in mathematical terms, *A la recherche du temps perdu* might be described as an elaborate, tripartite 'equation' (*PTD*, 11), juxtaposing habitual behaviour and both positive and negative modes of non-habitual actions, be these artistic, non-artistic, or 'social'. Charting a hierarchy of existential possibilities which range from the graceful harmony of those actions evincing 'poetry' and 'innocence' (II.160) to the graceless agitation of those negative actions which lead to the nihilistic inertia from which it is impossible to escape, 'even with the best will in the world' (I.287), Proust's novel, and its peculiarly positive' relativism, may now be summarized diagrammatically, in the following manner, in terms of its subtly symmetrical analyses of both positive and negative modes of existence.

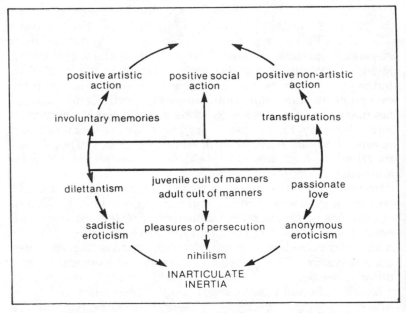

The Parameters of Proust's 'dualism in multiplicity'

The following chapters will now consider the unusual strategies that Beckett employed in his essay on Proust in order to validate his assertion that, far from evincing an optimistic, 'positive relativism', Proust's *A la recherche du temps perdu* advocates the peculiarly pessimistic pearls of 'the wisdom that consists ... in the ablation of desire' (*PTD*, 18).

5

BECKETT'S PROUSTS —
THE SINGULAR AND THE MULTIPLE

One is sometimes led to wonder whether any study of influence is truly justified unless it succeeds in elucidating the particular qualities of the borrower, in revealing along with the influence, and almost in spite of it, what is infinitely more important: the turning point at which the writer frees himself of the influence and finds his originality. [1]

As Anna Balakian suggests, most writers worthy of critical attention eventually reveal their originality by rejecting early influences, biting the hands that feed them. Beckett is no exception to this rule, and his essay on Proust, though fascinating as an analysis of Proust's ideas, is perhaps even more interesting as a record of the 'turning points' at which Beckett rejected many of Proust's ideas and, in the process, manifested the first substantial signs of his own originality. Far from affording a faithful account of Proust's vision, and thereby demonstrating that Beckett is somehow a Proustian disciple, this eccentric essay repeatedly offers an extremely heretical account of what one might think of as the Proustian 'faith', interweaving breathtakingly perceptive analyses of those few Proustian ideas with which Beckett concurred, with seductively deceptive exegeses of those many Proustian ideas with which he begged to differ.

Now that Beckett has donated his own annotated copies of *A la recherche du temps perdu* to the Beckett Collection at Reading University, it is possible to trace some of the sources from which the conclusions of this essay of 1931 almost certainly derive. [2] Beckett repeatedly underlines and annotates the most misanthropic meditations of Proust's narrator-hero, Marcel. As one very singular segment of both Marcel's multiple experiences, and of the multiple experiences of Proust's legions of other characters, these pessimistic speculations are by no stretch of the imagination representative of the implied vision generated by the entirety of the novel. Yet, more often than not, it is upon this very limited testimony that Beckett's analysis of *A la recherche du temps perdu* rests its case. Paradoxically, few of Beckett's critics have ever cared to draw attention to this bizarre approach to Proust's vision; indeed Beckett's *Proust* usually enjoys a quite undeserved and quite confusing reputation as an exemplary guide to the works of both its author and its subject. As a result, Beckett's critics have tended to conflate both the author and the subject of his essay, rather than attending to the crucial differences between their respective visions and priorities.

With the exception of Frank Kermode, who boldly argued that Beckett's *Proust* was 'not, as criticism should be, in the service of the work it undertakes to elucidate',[3] the majority of Beckett's early critics somehow persuaded themselves that this essay was, more or less, an accurate and quite acceptable account of Proust's ideas, and only in recent years have one or two critics tentatively drawn attention to the specific shortcomings of this essay. One of the most perceptive of these critics, Steven J. Rosen, has gently hinted that Beckett 'Consistently, and not always fairly ... strives to make the many-sided Proust seem little more than a pessimistic sage',[4] while John Pilling rather more indulgently argues that Beckett's undeniably reductive analysis 'does not so much misrepresent Proust's insight into personality as give it a one-sided emphasis'.[5]

In this respect, it is perhaps unfortunate that while critics now enjoy access to Beckett's annotated copies of *A la recherche du temps perdu*, they do not share similar access to the annotated copy of Beckett's *Proust* described by Deirdre Bair in her biography of Beckett. Relating that a copy of this essay 'surfaced in a second-hand bookstore in Dublin with comments and emendations in Beckett's handwriting scattered throughout', Deirdre Bair refers to the title page, which is revealingly inscribed with the words: 'I have written my book in a cheap flashy philosophical jargon'.[6] Nevertheless, like so many of Beckett's critics, Deirdre Bair finally observes:[7]

Throughout the essay one is aware of a smoothness in the writing, the ease with which Beckett glides from idea to idea. The syntax is clear, flowing and lucid, definite progress from the schoolboy preciosity of 'Dante ... Bruno. Vico .. Joyce'. The vocabulary is intelligent and restrained, avoiding the verbal pyrotechnics that characterize the earlier essay.

This verdict is surely over-generous. As Deirdre Bair very

kindly indicated in a letter regarding this annotated copy of
Proust,[8] Beckett also annotated other pages of the essay with
such ferocious comments as: 'Dog vomit', 'terrible jargon', and
the very telling reflection:[9]

"too abstract" indeed. The use of mainly concrete nouns and active
verbs instead of all this abstract jargon would have gone a long way to
"clarify" the argument.

Deirdre Bair does not quote these subsequent annotations in her
biography, but as careful analysis of the essay reveals, Beckett
quite rightly condemns it now and then for its 'terrible' and
excessively 'abstract' jargon. As the following chapters will
indicate, Beckett's argument and terminology are frequently far
from 'clear', 'flowing', and 'restrained'.

At its best, the essay is certainly both lucid and engaging, and
it is to Beckett at his best that most critics have given their
attention. Unfortunately, something very close to infatuation
with those choice paragraphs and pages in which Beckett
elegantly summarizes many of Proust's most basic concepts has
led countless critics to neglect the ways in which the remainder
of this essay systematically misrepresents Proust's vision by
reducing it to Beckettian terms. It is all the more ironic, then, that
a critic such as John Pilling, who seems admirably sensitive to
Beckett's one-sided approach to Proust, should conclude that
this kind of approach constitutes a 'legitimate' critical
manoeuvre.[10]

Viewed in a very general context, this assumption is far from
convincing, and considered in the context of Beckett's essay on
Proust this defence of one-sided criticism makes no sense at all. In
the very first sentence Beckett insists that Proust's vision is far
more complex than any one-sided thesis, declaring: 'The
Proustian equation is never simple' (11). Lest the reader fails to
grasp this distinction, the fifth sentence stipulates that, far from
being a one-sided thinker, Proust was the master of the many-
sided perspective that Beckett beautifully defines as 'dualism in
multiplicity' (11). The fundamental tension — and, perhaps, the
fatal tension — in *Proust*, arises precisely from the curious dialectic
between Beckett's perspicacious awareness that 'Proust respects
the dual significance of every condition and circumstance of life'
(69), and Beckett's antithetical compulsion to demonstrate that
the reverse is true, and that Proust viewed the world in terms of a
one-sided, amoral, and utterly pessimistic perspective.

The tension between these two approaches to *A la recherche du temps perdu*, and the curious process by which the latter approach reduces the complex 'Proustian equation' to the kind of 'pre-conceived equation' deplored by Beckett in his lectures at Trinity College, [11] rapidly becomes apparent when one considers the content and the continuity of Beckett's argument in the seven sections of *Proust*. The first four sections successively discuss Proust's theories of time, habit, memory, and the 'salvation' of involuntary memory. The fifth section examines his concepts of love and friendship; the sixth section returns to his notion of in-voluntary memory, with particular reference to Marcel's final revelations at the Guermantes' matinée; and the seventh section offers Beckett's conclusion to the essay.

Had Beckett wished to reveal the complexity of the Proustian 'equation', then one might reasonably expect each of the sections of his essay to analyse their subject in a dualistic manner, with equal regard to the positive and the negative dimensions of time, habit, memory, involuntary memory, and so on. But instead of employing this dualistic analytical approach, the essay attempts to imitate the one-sided nature of Marcel's laborious sentimental and perceptual education. In other words, just as Marcel incom-petently progresses from blunder to blunder and from confusion to confusion, until at long last he finally stumbles into the domain of extra-temporal wisdom right at the very end of his adventures, at the Guermantes' matinée, the early sections of *Proust* catalogue negative revelation after negative revelation and failure after failure, delaying all comprehensive discussion of their positive counterparts until the sixth section, which is devoted to Marcel's discoveries at the Guermantes' matinée.

Blithely refusing to reveal the positive terms of Proust's 'equations' regarding time, habit, memory and involuntary memory, Beckett repeatedly insists that consideration of these positive concepts can 'wait a little longer' (39), until they will be 'discussed in their proper place' (15), by which he means the penultimate section of his essay. Accordingly, his argument assumes relatively dualistic dimensions only in the last two of its sections, when the complexity of Proust's vision has been repeatedly caricatured in terms of the misanthropic passages that Beckett underlined in his copies of *A la recherche du temps perdu*. Far from revealing the subtlety of the carefully balanced vision that he subsequently associates with 'Proust ... the dialectician', [12] the early sections foreground the unbalanced, lovelorn introspection that Nabokov's Humbert Humbert wittily associates with Proust's 'internal combustion martyr'.[13]

Remarkable as Marcel's anguished meditations may be, they should not be confused with the implied vision of Proust's novel as a whole, for as Proust explains in his correspondence with Jacques Rivière, Marcel's conclusions repeatedly 'depict errors'.[14] Like many of Proust's critics, Beckett overestimates the significance of Marcel's testimony, confuses Marcel's errors with Proust's truths, and neglects the significance of those many other characters who implicitly or explicitly evince the Proustian truths that the immature Marcel invariably overlooks. But whereas most critics tend to overvalue Marcel's positive affirmations (thereby neglecting their negative counterparts), Beckett refreshingly reverses this process, emphasizing the pessimistic portion of Proustian thought which few other critics have ever explored. Thus, while Beckett's *Proust* repeatedly betrays his crucial initial insight into the dualistic quality of Proust's vision, his single-minded excavation of the pessimistic dimension of *A la recherche du temps perdu* consistently complements orthodox criticism with a dazzling analysis of the neglected negative modes of non-habitual perception with which Proust complements his celebration of positive revelations in order to complete his epic study of the 'damnation and salvation' to which Beckett obligingly alludes in his opening remarks in *Proust*.

This crucial dualistic concept appears when Beckett introduces his analysis of the way in which time contributes to Proust's 'dualism in multiplicity' by defining time in terms of its antithetical properties as a 'double-headed monster of damnation and salvation' (11). Stressing the former property, he explains that Proust's characters are the 'victims' (12) of time, insofar as time constantly changes them, thereby invalidating their joys, fears, beliefs, and all the other trappings of their identity: 'We are not merely more weary because of yesterday, we are other, no longer what we were before the calamity of yesterday' (13). Or, as Estragon puts it in *Waiting for Godot*, 'It's never the same pus from one second to the next' (*WFG*, 60). Accordingly, Proust's characters constantly discover that 'The aspirations of yesterday were valid for yesterday's ego, not for to-day's' (13).

Turning to the implications of this problem, Beckett appears to suggest that Proust's characters continually — and inevitably — fail to realize their desires. By the time the object of desire is realized, the desiring subject has almost certainly changed, so that it might be said that they have 'died — and perhaps many

times — on the way' (14). Moreover, even when, 'by one of those
rare miracles of coincidence', the object of desire materializes
before the desiring subject has had time to change, Beckett
argues that this hypothetical fulfilment of desire is still flawed,
since the very incidence of realized desire so completely eclipses
the preceding period of unfulfilled desire that all memory of this
period of unfulfilment disappears. The concept of *before* no
longer exists to validate the *after*-effect of fulfilment and, in
Beckett's terms, 'we are incapable of appreciating our joy by
comparing it with our sorrow' (14).

Although he gives the impression that these observations
account for the entirety of Proust's vision, they are valid only
insofar as they apply to the limited world of habitual perception.
As Beckett demonstrates later in his essay, in his discussion of
Marcel's love for Albertine, the desiring subject does not always
rapidly die 'many times' (as these early pages claim), but often
survives to experience various kinds of non-habitual experience,
such as Marcel's prolonged bouts of unrequited love. In other
words, the early pages exaggerate the speed with which time's
'Deformation' (13) eliminates desire and memory. At the same
time, though, Beckett's comments anticipate the way in which
the ravages of time create the day-to-day confusions of his own
plays, in which a bare tree can become covered with leaves 'In a
single night' (*WFG*, 66), and in which such characters as Vladimir
can complain: 'Was I sleeping ... Am I sleeping now?
Tomorrow, when I wake, or think I do, what shall I say of today?'
(*WFG*, 90).

As his analysis of the Proustian concept of time advances,
Beckett admits that his discussion has focused upon 'vulgar
perception' and 'vulgar phenomena' (17), or the habitual
concepts that derive from 'conscious intellectual effort' (14).
Paraphrasing Proust's critique of the superficiality of logical and
imaginative perception, and addressing the concomitant
problem of the habitual and logical process of voluntary
memory, he specifies that this mode of 'conscious intellectual'
memory is 'of no value as an instrument of evocation, and
provides an image as far removed from the real as the myth of
our imagination or the caricature furnished by direct perception'
(14).

As is so often the case, Beckett's summary of Proust's thought
seems extremely judicious. Although his copy of volume one of
A l'ombre des jeunes filles en fleurs is missing from his annotated
copies of *A la recherche du temps perdu* in the Reading University

Beckett Collection, his specification almost certainly derives from
the passage in which Marcel reflects that:

le monde visible . . . n'est pas le monde vrai, nos sens ne possédant par
beaucoup plus le don de la ressemblance que l'imagination. (I.548)
(the world that we perceive visually . . . is not the real world, since our
senses are only marginally more accurate than our imagination.)

Yet, at the same time, Beckett is also capable of juxtaposing
exemplary accuracy with exasperating ambiguity. Having
defined the vulgar modes of perception in Proust's novel, and
having alluded to the problem of perceiving 'the real', he
perversely evades the task of defining authentic modes of perception by cryptically concluding:

There is only one real impression and one adequate mode of evocation.
Over neither have we the least control. That reality and that mode will
be discussed in their proper place. (14–15)

The last of these sentences is typical of Beckett's mischievous
'delaying tactics' in this essay. Of more interest at this particular
point in his argument is the statement that Proust's characters
have not the least control over authentic modes of perception
and communication (which is presumably what Beckett means
by 'real impression' and by 'adequate mode of evocation'). His
assertion is partially accurate, insofar as these processes are to
some extent involuntary, or beyond voluntary control. But as our
analysis of exemplary perceptions and exemplary communication in *A la recherche du temps perdu* has suggested, Proust
intimates that such ideal modes of self-realization may be
controlled, insofar as they may be accelerated or decelerated
according to the extent to which moral values are consciously
respected or neglected. For example, although Marcel experiences his celebrated revelation of time past when quite young,
upon savouring what Beckett calls 'the famous madeleine' (38),
this 'real impression' is only partially 'adequate', since Marcel
fails to analyse it and fails to convert it into a work of art. Put
another way, his moral immaturity makes him incapable of
guiding this revelation towards its fulfilment in a work of art, and
leaves him vulnerable to the various 'vulgar' distractions that
delay his artistic vocation for hundreds of pages, until his final
decision to dedicate himself to literature extricates him from the
limbo of complacency.

Beckett's essay persistently denies that such moral con-

siderations inform *A la recherche du temps perdu*, and stubbornly
asserts that Proust's characters are 'active with a grotesque predetermined activity, within the narrow limits of an impure
world' (89). Even Marcel, whom Beckett takes to be the one pure
exception among this impure breed, is defined in terms of his
'complete indifference to moral values and human justices' (89).
One of its few footnotes specifically indicates the source of this
observation, referring to Marcel's confession: 'le sentiment de la
justice, jusqu'à une complète absence de sens moral, m'était
inconnu' (III.291) (my lack of any sense of justice amounted to a
complete absence of morality).

But, as Proust observed, Marcel makes many erroneous
statements, and this confession of moral insensibility seems no
more convincing than his similarly phrased and equally drastic
confession of 'mon absence de dons littéraires' (III.854) (my lack
of any literary talent). At worst, these statements are very stupid.
At best, they are relative rather than absolute, and refer to
Marcel's indifference towards the superficiality of conventional
moral and artistic norms (or to vulgar morality and vulgar art),
rather than demonstrating his indifference to moral and artistic
absolutes. As becomes evident in his subtle comments upon
such ethical issues as the 'falsely evil' quality of Charlus (III.317),
Marcel is capable of extremely sensitive moral discriminations.

Nevertheless, Beckett seems to have had no difficulty in taking
Marcel's confession of amorality quite literally, and several times
he reminds the reader that Proust's characters can no more
control their adequate perceptions than they can control their
inadequate perceptions. As a rule, these reminders take the form
of relatively unobtrusive comments. For example, as Beckett
discusses the devastating influence of time, he somewhat
mechanically insists that its victims can do nothing to help themselves, noting that the 'mood is of no importance' and that the
'good or evil disposition of the subject has neither reality nor
significance' (13). Collectively, though, these discrete refrains
accumulate to form an analytical leitmotiv that evades, and
thereby obscures, all contrary evidence, thus consolidating the
disproportionate emphasis upon negative modes of experience
that Beckett once again exhibits in the next subsection of his
discussion of time.

This subsection refers to Proust's fascination with the ways in
which the uncertainties of the future may be quite as baffling as
the discrepancies between the present and the past, once 'any
temporal specification (allows) us to measure the days that

separate us from a menace — or a promise' (15–16). Put more plainly, Beckett refers to the anxiety that arises once the perceiver ceases to be indifferent towards the future and awaits a specific event, be this a negative 'menace' or a positive 'promise'. Significantly, Beckett elects to exemplify this anxiety exclusively in terms of menaces.

His first example refers to the anguish with which Swann contemplates the months which will separate him from Odette, when she is about to travel to Egypt in the company of his rival, de Forcheville. In such circumstances, Swann 'suffers more grievously than even at the misery of his present condition' (16). In much the same way, Beckett refers to the way in which Marcel's habitual indifference towards the daily departure of Albertine 'is transformed into the most horrible anxiety' (16) when he overhears her making a disturbingly ambiguous rendezvous with a potential rival with the words, 'Tomorrow, then, at half-past eight' (16). The problem with these illustrations is that they reduce the multiplicity of Proust's terms to a pessimistic, Beckettian dialectic. Instead of examining the ways in which Proust analysed the tripartite variations of habitual indifference, and non-habitual modes of promise and menace, Beckett reduces Proust's terms to the dreary dialectic between habitual 'indifference' and non-habitual 'anxiety'.

Compounding this pessimistic caricature of Proust's vision, Beckett stipulates that this anxiety shatters Marcel's confidence in his ability to determine his existence, when the 'tacit understanding that the future can be controlled is destroyed' (16), and leaves the reader with the impression that Proust's novel is primarily about Marcel's discovery of ever more depressing nuggets of self-knowledge. In the specific context of this episode, Beckett's conclusion seems extremely persuasive, insofar as it is obvious that Marcel cannot hope to control Albertine's future movements. But on other occasions, such as the moment when Marcel contemplates the beauty of blossoming pear trees and cherry trees, his meditations upon the future are much more positive. Reflecting upon the way in which 'la réalité n'est pas ce qu'on croit' (II.160) (reality is not what we suppose it to be), Marcel very interestingly formulates his conviction that his own future movements *may* be meaningfully controlled and directed, since

la splendeur de la poésie . . . (et) l'éclat merveilleux de l'innocence . . . pourront être la récompense que nous nous efforcerons de mériter. (II.160–61)

(the splendour of poetry . . . and the marvellous radiance of innocence
. . . may be the reward that we should make every effort to merit.)

This quintessential statement clearly testifies to Marcel's
eventual awareness of life's promise; to his discovery of the
existential values of 'poetry' and 'innocence'; and to his crucial
realization that these values must be earned by conscious
application. Few other passages in Proust's novel formulate the
positive implications of his 'relativism' more clearly. Yet the
reader searches in vain for any reference to this passage in
Beckett's *Proust*. Quite simply, Beckett seems to have ignored
such moments of 'baffled ecstasy' (76), although his awareness
of their existence sporadically surfaces when his early novels,
such as *Molloy*, pillory Marcel's mysticism. For example, while
Marcel transforms his love of hawthorns into something
bordering upon a religious cult, likening a hawthorn hedge to
'une suite de chapelles' (I.138) (a series of chapels), Beckett's
Molloy deftly denigrates both terms of Marcel's pious metaphor.
Glibly announcing 'chapel, that's the word', in order to describe
the 'two recesses, no, that's not the word, opposite each other,
littered with miscellaneous rubbish and with excrements, of dogs
and masters' in a public lavatory (*Molloy*, 61 and 60–61), he also
pointedly confides: 'The white hawthorn stooped towards me,
unfortunately I don't like the smell of hawthorn' (*Molloy*, 27).

The final subsection of Beckett's discussion of time addresses
the perceptual confusion that arises from the 'unceasing
modification' (15) of the perceiver — that is, the mobility of the
perceiver's perceptions. Even if the perceived is immobile, it will
appear to be mobile because it is perceived in different ways on
different days by a mobile perceiver. In this respect, the
'observer infects the observed with his own mobility' (17). Once
again, a minor Proustian complaint anticipates a major
Beckettian dilemma. If Marcel is at times bemusedly baffled by
his varied visions of immobile objects (such as his vacillating
impressions of the stained-glass windows of the church at
Combray (I.60)), Beckett's Watt is incessantly tormented by such
contradictions as 'the stairs that were never the same and of
which even the number of steps seemed to vary, from day to day'
(*Watt*, 80). Briefly, the perceptual problems of Beckett's fiction
might be likened to Proustian clouds drastically darkened and
stripped of their silver lining.

As Beckett subsequently explains, such perceptual 'infection'
becomes even more excruciating 'when it is a case of human

intercourse' (17), and a mobile subject avidly contemplates an equally mobile human object. For, according to the next sub-section of the essay, Proust maintained that people can never hope to understand one another, since they evolve at different speeds and interpret each other from utterly incompatible points of view. In Beckettian terms, the perceiver and the perceived are 'two separate and imminent dynamisms related by no system of synchronisation' and, as a result, 'whatever the object, our thirst for possession is, by definition, insatiable' (17).

Apparently forgetting that he has already stipulated that Proust's characters sometimes have access to some sort of 'real impression' (14), Beckett argues that their understanding of both animate or inanimate 'objects' is at most fragmentary, since:

At the best, all that is realised in Time . . . whether in Art or Life, can only be possessed successively, by a series of partial annexations — and never integrally and at once. (17–18)

At this point Beckett might once again have specified that such 'laws' are only true with regard to the limited observations that he previously equated with 'vulgar perception' (17), and that any 'wisdom' predicated upon such 'vulgar' laws could only offer a partial account of Proust's complex vision. For, as he acknow-ledges in the penultimate section, Proust also envisages adequate modes of perception 'annihilating every . . . temporal restriction' and unveiling reality in all its 'integral purity' (72).

Paradoxically, Beckett attempts to define Proust's wisdom without regard to either the pure mode of artistic perception to which he refers above, or the pure modes of interpersonal perception that Marcel associates with the finest moments in his relationships with his grandmother and with Saint-Loup. Far from considering the implications of these paragons of authentic perception and communication, Beckett truculently travesties Proust's account of human relationships by abruptly announcing that the 'tragedy of the Marcel-Albertine liaison is the type-tragedy of the human relationship whose failure is preordained' (18). From this preposterous premise, which Beckett self-consciously defines as a 'too abstract and arbitrary statement of Proust's pessimism' (18), it is but a short step to his still more abstract and arbitrary conclusion that Proust, like 'all sages', advocates 'the wisdom that consists not in the satisfaction but in the ablation of desire' (18).

As Swann testifies, Proust rather more optimistically

conceived of his fictional species as 'imperfect, but at least perfectible' (I.290). He envisaged their positive actions as the realization of positive desires, facilitated by the sacrifice of negative desires (while envisaging their negative actions as the consequence of the antithetical, negative sacrifice of positive desires). Neglecting the subtlety of this vision, Beckett's wayward account of Proust's wisdom brings this first section of his essay to what one might well think of as its preordained pessimistic conclusion.

In the second section of his essay, Beckett examines the function of habit in the fictional world of *A la recherch du temps perdu*. As in his discussion of time, his analysis begins relatively accurately, and then degenerates into a reductive argument, illustrated by one-sided examples. Beckett's best general definition of habit appears almost twenty years after the composition of *Proust* in *Waiting for Godot*,[15] in which Vladimir gratefully reflects that 'habit is a great deadener' (*WFG*, 91). Put another way, habit is the familiar force that deadens the pleasant or unpleasant shock of the new, a perceptual anaesthetic that 'paralyses our attention' (20) and offers 'the guarantee of a dull inviolability' (21). Habit, then, is 'a screen to spare its victim the spectacle of reality' (21).

The advantage of this habitual 'screen' is that it shelters the perceiver within the vulgar reality of the 'comfortable and familiar' (21), wherein everything is effortlessly reducible to 'the sanity of a cause' (23). The disadvantage of habitual reality is that it is extremely 'dull' (21) and extremely prejudiced, insofar as it rejects all symptoms of authentic reality. In Beckett's terms, the 'creature of habit', who 'turns aside from the object that cannot be made to correspond with one or another of his intellectual prejudices' (23), is blighted by the same limited perspective as the vulgar 'conscious intellectual effort' (14) that he subsequently derides as being:

conditioned by the prejudices of the intelligence which abstracts from any given sensation, as being illogical and insignificant ... whatever ... cannot be fitted into the puzzle of a concept. (71-2)

Yet despite this unflattering evocation of the dull and unpleasantly prejudiced quality of habitual modes of perception, Beckett's subsequent paragraphs gradually suggest that the boredom and the inadequacies of habitual reality are infinitely preferable to the suffering that he almost invariably associates with the spectacle of non-habitual reality.

At first Beckett seems to respect the parameters of Proust's rather more complex perspective, acknowledging that for Proust habitual reality deadens two distinct modes of non-habitual reality. For example, Marcel specifies that the 'secondary' reality of habitual vision hides both the pain and the pleasure of 'primary', non-habitual reality, observing:

si l'habitude est une seconde nature, elle nous empêche de connaitre la première, dont elle n'a ni les cruautés ni les enchantements. (II.754).

Faithfully translating this key statement, Beckett's essay un-ambiguously asserts that:

if Habit . . . is a second nature, it keeps us in ignorance of the first, and is free of its cruelties and enchantments. (22)

Nevertheless, having dutifully presented this accurate account of Proust's dualistic concept of non-habitual reality, Beckett immediately dissociates himself from the positive concept of enchanting modes of non-habitual reality, by adding the incredulous rejoinder: ' "Enchantments of reality" has the air of a paradox' (22). In much the same way, he casts doubt upon Curtius's troublesome concept of Proust's positive relativism by remarking: 'I think the term "positive relativism" is an oxymoron' (85). In both of these somewhat petulant objections to Proust's more positive and optimistic precepts, Beckett very revealingly places his pessimistic cards on the critical table. Quite simply, it seems that the possibility of enchanting modes of non-habitual reality and of positive modes of relative vision surpassed his credence. Although Beckett occasionally reiterates Proust's distinction between the 'advantages and . . . dis-advantages' (21) of non-habitual reality, his argument gradually obscures all reference to the advantages and the enchantments of non-habitual reality, and surreptitiously superimposes his own peculiarly negative relativism upon Proust's far more complex, positive relativism.

This subtle metamorphosis is not obvious at first glance. However, its action may be traced by examining Beckett's account of those transitional moments when man leaves one mode of habitual 'living', and temporarily finds himself exposed to the 'dangerous' and 'fertile' domain of non-habitual 'being'. Almost imperceptibly, the key concept of non-habitual enchantment — or the 'fertile' non-habitual reality that Beckett initially juxtaposes with 'dangerous' non-habitual reality — goes missing in action between the lines, as he equates all non-habitual 'being' with suffering:

The periods of transition that separate consecutive adaptations (of habit) ... represent the perilous zones in the life of the individual, dangerous, precarious, painful, mysterious and fertile, when for a moment the boredom of living is replaced by the suffering of being. (19)

Having established that Proust opposes boredom and suffering, Beckett 'rides the antithesis to death' (to borrow a Beckettian phrase from 'Proust in Pieces').[16] The reader is reminded of the 'suffering of being: that is, the free play of every faculty' (20) and, at the end of this section on habit, Beckett generously serves yet another double-helping of this definition. Alluding to the 'duty of Habit', Beckett explains that 'Suffering represents the omission of that duty ... and boredom its adequate performance'; and, by way of encore, adds that:

The pendulum oscillates between these two terms: Suffering — that opens a window on the real and is the main condition of the artistic experience, and Boredom. (28)

But, as we have observed, Proust's pendulum traverses a wider arc, moving from the pole of suffering, via the stationary point of boredom, to the pole of enchantment. Moreover, though the Proustian artist sometimes gains inspiration from suffering, Marcel's final moment of creative inspiration (which is surely the most important in Proust's novel), results from his non-habitual felicity at the Guermantes' matinée. Marcel undoubtedly alludes to the creative stimulus offered by suffering (III.909). But he also concurrently conceives of an antithetical mode of inspiration, and refers elsewhere to the way in which certain artists never require the painful non-habitual experience that Beckett dubs the 'main condition of the artistic experience' (28), remarking that 'quelques grandes génies' (certain great geniuses) seem capable of creativity 'sans qu'il y ait besoin ... pour eux des agitations de la douleur' (III.897) (without requiring ... the stimulation of suffering). But of this Beckett says nothing, or next to nothing.

Perhaps such critical misdemeanours are inevitable. Viewed as an analytical hare, the critic can never hope to catch up with the textual tortoise he pursues. Proliferation of such clichéd conceits might easily lead one to conclude, then, that Beckett's analytical aberrations are more or less 'a common, and legitimate, critical manoeuvre'.[17]

Were this indeed the case, then there might be grounds for terminating this critique of Beckett's *Proust* on the spot, with a resigned reference to the way in which this Irish scallywag's critical practice is no better, and no worse, than it should be. Significantly, though, the very terms with which Beckett pinpoints two of the most prevalent failings of 'vulgar perception' in Proust's novel also permit more rigorous evaluation of his own critical manoeuvres, insofar as they rebound to identify the two principal imperfections in his analysis of Proust's vision.

Firstly, like the Proustian 'creature of habit' (23), Beckett is a critic of habit, or more specifically, a critic of pessimistic habit. And just as the Proustian creature of habit 'turns aside from the object that cannot be made to correspond with one or other of his intellectual prejudices' and 'that resists the propositions of his team of synthesis' (23), so too does Beckett's argument resist all reality residing outside his particular 'team of synthesis' — the team of 'Suffering' and 'Boredom' (28). Thus, as we have just observed in Beckett's account of creativity, he 'turns aside' from all mention of creativity predicated upon 'Enchantment', and doggedly 'resists' Marcel's specific references to the ways in which certain great geniuses offer significant exceptions to the Beckettian thesis that suffering is 'the main condition of the artistic experience' (28).

Secondly, like the Proustian creature of habit, and more particularly like the immature Marcel, Beckett is prone to generate the most misleading associations from 'the mirage of imagination' and the 'mirage of memory' (40). Just as Marcel conflates contradictory data, and equates partial reality with reality as a whole, whenever he contemplates Albertine in terms of 'the arbitrary images of memory and imagination' (53), and promptly generates the delusions that Beckett dismisses as 'an artificial fiction' (53), Beckett likewise creates critical 'fictions' whenever he formulates over-imaginative conclusions on the basis of carelessly remembered — or perhaps, callously conflated — quotations from Proust's novel. His assertion that Proust envisaged existence as a pendulum oscillating between 'Suffering ... and Boredom' (28) typifies this errant exegesis.

Far from deriving from any single Proustian statement, this evocative, provocative, and ultimately very Beckettian statement derives from several discrete sources in *A la recherche du temps perdu*, which by absent-mindedness, or by bloody-mindedness, Beckett first conflates, and then equates with Proust's 'wisdom'. The juxtaposition of 'Suffering ... and Boredom' emerges, it seems, from a particularly gloomy meditation in *Le Côté de Guermantes*, in which Marcel situates friendship 'entre la fatigue et l'ennui' (II.395) (between weariness and boredom), although on other occasions he appears full of praise for Saint-Loup's 'parfaite amitié' (II.415) (perfect friendship). The image of a pendulum, however, seems to spring from Marcel's equally gloomy meditations upon lost love, in *La Fugitive*, where he likens his torments to 'l'oscillation du pendule' (III.425) (the oscillations of the pendulum). Neither of these sources addresses life in general, yet via Beckett's imagination, and via the accidents or designs of his memory, they become transformed into his confusing conviction that Proust conceived of existence in terms of fluctuations between the monotony of boredom and the shock of suffering, anticipating, as it were, the Beckettian hero's parallel postulation that life might best be defined as 'a deep and merciful torpor, shot with abominable gleams' (*Molloy*, 54).

The same heady mixture of pessimistic prejudice and of carelessly or callously imaginative exegesis informs the next subsection of Beckett's analysis of the function of habit in *A la recherche du temps perdu*. Here, he turns his attention to the ways in which habit appears to nullify all human relationships, and attempts to illustrate this process with two examples drawn from Marcel's relationship with his grandmother. On each occasion, Beckett emphasizes the 'cruelties' of certain moments of non-habitual lucidity during this relationship. As one might anticipate, he makes no effort to complement these one-sided observations with examples of those equally non-habitual moments of 'enchantment' which give this relationship its positive value and which seem, indeed, to eclipse the negative implications of the incidents that he discusses.

The first of these examples springs from Marcel's reflections, during his first visit to Balbec, upon his own mortality and upon the mobility of the personality, when his discovery of his ability to discard old habits and develop new habits makes his dearest relationships appear alarmingly impermanent. According to Beckett, this discovery makes Marcel keenly aware of a number of specific issues, when

he thinks how absurd is a dream of a Paradise with retention of personality, since our life is a succession of Paradises successively denied, that the only true Paradise is the Paradise that has been lost. (26)

Beckett's conclusion is more than a trifle tiresome.

Firstly, although it is true that Marcel meditates upon the unlikelihood of a paradise in which the personality may be retained
in its habitual state, and although he also undoubtedly concludes
that the only true paradises are the paradises that we have lost,
neither of these thoughts comes to him on this occasion at Balbec,
as Beckett professes. The first of them occurs much later, in
Sodome et Gomorrhe, when Marcel ponders Albertine's
bewildering identity (II.859), while the second of these choice
observations occurs at the very end of Marcel's narrative, in *Le
Temps Retrouvé*, during his revelations at the Guermantes'
matinée (III.870). Still more vexing than this attempt to both
accelerate and exaggerate the quality of Marcel's pessimistic
introspection at Balbec is Beckett's flagrant inattention to the way
in which Marcel's visit to Balbec not only prompts his morbid
suspicion of the unlikelihood of 'une survie comme celle que
Bergotte promettait aux hommes dans ses livres' (I.670) (an
afterlife, such as the one that Bergotte promised to mankind in
his books), but also prompts his celebration of his loving
relationship with his grandmother.

On the very same page upon which Marcel formulates his
doubts regarding the permanence of the personality, he also
very significantly describes the miraculous tapping communication by means of which his grandmother communicates her
peerless affection, and by which he apprehends: 'l'âme de ma
grand'mère tout entière' (I.670) (the entirety of my grandmother's soul). Of course, this gestural communication is just one
of a number of ways by which Marcel's grandmother successfully
communicates her benevolence to Marcel. Later, during Marcel's
visit to Saint-Loup at Doncières, she once again communicates 'sa
douceur même' (II.135) (her very affection), when he telephones
her, and senses her benevolence in the intonation of her voice,
rather than in the intonation of her fingers on a partition.

It is strange that Beckett should make no mention of the
momentous quality of this tapping communication when
discussing Marcel's sufferings at Balbec, since in later works,
such as *Footfalls*, he is particularly sensitive to the ways in which
faint sounds may permit communication between different
generations.[18] Moreover, it seems almost certain that Beckett
was aware of the significance of this tapping communication,
since he not only underlines subsequent references to the
partition upon which Marcel and his grandmother tap to one
another, but also annotates Marcel's reference to the way in

which the same partition that allowed him to communicate with
his grandmother subsequently separates him from Albertine,
observing: '2 aspects of cloison'.[19] Predictably, Beckett's essay
only emphasizes the negative function of this partition.

In much the same way, Beckett's subsequent fiction elaborates
negative variants of the miraculous tapping communication
which allows Marcel and his grandmother to transcend both
spatial barriers and the discursive barrier of habitual
conversation. Submitting Marcel's tender 'trois petit coups'
(I.669) (three little taps) to the full force of his parodic irony,
Molloy triumphantly records the successful way in which he first
'got into communication' with his mother, when 'knocking her
on the skull'. He adds that he perfected this process upon
discovering 'a more effective means', which 'consisted in
replacing the first four knocks of my index knuckle by one or
more . . . thumps of the fist, on her skull' (*Molloy*, 18).

The Unnamable similarly exemplifies a negative variant of
Marcel's tapping communication, when comparing himself with
a partition. Far from employing this image in the context of
authentic communication, as Marcel does, when describing the
way in which the partition separating him from his grandmother
becomes 'pénétrée de tendresse et de joie' (I.670) (penetrated
with tenderness and joy), and thus the very means by which he
and his grandmother commune with one another, the
Unnamable uses the metaphor of the partition to emphasize his
isolation from both exterior and interior reality and, it seems, to
celebrate his immunity to the whole problem of communication,
reflecting:

perhaps that's what I feel, an outside and an inside and me in the
middle, I'm the partition . . . I'm the tympanum, on the one hand the
mind, on the other the world, I don't belong to either. (*The
Unnamable*,386)

If Beckett was clearly very impressed by Marcel's partition
image, and was equally clearly aware of the '2 aspects' of this
image, it also seems clear that he was quite disinclined to docu-
ment — let alone, accentuate — the positive aspect of this image.

While Beckett's refusal to acknowledge the triumphant quality
of the grandmother's tapping communication may seem strange,
it seems still more strange that Beckett should similarly suppress
all reference to her equally triumphant telephonic communication with Marcel, when discussing Marcel's telephone call to
his grandmother as part of his second example of the ways in

which the forces of habit invalidate all human affection. This telephone call appears to have fascinated Beckett as a particularly pregnant example of non-habitual dialogue. For, as Beckett observes, when Marcel converses with his grandmother, he hears her voice independently of her habitual facial expression, just as she too responds to Marcel as a particularly distant, disembodied interlocutor. As one might expect, such non-habitual communication has '2 aspects', and Beckett's initial comments appear to foreground the advantages of this non-habitual conversation by specifying that Marcel hears his grandmother's voice 'in all its purity and reality' (27). But Beckett hastens to add:

It is a grievous voice, its fragility unmitigated and undisguised by the carefully arranged mask of her features, and this strange real voice is the measure of its owner's suffering. He hears it also as the symbol of her isolation, of their separation. (27)

One might well infer, then, that the voice of Marcel's grandmother is most significant as an index of her misery, and as further evidence of the futility of human affection. The reckless reader might even liken it to the disembodied utterances of Beckett's 'Mouth', whose voice rather more explicitly sums up its owner's sufferings in the reminiscence:

so no love ... spared that ... no love such as normally vented on the speechless infant ... in the home ... no ... nor indeed for that matter any of any kind ... no love of any kind ... at any subsequent stage ... (*Not I*, 6)

Yet despite the fact that Marcel comments upon the sadness in his grandmother's voice, he does not simply refer to her sadness and sufferings, as Beckett's essay might lead the unwary reader to suppose. On the contrary, he takes pains to indicate the way in which the gentle and utterly selfless qualities of her voice allow her to offer him precisely the kind of love that 'Mouth' claims never to have known:

Elle était douce, mais aussi comme elle était triste, d'abord à cause de sa douceur même, presque décantée, plus que peu de voix humaines ont jamais dû l'être, de toute dureté, de tout élément de résistance aux autres, de tout égoïsme! (II.135)
(How gentle it was, and how sad, firstly because of her very affection, which was almost completely decanted, more so than almost any other human voice can have been, of all traces of opposition to other people, of all egotism!)

In other words, far from offering an epitome of existential failure, and far from testifying to Beckett's thesis that Proust's characters are doomed to isolation and separation, and that 'There is no communication because there are no vehicles of communication' (64), Marcel's grandmother offers an epitome of selfless, and utterly successful, gestural communication. In this respect she differs from such selfish characters as Charlus, whose failure to offer his talents adequate realization prompts Marcel's moralizing musing:

s'il eût fait des livres on aurait eu sa valeur spirituelle isolée, decantée du mal, rien n'eût gêné l'admiration. (III.209)
(if he had written books then his spiritual value would have been isolated, decanted of all evil, and open to unqualified admiration.)

The great failing of Charlus is that he neither 'isolates' his positive potential nor reveals his 'spiritual value', whereas the great achievement of Marcel's grandmother is that she realizes these ideals on several occasions. Yet, for reasons best known to himself, Beckett makes no mention of this achievement, intimating instead that Marcel's grandmother simply stands as Proust's symbol of 'suffering', 'isolation' and 'separation' (27).

Once again, in this subsection of his analysis of habit, as elsewhere in his essay, Beckett paints the gloomiest of pictures of the Proustian vision, suggesting that Proust found communication to be impossible, affection to be futile, and man and woman incapable of determining their destiny or of making morally consequential decisions. Accordingly, as Beckett hints at the beginning of his meditations upon habit, there is virtually nothing to be done, since 'An automatic adjustment of the human organism to the conditions of its existence' — by which Beckett seems to mean the renovation of habit — 'has as little moral significance as the casting of a clout when May is or is not out' (20). And thus, 'the exhortation to cultivate a habit' makes 'as little sense as the exhortation to cultivate a coryza' (20).

Beckett's reference to a *coryza* (in layman's terms, a runny nose or catarrh) amusingly anticipates the wealth of nasal references in the novel that Beckett wrote immediately after *Proust*, *Dream of Fair to Middling Women*, in which he repeatedly refers to his hero's craving to 'pick his nose thoroughly' (*Dream*, 14), or else lovingly details the way in which the 'Solitary meditation' of his hero's lady love 'furnished her with nostrils of a generous bore' (*Dream*, 160). Nevertheless, for all its merit as an intimation of the nasal motifs in Beckett's first novel, this reference has the demerit of blurring the 'moral significance' of Proust's vision, by suggesting that all habitual actions are equally insignificant and equally unworthy of 'exhortation'. This is a contention which either consciously or unconsciously overlooks Marcel's crucial exhortation of the three cardinal 'good habits' of 'la bonté, le scrupule, le sacrifice' (III.188) (goodness, scrupulousness, sacrifice).

Beckett concludes his confusing account of the workings of habit by offering the reader 'an apéritif of metaphors' (29), by way of prelude to his revelation of the Proustian aesthetic. The most striking of these metaphors suggests that despite Beckett's repeated allusions to the cruelties and the sufferings of non-habitual perception, a process of 'poetical excavation' para-doxically affords a desirable mode of non-habitual perception and somehow reveals 'the heart of the cauliflower or the ideal core of the onion' (29). Attractive as this process may appear, its precise conditions remain far from clear, since Beckett refrains from diluting this *apéritif* with further details, and rapidly brings this section of *Proust* to a close. Beckett does not seem to have intended to offer clear accounts of successful 'poetical excavation' — or indeed clear accounts of successful *anything* — at this juncture of his essay.

The third section of *Proust* discusses the workings (or misworkings) of voluntary memory. Unlike the preceding section, it is not illustrated by substantial examples, but instead is deftly delineated in terms of a number of abstract and metaphorical notions which seem to have caught Beckett's imagination to such an extent that they culminate in one of his most sympathetic accounts of involuntary memory. Nevertheless, like the preceding section, this part of *Proust* insists upon the painful potential of involuntary revelations.

As Beckett hinted when associating habitual perception with 'intellectual prejudices' and with the 'sanity of a cause' (23), voluntary memory is above all a rational, causal process, or 'the uniform memory of the intelligence' (32). As such, it ignores 'the mysterious' and registers only 'those impressions of the past that were consciously and intelligently formed' (32). As a function of what Beckett sneeringly terms man's 'impeccable habit' (30) — that is, his rational habit — voluntary memory is at best a device for registering the limited, vulgar perceptions of habitual reality. Put another way, it is a boring 'instrument of reference', rather than an 'instrument of discovery' (30) boring into the depths of non-habitual reality.

By contrast, involuntary memory, a process which Beckett evokes in the most abstract terms and refuses to define in any detail, appears to retrieve the mysterious reality that he optimistically evinces at this point as 'the best of our many selves' and as our 'fine essence' (31), by rescuing it from the 'deep source' (32) that he envisages as 'that ultimate and inaccessible dungeon of our being to which Habit does not possess the key' (31). This is the zone of our 'inattention' (31) or, at least, of mysterious perceptions which habitual memory cannot reduce to comforting causes and effects, and which it therefore finds unworthy of attention; a notion which nicely paraphrases Marcel's references to those 'profondeurs où ce qui a existé réellement gît inconnu de nous' (III.896) (depths where, unbeknown to us, everything that really exists resides). Rediscovered by involuntary memory, rather than by voluntary memory, this deep reality is 'accumulated .. under the nose of our vulgarity' (31), and it is precisely upon rediscovering its 'pearl' that we also rediscover the paucity — or 'paste and pewter' (31) — of our vulgar 'utilitarian considerations' (31).

For a brief interval, this section of *Proust* offers a surprisingly faithful and a surprisingly sympathetic account of the enchantments of the non-habitual reality that Marcel unreservedly eulogizes as 'l'immédiate, délicieuse et totale déflagration du souvenir' (III.692). Indeed Beckett even goes so far as to translate this paean to involuntary memory, by specifying that it 'is explosive, "an immediate, total and delicious deflagration" ' (33). Elaborating Marcel's archetypal mystical images of the fires and the luminosity of involuntary memory, Beckett additionally explains that the purity of involuntary memory derives from the way in which it both transcends and destroys the vulgarity of voluntary perception,

because in its flame it has consumed Habit and all its works, and in its brightness revealed what the mock reality of experience never can and never will reveal — the real. (33)

As is frequently the case in his book reviews written after *Proust*, Beckett seems compelled to qualify such accounts of the advantages of non-habitual, mystical experience with an immediate rejoinder referring to the infrequency of non-habitual bliss, or emphasizing the imminence of non-habitual torment. On this occasion, Beckett adopts the latter strategy, and promptly reminds the reader that Marcel's enthusiasm for the miracle of involuntary memory is but one possible response to this force, since involuntary memory 'restores . . . the Lazarus' that the past 'charmed or tortured' (33), and is thus a potential source of both non-habitual charm and non-habitual torture. As Beckett's first three fictional works all indicate, Beckett seems to have concluded that one should refrain from reactivating the past, and let sleeping Lazaruses lie, rather than running the risk of resuscitating long-forgotten torments. Accordingly, in both *Dream of Fair to Middling Women* and *More Pricks Than Kicks*, the 'Polar Bear' scathingly derides the raising of Lazarus as 'a piece of megalomaniacal impertinence', while Murphy similarly considers this miracle to be 'the one occasion on which the Messiah had overstepped the mark'.[20]

In another such qualification, Beckett emphasizes the comparative rarity of involuntary memory, explaining:

Involuntary memory is an unruly magician and will not be importuned. It chooses its own time and place for the performance of its miracle. (33–34)

This specification springs in its turn from his insistence that the 'salvage' of involuntary memory is 'an accident'. Formally introducing the concept of involuntary memory in five teasingly brief sentences, he defines the mysteries of involuntary memory metaphorically, as 'a diver' salvaging aspects of the past; he explains that for the present he has no intention of defining this 'diver' in any more detail; and finally he rather peevishly concedes that Proust discussed this process not so much in diving metaphors as in terms of 'involuntary memory'. Offering a fine example of Beckett's tendency to write what one might think of as 'involuntary exegesis', these sentences condescendingly confide:

His work is not an accident, but its salvage is an accident. The conditions of that accident will be revealed at the peak of this prevision. A second-hand climax is better than none. But no purpose can be served by withholding the name of the diver. Proust calls him 'involuntary memory'. (32)

Taken as a whole, this section of Beckett's essay offers a fairly clear account of the shortcomings of voluntary memory, and a characteristically mixed account of its involuntary counterpart, ranging from his sympathetic, but highly abstract, evocation of its impact, to his stubborn refusal to offer any precise analysis of its function. Surprisingly, the next section, which is notionally

consecrated to involuntary memory, proves equally reluctant to
define its function as an 'immediate, total and delicious
deflagration' (33).

This fourth section, which seems to have set out with the
sterling intention of explicating the miracle of involuntary
memory, begins with a barrage of antitheses and abstractions
sufficient to give semantic shell-shock to all but the most hardy
readers. Beckett proclaims:

From this Janal, trinal, agile monster or Divinity: Time — a condition of
resurrection because an instrument of death; Habit — an infliction in so
far as it opposes the dangerous exaltation of the one and a blessing in so
far as it palliates the cruelty of the other; Memory — a clinical laboratory
stocked with poison and remedy, stimulant and sedative: from Him the
mind turns to the one compensation and mirace of evasion tolerated by
His tyranny and vigilance. (35)

Somewhat like 'Mrs. W', in Beckett's *Footfalls*, the reader might
well exclaim: 'What do you mean . . . to put it mildly, what can
you possibly mean?' (*Footfalls*, 13).

Tracked down to its sources in *A la recherche du temps perdu*, this
perplexing personification of 'Time', 'Habit' and 'Memory'
appears to derive from two passages in which Marcel ponders
upon the ambiguities of Albertine, rather than from any
definition of involuntary memory.[21] Yet again, Beckett misleadingly transposes Proustian concepts from one context to
another. Picked at with the scalpel of close analysis, the passage
offers an awesome mixture of imprecise antitheses, ambiguous
metaphors, impenetrable cross-references, and incongruous
personifications. But, considered in its own terms, it simply
seems to postulate that the 'accidental and fugitive salvation . . .
of involuntary memory' (35) affords the 'one compensation' for
the positive and negative effects of time, habit and memory. As
we have observed, Beckett conflates and personifies these effects
as a 'Janal, trinal, agile' being, in order to create a new binary
opposition between the 'salvation' of involuntary memory and
the disorientating influences of his horrible 'Janal, trinal, agile
Monster or Divinity' (to give the brute its full, unwieldy name).

This binary opposition appears both unnecessary and un-
tenable. It makes no sense to contrast involuntary memory with
a personification of the positive and negative aspects of time,
habit and memory, because involuntary memory pertains to this
personification. Put another way, involuntary memory is the
product or synthesis of the positive aspects of time, habit and

memory. Time's 'resurrection', and Habit's 'dangerous exaltation' are the very conditions and constituents of involuntary memory. Accordingly, the principal dichotomy within Proust's vision resides not so much in the pseudo-dichotomy that Beckett constructs between involuntary memory and a bizarre personification of voluntary and involuntary perceptions, as in Proust's crucial distinctions between positive and negative variants of each and every mode of perception, and each and every mode of self-realization.

Beckett's pseudo-dichotomy typifies his compulsion to define involuntary memory as the single pure mode of perception in Proust's novel. This compulsion appears to derive from Beckett's assumption that Proust conceived of salvation exclusively in terms of the artistic or perceptual salvation afforded by involuntary memories. And this assumption seems to be predicated in its turn upon Beckett's refusal to concede that Proust either conceived of a plurality of artistic and non-artistic modes of salvation, or located these examplary actions within a hierarchy of morally differentiated actions.

Reconsidered in the context of these observations, it would seem that Beckett's distinction between the 'salvation' of involuntary memory and the 'damnation' arising from all other modes of perception is not only consistent with his refusal to acknowledge moral values and non-artistic modes of salvation in Proust's fictional universe, but is also dependent upon these pessimistic prejuduces (rather than upon any internal evidence drawn from *A la recherche du temps perdu*). Having introduced this strategic — and ultimately fallacious — distinction, Beckett turns his attention to more specific aspects and examples of involuntary memory in order to consolidate his interpretative prejudices.

Before listing examples of involuntary memory, he meditates upon the musical quality of 'this mystic experience' (35) in a succession of both flattering and unflattering observations. On the one hand, he volunteers the suggestion that involuntary memory functions 'as the Leitmotiv' of Proust's novel. But, on the other, he adds that it 'recurs like . . . a neuralgia rather than a theme' (35), somewhat as his subsequent criticism compares the entire narrational trajectory of *A la recherche du temps perdu* with 'the chart of an ague',[22] and somewhat as Belacqua, the hero of *Dream of Fair to Middling Women*, suffers from a haunting musical phrase which he describes as 'moaning in his memory' and 'coming now to a head in . . . a stress of remembrance'

(*Dream*, 204). In other words, despite the fact that Beckett subsequently argues that music saves Marcel from despair and 'asserts to his unbelief the permanence of personality and the reality of art' (92), Beckett's unbelief refused to be convinced by Proust's argument; and both here in *Proust*, and subsequently in *Dream of Fair to Middling Women*, he insisted upon registering his incredulity by characterizing music as a source of irritation rather than as a source of revelation.

This tendency becomes particularly clear if one considers Beckett's use of the concept of 'grace-notes', an image that he perhaps borrowed from the passage in Joyce's *A Portrait of the Artist as a Young Man* in which Stephen Dedalus's father explains that the Joycean musical archetype of a 'strange sad happy air' festooned with 'tender tremors' sounded even more beautiful when sung by one Mick Lacy, who 'had little turns for it, grace notes that he used to put in that I haven't got'.[23] Beckett applies this term quite respectfully in *Proust*, alluding to the way in which the leitmotiv of involuntary memory is 'enriched with a strange and necessary incrustation of grace-notes' (35). But one year later, as if regretting this respectful reference to an alien ideal, he systematically ridiculed it in *Dream of Fair to Middling Women*, in which Belacqua not once, but twice 'suffered the shakes and gracenote strangulations and enthrottlements of the Winkelmusik of Szopen or Pichon or Chopinek or Chopinette or whosoever it was' (*Dream*, 61 and 12–13).[24] In much the same way, Beckett's eventual discussion of Marcel's involuntary memories commences with his dutiful description of their advantages, and then rapidly degenerates into an analysis of the kind of involuntary anguish which proves both an exception to the rule of the Proustian 'mystic experience' (35), and a prefiguration of the perceptual chaos that Beckett subsequently associates with his own particular species of 'dud mystic' or 'mystique raté' (*Dream*, 166).

At first Beckett offers nominal recognition to the positive potential of involuntary memory, acknowledging that it affords 'an essential statement of reality', and that it 'climbs through a series of precisions and purifications to the pinnacle from which it commands and clarifies ... and delivers its triumphant ultimatum' (35–6). Having already announced in a rather off-hand manner that 'I do not know how often this miracle recurs' (34), he lists eleven authentic examples of what he now almost disdainfully prefers to term Proust's 'fetishes' (36); adds three 'tentative and abortive experiences' (37) to this list; concedes that most critics discuss 'the famous madeleine' (38); and then devotes the remainder of this section to the perceptual 'neuralgia' (35) generated by the one impure, imprecise and 'poisoned' (42) involuntary memory in *A la recherche du temps perdu*, acclaiming it a prize example of 'the erratic machinery of habit and memory as conceived by Proust' (39). Lest the reader protest that this peculiarly 'poisoned' and 'erratic' example of involuntary memory is atypical of the workings of such positive involuntary memories as those precipitated by 'the famous madeleine' (38), Beckett triumphantly announces that his discussion of the workings of involuntary memory (or what he terms the 'Proustian *Discours de la Méthode*') has once again been postponed, adding the equally teasing suggestion that the reader should both accept such critical cake and *not* eat it. In Beckettian terms:

Albertine and the Proustian *Discours de la Méthode* having waited so long can wait a little longer, and the reader is cordially invited to omit this summary analysis of what is perhaps the greatest passage that Proust ever wrote. (39)

Beckett begins his analysis of this 'greatest passage' in *A la recherche du temps perdu* by explaining that Marcel's second visit to Balbec is highly significant as an illustration of the illusions of voluntary memory. Marcel no longer misinterprets Balbec with the 'mirage of imagination', by depicting it in terms of the associations prompted by the syllables of its name, but reduces it to erroneous habitual categories with the 'mirage of memory' (40). Put another way, Marcel envisages Balbec in terms of the 'uniform memory of intelligence', a perceptual practice which, as Beckett previously observed, selects 'images . . . as arbitrary as those chosen by imagination, and . . . equally remote from reality' (32).

Marcel confesses that his second approach to Balbec illustrates the way in which we manage to 'poser sur les choses l'âme qui nous est familière au lieu de la leur qui nous effrayait' (II.764) (impose familiar souls upon things, in the place of their own souls, which once frightened us), and Beckett faithfully paraphrases this statement, alluding to the manner in which Marcel's habitual memories effect 'the imposition of our own familiar soul on the terrifying soul of our surroundings' (40–41). But what interested Beckett still more than this demonstration of the ease with which habit superimposes its comforting categories upon unfamiliar reality was the way in which Marcel's second visit also introduced the alarming process by which certain erratic modes of involuntary memory might suddenly superimpose intolerably contradictory images of the past.

In this respect, this incident from *A la recherche du temps perdu* probably fascinated Beckett most of all in terms of the way in which it seemed to illustrate his thesis that involuntary memory was a very mixed blessing insofar as it resurrected perceptions that both 'charmed' and 'tortured' (33). Leaning over his boots, Marcel is suddenly intensely charmed by an unusually vivid memory of the benevolent way in which his grandmother used to help him to unbutton his boots. But, at the same instant, he is also *tortured* by his sudden, equally vivid awareness that his grandmother is dead, and therefore 'for ever incapable of any tenderness' (42). Simultaneously exposed to two incompatible revelations, Marcel finds that 'This contradiction . . . is intolerable' (42).

Like many of Proust's critics, Beckett acknowledged that the 'rhetorical equivalent of the Proustian real is the chain-figure of the metaphor' (88), or what Marcel refers to as 'un certain rapport entre . . . ces souvenirs qui nous entourent simultanément' (III.889) (a certain relationship between . . . the memories that simultaneously surround us). But unlike most of Proust's critics, he also realized that another important aspect of the 'Proustian real' might be envisaged as a failed or flawed metaphorical vision — or metaphor *manqué* — in which involuntary memories clash in a state of intolerable conflict. Beckett's interpretation of this perceptual conflict is as audacious as it is perspicacious.

While the perspicacity of Beckett's judgment led him to demonstrate that Proust not only conceived of harmonious metaphorical visions of essential reality, but also complemented such idyllic non-habitual revelations with the equally non-habitual flawed metaphorical insights that Marcel defines as a 'douloureuse synthèse' (II.760) or, in Beckettian terms, a 'dolorous synthesis' (42), the rare audacity — or the madness — of Beckett's method led him to confuse such dolorous syntheses with the substance of Proust's vision. Responding over-literally to Marcel's moments of confusion and delusion, and overestimating their significance, he argues that Marcel's contradictory memories of his grandmother reveal that their relationship has no special value after all and is at best 'an accident', since Marcel 'meant nothing to her before their meeting' and likewise 'can mean nothing to her after her departure' (42). In a sense, Beckett seems convincing.

Marcel certainly momentarily persuades himself that his

relationship with his grandmother was nothing more than an illusion, and disconsolately concludes:

Elle était tout dans ma vie; les autres n'existaient que relativement à elle, au jugement qu'elle me donnerait sur eux; mais non, nos rapports ont été trop fugitifs pour n'avoir pas été accidentels. Elle ne me connaît plus, je ne la reverrai jamais. Nous n'avions pas été crées uniquement l'un pour l'autre, c'était une étrangère. (II.775)
(She was everything in my life; others existed only in relation to her, in relation to the verdict upon them that she would give to me; no, on the contrary, our relationship was too fugitive not to have been accidental. She no longer knew me, I would never see her again. We were not created uniquely for each other, she was a stranger.)

Yet, viewed in a wider context, this testimony carries rather less conviction. For, as Beckett observes, Marcel's ruminations 'bristle with alternatives' (81), and, as we have observed, these alternatives include Marcel's crucial assertion that his grand-mother means a great deal to him, both generally, as one of 'ces êtres qui m'avaient révélé des vérités' (III.902) (those persons who revealed truth to me), and more specifically, as 'l'être ... qui me sauvait de la sécheresse de l'âme' (II.755) (the person who saved me from aridity of soul). And, as we have demonstrated, Marcel's grandmother is also exceptionally significant as one of the few non-artists in *A la recherche du temps perdu* who successfully communicates their benevolence and affection to Marcel.

Yet both here, in his analysis of the workings of involuntary memory and in the subsequent section of *Proust*, in which he examines Marcel's relationships with Albertine and Saint-Loup, Beckett doggedly defends his thesis that Proust depicts a fictional world in which meaningful relationships and authentic com-munication are unknown, and in which man's only certainty with regard to human relationships is the certainty that their 'failure is preordained' (18). Once again, then, Beckettian analysis of *A la recherche du temps perdu* transforms the peculiar 'multiplicity' (11) of Proust's vision into the peculiar singularity of the Beckettian vision and reduces existence to the sorry condition that the narrator of *Dream of Fair to Middling Women* deplores as: 'a gehenna of sweats and fiascos and tears and an absence of all douceness' (*Dream*, 16).[25].

6

BECKETT'S INTERPRETATION OF THE 'ALBERTINE TRAGEDY'

Most of the fifth section of Beckett's *Proust* discusses Marcel's ill-fated infatuation for Albertine, the relationship that Beckett prefers to refer to as the 'Albertine Tragedy' (45). Most of Beckett's confusions regarding Proust's vision spring from his curious conviction that this 'Tragedy' is 'the type-tragedy of the human relationship' (18).

Arguably, Swann's fervent passion for Odette typifies the human relationship, if the human relationship is in turn to be typified by unrequited love. Certain 'scenes' of the 'Albertine Tragedy' certainly illustrate the ways in which the successive phases of passionate love first multiply, and then remultiply, the typical perceptual errors of the typical passionate lover. But the 'stupefying antics'[1] with which Albertine torments Marcel in the 'Albertine Tragedy' are so atypical of average human behaviour in Proust's novel that they cannot possibly be confused with 'the type' of the human relationship in *A la recherche du temps perdu*.

Beckett's blunder — or Beckett's bluff — is to assert that Proust 'extends' the implications of Marcel's misadventures with the inscrutable Albertine 'to all human relations' (85). Proust does no such thing. As the sole substantial example of the permanent, and thus 'imperfectible', existential immaturity that Swann associates with 'une eau informe' (I.290) (formless water), Albertine is the very antithesis of the average Proustian character, and is in turn quite incapable of contributing to anything approximating an average relationship between average characters. Quite simply, she is not that kind of girl.

Yet it is easy to see why Beckett may have thought of the 'Albertine Tragedy' as the 'central catastrophe' in Proust's novel. In the course of his thankless pursuit of Albertine, Marcel conveniently exemplifies nearly all of the perceptual torments that Beckett introduces in the first four sections of his essay, becoming painfully familiar with the slings, arrows, and outrageous misfortunes brought about by time, habit, and voluntary and involuntary memory. Beckett's analyses of these torments are usually exemplary until that pivotal point when his argument overlooks his previous injunction that the 'danger' of all criticism 'is in the neatness of identifications',[2] and he attempts to identify Marcel's sufferings with 'all human relations' (85).

Beckett's analysis of the 'Albertine Tragedy' begins by astutely indicating the way in which Marcel initially misinterprets Albertine with the mirages of his imagination and of his voluntary memory, somewhat as he misinterprets Balbec by considering it with these faulty faculties. Described in Beckett's metaphorical terminology, Marcel's imagination first 'weaves its cocoon about this frail and almost abstract chrysalis' (46) by associating Albertine with the sea, 'co-ordinating her with another image' (46). Or, defined in William Burroughs's terms, Marcel becomes dependent upon a maritime 'image fix'.[3] For henceforth, Albertine must evince the sea, in order to offer Marcel perceptual satisfaction. He is 'addicted' to this image.

Marcel's perceptual torments begin when he is denied this 'image fix'. This occurs as he gradually becomes aware of the contradictions and the conflict between his favourite, imaginary, maritime image of Albertine, and the alternative images offered by his varied voluntary memories. At this point, Marcel suffers from the 'shifting superficies' and 'pictorial multiplicity' (47) of Albertine; and, as Beckett explains, he is very much the author of his own sorrows, since they are 'an effect of the observer's angle of approach' (48). Like two distinct viruses, Marcel's imagination and his voluntary memories first 'infect the observed' (17) and then afflict each other.[4]

But as Beckett subsequently explains, Albertine's ambiguity — or 'pictorial multiplicity' — is also an effect of her own 'immanent dynamism' (17). Puzzled by her unpredictable behaviour, Marcel finds that there is 'no common measure' (48) between her different attitudes. And, to make matters worse, he gradually becomes aware that Albertine is 'a natural liar' (51). As we have suggested, it is precisely these traits that distinguish Albertine from Proust's other characters, and identify her as an exception to the 'rule' rather than as the 'type' of any general pattern of behaviour in the Proustian universe.

If Marcel's relationship thus far confirms Beckett's earlier reference to the human relationship as the confusion between 'two separate and immanent dynamisms related by no system of synchronisation' (17), this confusion becomes further intensified when Marcel falls in love with Albertine, and she becomes what Beckett defines as 'a cardiac and no longer a visual stimulant' (49). In other words, she becomes an emotional rather than a purely intellectual or 'pictorial' problem, and Marcel 'listens for her step . . . not with his ear and mind, but with his heart' (50). Or, as Beckett observes in yet another of his illuminating antitheses, Albertine is no longer 'all surface', but becomes 'a multiplicity in depth' (47) and the source of the profound, irremediable confusions that he describes as: 'a turmoil of objective and immanent contradictions, over which the subject has no control' (47).

This 'turmoil of objective and immanent contradictions' becomes most unbearable on the occasion when Marcel's cherished image of 'the first Albertine, the beach flower' (47) clashes violently with his equally intense suspicion that Albertine, like Mlle Vinteuil, might be participating in lesbian orgies. Simultaneously 'co-ordinating' the image of Albertine with both the beauty of the sea and the disquieting memory of Mlle Vinteuil's lesbian frolics at Montjouvain, Marcel discovers that these two images eventually become so helplessly entwined that he is incapable of either enjoying the sea in its own right, or of conjuring up comforting maritime images of Albertine in order to satisfy his 'addiction' to this image. For, as Beckett explains, both the sea and Marcel's maritime image of Albertine are 'poisoned' by his image of Albertine's lesbianism, so that finally:

The strand and the waves exist no more, the summer is dead. The sea is a veil that cannot hide the horror of Montjouvain, the intolerable vision of sadistic lubricity. (53)

In other words, Marcel's first metaphorical vision of Albertine becomes horrifyingly out of focus, as it is eclipsed by an 'intolerable vision', or counter image, over which he 'has no control' (47).

This evocation of intense perceptual confusion perhaps testifies more than anything else to the subtlety of the Proustian vision. At first sight, Proust appears to be an archetypally Modernist writer, in so far as he celebrates the Symbolist sacrament, and evinces ideal, harmonious perceptions in which 'Les parfums, les couleurs et les sons se répondent' (Perfumes, colours, and sounds answer one another).[5] But as this evocation of Marcel's contradictory perceptions indicates, Proust also anticipates the ways in which certain Post-Modernist novelists have given attention to quite antithetical, unharmonious conditions, in which conflicting sensations, perceptions and emotions, deflate, negate and nullify one another.

On the one hand, writers like Beckett have explored the private, solipsistic confusion afflicting characters such as Malone, who finds that 'Words and images run riot in my head' (*Malone Dies*, p.198). On the other hand, writers such as Burroughs have elaborated more public, apocalyptic visions of 'words and images run riot', when, in Burroughs's somewhat indelicate terms, 'the whole fucking shit house goes up'.[6] More often than not, such novels implode and explode with visions of universal chaos, as in the following passage from *Nova Express*:

Electric storms of violence sweep the planet — Desperate position and advantage precariously held — Governments fall with a whole civilisation and ruling class into streets of total fear — Leaders turn on image rays to flood the world with replicas — Swept out by counter image —[7]

As this telegrammatic account of warfare between 'image rays' and 'counter image' suggests, and as Burroughs himself specifies, his fiction frequently reflects an interest 'in precisely how word and image get around on very, very complex association lines'[8] — a process which similarly constitutes one of the central concerns of both Proust's and Beckett's writing. Stipulating that his work aspires to 'look outside', or explore means of social control, whereas 'Beckett wants to go inward',[9] Burroughs also nicely pinpoints the way in which Beckett, like Proust, is primarily an explorer of that inner space in which intense images and perceptions of others and of the self 'get around on very, very complex association lines.'

The problem with Beckett's analysis of Proust's vision is that all too often he responds over-literally to Marcel's testimony, rather than taking account of the 'very, very complex, association lines' of Proust's vision as a whole. Having offered impeccable analyses of Marcel's 'pictorial' and 'cardiac' confusions, Beckett misinterprets their significance by indiscriminately reiterating a number of Marcel's exceedingly pessimistic and unreliable statements. Marcel temporarily persuades himself that 'tous les jours qui viendraient ensuite ne m'apporteraient plus jamais l'espérance d'un bonheur inconnu, mais le prolongement de martyre' (II.1117) (all of the days to come would bring me no trace of unknown joy, but merely prolong my martyrdom), and Beckett similarly avows that Marcel envisages 'a succession of joyless dawns, poisoned by the tortures of memory and isolation' (53).

Such a summary of Marcel's moods would be perfectly legitimate had Beckett indicated that it was merely of temporary validity, and that Marcel subsequently asserted more positive beliefs, such as his suggestion that 'le chagrin . . . développe les forces de l'esprit' (III.906) (grief . . . cultivates spritual strength). Instead, Beckett takes Marcel's pessimistic outbursts very seriously, and dogmatically asserts that his 'pictorial' and 'cardiac' sufferings demonstrate the way in which

No object prolonged in this temporal dimension tolerates possession, meaning by possession total possession, only to be achieved by the complete identification of object and subject. (57)

From this 'law', it would seem to follow that:

All that is active, all that is enveloped in time and space, is endowed with what might be described as an abstract, ideal and absolute impermeability. (57–8)

Taken in tandem, these assertions suggest, then, that no object or person can ever be known, since all objects and all persons are utterly impermeable.

There can be no denying that Marcel repeatedly alludes to the impossibility of possessing anyone or anything. Deriding the concept of sexual possession, he refers to 'l'acte de la possession physique — où d'ailleurs l'on ne possède rien' (I.234) (the act of physical possession — when, moreover, one possesses nothing), just as he dismisses Swann's vain desire for 'la possession, toujours impossible, d'un autre être' (I.364) (the possession, forever impossible, of another being). Subsequently, he even suggests that such artistic works as Vinteuil's sonata defy possession: 'cette Sonate, je ne la possédai jamais tout entière: elle ressemblait à la vie' (I.530) (that sonata, I never really possessed it entirely: it was just like life).

Significantly, though, most of his references to the impossibility of ever totally possessing or totally knowing anything or anyone are predicated upon logical concepts, which are in turn aspects of a 'vulgar', logical fallacy. These concepts insist that possession or knowledge is dependent upon awareness of *all* the successive parts of any whole, and derive from his definition of the loved one as: 'l'extension de cet être à tous les points de l'espace et du temps que cet être a occupés et occupera' (III.100) (in Beckett's translation: 'the extension of that being to all the points of space and time that it has occupied and will occupy' (58)). Marcel concludes:

Si nous ne possédons pas son contact avec tel lieu, avec tel heure, nous ne le possédons pas. Or nous ne pouvons toucher tous ces points. (III.100)

and Beckett faithfully translates:

If we do not possess contact with such a place and with such an hour we do not possess that being. But we cannot touch all these points. (58)

However, the fearful symmetry of this argument becomes short-circuited once Marcel discovers that profound reality does not consist of an accumulation of the 'vulgar' data that man defines as tangible 'points of space and time'. To his relief, he finally realizes that successful communication *may* occur when certain forms of artistic and non-artistic discourse transcend the limitations of logical language and perception, and he denounces logical categories as 'un misérable relevé de lignes et de surfaces' (III.885) — as Beckett freely admits, when alluding to Marcel's contempt for 'the grotesque fallacy of . . . "the miserable statement of line and surface" ' (76).

For all his doubts about the possibility of total possession and total communication, Marcel eventually discovers the way in which the gestural discourse of his grandmother's tapping communicates 'l'âme de ma grand'mère tout entière' (I.670) (the entirety of my grandmother's soul), just as he similarly discovers the way in which the musical discourse of Vinteuil's compositions permits 'la communication des âmes' (III.258) (the communication of souls). In other words, despite his initial logical assumption that communication is impossible, he realizes that total communication is at least temporarily attainable by both the artist and the non-artist. To extend Beckett's formulae, if 'Music asserts to his unbelief the permanence of the personality and the reality of art' (92), the benevolent gestures of his grandmother and of Saint-Loup similarly reveal the reality of human affection and testify to the possibility of its communication.

Unfortunately, this final allusion to the way in which Marcel perspicaciously peers beyond the parameters of his 'unbelief' appears only at the end of the penultimate page of *Proust*, when it is far too late for it to offer an effective antidote to Beckett's previous partisan accounts of Marcel's pessimism. These misleading, partisan responses to Marcel's complaints reach their climax at the end of Beckett's analysis of the 'Albertine Tragedy', when he nonchalantly asserts that:

as before, wisdom consists in obliterating the faculty of suffering rather than in a vain attempt to reduce the stimuli that exasperate that faculty. (63)

The implications of this sentence are extraordinary. If Beckett is to be taken seriously, and if it is indeed the case that Proust's wisdom consists in 'obliterating the faculty of suffering', then it follows that Proust's wisdom must also consist in the cultivation of habitual reality, or 'the boredom of living'. For, as Beckett stipulates, such vulgar, habitual, 'living' offers the only alternative to non-habitual existence, or the 'suffering of being' (20), when man attains his 'maximum value' (21) and experiences 'the free play of every faculty' (20). Put another way, the obliteration of man's faculty of suffering necessitates the obliteration of the 'free play of every faculty' (20) in which man is exposed to the 'advantages and ... disadvantages' (21) and to the 'cruelties and enchantments' (22) of non-habitual existence.

This may be Beckett's wisdom, but it is certainly not Proust's. Beckett's characters consistently advocate the lethargy of habitual 'living', making such asides as 'it suddenly occurs to us that the real problem of waking hours is how soonest to become sleepy' (*Dream*, 109), and a handful of Proust's nihilistic characters likewise crave for 'l'inertie absolue' (I.50) (absolute inertia). But Proust's wisdom can best be represented in terms of Elstir's suggestion that man should cultivate authentic modes of 'being' by engaging every faculty in the kind of existential struggle that he memorably associates with 'un combat et une victoire' (I.864) (a battle and a victory).

Having travestied Proust's 'wisdom' in this wayward conclusion to his analysis of the 'Albertine Tragedy', Beckett introduces his discussion of Marcel's friendship with Saint-Loup with the equally wayward suggestion that love exhibits the 'nobility' of a 'tragic' failure, or 'the failure to possess' (63), whereas friendship apparently reveals the 'simian vulgarity' and the 'horribly comic' quality of 'the attempt to communicate where no communication is possible' (63). One can only speculate that this peculiar distinction arises from his misreading

of the enigmatic passage with which he ornaments his conclusion to the 'Albertine Tragedy', when quoting Marcel's
mysterious affirmation that:

"One desires to be understood because one desires to be loved, and one
desires to be loved because one loves. We are indifferent to the
understanding of others, and their love is an importunity." (63)

Beckett neither introduces nor comments upon these
statements, so their function remains far from clear. It seems
most likely, however, that he took them to be proof that the lover
more or less eschews communication with the loved one and
remains indifferent to others, and is thus more or less innocent of
the friend's incorrigible impulse to communicate. As we have
hinted, this kind of distinction between the lover and the friend
is predicated upon a misinterpretation of Proust's text. Marcel
admits that he is not so much in love with Albertine's intrinsic
qualities, as in love with the concept of 'la possession totale
d'Albertine' (III.496) (the total possession of Albertine), but he
also alludes to the way in which 'J'avais rêvé d'être compris . . .
par elle' (III.496) (I dreamed of being understood . . . by her), and
he refers to the way in which his exclusive preoccupation with
Albertine made him indifferent to 'tant d'autres' (III.496) (so
many others) who might willingly have reciprocated his love.

In this respect, the passage does not simply demonstrate that
the lover seeks possession, but not communication, as Beckett
postulates. Rather, it appears to reflect both upon the strange
way in which the lover's desire for possession eclipses the desire
for communication, and upon the ironic way in which the lover's
obsessive desire to communicate with the loved one, and only
the loved one, leads him to overlook the more readily accessible
affection of 'so many others'. Nevertheless, having transformed
this relative observation into an absolute distinction between
lovers (who apparently have no desire to communicate with
anybody) and friends (who apparently monopolize the 'horribly
comic' (63) impulse to communicate), Beckett elaborates this
derisory definition of friendship in a series of simplistic
comparisons that serve to extoll the virtues of the artistic
vocation.

These comparisons are predicated upon the precept that
'Friendship implies an almost piteous acceptance of face values'
(63). From this supposition, it follows that friendship 'has no
spiritual significance' (63–4), and that it can therefore be
distinguished from the work of the artist, 'who does not deal in

surfaces' (64). Accordingly, friendship apparently works with the 'material and concrete', whereas the artist effects 'the spiritual assimilation of the immaterial' (65). Bearing these dogmatic distinctions in mind, Beckett proceeds to one of his most majestic affirmations:

The only fertile research is excavatory, immersive, a contraction of the spirit, a descent. The artist is active, but negatively, shrinking from the nullity of extracircumferential phenomena, drawn in to the core of the eddy. He cannot practice friendship, because friendship is the centrifugal force of self-fear, self-negation. (65-6)

Most of Beckett's critics probably know at least the first sentence of this statement by heart, and many could probably recite it backwards. Yet few passages by Beckett have precipitated more confusion and misunderstanding.

Nearly all critics argue that these sentences anticipate the way in which Beckett's own excavatory and immersive work was to undertake and advocate the exploration of 'the core of the eddy'. But Beckett's work work is not so simple. As his first hero, the archetypal Belacqua, embarrassingly indicates, Beckett's characters tend to aspire not so much to this ideal, deep, spiritual reality, as to that neutral, vacuous, absence of reality that Belacqua defines as being neither 'centrifugal' nor 'centripetal', but 'not' (*Dream*, 107). This passage is therefore doubly ambiguous. On the one hand, it has given rise to an over-simplistic reading of Beckett's work, while, on the other, it oversimplifies the quality of Proust's vision by suggesting that only the Proustian artist attains sprritual significance.

It is surprisingly easy to overlook the reductive quality of Beckett's argument. *Proust* is, after all, a treasure-house of beguiling half-truths and, at first sight, these three sentences seem to make perfect sense in the general context of the Proustian vision. The only 'fertile' activity for the Proustian artist (or indeed, the Proustian non-artist) is 'a contraction of the spirit' necessitating a retreat from the superficiality of 'extra-circumferential phenomena'. When Proust's exemplary artists (or exemplary non-artists) reveal what Beckett terms 'the best of our many selves' (31), they do so by shrinking from 'the nullity' of vulgar, egotistical reality. In other words, the first two sentences in this eloquent summary of Proust's existential ideals lucidly lend themselves to both the artistic and the non-artistic spiritual development that Marcel advocates as 'la récompense que nous nous efforcerons de mériter' (II.161) (the reward that we should make every effort to merit).

Beckett's argument goes off the rails, however, in his third sentence, where he conflates the moral implications of the word 'extracircumferential' with the more neutral adjectival connotations of the concept of 'the centrifugal'. As we have remarked, the word 'extracircumferential' refers to the superficial reality which man must reject in order to realize himself in a 'fertile' manner. And, as Beckett previously specifies, 'the only possible spiritual development is in the sense of depth' (64), or in the sense of a retreat from the extracircumferential. But to this moral distinction, Proust also adds the more neutral distinction between two modes of morally 'deep' self-realization: the vocations of art and of friendship. Marcel defines the artist in terms of 'ceux d'entre nous dont la loi de développement est purement interne' (I.907) (those among us who realize themselves according to purely internal laws), introducing the concept of the artist's centripetal mode of spiritual development.

But at the same time, Marcel also acknowledges that certain non-artists, such as Saint-Loup, may in turn attain an analogously deep mode of self-realization by means of external or centrifugal actions. And during certain moments of rare perspicacity and equanimity, such as his meditation upon the mutually exclusive advantages of his own artistic vocation and of the non-artistic vocation of Saint-Loup, Marcel defines the virtues of Saint-Loup's friendship in terms of:

cette grande pureté morale qui ... ne rencontrant pas ... en lui l'impossibilité qui existait par exemple en moi de trouver sa nourriture spirituelle autre part qu'en soi-même, le rendait vraiment capable, autant que moi incapable, de l'amitié. (I.779)
(this great moral purity which ... did not feel ... constrained, as I did, to obtain its spiritual nourishment from within, made him as truly capable, as I was incapable, of friendship.)

In this respect, Beckett quite rightly annotated his copy of *A l'ombre des jeunes filles en fleurs* with the comment 'Artist not a friend',[10] for, as this passage clearly indicates, the artist and the friend exemplify two quite distinct modes of self-realization. Beckett's error is to react over-literally to Marcel's more pessimistic assessments of friendship, such as his avowal that for the artist 'l'amitié n'est pas seulement dénuée de vertu comme la conversation, elle est de plus funeste' (I.907) (friendship is not only worthless like conversation, but is downright dangerous). It is this kind of statement that prompts Beckett's annotation 'artist not a friend', and it is this kind of denunciation of friendship that seems to have misdirected his entire understanding of friendship in *A la recherche du temps perdu*.

At most, Marcel's derision of friendship expresses a half-truth. Friendship is certainly fatal for the artist, since the artist cannot simultaneously practice art and friendship. But, reciprocally, it might be argued that art is fatal to friendship. Accordingly, it follows that neither art nor friendship are representative of existence as a whole. In much the same way, Proust's hierarchical conception of positive and negative variants of both of these vocations indicates that neither art nor friendship is intrinsically salutary. Unfortunately, Beckett's argument obfuscates these distinctions by obstinately confusing Marcel's comments upon art with Proust's concept of existence as a whole, and by assuming that the artist can no more do wrong than the non-artist can do right.

Beckett's misleading interpretations of Marcel's aesthetic theories are nicely illustrated by his very free translation of Marcel's suggestion that the artist can only attain self-realization by using the internal material that he likens to the sap of a tree. Marcel reflects:

nous ne sommes pas comme des bâtiments à qui on peut ajouter des pierres du dehors, mais comme des arbres qui tirent de leur propre sève le noeud suivant de leur tige, l'étage superièure de leur frondaison. (I.907)
(we are not buildings that can be extended with stones from the outside, but are like trees that draw the next knot in their trunk and the next layer of their leaves from their own sap.)

Such, then, are the 'internal laws' of artistic self-realization. But where Marcel proposes, Beckett disposes. Transmuting the artistic 'we' into the more general 'Man', and transforming the specificity of Marcel's artistic point of view into the generality of 'Proust', he implies that this statement represents one of the general existential tenets of *A la recherche du temps perdu*, and announces:

"Man", writes Proust, "is not a building that can receive additions to its superficies, but a tree whose stem and leafage are an expression of inward sap". (66)

Yet despite his sly interpolation, Beckett's translation still rings with a certain truth, insofar as Elstir emphasizes that authentic existence comes from the self rather than from without, 'après un trajet que personne ne peut faire pour nous' (I.864) (after a journey that nobody else can make in our place). But whereas Elstir uses this distinction in order to introduce exemplary modes of both artistic and non-artistic self-realization, characterizing the latter in terms of 'les attitudes que vous trouvez nobles' (I.864) (the attitudes which you consider to be noble), Beckett reductively argues that these internal laws demonstrate that man cannot communicate, that friendship is indeed 'horribly comic' (63), and that 'We are alone. We cannot know and we cannot be known' (66). Just to make matters perfectly clear, he adds Marcel's cheerless dictum that: 'Man is the creature that cannot come forth from himself, who knows others only in himself, and who, if he asserts the contrary, lies' (66). This time, Beckett's translation is impeccable. Marcel unambiguously states that 'L'homme est l'être qui ne peut sortir de soi, qui ne connaît les autres qu'en soi, et, en disant le contraire, ment' (III.450).

Yet, once again, Beckett proffers a half-truth. This most morbid of Marcel's meditations derives from his realization that despite all the illusions of love and friendship, 'nous existons seuls' (III.450) (we exist alone), and in a sense this is true. Neither affection nor art appear to offer permanent solutions to solitude. Grandmothers have a tendency to die, and art itself is vulnerable to mortality, insofar as 'La durée éternelle n'est pas plus promise aux oeuvres qu'aux hommes' (III.1043) (Eternal life is no more promised to works of art than to man). Nevertheless, both grandmothers and works of art offer temporary moments of communication with others, and in this respect grandmothers and artists successfully 'sortir de soi' (come forth from themselves) and add to the lives of others.

Yet, according to Beckett, communication quite simply does not take place in *A la recherche du temps perdu*. Intoning a litany of unbelief, he grimly insists that:

There is no communication, because there are no vehicles of communication. Even on the rare occasions when word and gesture happen to be valid expressions of personality, they lose their significance on their passage through the cataract of the personality that is opposed to them. (64)

Beckett almost certainly derived this 'law' from the occasion upon which Marcel despairingly observes that his words to Gilberte are continually deflected by 'le rideau mouvant d'une cataracte' (I.612) (the moving curtain of a cataract), and very tellingly annotated this phrase as 'Tragic'.[11] At the same time, Proust — or perhaps both Proust and Beckett — may also have borrowed this striking image from Walter Pater's suggestion that:[12]

Experience, already reduced to a swarm of impressions, is ringed round for each one of us by that thick wall of personality through which no real voice has ever pierced on its way to us, or from us to that which we can only conjecture to be without.

Significantly, though, Pater also envisages exceptions to this dreadful rule, speculating that on those occasions when man sees with his 'finest senses' and transcends 'the stereotyped world',[13]

we may well catch at any exquisite passion, or any contribution to knowledge that seems, by a lifted horizon, to set the spirit free for a moment, or any stirring of the senses, strange dyes, strange flowers, and curious odours, or work of the artist's hands, or the face of one's friend.

As on other occasions, Pater's concepts and images coincide very closely with those of Proust. In this instance, they prefigure the latter's emphasis upon the ways in which a number of kinds of non-habitual perceptions, or moments of 'exquisite passion', permit the perceiver to transcend the banality and the impermeability of habitual reality. For example, Pater's reference to the non-habitual 'knowledge' brought about by the 'work of the artist's hand', and by such 'stirring of the senses' as the stimuli of 'curious odours', fascinatingly foreshadows Proust's celebration of the insights afforded by exemplary works of art and by the involuntary memories which precede such art. And in much the same way, Pater's allusions to the non-artistic illumination of 'the face of one's friend', and to certain non-habitual circumstances during which the equivalent of 'a lifted horizon' seems 'to set the spirit free', portend the Proustian commemoration of the friendship and affection communicated by such non-artistic, gestural 'language' as Saint-Loup's leaping movements, and by more fleeting, involuntary revelations of benevolence, such as Odette's 'transfiguration' (which occurs 'comme une campagne grise, couverte de nuages qui soudain s'écartent' (I.314) (like a grey, overcast horizon, which the clouds suddenly unveil)).

Beckett's published works make no reference to Pater's ideals, so it is uncertain how he would have reacted to the passage above from the conclusion to *The Renaissance*. But if his response to Marcel's conclusions are anything to go by, his comments would almost certainly have been what the early Belacqua terms 'a fine stinger' (*Dream*, 57). For, despite his earlier suggestion that the cataract of personality prohibits all communication, Marcel finally argues that the novel that he is about to write may well remedy the perceptual problems that Beckett found to be so 'Tragic' by offering its readers 'le moyen de lire en eux-mêmes' (III.1033) (the means of reading into themselves). Far from delightedly annotating this hypothesis with a noun such as 'Blessing', or 'Antidote' or 'Advantage', or indeed with a more modest comment such as 'Not Tragic', Beckett responded to this optimistic speculation with the rude rejoinder: 'Balls'.[14]

To be sure, Beckett's objections to Proust's optimism are never formulated quite so bluntly in *Proust*. Indeed, on several occasions, he dutifully describes the advantages of involuntary memory in quite glowing terms. But, as we have seen, he continually removes the gilt from the Proustian gingerbread by insisting that Proust's universe is bereft of all signs of authentic affection and authentic communication. Accordingly, Beckett's brief analysis of Saint-Loup's friendship for Marcel insists that this friendship is quite literally nothing out of the ordinary.

Like most of Proust's critics, he staunchly maintains that Saint-Loup's benevolent leaping gestures are nothing more than the predictable consequence of a predictable training. Arguing that Marcel assumes that all aristocrats are, almost axiomatically, astounding leapers, Beckett concludes:

the beauty and ease of his tenderness for the narrator — as when, for example, he accomplishes the most delicate and graceful gymnastics in a Paris restaurant so that his friend shall not be disturbed — are appreciated not as the manifestation of a special and charming personality, but as the inevitable adjuncts of excessively good birth and breeding. (66)

This conclusion seems very much at odds with Marcel's stipulation that Saint-Loup's movements are admirable precisely because they transcend mere 'gymnastics' — or what Marcel derisively defines as 'La simple gymnastique élémentaire de l'homme du monde' (I.202) (The simple, elementary gymnastics of high society), and precisely because they reveal the 'special personality' that Marcel associates with 'une réelle humilité morale' (II.415) (a real moral humility) and with 'quelque chose de plus élévé que la souplesse innée de son corps' (II.414) (something more elevated than the innate suppleness of his body). [15] But, as we have observed, Beckett appears to have been in no mood to entertain such concepts as 'real moral humility'. It comes as no surprise to find that the final paragraph to this discussion of friendship in *A la recherche du temps perdu* commences with yet another chorus of the familiar refrain:

Here, as always, Proust is completely detached from all moral considerations. There is no right and wrong in Proust nor in his world. (66)

Consolidating this distortion of the Proustian vision by relentlessly reducing its scale to that of the 'cataract' of the Beckettian personality, this closing paragraph asserts that Proust ultimately envisaged life as 'an expiation' of the 'Tragedy' of 'original sin', or 'the sin of having been born'. It is difficult to reconcile this statement with Marcel's own final suggestion that, far from deeming existence as tragic, man should 'considérer la vie comme digne d'être vécue (III.1032) (consider life as being worthy of living). And while innumerable Beckettian characters share the Unnamable's suspicion that the sufferings of existence constitute 'a punishment for having been born' (*The Unnamable*, 312), it is equally difficult to locate any reference to this 'original sin' in *A la recherche du temps perdu*. Doubtless, this is why Beckett made no attempt to do so, and instead simply concluded this section of his essay by quoting Calderón's lines:

"Pues el delito mayor
  Del hombre es habor nacido." (67)

While Calderón may have considered that 'Man's greatest sin is to have been born', this conviction is not at home among the beliefs that Beckett dubbed 'Proust's treasury of nutshell phrases' (29). A Beckettian cuckoo in the Proustian nest, it offers yet another example of the extent to which he was prepared to redefine Proust's thought in order to bring it into line with the very different dictates of his own emergent vision.

7

BECKETT AND THE 'PARADOX' OF
THE 'MYSTICAL EXPERIENCE'

According to John Fletcher, Beckett said that he 'hated' the task of writing his essay on Proust. [1] It is tempting to speculate that he found the last two sections of *Proust* to be the most hateful part of this enterprise. For it is here that Beckett, the incipient 'dud mystic' (*Dream*,166), found himself obliged to contemplate and explicate the 'exaltation' (75), the 'transcendental aperception' (90) and the 'pure act of understanding' (91), which accompany the involuntary 'mystical experience' (69) of the Proustian hero.

As Beckett subsequently indicated in a book review of 1934, when discussing Rilke's poetry, this kind of 'mystical experience' was not something that he relished. Becoming increasingly impatient with the concept of Rilke's 'mystical heart' and belittling the mystic's vocation as the wish 'to save his bacon (oh in the very highest sense)', he indignantly concluded:

He has the fidgets, a disorder which may very well give rise, as it did with Rilke on occasion, to poetry of a high order. But why call the fidgets God, Ego, Orpheus and the rest? This is a childishness to which German writers seem specially prone. [2]

Beckett's intolerance of such mystical 'childishness' becomes most explicit, however, in his poem 'Casket of Pralinen for a Daughter of a Dissipated Mandarin', which was published the same year — 1931 — as *Proust*, in Samuel Putnam's *European Caravan*. Abandoning the attempt to contemplate the Proustian 'paradox' (22) with critical equanimity, and introducing one of the most enduring images in Beckett's work, this poem scathingly invoked involuntary memory as: [3]

... my memory's involuntary vomit —
violently projected,
oh beauty!

This cynical allusion to the discomforts of involuntary memory is
at once both a passing jest and an uncannily prophetic evocation
of Beckett's literary vocation and subject-matter. Some fifteen
years after he first composed these lines, he employed almost
identical̄ terminology when deploring the fact that he 'was
doomed to spend the rest of (his) days digging up the detritus of
(his) life and vomiting it out over and over again'.[4] And more
recently, some forty-one years after his first articulation of the
concept of the memory's violently projected 'involuntary vomit',
the first production of *Not I* gave it theatrical representation, as
'Mouth' disgorges the words:

sometimes sudden urge . . . once or twice a year . . . always winter some
strange reason . . . the long evenings . . . hours of darkness . . . sudden
urge to . . . tell . . . then rush out stop the first she saw . . . nearest
lavatory . . . start pouring it out . . . steady stream . . . mad stuff . . . half
the vowels wrong . . . no one could follow . . . till she saw the stare she
was getting . . . then die of shame . . . (*Not I*, 14–15)

It is in the context of these conceptions of the literary vocation
and of involuntary memory that the final sections of *Proust*
should be considered. Here, as nowhere else in this essay,
Beckett was writing against the grain of his own beliefs and
intuitions. Not surprisingly, the penumbra of Beckettian
pessimism frequently colours — or, more precisely, discolours —
the optimistic aura of Marcel's mystical revelations.

The sixth section of *Proust* finally bites the mystical bullet, and
describes Marcel's beatific involuntary memories at the *matinée
des Guermantes*. Marcel specifies that these revelations follow his
most intense period of depression, shortly after his prolonged
sojourn in a sanatorium during the post-war years,[5] at a time
when he becomes firmly convinced that he is 'sans valeur'
(III.855) (worthless). He morbidly ponders upon: 'mon absence
de dons littéraires' (III.855) (my lack of any literary talent); 'la
vanité . . . de la littérature' (the vanity . . . of literature); and
'l'inexistence de l'idéal auquel j'avais cru' (III.855) (the
inexistence of my most cherished ideal).

The reader of *Proust* might easily underestimate the nature of
this crisis. For in the wake of example after example of Marcel's
delusions, illusions and 'intolerable' revelations, the suggestion
that he feels that 'everything is lost' (67) and 'utterly bereft of any
individual and permanent necessity' (68) simply recapitulates
the *déjà lu*. At most, the reader learns that Marcel is now
additionally persuaded of his 'incurable lack of talent' (68). But

for this detail, Beckett's disproportionately bleak account of Marcel's previous life suggests that like 'the Ottolengthi', in 'Dante and the Lobster', Marcel might well claim to be: 'where we were, as we were' (*MPTK*, 20).

Compounding this misrepresentation of Marcel's earlier experiences, Beckett recounts that after 'years of fruitless solitude' (68) Marcel finally receives:

the oracle that had invariably been denied to the most exalted tension of his spirit, which his intelligence had failed to extract from the seismic enigma of tree and flower and gesture and art. (69)

Once again, Beckett's predeliction for overstatement conflicts with the complexity of Proust's thought. Marcel is not so much innocently 'denied' the oracle of involuntary memory, as guilty of being too lazy to interpret his previous oracles. Alluding to this indolence, Marcel revealingly reflects:

cette fois, j'étais bien décidé à ne pas me resigner à ignorer pourquoi, comme je l'avais fait le jour ou j'avais goûté d'une madeleine trempée dans une infusion. (III.867)
(this time, I was determined not to resign myself to ignorance, as I had done the day when I tasted a madeleine dipped in tea.)

Having obscured Marcel's moral culpability by suggesting that he is not so much the victim of his own passivity, as the passive victim of inadequate oracles, Beckett oversimplifies matters still further by referring to Marcel's failure to 'extract . . . the seismic enigma of tree and flower and gesture and art' (69).

Beckett's allusions are themselves so excruciatingly enigmatic that it is by no means clear precisely what trees or, for example, what gestures he has in mind. Perhaps he refers to the enigmatic Hudimesnil trees (I.717) and to the stupefying gestures of Albertine — two prospects which undoubtedly leave Marcel extremely baffled. But, as Marcel's narrative repeatedly indicates, he is not *invariably* confused by trees and gestures. On other occasions he dexterously and delightedly decodes their 'enigmas', perceiving both the optimistic implications of the pear and cherry trees that he contemplates with Saint-Loup (II.160−61) and the ethical and amical significance of Saint-Loup's graceful leaping gestures (II.414−15).

The maddeningly erratic quality of Beckett's analysis is typified by the way in which this myopic allusion to Marcel's 'invariably' enigmatic oracles is followed by the highly sensitive — and contradictory — suggestion that 'at the end as in the body of his work, Proust respects the dual significance of every condition and circumstance of life' (69). He refers here to the contrast between Marcel's extra-temporal and temporal revelations. Having discovered the timeless realm of involuntary memory, Marcel discovers the temporal reality of 'Time made flesh' (76), as he surveys the sour cream of Parisian society, and contrasts their present debilities with their former glory.

Sensing the comic potential of Proust's corroboree of senile delinquents, and savouring the childish puns of the 'unspeakably insolent Charlus' (77), Beckett refers to Charlus's allusions to such imaginary aristocrats as 'la comtesse Caca' and 'la baronne Pipi' (II.1090) (crudely translated: 'the Countess of Crap' and 'the Baroness of Piss'), transposing these terms into 'the *Duchesse de Caca*' and 'the *Princesse de Pipi*' (77). He resurrects these jokes in *Molloy*, when Molloy refers to his sole surviving and aged parent as 'Ma, Mag or the Countess Caca' (*Molloy*, 18), and when Moran claims that he is on a pilgrimage to 'la madonne de Shit', [6], or 'the Turdy Madonna' (*Molloy*, 174).

Molloy is one of the few places where Beckett commemorates phrases or images that caught his fancy while he was writing *Proust*. More often than not, his fictions tend to parody and generally deride Proust's discourse. Sometimes they ridicule episodes which he must have instinctively questioned, but nevertheless felt obliged to discuss objectively. But, on other occasions, they subvert key Proustian concepts which Beckett almost certainly had in mind when writing *Proust*, but which seem to have disturbed him to such an extent that he makes no explicit reference to them there. In both these instances, his allusions to *A la recherche du temps perdu* offer valuable pointers to the dissension that variously informs and deforms the final sections of his essay.

The transition from objective description to parodic deflation is conveniently illustrated by Beckett's critical and fictional responses to the incident in which Marcel stumbles upon the first of his involuntary memories outside the hôtel de Guermantes, when the sensation of carelessly stubbing his toe on a cobblestone awakens memories of his holidays in Venice. Marcel refers to the way in which he hovers on one leg while concentrating upon this revelation, much to the amusement of 'la foule innombrable des wattmen' (III.867) (the crowd of innumberable wattmen) towards whom he has become blissfully oblivious, and Beckett soberly relates: 'His surroundings vanish, wattmen, stables, carriages ... disappear' (70). Only afterwards does Beckett parody this idyll, when Belacqua similarly stumbles in *Dream of Fair to Middling Women* and, in the absence of any illumination, derisively mutters: 'The wattmen tittered as I tottered on purpose for radiant Venice to solve my life' (*Dream*, 73).

As we have suggested, Beckett also parodies Proustian concepts which he found it politic to banish from the pages of *Proust*. The most important of these suppressed concepts is probably Marcel's suggestion that man's rational faculties are necessary to successful self-realization, insofar as they not only very helpfully eliminate 'vulgar' distractions, but also, still more helpfully, eliminate themselves of their own volition. This troublesome argument finds formulation in Marcel's thesis that spiritual development should 'commencer par l'intelligence et non par un intuitivisme de l'inconscient' (begin by employing the intelligence and not with the intuitions of the unconscious). According to this thesis, the intelligence first prepares the way for 'des puissance autres' (other powers), and then of its own volition, 'abdique, par raisonnement, devant elles et accepte ... de devinir leur servante' (III.423) (abdicates, rationally, before these forces and accepts ... to be their servant).

A thorn in the side of Beckett's pessimistic hypotheses, this passage must have troubled Beckett considerably. For its four-fold optimism asserts that man may partially determine his destiny; that man's rational volition may effect this self-determination; that existence is therefore not simply accidental or contingent upon unconscious, instinctive reactions; and that insofar as such rational volition springs from the best of man's intelligence, or 'l'intelligence positive' (I.236) (the positive intelligence), existence is not simply the amoral process that one might at first assume it to be. Beckett's response to this optimistic thorn is to suppress it, rather than examine it in any detail.

Suppressed thorns are far from comfortable, and Beckett only suppressed this 'thorn' with partial success. After first marking the relevant passage in his copy of *Albertine Disparue* with a vertical line,[7] he avoided almost all mention of it in his essay, except for a page reference in a footnote citing Proust's 'anti-rational tendency' (81). But once Beckett turned from the critical conventions of *Proust* to the fictional freedom of *Dream of Fair to Middling Women*, he compulsively parodied and picked at this passage. The narrator persistently taunts himself with such questions as: 'How could the will be abolished in its own tension?' (*Dream*, 110), and the equally 'wretched Belacqua' wrestles in his turn with this perplexing paradox, regretting that he 'could not will . . . his enlargement from the gin-palace of willing' (*Dream*, 109). Beckett clearly had Marcel's arguments in — or just under — his mind when writing *Proust*. Yet despite Marcel's advocacy of man's rational volition, and despite his concomitant indifference to 'the intuitions of the unconscious', the final section of *Proust* asserts that 'will . . . is not a condition of the artistic experience' (90), that Proust 'affirms the value of intuition' (86), and that his characters evince 'a grotesque predetermined activity' (89).

It is tempting to argue that this 'grotesque' reading of *A la recherche du temps perdu* derives from the 'predetermined' prejudices of Beckett, rather than from the substance of Proust's novel. Arguably, though, there is a certain method in Beckett's madness. Beckett's suggestion that Proust's universe is irrational, amoral, accidental, intuitive and predetermined, seems to elaborate and stem from his erroneous conflation of the conditions of involuntary memory (which, as he observes, are more or less irrational, amoral, etc.), with the very different conditions of existence as a whole in Proust's fictional universe. In this respect, the only blatantly 'grotesque predetermined' conviction in *Proust* is Beckett's conviction that all exposure to non-habitual existence reveals 'reality, intolerable' (22). This archetypal Beckettian thesis reaches its climax at the beginning of the long-delayed analysis of the conditions of involuntary memory with which he concludes the sixth section of his essay.

First of all, having introduced involuntary memory in terms of his sober description of Marcel's close encounter with a cobble-stone, Beckett stealthily insinuates that Marcel's involuntary memories are not so much 'delicious' (33), as he previously suggested, as they are an unpleasant and unwelcome intrusion into the privacy of Marcel's mind. As before, Beckett's analysis begins accurately, but then falls prey to rampant interpolation, as he infiltrates more and more negative nouns, verbs and adjectives into his exegesis. Marcel eulogizes his revelations as 'céleste nourriture' (III.873) (celestial food), and having both underlined this term and annotated it with the word 'host' in his copy of *Le Temps Retrouvé*,[8] Beckett concedes that Marcel is some kind of 'communicant' (75).

But, Beckett could not be relied upon to share Marcel's reverence for such concepts as 'celestial food', as one gathers from *Watt*, in which Mr Spiro ponders upon the letter in which Martin Ignatius MacKenzie cogitates:

A rat . . . eats of a consecrated wafer.
1. Does he ingest the Real Body, or does he not?
2. If he does not, what has become of it?
3. If he does, what is to be done with him? (*Watt*, 26–7)

Gradually transforming Marcel's bliss into its antithesis, Beckett suggests that Marcel must 'suffer a religious experience' (69), that this experience invades his mind as 'a bright and vehement interloper' (70), and that it painfully imposes the 'luminous and fleeting domination' (71) of its 'intolerable brightness' (70). Accidently or deliberately forgetting the beatific quality of Marcel's 'transcendental aperception' (90), Beckett transforms this Proustian miracle into the kind of Beckettian nightmare that Molloy dreads as a 'brief abominable gleam' (*Molloy*, 54). At the same time, his strategic choice of the adjective 'intolerable' defuses Proust's distinction between this unpoisoned involuntary memory and Marcel's previous poisoned percept-ions, by conflating the supposedly 'intolerable' brightness (70) of this final revelation with Marcel's 'intolerable' memories of his grandmother (42) and of Albertine (53). Here, as nowhere else in the essay, the Proustian vision becomes totally eclipsed by the 'grotesque predetermined' pessimism that makes the Beckettian hero 'intolerant of light' (*Dream*, 72).

Having made this strange attempt to add Marcel's unpoisoned involuntary memories to his catalogue of intolerable non-habitual perceptions in *A la recherche du temps perdu*, Beckett attempts to define the precise conditions of this alarming experience, by offering a bevy of negative definitions. The non-habitual reality evoked by involuntary memory is thus defined as being 'rejected by the imperious vulgarity of a working-day memory' (70); as a 'mysterious element that the vigilant will rejects' (72); as something 'illogical' which 'cannot be fitted into the puzzle of a concept' (72); and thus something that Marcel's 'will . . . rejected as extraneous to its immediate activity', and something which is similarly 'rejected by our intelligence' (73).

Collectively, these concepts define involuntary memory as something transcending habit, reason, and volition, and lead in turn to Beckett's assumption that involuntary memory occurs 'by accident' or 'instinctively' (72). It is therefore independent of all moral considerations. In Beckett's terms, 'the mood, as usual, has no importance' (73). With these stipulations in mind, he fleetingly intimates that non-habitual reality is incompatible with the habitual categories of nineteenth-century realism, remarking upon the way in which Marcel finally understands ... more clearly than ever the grotesque fallacy of a realistic art — 'the miserable statement of line and surface', and the penny-a-line vulgarity of a literature of notations. (76)

Elegantly incorporating Beckett's translation of Marcel's contemptuous reference to modes of realistic fiction which merely afford 'un misérable relevé de lignes et de surfaces' (III.885), this striking statement serves as an overture to the seventh and final section of *Proust*, which turns from the conditions of involuntary memory to Proust's conception of the conditions of the artistic process and his conception of existence as a whole.

Beckett begins this section of his essay by elaborating his reference to Marcel's contempt for 'the grotesque fallacy of a realistic art' with its 'literature of notations' (76). Explaining that Marcel is 'incapable of recording surface' (82) he draws particular attention to:

his contempt for the literature that 'describes', for the realists and naturalists worshipping the offal of experience ... and content to transcribe the surface, the facade, behind which the Idea is prisoner. (78–9)

Like the famous definition of the 'only fertile research' (65), this summary of Proust's literary priorities is another text which most of Beckett's critics certainly know by heart, and which is invariably interpreted as an indication and intimation of Beckett's own contempt for literature which merely transcribes the 'facade' of reality, rather than descending to 'the ideal core of the onion' (29). It is certainly pleasant to suppose that his literary values coincide with those of Proust, just as it is 'soothing' — as Beckett remarks elsewhere — to contemplate 'a carefully folded ham-sandwich'.[9]

Upon inspection, however, one discovers 'faults' between the 'folds' of Proust's and Beckett's literary ideals. The latter both share and subvert Proust's values. On the one hand, Beckettian heroes such as Murphy reject the 'penny-a-line vulgarity ... of notations' (76) and deplore the prospect of 'doing sums with the petty cash of current facts' (*Murphy*, 123), just as Beckett's early book reviews sneeringly dismiss the superficiality of the 'chartered recountant' and of literary 'book-keeping'.[10] But, on the other hand, despite the widespread conviction that his characters invariably explore the 'core' of reality, it seems patently clear that nearly all of them beat a hasty retreat once they discover its intolerable quality. Far from rejecting superficial, 'penny-a-line' reality, they wallow in it.

For example, far from 'descending' into the 'deep' reality of two intense memories which he has 'never forgotten',[11] the narrator of *Company* complacently 'ascends' to the superficiality of meaningless mathematics:

> You close your eyes and try to calculate the volume. Simple sums you find a help in times of trouble. A haven . . . still in the timeless dark you find figures a comfort. (*Company*, 54–5)

And far from declining to combine such 'sums' with 'petty facts', this narrator desperately attempts to alleviate his profound awareness of 'the woes of your kind' (80), by turning 'chartered recountant' in such stifling descriptions as the observation:

> Your eyes light on the watch . . . they follow round and round the second hand now followed and now preceded by its shadow . . . At 60 seconds and 30 seconds shadow hidden by hand. From 60 to 30 shadow precedes hand at a distance increasing from zero at 60 to maximum at 15 and thence decreasing to new zero at 30 . . . And so on and on. (*Company*, 80–82)

Similarly, while Marcel repeatedly repudiates 'the vulgarity of a plausible concatenation' (81–2) and 'the myth of our imagination' (14), the narrator of *Company* asks for nothing more than to escape into the 'haven' of such concatenations and myths, remarking: 'So with what reason remains he reasons and reasons ill' (*Company*, 14), and: 'So he imagines . . . But further imagination shows him to have imagined ill' (*Company*, 44). Far from being particularly disturbed by the fallible quality of such reasoning and such imagination, the narrator of *Company* appears particularly grateful for any inoffensive concept that happens to provide 'company . . . In which to escape from his own' (*Company*, 77). This evasive strategy typifies the ironic manner in which Beckett's heroes invariably fall victim to 'the centrifugal force of self-fear, self-negation' (66), and finally retreat from the centripetal reality of the self to the centrifugal 'company' of the very 'nullity of extracircumferential phenomena' (65) that they initially despise as 'miserable . . . line and surface' (76). Suffice it to remark that there is frequently all the difference in the world between the Proustian ideals that Beckett summarizes in *Proust* and the Beckettian ideals that emerge in works from *Dream of Fair to Middling Women* to such recent texts as *Company*.

Having introduced Proust's aesthetic values in terms of
Marcel's derision for 'the literature that "describes"' (78),
Beckett turns to the characteristics of Proust's literary style. At its
most pugnacious, his analysis erupts in a splendidly sweeping
broadside directed both at Proust's more obtuse critics and at the
unfortunate publishers of what Beckett previously reviled as 'the
abominable edition of the *Nouvelle Revue Française*' (9). According
to Beckett:

Proust's style was generally resented in French literary circles. But now
that he is no longer read, it is generously conceded that he might have
written an even worse prose than he did. At the same time, it is difficult
to estimate with justice a style of which one can only take cognisance by
a process of deduction, in an edition that cannot be said to have trans-
mitted the writings of Proust, but to have betrayed a tendency in that
direction. (87)

The most pertinent observation in this diatribe — the
suggestion that one can only take cognisance of Proust's style 'by
a process of deduction' — seems to allude to the crucial acausality
of Proust's style; a factor which Beckett associates with its
metaphorical, impressionistic and relativistic characteristics.
Beckett's provocative analyses of these traits repeatedly portend
the singularly Beckettian — or un-Proustian — ways in which his
own subsequent fiction takes up and transforms these acausal
modes of writing.

As we have observed, Marcel introduces the primacy of
metaphorical writing when he postulates that reality resides not
so much within the logical causality of discursive statements, as
in the relationship between more distant and disparate
sensations. Accordingly:

Ce que nous appelons la réalité est un certain rapport entre ces
sensations et ces souvenirs qui nous entourent simultanément ...
rapport unique que l'écrivain doit retrouver pour en enchaîner à jamais
dans sa phrase les deux termes différents ... la vérité ne commencera
qu'au moment où l'écrivain prendra deux objets différents, posera leur
rapport ... et les enfermera ... dans une métaphore. (III.889)
(That which we call reality is a certain relationship between those
sensations and memories which surround us simultaneously ... a
unique relationship which the writer must discover in order to enchain
the two terms together forever within his phrase ... truth only begins
to be expressed when a writer takes two different objects, reveals their
relationship ... and encloses them ... in a metaphor.)

Deftly summarizing this passage as Proust's defence of 'the indirect and comparative expression of indirect and comparative perception', Beckett concludes:

The Proustian world is expressed metaphorically by the artisan because it is apprehended metaphorically by the artist ... The rhetorical equivalent of the Proustian real is the chain-figure of the metaphor. (88)

In a curious coda to this summary, he adds that 'It is a tiring style, but it does not tire the mind', explaining:

One is exhausted and angry after an hour, dominated by the crest and the break of metaphor after metaphor: but never stupefied. The complaint that it is an involved style, full of periphrasis, obscure and impossible to follow, has no foundation whatsoever. (88)

Considered more than half a century after its composition, this generous defence of Proust's style, along with its complaint that it exhausts the reader, causing 'a fatigue of the heart, a blood fatigue' (88), irresistibly begs the question of the 'exhausting' quality of Beckett's style and, indeed, the exhausting quality of Post-Modern literature in general. As we have suggested, if many Post-Modern writers — such as Beckett and Burroughs — appear especially difficult to read, this is precisely because they evoke simultaneous perceptions which fail to resolve themselves within 'metaphor after metaphor' (88), and which generate the perceptual confusions that we have associated with a kind of anti-metaphor or metaphor *manqué*.

Although he does not consider the perceptual pandemonium of Beckett and Burroughs, Roland Barthes perceives a similar anti-metaphorical paradigm within the more vacuous Post-Modern fictions of Alain Robbe-Grillet. Insisting upon the superficiality of his fictions, as though this were some sort of value, Barthes' early essays on Robbe-Grillet cheerfully claim that:

L'écriture de Robbe-Grillet est sans alibi, sans épaisseur et sans profondeur: elle reste à la surface de l'objet et la parcourt également, sans privilégier telle ou telle de ses qualités: c'est donc le contraire même d'une écriture poétique.
Robbe-Grillet's writing has no alibi, no density and no depth: it remains on the surface of the object and inspects it impartially, without favouring any particular quality: it is the exact opposite of poetic writing. [12]

While Beckett argues that the clarity of Proust's phrase is 'explosive' (88), and while one might well argue that the solipsistic and apocalyptic incoherence of Beckett's and Burroughs's respective 'poetry' is equally explosive, Barthes insists that Robbe-Grillet's defused data 'n'explose pas' (does not explode),[13] and does not in fact 'do' anything:

cet univers ne connaît ni la compression ni l'explosion, rien que la rencontre, des croisements d'itinéraires, des retours d'objets.
this universe knows neither compression nor explosion, nothing but encounters, intersections of itineraries, returns of objects.[14]

In the absence of attraction or repulsion, or of 'compression' and 'explosion', Robbe-Grillet's subjects and objects merely evince 'des liens superficiels de situation et d'espace' (superficial links to situation and space), and in this respect

il leur enlève toute possibilité de métaphore, les coupe de ce réseau de formes ou d'états analogiques qui a toujours passé pour le champ priviligié du poète.
he removes any possibility of metaphor, cuts them off from that network of analogical forms or states which has always passed for the poet's privileged terrain.[15]

Put another way, 'si Robbe-Grillet décrit quasi-géométriquement les objets, c'est pour ... les corriger de la métaphore' (if Robbe-Grillet describes objects quasi-geometrically, it is in order to ... correct them of metaphor).[16]

Barthes intimates, then, that Alain Robbe-Grillet is the Thomas Gradgrind of Post-Modern fiction. 'Corrected' and 'cut off' from the world of metaphorical convergences and divergences (somewhat as the hapless pupils of Dickens's Thomas Gradgrind are 'corrected' of all 'fancy' in the aptly titled *Hard Times*), Robbe-Grillet's neutral narratives neither culminate in the 'infallible proportion' (72–3) which Beckett associates with Proust's modes of 'positive synthesis' (85), nor disintegrate or run riot like Beckett's and Burroughs's variants of the 'dolorous synthesis' (42). Rather like the 'cold eyes' of Gradgrind's star pupil, the incipient structuralist, Bitzer, 'whose skin was so unwholesomely deficient in the natural tinge, that he looked as though, if he were cut, he would bleed white', Robbe-Grillet's fictions seem fated to register 'Facts ... nothing but Facts'. As Barthes approvingly concludes, Robbe-Grillet's Bitzeresque point of view 'ne peut fonder ni correspondences ni réductions, seulement des symétries' (cannot establish either correspondences or reductions, only symmetries). [17]

It might be more accurate to argue that Robbe-Grillet's novels both propose and depose such superficial 'symmetries'. For if Robbe-Grillet's variant of Post-Modern fiction lacks any sense of metaphorical synthesis or correspondences (be these 'positive' or 'dolorous'), then this is because it incessantly generates the kind of superficial contradictions, or asymmetries, that Beckett's *Molloy* defines as 'dutiful confusions' (*Molloy*, 15). Happily, the beauty of Barthes' observations resides beyond such contentious detail, in his marvellous implicit allusion to the general way in which much of Post-Modern writing neutralizes or subverts the poetic resonance of the metaphor, thereby inaugurating and inhabiting an era characterized by modes of anti-metaphor, or metaphor *manqué*. And as subsequent chapters will indicate, the 'beauty' of Beckett's Post-Modernity resides in the way in which his fictions, like those of Burroughs, allow a bull to rampage in the metaphorical china-shop of Modernism, rather than merely transforming the metaphorical chinaware of Modernism into the tedious fictional tupperware of Robbe-Grillet's 'surface' and 'facade' (74).

While Beckett's analyses of Proust's metaphorical descriptions consider the way in which Marcel makes sense of quite distant sensations, his analysis of Proust's impressionism considers Marcel's acausal responses to several successive observations, or:

his non-logical statement of phenomena in the order and exactitude of their perception, before they have been distorted into intelligibility in order to be forced into a chain of cause and effect. (86)

Beckett's examples of this crucial process are restricted to a five-line footnote, in which he cryptically refers to such immediate perceptual confusions as 'a napkin in the dust taken for a pencil of light' (86). Marcel's 'impressionism' might be illustrated more clearly in terms of those occasions when he considers a number of ambiguous impressions before apprehending their cause, such as the passage in *Du Côté de chez Swann* in which he successively observes:

Un petit coup au carreau, comme si quelque chose l'avait heurté, suivi d'une ample chute légère comme de grains de sable qu'on eût laissés tomber d'une fenêtre au-dessus, puis la chute s'étendant, se réglant, adoptant un rythme, devenant fluide, sonore, musicale, innombrable, universelle: c'était la pluie. (I.101–2)

(A small tap upon the windowpane, as if something had struck it, followed by a prolonged light falling sound, as if sand were being sprinkled from a window overhead, after which the falling sound seemed to spread out, becoming more regular, more rhythmic, more fluid, sonorous, musical, infinite and universal: it was raining.)

In somewhat the same way, such heroes as Malone employ a similarly 'impressionistic' narrative technique. But whereas Marcel's impressionistic perspective is often the pretext for an avalanche of charmingly metaphorical misperceptions as, for example, when rain becomes confused with the sound of falling sand or with something musical, akin to drumming, Malone's impressionistic observations prove the occasion for mercilessly ironic meditations upon such romantic clichés as the unspeakable beauty of requited love. Inauspiciously announcing that he is unfortunately 'not one of those people who can take in everything at a single glance' (*Malone Dies*, 238), Malone regales the reader with the following account of the couple inside the room opposite his window:

they cleave so fast together that they seem a single body, and consequently a single shadow. But when they totter it is clear they are twain, and in vain they clasp with the energy of despair, it is clear we have here two distinct and separate bodies, each enclosed within its own frontiers, and having no need of each other to come and go and sustain the flame of life, for each is well able to do so, independently of the other. Perhaps they are cold, that they rub against each other so . . . It is all very pretty and strange, this big complicated shape made up of more than one, for perhaps there are three of them . . .

Elaborating these vague impressions for several lines, Malone finally brings his observations to their awful climax, with the sudden realization:

Ah how stupid I am, I see what it is, they must be loving each other, that must be how it is done . . . They have loved each other standing like dogs. Soon they will be able to part. Or perhaps they are just having a breather, before they tackle the titbit. Back and forth, back and forth, that must be wonderful. They seem to be in pain. (*Malone Dies*, 238–9)

Like the 'death dwarf' in Burroughs's *Nova Express* (who cynically expostulates: 'Beauty — Poetry . . . What good is all that to me?', gloating: 'Shit — Uranian shit — That's what my human dogs eat — And I like to rub their noses in it'), Beckett's narrator-heroes seem to be similarly indifferent to beauty and truth, and similarly inclined to lead the reader by the nose 'headlong into the shit, without knowing who was shitting against whom' (*Molloy*, 32).[18] In other words, if Marcel's impressions tend to reflect and refract 'la vie en rose', those of the Beckettian narrator-hero evince 'la vie en merde'.

Beckett's account of Proust's relativism invites the same kind of comparison between Proust's and Beckett's use of this 'anti-intellectual attitude' (85). Whereas Proust's 'impressionism' arises from Marcel's tendency to work towards conclusive observations by way of a number of tentative impressions, his 'relativism' seems to derive from those completely inconclusive hypotheses that Beckett describes as 'experimental and not demonstrative' (87). With these relative explanations Marcel never actually explains things, but 'explains them away', and therefore allows them to 'appear as they are — inexplicable' (87). Marcel frequently loses himself and his object within labyrinths of logical alternatives, as he exhaustedly and exhaustingly examines explanation after explanation hinging upon such equivalents of 'perhaps' as 'soit' or 'peut-être'.Throughout his copies of *A la recherche du temps perdu* Beckett equally industriously annotates such futile deliberations in terms of their 'timid logic' and their 'Finical pure logic'.[19]

This kind of 'timid logic' might be exemplified by Marcel's account of his failure to engage the 'lift' in conversation, on arriving for the first time at his hotel in Balbec. Inconclusively working his way through eight perfectly reasonable explanations for his silence, Marcel ponders:

Mais il ne me me répondit pas, soit étonnement de mes paroles, attention à son travail, souci de l'étiquette, dureté de son ouïe, respect du lieu, crainte du danger, paresse d'intelligence ou consigne du directeur. (I.665)
(But he made me no reply, perhaps because of his astonishment at my words, his attention to his work, his consideration for etiquette, his hardness of hearing, his respect for the time and place, his fear of danger, his mental indolence, or his instructions from the management.)

Beckett claims that this relativistic perspective is 'negative and comic' (86) and that it is 'pessimistic ... and employed as an element of comedy' (85). As usual, he tends to oversimplify Proust's vision. One pole of Proust's anti-intellectual 'relativism' is certainly negative and comic and pessimistic, insofar as it ridicules man's confidence in his 'vulgar' intellectual perceptions. But, at the other extreme of Proust's vision, Marcel also discerns great beauty in the imprecise quality of such ambiguous prospects as the imagery of Elstir's paintings (I.835) and the mobility of the Martinville towers (I.182). A wholly — or predominantly — negative, comic and pessimistic variant of this relativism resides not so much in *A la recherche du temps perdu* as in the manic mansion of Mr Knott in *Watt*, Beckett's masterpiece of 'the comedy of ... exhaustive enumeration' (92).

An epic demonstration of the limitations of the 'chartered recountant', this chronicle of Watt's methodical attempts to unravel the 'knots' of his existence mercilessly lures the reader into the maze of such vertiginous verbal variations as:

But he thought that perhaps he felt calm and free and glad, or if not calm and free and glad, at least calm and free, or free and glad, or glad and calm, or if not calm and free, or free and glad, or glad and calm, at least calm, or free, or glad, without knowing it. (*Watt*, 133)

Such a sentence surely offers the quintessence of negative and comic relativism. On the one hand, it lets relativity run mad, as it permutates every combination of 'calm' and 'free' and 'glad'. On the other hand, it seems doubly negative, insofar as it not only trivializes the ideals of tranquillity, freedom, and happiness, by reiterating them within this mind-boggling permutation, but also adds the ironic stipulation that Watt's understanding of these absolutes occurs in the absence of all understanding, 'without knowing it'.

As if this were not enough, the narrator additionally specifies that Watt's most troublesome perceptions — such as his disquieting vision of the 'incident of the Galls father and son' (*Watt*, 73) — arise from sensations 'that he could neither think of ... nor speak of ... but only suffer, when they recurred' (*Watt*, 76). Watt's relativism is not simply confusing, painful, and comic, but, for good measure, it is something he may only suffer. Lest Watt or the reader should venture to wonder why exactly such suffering is never relieved by any kind of 'enchantment', the narrator intimates that suffering is Watt's natural lot, impatiently expostulating: 'One wonders sometimes where Watt thought he was. In a culture-park?' (*Watt*, 73).

The extravagance of Beckett's fictional discourse seems peculiarly illuminating. Despite the fact that Marcel, like Watt, must suffer the illusions and delusions of 'vulgar' modes of metaphorical, impressionistic, and relativistic perception, his sense of aesthetical and ethical values is constantly renewed by his exposure to exemplary modes of self-realization (or 'culture', in its widest sense). Unlike Watt, he is placed fairly and squarely within an extraordinary 'culture park'. Although he is frequently distracted, distresssed and depressed by the more painful phases of his existential adolescence, he finally discovers the way in which such creativity as Vinteuil's music 'asserts to his unbelief the permanence of personality and the reality of art' (92), just as the very trees in the 'park' testify to the permanent reality of 'the splendour of poetry' and 'the marvellous radiance of innocence' (II.160–161)

Watt's problem, like that of so many of Beckett's heroes, is that he is *not* located within this kind of 'culture park', but rather within an existential labyrinth from which there appears to be no exit, and within which his inevitable destination is that of *Worstward Ho*,[20] or 'the coming and being and going in purposelessness' (*Watt*, 57). Watt's 'unbelief' is therefore absolute, for it is never challenged. In consequence, Watt's relativism remains 'pessimistic . . . negative . . . and . . . an element of comedy' (85). By contrast, while Marcel's relativistic perspective certainly accentuates the tragedy and the comedy inseparable from 'the dual significance of every . . . circumstance' (69), it is perhaps most significant as a function of that 'inspired perception' (84) which transcends the confusions of 'vulgar' modes of metaphorical, impressionistic and relativistic vision, and reveals atemporal and acausal reality by 'annihilating every spatial and temporal restriction' (72).

While Beckett tentatively acknowledges the existence of this 'pure act of cognition' (73), he adamantly refuses to admit that Proust's vision is anything other than a mode of negative relativism: a concept which finds most forceful formulation in his piqued riposte to the antithetical hypotheses of the German critic Ernst Robert Curtius. In a sense, Beckett ought to have admired Curtius's interpretation of Proust. For, like Beckett, Curtius was particularly impressed by Proust's dualism — or, in his terms Proust's relativism — declaring this trait to be 'la forme essentielle selon laquelle s'organise l'expérience tout entière' (the essential form around which the entirety of experience is organized).[21]

Unlike Beckett, however, Curtius insists that Proust's vision is neither sceptical nor negative. Curtius initially reflects that 'relativism' is not simply a 'negative' perspective:

On confond volontiers 'relativisme' avec 'scepticisme'. 'Tout est relatif'

est considéré comme synonyme de 'Il n'y a rien qui vaille'. (135)
(One freely confuses 'relativism' with 'scepticism'. 'Everything is
relative' is often assumed to mean 'Nothing is valid'.)

With this distinction in mind, Curtius continues:

C'est précisément le contraire qui est vrai pour Proust. Pour lui tout est
relatif signifie que tout vaut, que chaque point de vue est fondé. (135)
(The very opposite is true for Proust. For him the idea that everything is
relative implies that everything is valid, that every point of view has
some foundation).

Curtius's argument stipulates, then, that Proust did not so
much consider all points of view as being of identical value, as he
maintained that all points of view had potential value. In this
respect, Proust is most important as a writer who extended the
frontiers of literary truths, since:

Le fait d'admettre une infinité de points de vue n'entraine point le
nivellement de la réalité objective, ni sa destruction, mais au contraire
une énorme extension de son domaine. (135)
(The recognition of infinite points of view implies neither the levelling of
all objective reality, nor its destruction, but on the contrary, an
enormous extension of its domain.)

Accordingly, Curtius convincingly concludes that Proust's
relativistic vision reveals 'un relativisme positif et fécond' (137) (a
positive and productive relativism), unlike the negative,
reductive relativism that he defines as: 'Le faux relativisme . . . le
relativisme sceptique et destructeur de valeurs' (136). (False
relativism . . . the sceptical relativism that destroys values.)

This conclusion could scarcely have pleased Beckett, and he
unleashes his irony in an attempt to discredit Curtius's
interpretation of Proust's relativism. Unfortunately, the barbs
are so fast, so furious, so haphazard, so fragmentary, and so
much off the mark, that it is very difficult to assess their value.
Here, perhaps, as much as anywhere in *Proust*, he vindicates
such rare admonitions of his essay as the Imagist poet F. S.
Flint's pithy rejoinder: 'If we could understand this essay, we
might be able to praise it'.[22] As Flint hints, the passion of
Beckett's thesis is as impressive as its impermeability.

Commencing with a botched Cartesian deliberation, Beckett
advances from 'I think' to 'I know' via an alarming mixture of
baffled erudition, studied scepticism and veiled allusion:

I think the phrase 'positive relativism' is an oxymoron, I am almost sure that it does not apply to Proust, and I know that it came out of the Heidelberg laboratory. (85)

Far from pausing to clarify these speculations, the next sentence abruptly asserts that Proust's vision must be pessimistic, since Marcel's response to the 'Albertine Tragedy' is pessimistic; and far from troubling to elaborate this avowal in any detail, Beckett then cryptically cites the 'law' which states that the perceiver cannot keep up to date with the perceived. These telegrammatic assertions only loom into focus when the reader has leaped through the hoops of two sets of parentheses, over one set of dashes, and around an abstruse reference to the concept *Blickpunkt*, in the following verbal obstacle-course:

We have seen how in the case of Albertine (and Proust extends his experience to all human relations) the multiple aspects (read Blickpunkt for this miserable word) did not bind into any positive synthesis. The object evolves, and by the time the conclusion — if any — is reached, it is already out of date. (85)

Such sentences are both a critic's nightmare and a poet's nightmare. It is almost certainly this kind of cryptic exposition that Bonamy Dobrée had in mind when he rebuked Beckett's essay for being 'a good deal too "clever"', and disfigured with pseudo-scientific jargon and philosophical snippets'; [23] and it is almost certainly the same abstruse discourse which frustrated the Imagist poet F. S. Flint, despite the fact that Flint's own theoretical writings advocated precision and enjoined poets to 'use absolutely no word that did not contribute to the presentation'. [24] The missing links between Beckett's lines may be partially reconstructed, however, by turning to his Proustian source, and to his working notes upon this material.

Beckett's final sentence seems most revealing in this respect, and may be traced back to the occasion in *A l'ombre des jeunes filles en fleurs* when Marcel formulates one of his first responses to the elusive quality of Albertine. Gradually defining the limitations of the successive, accumulative observations peculiar to vulgar perception, Marcel comments:

Ainsi ce n'est qu'après avoir reconnu . . . les erreurs d'optique du début qu'on pourrait arriver à la connaissance exacte d'un être si cette connaissance était possible. Mais elle ne l'est pas; car tandis que se rectifie la vision que nous avons de lui, lui-même, qui n'est pas un

objectif inerte, change pour son compte, nous pensons le rattraper, il se déplace, et, croyant le voir enfin plus clairement, ce n'est que les images anciennes que nous en avions prises que nous avons réussi à éclaircir, mais qui ne le représentent plus. (I.874)
(Thus it is only after one has recognized . . . one's initial errors that one can finally know somebody completely, were such knowledge attainable. But it is not; for while we are correcting our first impressions, the person we are observing, who is not a static object, changes in his own right, and though we think that we have finally caught up with him, he changes again, so that when we finally think we are perceiving him clearly, we have only succeeded in clarifying various outmoded images, which no longer represent him.)

Beckett clearly had this passage in mind while formulating his riposte to Curtius's interpretation of *A la recherche du temps perdu*, for he not only paraphrases it in the third of the sentences quoted above, but also very revealingly annotates it with the comment: 'Opposed to Curtius's view of Proust as a representative . . . of positive relativism.'[25]

While Marcel's meditation upon the impossibility of ever knowing Albertine is certainly extremely pessimistic, he does not extend his gloomy hypothesis 'to all human relations' (85), as Beckett would have the reader believe. Beckett quite rightly perceives that this pessimism conflicts with 'positive relativism', but quite wrongly equates this pessimism with Proust's existential vision in *A la recherche du temps perdu*. It would be more accurate to define this pessimism as a function of vulgar perception and, more specifically, as a function of Marcel's un-requited love for the elusive Albertine. For, as Beckett sub-sequently acknowledges, the wholesale pessimism of Marcel's initial 'unbelief' gives way to his realization that exemplary works of art may communicate 'the permanence of personality and the reality of art' (92), and as Marcel (if not Beckett) also testifies, exemplary gestural discourse similarly communicates the reality and affection of the 'non-artistic' personality.

Beckett's disjointed rejoinder to Curtius's conclusions forms the climax to his attempt to conflate the Proustian vision with Marcel's pessimistic responses to the 'Albertine Tragedy'. Hereafter, the remaining pages of the essay consolidate this travesty of Proust's 'dualism in multiplicity' (11) by making a number of references to the ways in which the Proustian universe is arbitrary, amoral, and — so it seems — alarmingly monodimensional. These references begin with the postulation that, far from advocating any positive ethical values, 'Proust is positive only in so far as he affirms the value of intuition' (86).

Once again, Beckett conflates one partial aspect of Proust's aesthetic theories with his existential vision as a whole. Marcel certainly argues that 'l'instinct dicte le devoir' (III.879) (instinct dictates man's duty), and that 'à tout moment l'artiste doit écouter son instinct' (III.880) (at every moment the artist should pay attention to his instinct), just as he argues that 'Seule l'impression ... est un critérium de vérité' (III.880) (Only impressions ... offer a criterion for reality). In a sense, the artist's instincts and impressions *are* the best guides to extra-rational reality. But, as Marcel emphasizes again and again throughout *A la recherche du temps perdu*, the successful evocation of such instinctive and impressionistic insights depends upon the artist's adherence to the three cardinal virtues of 'goodness, scrupulousness, and sacrifice' (III.188).

Arguably, then, Beckett's contention that 'Proust is positive only in so far as he affirms the value of intuition' (86) is flawed at a number of levels. Even within the restricted context of creativity, intuitive perception is not unconditionally positive, since, as we have just remarked, ideal creativity is contingent upon ethical restraint. As we have also observed, Marcel similarly stipulates that man's positive, self-sacrificing intelligence is of more value than 'the intuitions of the unconscious' (III.423). Elsewhere, when evaluating different kinds of instinctive, intuitive and improvised actions and reactions within the lower depths of high society, he frequently emphasizes their depravity and cruelty. Charlus, for example, appears 'en proie au démon de l'inspiration' (II.1066) (the victim of demonic inspiration), while Mme Verdurin likewise evinces 'un certain don d'improvisation quand la malveillance l'inspirait' (III.280) (a certain gift for improvisation when inspired by malevolence).

Beckett reveals the same kind of indifference to Proust's ethical criteria when he subsequently insists that Proust dissociates stylistic felicity from all moral considerations: 'For Proust the quality of language is more important than any system of ethics or aesthetics' (88). Marcel certainly rejects conventional systems of ethics and aesthetics, just as he rejects other superficial values. But this initial, scrupulous rejection of habitual values only serves to facilitate Marcel's exploration of more profound modes of absolute value. Far from rejecting ethics and aesthetics in favour of some kind of intuitive or instinctive literary anarchy, he speculates that the 'quality' of literary language lies not so much

in conventional academic categories, as in a more ethereal mode
of intellectual and moral attainment:

Et peut-être est-ce plutôt à la qualité du langage qu'au genre
d'esthétique qu'on peut juger du degré auquel a été porté le travail
intellectuel et moral. (III.882)
(And perhaps it is in terms of this quality of language rather than in
terms of aesthetics and genre that one can judge the degree to which the
work embodies intellectual and moral effort.)

In its indecent haste to dissociate Proust's vision from any kind
of values (be they superficial or deep, or aesthetic, moral or
intellectual), Beckett's argument both obscures the way in which
Proust elaborated an ethical system predicated upon the value of
'intellectual and moral effort', and prepares the way for the final
announcement that Marcel exhibits 'complete indifference to
moral values and human justice' (89). A footnote to this assertion
indicates that it arises from Marcel's claim that he suffers from
'une complète absence de sens moral' (III.291) (a complete
absence of morality). As we have observed, this confession is
among Marcel's silliest statements. Marcel is forever weighing
the moral value of his acquaintances, and proves the champion
of 'ces lois dont tout travail profond de l'intelligence nous
rapproche et qui sont invisibles seulement ... pour les sots'
(III.188) (those laws towards which all profound works of the
intelligence draw us, and which are only invisible ... for fools).
Among Proust's characters the most notable example of this
latter category is the amoral Albertine, whom Marcel associates
with 'la vie inconsciente des végétaux' (III.70) (the unconscious
existence of vegetables), and who seems to offer the perfect
example of Swann's concept of the ethically neutral being who is
'même pas une personne, une créature définie' (not even a
person, a definite being), but 'une eau informe qui coule selon la
pente qu'on lui offre' (I.290) (formless water, flowing with the lie
of the land). Having read rather too much Schopenhauer, and
rather too little of A la recherche du temps perdu, Beckett reaches the
astonishing conclusion that all of Proust's characters resemble
such foolish, formless, unconscious matter. Conceiving of
'Proust's men and women' as hopelessly and helplessly amoral
vegetation, and claiming that Proust 'assimilates the human to
the vegetal', Beckett informs the reader:

Flower and plant have no conscious will. They are shameless, exposing
their genitals. And so in a sense are Proust's men and women, whose

will is blind and hard, but never self-conscious, never abolished in the pure perception of a pure subject. They are victims of their volition, active with a grotesque predetermined activity, within the narrow limits of an impure world. But shameless. There is no question of right and wrong. (89)

Viewed in a very general perspective, this account of Proust's characters appears grotesquely reductive. For Beckett all but transforms Proust's 'indeterminates'[26] into the kind of over-determined automaton that the narrator of *Dream of Fair to Middling Women* ridicules as 'clockwork cabbages' (*Dream*, 106), which may be relied upon to advance 'at whatever speed in whatever direction (the author) chooses' (*Dream*, 107). As Marcel emphasizes when discussing such characters as the Verdurins, the peculiarity of Proust's characters resides not so much in their 'grotesque' or 'predetermined' or 'narrow' or 'impure' activity, as in their unpredictable capacity to fluctuate between impure and pure activities, or between cruelties and 'Une bonté partielle' (III.327) (Partial goodness).

Viewed in the more specific context of Schopenhauer's writings, Beckett's 'vegetal' description of 'Proust's men and women' seems the consequence of a bad case of intertextual indigestion. Put more simply, he misrepresents Proust's characters by conflating their complexity with Schopenhauer's terminology, just as he previously misrepresented Proust's vision by conflating it with Calderón's concept of 'the sin of having been born' (67). As James Acheson persuasively argues,[27] Beckett seems to owe his 'vegetal' image of Proust's characters to Schopenhauer's *The World as Will and Idea* rather than to *A la recherche du temps perdu*. For despite the learned overtones of his assertion that 'the majority of (Proust's) images are botanical' (88–9), Beckett's botanical evocation of Proust's characters is not so much Proustian in origin, as what Acheson terms 'a direct echo' of the lines in which Schopenhauer reflects:

The plant reveals its whole being at the first glance, and with complete innocence, which does not suffer from the fact that it carries its organs of generation exposed to view on its upper surface.[28]

Unfortunately, the critical implications of this echo are both indistinct and confusing. The Proustian character corresponds neither to Schopenhauer's paradigm of completely 'innocent' vegetation nor to Beckett's concept of 'impure' vegetation, but, as Swann remarks, is usually 'imparfaite, mais du moins perfectible' (I.290) (imperfect, but at least perfectible). As Beckett subsequently concedes, in a book review of 1934, Proust's progeny are capable of being 'a saint and a snob in the one breath',[29] and are thus constantly susceptible to analysis in terms of a 'question of right and wrong' (89).

The fundamental flaw of Beckett's argument in *Proust* is, of course, that it makes no provision for any kind of 'saintly' action or perception. Trapped within 'the narrow limits of an impure world' (89), Proust's characters seem to have no opportunity of attaining 'pure ... cognition' (73) or 'pure ... understanding' (91). For if Beckett's analysis is to be taken seriously, they are incurable victims of 'the impurity of will' (90) — another concept borrowed from Schopenhauer, which, as Acheson observes, seems to correspond to the Proustian concept of 'Habit' or 'the will to enjoy pleasure and avoid pain'.[30] As we have seen, Beckett's final diagnosis of the Proustian patient insists that '(his) will is blind and hard' and 'never abolished in the pure perception of a pure subject' (89).

In this respect, there seems very little difference between Beckett's critical account of human existence in *A la recherche du temps perdu* and his fictional account of human existence (if this is still the correct term) in such infernos as the environment of *The Lost Ones*, in which the characters are denied all trace of aesthetic and human understanding. Just as the 'Lost Ones' can never savour the aesthetic 'harmony' available only to those attaining the unattainable 'perfect mental image of the entire system' (*TLO*, 11–12), Beckett insists that the perceptions of Proust's characters never 'bind into any perfect synthesis' (85). And just as the 'Lost Ones' similarly suffer from a gloom in which 'Man and wife are strangers two paces apart', and do 'not appear' to recognize one another even when 'close enough to touch' (*TLO*, 36), he insists that 'Proust's men and women' are 'separate ... dynamisms related by no system of synchronisation (17), a phrase anticipating the way in which Beckettian men and women in *Dream of Fair to Middling Women* are 'two separate non-synchronised processes each on his and her side of the fence' (*Dream*, 149). If this is indeed the case, then one might well wonder how Marcel manages to look over 'his side of the fence', and how on earth he succeeds in 'synthesising' and 'synchronising' his perceptions.

Beckett's answer to this problem is childishly simple. Marcel enjoys pure cognition and pure perception because he is a 'pure subject' (90), and thus an exception to the rule of Proust's 'impure world' (89). Put slightly more tentatively, Marcel enjoys 'a pure act of understanding, will-less' (91), because, for reasons which remain a mystery, he is 'almost exempt from the impurity of will' (90). Like the narrator of *Dream of Fair to Middling Women*, Beckett might have congratulated himself for formulating this charming solution by adding: 'Is that neat or is it not?' (*Dream*, 107). The reader might then reply: 'Alas, too neat, too neat for comfort'. For Marcel is neither a 'pure subject' nor 'almost exempt from the impurity of will', but like a great many other Proustian characters he is simply an impure subject who is occasionally exempt from the impurity of will.

While Marcel's failure to interpret his early involuntary memories testifies to his 'impurity of will' and deflates Beckett's naively exaggerated estimate of his purity, his discovery that 'Music ... asserts ... the permanence of personality and the reality of art' (92) equally significantly testifies to the 'will-lessness' of other characters, such as the composer Vinteuil, and deflates Beckett's naively exaggerated estimate of their impurity. At this juncture, the entirety of Beckett's argument in *Proust* threatens to topple like a well-wobbled house of cards, as the reader realizes that Marcel is not the only significant character in *A la recherche du temps perdu*, but merely one of the many artists and non-artists who variously realize their varied talents within the vast parameters of Proust's hierarchy of positive, negative, and nihilistic actions.

Beckett concludes his essay with yet another assertion which at once seems pregnant with relevance to his own subsequent work and of very dubious relevance to *A la recherche du temps perdu*. He suggests that music (or 'the ideal and immaterial statement of ... a unique beauty'), far from being most important as a force which shatters 'unbelief' and testifies to 'the permanence of personality' and to 'the reality of art' (92) is most significant as:

the 'invisible reality' that damns the life of the body on earth as a pensum and reveals the meaning of the word: 'defunctus'. (93)

'Pensum' is not a Proustian word, and Proust's characters never indicate that they consider existence to be, in the definition of the *Concise Oxford Dictionary*, a 'charge, duty, or alloted task; a school task to be prepared; also ... a piece of work imposed as a punishment'. And although Marcel becomes horribly aware of his own physical fragility after his final revelations — 'j'avais un corps ... Et avoir un corps, c'est la grande menace pour l'esprit'

170   *Beckett and Proust*

(III.1035) (I had a body . . . And the body poses the gravest threat to the mind) — he unambiguously argues that life is 'digne d'être vécue' (III.1032) (worthy of living), rather than deploring existence and 'Gnawing to be gone' (*WH*, 42), like Beckett's narrator-heroes.

'Pensum' is, however, a very Beckettian word, and Beckett's heroes frequently evoke existence as a pensum which they partially accept as some sort of punishment for the sin of being born, and which they partially reject by attempting to attain the relief which the narrator of *The Lost Ones* associates with 'brief losses of consciousness' (*TLO*, 10). 'Craving to enter' a 'torpor', Murphy associates such respite with those moments when

he slipped away, from the pensums and prizes, from Celia, chandlers, public highways, etc., from Celia, buses, public gardens, etc., to where there were no pensums and no prizes. (*Murphy*, 74)

In much the same way, the Unnamable ardently anticipates the 'bliss of coma' (*The Unnamable*, 327) and grimly ponders:

I want to go silent . . . My speech-parched voice at rest would fill with spittle, I'd let it flow over and over, happy at last . . . my pensum ended, in the silence . . . Yes, I have a pensum to discharge, before I can be free . . . I was given a pensum, at birth perhaps, as a punishment for having been born perhaps. (*The Unnamable*, 312)

Anticipating the priorities of his own subsequent writings, and combining his theories that life is a 'pensum' and that existence is ultimately man's punishment for 'the sin of having been born' (67), Beckett's conclusion to *Proust* seems to be as 'Beckettian' as his opening allusion to Proust's 'dualism in multiplicity' (11) is 'Proustian'. Put another way, this tantalizing essay, which begins, innocently enough, by analysing the values of Proust and which concludes, somewhat less innocently, by adumbrating the antithetical values of Beckett, offers a striking example of the process by which 'The observer infects the observed' (17).

Considered as literary criticism, this eccentric essay is a strange mixture of the productive and the reductive, and of the enthralling and the appalling. On the one hand, Beckett offers supremely sensitive analyses of the complex modes of perceptual failure described in Proust's novel. But, on the other hand, Beckett also turns false prophet, and treats the reader to supremely pig-headed misreadings of Proust's theories of positive modes of perception, communication, and self-realization. In a nutshell, the virtues and the vices of the essay are equally spectacular.

That the majority of Beckett's critics should have read *Proust* so uncritically is one of the enigmas of twentieth-century scholarship. For all the perils of the intentional fallacy, it is perhaps chastening to recollect that neither Beckett nor his characters ever suggest that their writings are very much more than the kind of amalgam that Arsene defines as 'what I have said ill . . . and what I have said well . . . and what I have not said' (*Watt*, 62). Rather than adulating *Proust* for its accuracy, perspicacity and whatnot, Beckett's critics might have been better advised to take its conclusions with a hefty pinch of salt, somewhat as Beckett subsequently advised the Irish novelist Aidan Higgins that:

What I have said is much too abstract and personal and black and white, that's what comes of trying to get down to the root. It's a terrible effort for me to write such stuff and I hope you disagree with it.[31]

Beckett's *Proust* is written with all the advantages and the disadvantages of poetic licence, and there seems no point in pretending that everything in it is 'said well'. Much of *Proust* is 'said ill', and there is much that this essay leaves 'not said'. At the same time, it seems both desirable and possible to define the quality of Beckett's poetic licence, by making further reference to his correspondence. If Beckett's essay caricatures Proust as a pessimistic sage espousing negative relativism, then this reading of *A la recherche du temps perdu* almost certainly reflects Beckett's growing awareness of his own 'dud' mysticism, and of his own compulsion to elaborate a poetry — or fiction — of 'dud' mysticism, pessimism and negative relativism.

This realization appears to have crystallized some fifteen years after *Proust*, in the mid-forties. For in the same letter of 1946 in which Beckett speculated that he was 'doomed to spend the rest of my days digging up the detritus of my life and vomiting it out over and over again', he also alludes to his discovery that his fiction was similarly fated to depict the gloomy reality that Malone associates with 'the black joy of the solitary way' (*Malone Dies*, 279). Beckett movingly concludes:

Optimism is not my way. I shall always be depressed, but what comforts me is the realization that I can now accept this dark side as the commanding side of my personality. In accepting it, I will make it work for me.[32]

In more recent years, Beckett has qualified his position somewhat, to the extent of admitting to Charles Juliet that he admires the 'illogisme brûlant' (burning anti-logic) of mystics such as Saint John of the Cross and Master Eckhart and sometimes shares their 'façon de subir l'inintelligible' (way of apprehending the unintelligible).[33] As will become evident, Beckett's writings of the seventies and eighties are far more benign in temper than the fiercer, gloomier writings with which he began his literary career.

The following chapter will examine the ways in which the 'dark side' of Beckett's personality gradually surfaced in his early critical writings, during the decade following the publication of *Proust*, when, like Krapp, he put pen to paper in the hope of 'Getting known'.[34]

8

BECKETT AND CRITICAL PERSPECTIVES

So far as one can tell, Beckett almost certainly told Tom F. Driver that 'The key word in my plays is "perhaps" '.[1] The same relativity similarly informs Beckett's fiction. For example, Watt concedes that 'Mr. Knott was a good master, in a way' (*Watt*, 64). Hunchy Hackett equally cautiously admits that he enjoys the sensation of striking his stick against the pavement, because the feel of the thudding rubber 'appeased him, slightly' (*Watt*, 5).

For all his subsequent antipathy towards the 'crritic' (*WFG*, 75), Beckett initially seems to have persuaded himself that literary criticism may also occasionally prove quite 'good . . . in a way', and for one reason or another he wrote a number of book reviews throughout the 1930s, in the years following the publication of *Proust*. Sometimes these reviews imply that art, too, appeases 'slightly', although Beckett never really shares Proust's unqualified confidence in 'the magic of literature' (*PTD*, 83), and sometimes they hint that the reverse is true, and that artistic mysticism is merely 'a childishness', since 'all writing, *qua* writing, is bound to fail'.[2].

Both of these latter hypotheses appear in book reviews published in 1934, some fifteen years before Beckett's formulation of his mature literary pessimism in his *Three Dialogues* with Georges Duthuit (1949), in which he gloomily confessed both to being 'weary of pretending to be able', and to having 'no power to express, no desire to express, together with the obligation to express'.[3] Significantly, though, this pessimism was by no means absolute in the early 1930s. For in another review of 1934, Beckett enthusiastically praised the essays collected in Ezra Pound's *Make it New* as 'a galvanic belt of essays, education by provocation', which would make Sir Philip Sidney's prescriptions 'move up a little in the bed'.[4] And as late as 1945, a review of Thomas MacGreevy's *Jack B. Yeats, An Appreciation and an Interpretation* defended both criticism and art in terms of their capacity to proffer a certain illumination, or at least for the way in which it might be claimed that their content 'reduces the dark'.[5]

Addressing the virtues of Thomas MacGreevy's critical insights, Beckett reflected:

It is difficult to formulate what it is one likes in Mr. Yeats's painting, or indeed what it is one likes in anything, but . . . There is at least this to be said for mind, that it can dispel mind. And at least this for art criticism, that it can lift from the eyes . . . some of the weight of congenital prejudice.[6]

And meditating upon the merits of Jack B. Yeats's painting, he argued that Yeats, too, lifted 'some of the weight of congenital prejudice', and that

He is with the great of our time . . . because he brings light, as only the great dare to bring light, to the issueless predicament of existence.[7]

Beckett employs analogous imagery in a letter of 1954 enjoining MacGreevy to 'Tell Jack Yeats he has lit a fire that will spread'; and writing to H.O. White in 1957 shortly after the death of Jack B. Yeats, Beckett once again alluded to the 'light' of Yeats's creativity: 'The light of Jack Yeats will always come with me'.[8]

As John Pilling has observed, Beckett's 'Hommage à Jack B. Yeats' (1954) also suggests that Yeats's paintings permit 'illuminations', albeit from the 'darkest' part of the spirit.[9] With this consideration in mind, Pilling postulates that 'The hint that illumination is still possible . . . is the first indication that Beckett is emerging from the poetics of the *Three Dialogues*', and concludes that 'Beckett began to see, in the late 1950s, that there might be an exit from the predicament that he once considered "issueless" '.[10] Pilling is surely mistaken.

Beckett always seems to have associated Yeats's work with a certain sense of illumination, regardless of his declarations in the *Three Dialogues* with Georges Duthuit. Put another way, the *Three Dialogues* represent a personal poetics, whereas Beckett's comments upon the 'light', 'fire', 'illuminations', 'radiance' or whatever, in the works of creators like Yeats, Proust, MacGreevy or whoever, pertain to a more detached and more impersonal mode of critical writing, in which he seems to have been prepared to formulate values which patently contradicted the pessimism and 'dud mysticism' inseparable from the 'dark side' of his mature creative vision.

In this respect, it makes very little sense to conflate Beckett's personal poetics with the ideals which he occasionally attributes to the subjects of his criticism and book reviews, although it makes perfect sense to examine the way in which his early critical texts not only acknowledge the ideals of their subjects, but also make every effort to dissociate their author from his subjects. For, as Beckett himself hinted in one of his book reviews, 'Analysis of what a man is not may conduce to an analysis of what he is'.[11] Conveniently confirming this hypothesis, analysis of the tension between his own values and the values of the authors discussed in his early book reviews proves particularly conducive to an understanding of the peculiarities of Beckett's highly individual fictional vision.

Beckett's critical writings contain few indications that he ever considered, or 'began to see', an 'exit' from the predicament of existence: more often than not he is careful to curtail any suggestion that his vision countenances any kind of 'exit'. Perhaps one of his most unambiguous statements of allegiance to literary mysticism is his appearance among the nine signatories to Eugene Jolas's manifesto 'Poetry is Vertical' (1932), which successively rejected 'the hypnosis of positivism' and 'the renewal of the classical ideal' in favour of 'the autonomy of the poetic vision', 'the immediacy of the ecstatic vision', 'the a-logical movement of the psyche', and the revelations of 'The transcendental "I"' and of 'the mystic-gnostic trance'.[12]

Deirdre Bair reports that 'In conversation forty years later, Beckett dismissed his signature as "not worth talking about" ',[13] and it seems likely that he felt in two minds about the manifesto from the very moment of his agreement to sign Eugene Jolas's articles of faith to the doctrine of 'mantic' language.[14] Nevertheless, his signature *is* worth talking about, because it helps to exemplify his typical fluctuations between luke-warm mysticism and icy cynicism. Somewhat as Jolas argued that a 'Vertical' mode of writing might overthrow positivistic, horizontal language, and assert 'the hegemony of the inner life over the outer life',[15] Beckett's first major fictional alter ego, Belacqua, the hero of *Dream of Fair to Middling Women* (which also dates from 1932), similarly ruminates upon the advantages of vertical — or 'perpendicular' — writing, until his rhapsodic digression about such masters of the perpendicular mode as Racine and Malherbe is gently deflated by the narrator's worldly irony. Belacqua meditates:

The uniform, horizontal writing, flowing without accidence, of the man with a style, never gives you the margarita. But the writing of, say, Racine or Malherbe, perpendicular, diamanté, is pitted, is it not, and sprigged with sparkles ... They have no style, they write without style, do they not, they give you the phrase, the sparkle, the precious margaret. Perhaps only the French can do it. Perhaps only the French language can give you the thing you want.

And the narrator retaliates: 'Don't be too hard on him, he was studying to be a professor' (*Dream*, 42).

This exchange is splendidly symptomatic of the contradictions in Beckett's early critical writings. Sometimes he appears to be reflecting quite seriously upon the ways in which writing may approach the 'perpendicular' and 'sparkle'. On other occasions, he seems to deride such suppositions as the excesses of an unfortunate 'studying to be a professor'. There is a constant dialectic between tentative mysticism and impatient cynicism, until that point between the mid-1930s and the early 1950s when this dialectic subsided, and Beckett turned from criticism to the creation of such characters as Murphy, Watt, Molloy, Malone and the Unnamable, who prefer to live without any kind of 'sparkles', cherishing those moments of obscurity that Moran eulogizes as 'Delicious moments, before one's eyes get used to the dark' (*Molloy*, 104).

The crucial characteristic of the early criticism is therefore its tendency to reject the ideals of its subjects, and the crucial development in Beckett's writing might be defined in terms of its astonishing *volte face* from a certain detached enthusiasm and bewildered tolerance for the 'gleam' of Proust's, Yeats's or MacGreevy's optimism, towards the obdurate 'gloom' of his own inconsolable pessimism. All too frequently this *volte face* has been overlooked. Beckett's critics have preferred to conflate his ideals with those of his subjects, seduced, as it were, by those paragraphs which faithfully summarize the ideals of their subjects. According to this one-sided school of criticism, Beckett's *Proust* becomes a 'table of the law for any student of either Proust, or Beckett'.[16]

Yet, as William Burroughs has recently suggested, Beckett and Proust appear 'about as far apart as you could possibly be'.[17] If they ever respond to the same law, then their responses are not so much in tandem, as Beckett's critics usually suppose, but, as Burroughs remarks, 'at opposite ends of the spectrum'.[18] Collectively, Beckett's writings subvert the whole Proustian enterprise, accumulating into a kind of *Contre Marcel Proust*, somewhat as Proust's early essays lent themselves to the title

Contre Sainte-Beuve. Over and over again, the fascination of Beckett's early critical writings springs from their subversive strategies. At first sight, Beckett often appears to reiterate Proustian values, and to celebrate the 'enchantments' of transcendental aperception. But upon further inspection, his purpose seems far more complicated and far more sinister.

For example, Beckett's review of Jack B. Yeats's *The Amaranthers* (1934) initially appears to be an obvious example of his conversion to the Proustian faith. Praising Yeats for refusing to join the ignoble army of 'chartered recountants' whose observations remain contorted within the 'corsets' of 'reportage'[19] — by which he presumably means the kind of logical statement of 'line and surface' (*PTD*, 76) that he avidly denounced in *Proust* — Beckett appears to give even more explicitly Proustian praise to Yeats's work when he applauds its 'discontinuity' in terms of its respect for:

the mobility and autonomy of the imagined (a world of the same order if not so intense as the "ideal real" of Prowst, so obnoxious to the continuity girls).[20]

Upon second reading, this passage seems far from innocent. Indeed, its eccentric mixture of flattering comparison and unflatteringly inaccurate spelling epitomizes the ambiguity of Beckett's response to transcendental values. On the one hand, he seems happy to cite Proust's values as the measure of Yeats's achievement. But, on the other hand, he also appears to take pains to dissociate himself from the heady mysticism of Proust's '"ideal real"', by carefully isolating this concept within the 'corsets' of quotation marks, and by carefully mis-spelling Proust's name in the Anglo-Irish manner.

A number of other reviews reiterate variants of Proust's distinction between superficial, 'chartered' reality, and more profound modes of 'ideal' reality. 'Dante ... Bruno. Vico .. Joyce' (1929) had already insisted that literary criticism should not be 'book-keeping'[21]; and his review of Eduard Moerike's *Mozart On The Way To Prague* (1934) likewise bewailed the way in which Moerike had brought all the trappings of book-keeping to bear on Mozart's genius without ever succeeding in doing anything but 'exhaust the inessential'.[22] Concluding that Moerike's book was ultimately 'a violation of its subject', and that there was 'nothing at all to be said for it', Beckett finally condemned it as:

an undertaking that has betrayed all the ingenuity and intelligence of
men very much more highly endowed than Eduard Moerike, and in
which all writing, *qua* writing, is bound to fail.[23]

If this anticipates the passage in *Watt* in which Arsene muses
that 'any attempt to utter . . . is doomed to fail, doomed, doomed
to fail' (*Watt*, 61), Beckett's reference to the futility of exhausting
'the inessential' anticipates a distinction which subsequently
serves as the very title of his book review of Sean O'Casey's
Windfalls: 'The Essential and the Incidental'. Like the review of
Yeats's *The Amaranthers*, which praised Yeats for respecting a
sense of 'discontinuity', this review of 1934 praises O'Casey as:

a master of knockabout in this very serious and honourable sense — that
he discerns the principle of disintegration in even the most complacent
solidities, and activates it to their explosion.[24]

The virtue of O'Casey's theatre, then, would appear to be its
fidelity to the 'essential' sense of 'dislocation' that Beckett
perceived in existence, and which he celebrated as 'this dramatic
dehiscence, mind and world come asunder in irreparable
dissociation'.[25]

In the same year Beckett's 'Proust in Pieces', a review of Albert
Feuillerat's *Comment Proust a composé son roman*, reaffirmed his
enthusiasm for the discontinuous vision and poured contempt
upon Feuillerat's ambition to excavate the narrative coherence of
A la recherche du temps perdu, in order 'to resolve the perturbations
and dislocations of the text as it stands'.[26] For, according to
Beckett, 'the essence of Proust's originality' becomes most
manifest precisely in terms of the presence of such 'perturbations', and in terms of the concomitant absence of all 'plausible
frills'.[27] Anticipating the way in which *Dream of Fair to Middling
Women* would ridicule the 'unreal permanence' and the 'chloroformed world' of Balzac (*Dream*, 106), he praises Proust above all
for his antipathy towards superficial modes of 'Uniformity,
homogeneity, cohesion', and for portraying 'the stupefying
antics of . . . indeterminates', within a narrative more like 'the
chart of an ague' than 'a respectable parabola'. In a nutshell,
Beckett considered Proust's finest achievement to be his rejection
of 'the sweet reasonableness of plane psychology *à la Balzac*'[28]

Like much of the argument in *Proust*, 'Proust in Pieces'
abounds in eloquent overstatement. While it qualifies Beckett's
previous assertion that Proust's characters are grotesquely
'predetermined' (*PTD*, 89) by alluding to his 'stupefying . . .

indeterminates', it tends to give the impression that the resolution to Marcel's 'search, stated in the full complexity of all its clues and blind alleys', in a world 'pulverized by time, obliterated by habit, mutilated in the clockwork of memory', is somewhat of a fraudulent anti-climax. For, according to Beckett, Marcel's perceptual confusions are only resolved when his 'dribs and drabs' of insight are finally 'cooked to give unity'[29] This jest in turn anticipates the way in which the narrator of *Dream of Fair to Middling Women* doubts, and even regrets, the possibility of such unity. Here, 'The only unity in this story is please God, an involuntary unity' (*Dream*, 118). Put more bluntly, all trace of unity, or of 'crazily spaced' disorder, is 'God's will . . . His will, never ours' (*Dream*, 111).

It thus appears that by the mid-1930's Beckett associated the literary vocation with two principal problems. Firstly, literature offered the task of formulating 'essential' reality rather than 'incidental' reality. Secondly, it offered the challenge of respecting and reflecting 'the full complexity' of existence, with its stupefying 'principle of disintegration'. Taken together, these two problems precipitated a third dilemma: the question of deciding whether or not a literature sensitive to the 'principle of disintegration' was compatible with the kind of 'essential' harmony that Beckett sometimes associated with the 'ideal real'.

By the early 1960s, when Beckett had written the trilogy of *Molloy*, *Malone Dies* and *The Unnamable*, his mature definition of reality appears to have become painfully clear. Talking with Tom F. Driver in 1961, he evoked existence as 'the mess' and defined the writer's function as the struggle to 'find a form that accomodates the mess'.[30] But in the mid-1930s, Beckett's definitions of essential reality seem to have been far more fluid. Sometimes it is defined positively, in terms of the 'brightness of art' (*PTD*, 76), and the 'radiant essence' (*PTD*, 76) and 'mystical experience' (*PTD*, 75) that he associated with the 'ideal core' (*PTD*, 29) of the Proustian vision. On other occasions, it is defined negatively, in terms of the 'discontinuity' that he admired in Jack B. Yeats's fiction; the 'disintegration', the 'dehiscence' and the 'dissociation' that he perceived in Sean O'Casey's plays; and the 'dissonances' and 'dislocations' within the general 'narrative trajectory' of *A la recherche du temps perdu*.[31]

This negative concept of essential reality may also be discerned in *Dream of Fair to Middling Women*, which illustrates Beckett's theories in terms of characters who spend their time 'coiling and uncoiling and unfolding and flowering into nothingness', affording the general spectacle of 'disintegrating bric-à-brac' (*Dream*, 104). Nevertheless, despite the fact that these latter texts all suggest that Beckett had already envisaged reality as an irremediable 'mess', two other reviews of 1934 still countenance the possibility that essential reality might conceivably consist of the same luminous harmony that he associated with the involuntary memories of Proust.

The first of these reviews, entitled 'Recent Irish Poetry', and published under the *nom de plume* of Andrew Belis in the 'Irish' issue of *The Bookman* (of August 1934), is probably one of Beckett's least known texts. Though the name 'Andrew Belis' may be unfamiliar, the preoccupations of the article are unmistakably Beckettian. Once again, he emphasizes the problems arising from his sensitivity to the relativity and discontinuity of perception. In Virginia Woolf's terms, he is acutely aware that reality is 'varying', 'unknown' and 'uncircumscribed', rather than 'a series of gig lamps symmetrically arranged'; while, in his own terms, this review of recent Irish poetry is primarily concerned with:

the degree in which the younger Irish poets evince awareness of the new thing that has happened, or the old thing that has happened again, namely the breakdown of the object. [32]

Acknowledging that this 'breakdown of the object' is concomitant with the 'breakdown of the subject', Beckett proposes to evaluate 'the younger Irish poets' in terms of their responses to the resultant 'rupture of the lines of communication' (325).

The most negative response seems to be that of those poets 'who are not aware of the rupture', or in whom 'the velleity of becoming so (is) suppressed as a nuisance', and who are thereby culpable of 'flight from self-awareness' (325). For such poets, poetry appears to be a matter of business as usual, or more precisely, the anachronistic, superficial, pre-Modernist business as usual that Beckett associates with 'the antiquarians, delivering with the altitudinous complacency of the Victorian Gael the Ossianic goods' (325). Still convinced, it seems, that reality may be 'symmetrically arranged', these poets purvey 'segment after segment of cut-and-dried sanctity and loveliness', in which there is little trace of the 'breakdown' and 'rupture' of perception for the simple reason that they maintain 'that the first condition of any poem is an accredited theme, and that in self-perception there is no theme' (325). Accordingly, their poems invoke 'accredited' centrifugal landscapes (rather than venturing into the unaccredited domain of centripetal mindscapes), and predictably present:

the correct scenery, where the self is either most happily obliterated or else so improved and enlarged that it can be mistaken for part of the *décor*. (325)

Subdividing contemporary Irish poets into 'antiquarians and others' (325), Beckett turns his attention to those poets who are aware of the problems arising from the relativity of perception and communication, and considers the ways in which this awareness may be expressed, beginning with those who merely evoke the symptoms, rather than the substance, of their distress. In a very general way, this kind of poet 'may state the space that intervenes between him and the world of objects' as 'no-man's land, Hellespont or vacuum, according as he happens to be feeling resentful, nostalgic or merely depressed' (325). While this option appears to consist of idiosyncratic responses to the 'break-down' in symmetrical perception, a second type of poet attempts to 'celebrate the cold comforts of apperception' (325), by which Beckett seems to refer to a more disciplined account of the tangible symptoms of perceptual confusion (or the kind of neutral, 'purely functional' description that Barthes attributes to Robbe-Grillet).[33] A third kind of poet may 'record his findings, if he is a man of great personal courage' (325). This final option seems to refer to the project of defining the substance, rather than the idiosyncratic or formal symptoms of perceptual crisis, or, in the terms of Beckett's *Proust*, to the project of recording the confusion at 'the core of the eddy' (*PTD*, 65–6).

Among his contemporaries, the poet whom Beckett most respects is his friend Thomas MacGreevy, who appears to accomplish the ideal compromise between sensitivity to the problems of language and perception in the era of the 'breakdown of the object', and mastery of these problems in poems which 'record his findings'. In Beckett's terms:

Mr. Thomas MacGreevy . . . neither excludes self-perception from his work nor postulates the object as inaccessible. But he knows how to wait for the thing to happen, how not to beg the fact of this 'bitch of a world' . . . And when it does happen and he sees, 'far as sensitive eyesight could see', whatever happens to be dispensed . . . it is the act and not the object of perception that matters. (236)

This analysis of MacGreevy's poetry makes two extremely interesting points. Firstly, it emphasizes that MacGreevy's revelations, like the involuntary memories in Proust's *A la recherche du temps perdu*, 'will not be importuned', but occur in their 'own time' (*PTD*, 34) according to the gradual process that MacGreevy must patiently 'wait for'. Secondly, quite unlike Beckett's subsequent fictions, it postulates that the intense, non-habitual *quality* of 'the act' of authentic self-perception is far more significant than 'the object of perception'. As will become evident, Beckett's narrator-heroes usually intimate that the reverse is true, insofar as they generally find that the 'object' — or content — of involuntary self-perception is sufficiently painful to render its hypothetical quality a very minor consideration. Indeed, far from desiring 'a high order' of mental activity, the Beckettian narrator-hero speculates that 'it might be argued the lower the better' (*Company*, 15). By contrast, Beckett's admiration for MacGreevy's poems stems from his conviction that their high order of mental activity justifies the avowal that they 'may be called elucidations' (236).

Beckett's article finally speculates that MacGreevy's poems are 'probably the most important contribution to post-war Irish poetry' (236). The same supposition informs 'Humanistic Quietism', an almost contemporary review of MacGreevy's *Poems*, in which Beckett suggests that they kindle 'a radiance without counterpart in the work of contemporary poets writing in English'.[34] This review begins with the astonishing assertion that 'All poetry . . . is prayer' (79), a statement which at once wings back to the mysticism of Proust, while also overlapping with the more recent 'manticism' of Eugene Jolas's *transition*. On the one hand, this concept finds antecedents in *A la recherche du temps perdu*, where Marcel muses that Vinteuil's music offers an amalgam of 'Prière, espérance' (III.255) (Prayer, hope), and in *Proust*, in which Beckett also specifies that Vinteuil's Sonata expresses its beauty 'as a prayer' (*PTD*, 93); and, on the other hand, it coincides with the argument of 'The Road through the Word', an article by Friedrich Marcus Huebner which appeared in *transition* 22 (1933). This article seems to function at a number of different levels. First and foremost, it offers a rejoinder to the linguistic theories of Fritz Mauthner by defending 'the magical' function of language which, Huebner argues, permits communication once 'words go beyond their purely rational tasks'.[35] Secondly, Huebner's argument appears to synthesize the theories of Eugene Jolas (indeed, Jolas annotates the essay with the footnote 'This is exactly the point I have tried to bring out in *transition* for some years' (110)). Thirdly, this argument also anticipates a number of the key points in Beckett's discussions of MacGreevy's poems, particularly when reflecting that 'Living words are spoken by prayer', that 'Living words are spoken by poetry', and that 'Living eloquence is a state of grace' which 'cannot be forced by our will' and which 'comes inadvertently' (111).

For the first two paragraphs of 'Humanistic Quietism', Beckett writes as if he were under the influence of some kind of transcendental aphrodisiac. Having defined all poetry as 'prayer', he further defines the condition of prayer as 'the grace of humility', adding for good measure that such prayer and grace is founded ' "not on misanthropy but on hope" ' (79). [36] Despite the fact that Beckett's subsequent fiction and criticism argue that art has little to do with prayer, grace, hope or any kind of clarity, this review repeatedly praises the 'endopsychic clarity' (80) and the 'equable radiance' of MacGreevy's poems, employing remarkably similar formulae to those with which Beckett evoked the 'radiant essence' (*PTD*, 70) of Marcel's 'mystical experience' (*PTD*, 75). Just as Marcel's revelations offer that process by which 'Darkness is obliterated in an intolerable brightness' (*PTD*, 70), the 'darkest' poem in MacGreevy's volume of 'shining' verse climbs to a 'blaze of prayer . . . obliterating the squalid elements of civil war' (79).

This is high praise indeed. Beckett's terminology not only echoes his preceding evocation of the Proustian revelation, but additionally revives the key terms in his suggestion that Joyce's language offers the 'inevitable clarity' of words that 'glow and blaze'. [37] At this point, Beckett probably sensed that he had over-lavishly eulogized MacGreevy's revelations, and the remainder of the review hints that the advantages of MacGreevy's insights, like his poetry, are 'intensely personal' (79) rather than something which others might share or attain. In much the same way, his specification that Marcel is a lone 'pure subject' (*PTD*, 90), within an otherwise 'impure world' (*PTD*, 89), intimates that his revelations are similarly solipsistic in quality. Contorted into something of a metaphysical tongue-twister, his final sentences confide:

To know so well what one values is, what one's value is, as not to neglect those occasions (they are few) on which it may be doubled, is not a common faculty; to retain in the acknowledgement of such enrichment the light, calm and finality that composed it is an extremely rare one. I do not know if the first of these can be acquired: I know that the second cannot. (80)

In simpler terms, Beckett appears to suggest that while the ability to take best advantage of certain fleeting moments of non-habitual revelation — and thereby 'not ... neglect' those rare occasions when one's habitual value is 'doubled' — may be mastered, only those with certain innate gifts may permanently 'retain' the 'light' from such experiences.

This tentative acknowledgement of the 'light, calm and finality' attending MacGreevy's revelations forms the swan-song to Beckett's brief flirtation with mystical values. While 'Dante ... Bruno. Vico .. Joyce' (1929) seems to share Vico's conviction that 'poetry is the foundation of writing',[38] and 'Humanistic Quietism' (1934) ventures to suggest that 'All poetry ... is prayer', Beckett's 'Denis Devlin' (1938) abruptly reverses this optimistic approach to literature. Condemning non-literary writing as 'linkwriting ... bound to sag', this review of Devlin's *Intercessions* commends the 'probity' arising from the 'minimum of rational interference' in Devlin's poetry, and then menacingly concludes:

The time is perhaps not altogether too green for the vile suggestion that art has nothing to do with clarity, does not dabble in the clear and does not make clear.[39]

Shallowly disguised as a casual aside by Beckett's self-deprecatory use of the adjective 'vile', this major statement is at once both a very sizeable step from his previous belief in 'the reality of art' (*PTD*, 92) and a very short step away from his subsequent suggestion that 'One can only speak of ... the mess'.[40] Having entertained two distinct concepts of the 'ideal real' — the one harmonious and clear, the other chaotic and obscure — Beckett seems to have detached himself from the triumphant mysticism of writers like Proust and MacGreevy, in order to explore the domain of literary unbelief which *Dream of Fair to Middling Women* aptly associates with the plight of the 'dud mystic' (*Dream*, 166).

Beckett elaborates this literary credo in his celebrated *Three Dialogues* with Georges Duthuit (1949), a series of dialogues which contain such gems as his celebrated invocation of:

an art turning away from (the plane of the feasible) in disgust, weary of puny exploits, weary of pretending to be able, of being able, of doing a little better the same old thing, of going a little further along a dreary road. (*PTD*, 103)

In much the same way as Wilde's dialogues in 'The Decay of Lying' and 'The Critic as Artist' offer a blueprint for Aestheticism, Beckett's *Three Dialogues* have been interpreted as a blueprint for a certain strand of European and North American Post-Modernism, particularly that strand composed of writers, critics, and writer-critics sharing Raymond Federman's conviction that many of the foremost contemporary novelists are:

more concerned with the problems of writing their books, of letting the difficulty of writing fiction transpire in the fiction itself . . . than . . . with the problems of man.[41]

According to Federman's argument, 'fiction today . . . tends to cancel itself . . . in order to denounce the imposture of traditional fiction'. It therefore follows that Beckett is one of the most eminent contemporary writers, because he 'has perfected the technique of cancellation of art to its ultimate degree'.[42] Beckett has probably encouraged this reading of his work by making such generalizations as: 'anyone nowadays who pays the slightest attention to his own experience finds it the experience of a non-knower, a non-can-er'; and by defining his work in terms of: 'complete disintegration. No "I", no "have", no "being". No nominative, no accusative, no verb'.[43] Yet despite the fact that these comments from 1956 conspire to confirm the suggestion in *Three Dialogues* that 'to be an artist is to fail, as no other dare fail' (*PTD*, 125), and despite the fact that Beckett has also defined his work as 'impotence, ignorance . . . something by definition incompatible with art',[44] there is something peculiarly unsatisfactory in the hypothesis that he is simply a grand master of the 'technique of cancellation'.

Were this simplistic and reductive hypothesis correct, then there might well be grounds for R. C. Kenedy's argument that Beckett is ultimately 'a minor writer' whose work has been misjudged by an audience 'which indulges itself in adulating things of little value during times when only things of little value receive adulation'.[45] Arguably, Beckett's work is more substantial than either Federman or Kenedy suggest, although Kenedy's diagnosis carries some conviction insofar as Beckett would seem to be a major writer plagued by critics obsessed with 'things of little value'. For, despite their good intentions, those critics who conflate Beckett's vision with the 'technique of cancellation' finally suggest that he is little more than an 'unchartered recountant', predictably misplacing his subject-matter within works that Virginia Woolf might have defined as 'asymmetrically arranged'. As Raymond Federman has demonstrated, even a 'crritic' can successfully follow this recipe for anti-literature.[46]

There is, of course, no denying that Beckett employs predictable cancellation techniques in his fictions. For example, *Worstward Ho* (of 1983) cancels the optimism of Kingsley's title with its own titular pun, and begins with the following cascade of antithetical snippets:

On. Say on. Be said on. Somehow on. Till nowhow on. Said nohow on. Say for be said. Missaid. From now on say for be missaid. (*WH*, 7)

Nevertheless, it seems clear that the unusual force of both this text and Beckett's other writings derives from something far more subtle, and far more complex, than self-negating rhetoric. Were this not the case, then Beckett would appear little more than a virtuoso of what Federman might dub the imposture of anti-fiction. Paradoxically, a surprising number of Beckett's critics have contentedly typecast him as precisely this kind of 'unchartered recountant' or 'chartered anti-recountant', hailing him as a literary Saint George battling against the dragons of language and of literary convention in an era informed by an 'overwhelming sense of the imminence of linguistic aridity'.[47] In this respect, Beckett has become something of a folk-hero in the literary global village, and critics have vied with each other to exaggerate the 'heroism' of his 'battle' against the limitations of language.

John Pilling, for example, remarks that if the 'long wrestle with language ends with something uncommonly like language winning ... the struggle, in it remorselessness and its courage, compels one's attention'; and in much the same way, Lawrence Harvey persuades himself that 'No one has succeeded as he has in winning for literature lands as strange and unknown as those conquered only in recent years by music and painting'.[48] These effusions are surely excessive. All experimental writers 'wrestle' with language, and many writers far more experimental than Beckett have produced works which he himself has acknowledged as 'refreshingly strange'.[49] Briefly, such enthusiasm for Beckett's 'remorseless' rhetoric has not proved particularly conducive to an understanding of his vision.

At the other extreme, a minority of Beckett's critics have taken his work to task for favouring 'failure' and 'disintegration'. Alan Rodway has accused him of 'exaggerating, making the worst of things', and Vivian Mercier has even more bluntly concluded that he offers 'a village-atheist oversimplification'.[50] John Fletcher somewhat similarly concedes that Beckett 'lacks too completely the moral, social, and political preoccupations of Cervantes, Swift, Fielding and Voltaire to be ranged finally with them', but concludes, nevertheless, on a surprisingly cheerful note, by asserting that his work accomplishes the 'no small feat' of being able 'to see our predicament' and 'see it whole'.[51]

This widespread emphasis upon the integral and inclusive quality of Beckett's vision almost certainly stems from the illusion that like Proust, he descends 'to the core of the eddy' (*PTD*, 65) in order to discover the 'whole' of reality. Thus, while Fletcher argues like Federman that 'Beckett's novels are about the impossibility of writing novels' and that his 'deepest pessimism is not about life ... but about literature',[52] these proposals eventually overlap with the suggestion that his literary explorations (like those of Proust) are essentially 'excavatory' (*PTD*, 65) and that therefore, he probes the limits of literature in order to probe the limits of life and of the self. According to this generous hypothesis, Beckett's work admirably fulfills his own definition of great art, since it shows 'concern ... with his expressive possibilities, those of his vehicle, those of humanity' (*PTD*, 120).

Briefly, Beckett's critics try to have their cake and eat it. First they insist that his work is solely concerned with the futility of literature, and then they announce that his abortive narrator-heroes also evince the search for 'whole' awareness. For example, Hannah C. Copeland postulates that 'Beckett's author-heroes seek self-knowledge through their creative efforts', and Francis Doherty likewise avows that 'Beckett traces the search for self ... by writers through writing'.[53] Numerous critics echo this seductive cliché, and the unwary reader might well assume that, like Marcel in *A la recherche du temps perdu*, the Beckettian hero is particularly anxious to accelerate self-awareness. A paragraph or two of examples should suffice to illustrate the prevalence of this misleading hypothesis.

According to John Fletcher, *Molloy* offers 'an epic of the search for one's real self'.[54] Ruby Cohn likewise alludes to the

Unnamable's 'preoccupation with self-knowledge', and Richard N. Coe refers to the Beckettian heroes' 'unending quest for a new concept of the Self', while Rosette Lamont discusses their 'infinite quest of their inner essence'.[55] Other critics make even more explicit references to the 'parallels' between Proust's and Beckett's vision, by appropriating the latter's critical terminology in order to suggest that — like Marcel — Molloy, Moran, Malone and company all voluntarily excavate 'the ideal core of the onion' (*PTD*, 29). For example, J. D. O'Hara argues that Beckett evokes 'the peeling of the self toward its ideal core', while Northrop Frye similarly conflates the Proustian and Beckettian enterprises in terms of the ambition that he evokes as: 'the core of the onion, the resolve to find in art the secret of identity, the paradise that has been lost'.[56] Explicitly comparing the search for self in Proust's and Beckett's novels, Melvin J. Friedman concludes that this quest is 'perfectly realized in *A la recherche du temps perdu*, bitterly and disappointingly unrealized in the Molloy trilogy'.[57]

Almost without exception, then, Beckett's critics have interpreted his work as the depiction of a search *for* self-knowledge, rather than an evocation of the kind of 'flight from self-awareness' and 'self-negation' that he derides in 'Recent Irish Poetry' (235) and in *Proust* (*PTD*, 66). Despite the fact that his early critical writings cast more and more doubts upon the possibility, and indeed, the very desirability of intense self-awareness and self-knowledge, Beckett's critics have stubbornly presented him as a kind of incompetent Proust, or 'the mystic denied, the man for whom the denied beatific vision is the sole essential object'.[58] Thus, according to Martin Esslin,[59]

Beckett's quest is the mystic's quest for the loss of the Self, or rather . . . through losing the Self to enter into Union with the ultimate essence of the universe which . . . is free from the frustrations and limitations of *being in the world*, of existence.

In other words, Esslin argues that Beckett's characters would transcend the 'incidental' self in order to commune with an 'essential', atemporal, *universal* self, somewhat as Marcel aspires to commune with 'l'essence des choses . . . en dehors du temps' (III.871) (the essence of things . . . beyond the dimension of time). This is certainly an attractive supposition. Nevertheless, one extremely significant objection comes to mind.

While the classical 'mystic's quest' might be defined as the attempt to attain a state of 'transcendental aperception' (*PTD*, 90) during which the mystic transcends the 'paste and pewter' of incidental reality, and enters into union with 'the pearl' (*PTD*, 31) of a higher, harmonious, essential mode of reality, Beckett's universe appears devoid of such 'pearls'. For the 'dud mystic' in Beckett's fiction, the only alternative to such habitual, workaday confusion as that within Murphy's 'Magdalen Mental Mercyseat', is the introspective anguish that the narrator of *Ill seen ill said* describes as 'the madhouse of the skull' (*Isis*, 20), or the intolerable condition that Robert Currie astutely defines as 'not a calm and contemplative nirvana but (a) terrible ascetic descendentalism', and which Theodor W. Adorno equally perceptively qualifies as 'counter-images of the indelible moments evoked in Proust's work'.[60]

Neither Currie nor Adorno elaborate their insights in any great detail, but, as the following chapters will indicate, the poignancy and the power of Beckett's vision derive from the peculiar tension informing a fictional cosmos in which the only alternatives to the frying pans of habitual existence are the intolerable fires of non-habitual perception. Beckett's 'dud mysticism' seems not so much an incompetent variant of orthodox mysticism, as most of his critics fondly assume, as a frightful mode of more or less lobotomized mysticism from which all traces of positive transcendence have been removed. In Proustian terms, Beckett presents a mode of negative relativism in which man vacillates between habitual 'Boredom' and non-habitual 'Suffering' (*PTD*, 28), without ever encountering anything approximating to the 'Enchantments' (*PTD*, 22) of non-habitual reality. Or, considered in terms of Beckett's analysis of Joyce's conception of the 'Purgatory' of existence, his vision appears to conceive of existence as a fluctuation between 'a flood' of habitual, purgatorial 'movement and vitality', punctuated by moments of 'Hell' — or 'unrelieved viciousness' — but devoid of any significant trace of the 'unrelieved immaculation' informing Joyce's 'Paradise'.[61]

Despite the fact that Beckett praised Proust's 'dualism in multiplicity' (*PTD*, 11), just as he praised Joyce's dialectical conjunction of 'two broad qualities',[62] Beckett's own work evinces an astonishingly impoverished metaphysics, in which things seem fated to go from bad to worse, and then, with luck, to bad again; and in which the only conceivable consolation is the paradoxical and unattainable idyll of those who 'know' that they are 'beyond knowing anything' (*Molloy*, 64). Far more complex than the celebrated 'impossibility of writing novels', and the very antithesis of the oft-cited 'search for self', this peculiarly anti-Proustian, and peculiarly Beckettian, ideal is first introduced in *Dream of Fair to Middling Women*.

9

BECKETT, PROUST, AND
DREAM OF FAIR TO MIDDLING WOMEN

Beckett's unpublished first novel, *Dream of Fair to Middling Women*, has long remained the Loch Ness Monster of Post-Modern fiction.[1] Most of Beckett's admirers have heard of it and believe that it first surfaced between 1932 and 1933; many of his critics have sighted it; but few comprehensive studies have been made of its substance and significance. Those critics who have examined it unanimously agree that it offers a crucial introduction to Beckett's subsequent writings, and usually argue that its hero, Belacqua, aspires to escape from 'a hostile external world' in order to 'retreat into the wider freedom of the mind' and to attain 'release into the microcosm'.[2] At best, such conclusions cultivate confusions.

Dream of Fair to Middling Women undoubtedly depicts Belacqua's initial attempts to retreat from macrocosmic, external reality in order to enter the microcosmic sanctuary of the mind, just as the nursery rhyme celebrating Old Mother Hubbard relates that this venerable dame went to her cupboard in order to fetch her poor dog a bone. But just as Mother Hubbard's cupboard proves bare, boneless, and a source of disappointment to all concerned, Belacqua's mind proves equally unsatisfactory as an alternative to the external world. Accordingly, Belacqua retreats from the microcosm, as well as from the macrocosm, towards an ideal and virtually unattainable state of nothingness, which is neither macrocosmic, nor microcosmic, but 'not' (107).

In other words, *Dream of Fair to Middling Women* does not so much advocate the Proustian ideal of 'immersive' (*PTD*, 65), non-habitual, introspective self-knowledge, as the paradoxical conscious absence of all knowledge that Beckett's essay on Proust associates with the 'ablation of desire' (*PTD*, 18), and which Belacqua craves as 'a Limbo purged of desire' (38). As the similarity between these terms suggests, *Dream of Fair to*

190

Middling Women abounds in phrases, images and thematic echoes from both *A la recherche du temps perdu* and Beckett's *Proust*. At first sight it is very tempting to conflate these works, and to assume that *Dream of Fair to Middling Women* elaborates the vision that Proust adumbrated in the pages of his novel and which Beckett subsequently summarized in the pages of his essay. For example, just as Marcel illustrates the limitations of habitual modes of perception when remarking upon the way in which the 'multiple aspects' of Albertine resist 'positive synthesis' (*PTD*, 85) and refuse to fall into any meaningful pattern, the narrator of *Dream of Fair to Middling Women* confesses that the contradictory traits of his characters similarly offer 'reluctance . . . to bind together and give us a synthesis' (105).

Yet, if *Dream of Fair to Middling Women* and *A la recherche du temps perdu* frequently address the same general problems arising from the limitations of habitual perception, their responses to what Tzvetan Todorov might term their shared 'prédicats de base' (basic predicates)[3] are very different. While Proust's narrator-hero reviles habitual perceptual categories, he also speculates that his writings may precipitate non-habitual self-knowledge by helping readers to discover 'le moyen de lire en eux-mêmes' (III.1033) (the means of reading into themselves). By contrast, the characters in *Dream of Fair to Middling Women* repeatedly anticipate the famous first line of *Waiting for Godot*, finding that there is 'nothing to be done' (3–4, 78, 79, 169). Rather than determining to do anything or to help anyone, they gradually despair of doing anything at all, prompting the narrator's cynical conclusion: 'How can you help people, unless it be on with their corsets or to a second or third helping' (110).

Like Beckett's essay on Proust, *Dream of Fair to Middling Women* teasingly generates a curious sensation of *déjà lu* and *jamais vu* — of the familiar and the unfamiliar — by transferring a number of problems, images and motifs from the peculiarly positive relativism of the Proustian fictional vision to the distinctively negative relativism of the Beckettian perspective. This disorientating sense of recognition and of surprise may best be exemplified in terms of Beckett's mischievous appropriation of one of Proust's most subtle images of idyllic rustic tranquillity.

As John Pilling has remarked, Beckett's annotations to *A la recherche du temps perdu* perceptively cross-reference Proust's duplicated allusion to the unusual 'impression de repos' (peaceful impression) that Marcel savours while listening to birds singing in a forest.[4] Marcel twice refers to the entrancing 'invisibilité des oiseaux qui s'y répondaient . . . dans les arbres' (I.720, II.994) (invisibility of the birds calling to one another . . . in the trees), and Beckett both redeploys and reverses this image when 'the Alba' — one of Belacqua's many 'Fair to Middling Women' — imagines herself to be within a forest in which:

> The birds would scuttle about bleeding in the tree-tops. A fizz of scampering birds . . . They would not fly, their wings were in tatters, she would not see them, desperately they would sprawl and flounder high overhead . . . a poor shoal of wounded noddies threshing aloft. (137)

Together with subsequent references to the inevitable decay of 'doomed flowers' (139), 'dying flowers' (154) and 'vanquished flowers' (155), this vision of terrified flight memorably introduces 'the mess' informing both Belacqua's world and the world of almost every subsequent Beckettian hero.[5] At the same time, it also typifies the way in which Beckett's writings compulsively parody Proust's paradigms of natural tranquillity and ridicule his confidence in man's capacity to attain similar serenity. Throughout *Dream of Fair to Middling Women*, the characters 'desperately . . . sprawl and flounder', without ever really relishing the kind of 'peaceful impression' beloved by Marcel. Their confusion may best be classified in terms of three general categories of experience.

Firstly, *Dream of Fair to Middling Women* depicts the frustrations of the artist or the would-be artist. Both Belacqua and the narrator exemplify the perils of those vulnerable to the creative impulse. Secondly, this novel evokes the vexations of human intercourse in terms of Belacqua's abortive friendships and issueless infatuations. Last, but not least, this novel examines the still more disagreeable experience of anguished introspection in terms of Belacqua's exposure to the sporadic 'inward glare' (110) of non-habitual self-awareness. The victim of these tripartite torments, Belacqua rapidly reassesses his initial enthusiasm for existence in the mind, and turns for solace to the two survival strategies to which almost all of Beckett's subsequent heroes instinctively resort. The most ambitious — and paradoxical — of these options attempts to elicit 'transcendental gloom' (5) by consciously attaining unconsciousness, and by willingly 'nilling' the will. Its more pragmatic counterpart endeavours to reduce all mental activity to comforting, 'boomerang' routines. Neither of these strategies meets with much success.

The problems of writing are not peculiar to Belacqua; rather, they are the abiding *bête noire* of almost every radical twentieth-century writer. But whereas Modernists like Woolf and Proust, and Post-Modernists like Beckett, all recoil before realist and naturalist conventions, and, in Lawrence Harvey's terms, are all 'quite sure of the kind of novel (they do) not want to write',[6] the narrators of Woolf and Proust also seem well aware of the new kinds of fiction that they *would* like to write. By contrast, such Post-Modern anti-heroes and anti-narrators as Belacqua and the narrator of *Dream of Fair to Middling Women* repeatedly remind the reader that their literary problems are somewhat graver, insofar as they fail to discover any kind of coherent creativity, are therefore unable to write, and are thus the sorrowful species that Beckett subsequently defined as the 'non-knower' and the 'non-can-er'.[7]

Anticipating Beckett's tendency to contrast his creative 'impotence' with the 'omnipotence' of Joyce,[8] the narrator ruefully distinguishes his earlier experiments from those of the great Modernist artists, confessing: 'we were once upon a time inclined to fancy ourselves as the Cézanne, shall we say, of the printed page, very strong on architectonics' (159). But, as the first pages of his narrative intimate, the narrator is no longer 'very strong' on anything. Far from encountering exemplary verbal 'architectonics', the reader soon stumbles upon such statements of failure as:

The fact of the matter is we do not quite know where we are in this story. It is possible that some of our creatures will do their dope all right and give no trouble. And it is certain that others will not. (7)

For example, the inauspiciously named 'Nemo' appears to defy all literary conventions (apart from the Beckettian convention of invariable incoherence), and 'cannot be made, at least not by us, stand for anything' (7). Elaborating a musical analogy in order to explain this dilemma, the narrator complains that the perplexing Nemo 'is not a note at all but the most regrettable simultaneity of notes' (8). As such, Nemo's incoherence prefigures the way in which the inconsistencies and contradictions of his fellow characters continually thwart all attempts to keep them in some kind of order, or 'up to their notes' (100), and eventually incites the outburst:

We call the whole performance off, we call the book off, it tails off in a horrid manner ... The music comes to pieces. The notes fly about all over the place, a cycle of electrons. And then all we can do, if we are not too old and tired by that time to be interested in making the best of a bad job, is to deploy a curtain of silence as rapidly as possible. (100)

In one way or another, Belacqua and the narrator relentlessly reiterate that almost all of life's problems are best placated by this kind of nihilistic 'curtain of silence'.

Like Nemo, the 'Smeraldina-Rima' — yet another of Belacqua's 'Fair to Middling Women' — tends to 'fly about all over the place' (100), making the narrator despair of finding 'a convenient term for ... the whole four of her and many another that have not been presented because they make us tired' (102). If one or two characters, such as the Smeraldina-Rima's mother, appear coherent and seem to produce 'the desired monotony' (103) rather than flying about all over the place, then it is only because this kind of character is excessively minor, excessively under-developed, and, in the narrator's terms, 'has had practically no occasion to be herselves' (103). Regretfully ruminating upon the way in which his characters evince 'a stew of disruption and flux' (104) fit to rival the 'stupefying antics' of Proust's 'indeter-minates',[9] the narrator explains:

Their movement is based on a principle of repulsion, their property not to combine but ... to scatter and stampede ... And not only to shrink from all that is not they, from all that is without and in its turn shrinks from them, but to strain away from themselves. (106)

From this observation, it follows that:

They are no good from the builder's point of view, firstly because they will not suffer their systems to be absorbed in the cluster of a greater system, and then, and chiefly, because they themselves tend to dis-appear as systems. (106)

Briefly, they obey and manifest the law of flight from both others and from the self — a law which seems the fundamental impulse of every one of Beckett's characters.

Yet at the same time — or, more accurately, from time to time — this process of disruption and flux is occasionally interrupted during certain moments of non-habitual stasis, moments which the narrator defines as 'odd periods of recueillement, a kind of centripetal backwash that checks the rot' (106). These unpre-dictable periods of 'nervous recoil into composure' (106) seem similar to the equally non-habitual moments of self-awareness or self-manifestation in *A la recherche du temps perdu*; most notably the involuntary memories of Marcel, and the 'transfiguration' of Odette. Significantly, though, these occasions are far from welcome in *Dream of Fair to Middling Women*. While Marcel regrets that they are 'trop rares' (III.898) (too rare), the narrator of Beckett's novel impatiently dismisses them as freak events which merely 'complicate things further', and which appear so atypical as to have 'little to do with the story' (106).

So far as the narrator is concerned, literature's first, and indeed only, task is to register the relativity of perception and the confusions of habitual existence, rather than attempt to hide such 'rot' beneath a veneer of implausible and improbable coherence. According to the narrator, realist fiction generates an 'unreal permanence of quality' (106). Bearing this criticism in mind, he deplores such realist writers as Balzac, insofar as:

The *procédé* that seems all falsity, that of Balzac, for example . . . consists in dealing with . . . this backwash, as though that were the whole story. Whereas in reality . . . one must be excessively concerned with a total precision to allude to it at all! (106)

The obvious weakness of this thesis is, of course, that it imputes an equally unreal impermanence of quality to existence. Undaunted by this problem, the narrator scathingly derides Balzac's 'chloroformed world', claiming that it is 'artificially immobilised in a backwash of composure' (106).

According to this argument, Balzac is nothing more than a chartered recountant who may 'juggle politely with irrefragable values, values that can assimilate other values like in kind and be assimilated by them' (106). By contrast, the characters in *Dream of Fair to Middling Women* are, at very least, what Beckett's Molloy dubs 'poliment perplexe' (*Molloy*, 20), or 'politely perplexing',[10] insofar as the narrator tends to 'juggle politely' with incompatible values which dutifully resist any kind of 'assimilation' or explanation.

It seems clear that the metamorphoses and contradictions of Beckett's characters are partially anticipated by Proustian 'indeterminates' such as Albertine, whom Marcel evokes in terms of 'cent' (III.479) (one hundred) Albertines, and in terms of 'des séries d'Albertines, séparées les unes des autres, incomplètes' (III.149) (many series of Albertines, separated one from the other, and incomplete). But whereas Marcel eventually manages to make some sense of most of his fellow characters (with the single and singular exception of Albertine), the narrator of *Dream of Fair to Middling Women* despairs of making the slightest sense of his offspring. As the reader discovers, 'Belacqua cannot be petrified in the moment of recoil, of back-wash into composure, any more than the rest of them' (110–11). 'At his simplest trine', Belacqua 'is no more satisfied by . . . three values . . . than he would be by fifty values, or any number of values' (111). To make matters worse, his very values are variable and unreliable, as the narrator vehemently complains:

Are they simple themselves? Like hell they are! Can we measure them once and for all like those imposters that they call mathematiciens? We can not. We can state them as a succession of terms, but we can't sum them and we can't define them. They tail off vaguely at both ends and the intervals of their series are demented. (111)

In this respect, Belacqua offers the very antithesis of the Proustian hero. As Beckett remarks in his essay on Proust, Marcel finally reveals himself to be a 'pure subject' (*PTD*, 90). For all his early confusions, Marcel eventually discovers the 'pure act of understanding' (*PTD*, 91) and thereby decodes the complexities of his existence, of Parisian society, and of such abstract questions as the nature of memory and of time. Belacqua, by contrast, remains an excruciatingly impure subject, as the narrator disconsolately observes in the course of elaborating yet another phase of his musical analogy. Alluding to his characters in terms male liŭ and female liū (or different kinds of notes), he reflects:

What is needed of course is a tuning-fork, faithful unto death . . . to mix with the treacherous liŭs and liūs and get a line on them. That is what we call being a liu on the grand scale . . . someone who could always be relied on for just one little squawk, ping!, just right, the right squawk in the right place, just one pure permanent liŭ or liū, sex no bar, and all might yet be well. Just one, only one, tuning-fork charlatan to move among the notes and size 'em up and steady 'em down and chain 'em together in some kind of nice little cantilena and then come along and consolidate the entire article with the ground-swell of its canto fermo. We picked Belacqua for the job, and now we find that he is not able for it. (112)

Like Belacqua, the narrator is quite incapable of functioning as a 'tuning fork' in the manner of the Modernist narrator-hero. While Proust's Marcel finds that music reveals 'the permanence of personality' and 'the reality of art' (*PTD*, 92), and in many respects orchestrates his narrative in a musical manner, with innumerable carefully interwoven themes, motifs and correspondences, the

narrator of *Dream of Fair to Middling Women* appears neither
willing nor able to 'size' and 'steady' and 'chain' his materials in
this kind of composition. On the contrary, he explicitly rejects
Marcel's musical aesthetic. Far from manifesting any enthusiasm
for the sonata, and far from asserting that such musical conventions permit the 'communication of souls' (III.258) and therefore afford paradigms for all authentic creativity, the narrator
dismisses the sonata as an inconsequential artifice that merely
prolongs the agonies of incompetent expression. Accordingly,
brevity is best. Thus, when faced with the annoyance of needing
to introduce the 'Syra-Cusa' — yet another of Belacqua's 'Fair to
Middling Women' — he tellingly explodes:

Why we want to drag in the Syra-Cusa at this juncture it passes our
persimmon to say. She belongs to another story, a short one . . . But she
remains . . . We could chain her up with the Smeraldina-Rima and the
little Alba . . . and make it look like a sonata, with recurrence of themes,
key signatures, plagal finale and all . . . She could be coaxed into most
anything . . . A paragraph ought to fix her. (43)

As the narrator has suggested, when referring to Belacqua's
inability to act as a 'tuning fork charlatan' (112), Belacqua is
similarly incapable of 'chaining' things together. While Marcel
finally unveils the secrets of 'Le Temps' (III.1048) (Time),
Belacqua's misadventures culminate in 'a panic of disorder'
which 'Gradually . . . got better' (214) as a voice, presumably
from some Dublin constable, 'enjoined him to move on'.[11]
Abruptly, and almost triumphantly announcing this short-
coming in his hero, the narrator comments: 'Had he any sense of
his responsibilities as an epic liŭ he would favour us now with an
incondite meditation on time. He has none and he does not'
(200). Not surprisingly then, Belacqua, like the narrator, resigns
himself to 'crazily spaced' creativity (111), conceding that if he
should ever happen to 'drop a book', it would be 'ramshackle,
tumbledown, a bone-shaker, held together with bits of twine'
(124). Just as the narrator dreams of resolving his creative crises
by deploying 'a curtain of silence as rapidly as possible' (100),
Belacqua contemplates equally nihilistic remedies when con-
fronted by the crises arising within the second major category of
experiences in this novel: the realm of human relationships.

Unlike the portrayal of the human condition in *A la recherche du
temps perdu*, *Dream of Fair to Middling Women* offers abundant
testimony to Beckett's suggestion, in *Proust*, that any two human
beings are doomed to remain 'two separate . . . dynamisms

related by no system of synchronisation' (*PTD*, 17). While the narrator dismisses Belacqua and the Alba as 'two separate non-synchronised processes' (149), Belacqua equally gloomily evokes their relationship as a 'slough of granny's bends' (152) and as a 'marsh of granny's bends' (157), suggesting that this liaison, like any book that he may eventually 'drop', is at best 'held together with bits of twine' (124). As the reader discovers, the 'essential incompatibility' (171) between Belacqua and the Alba springs from their respective repugnance for sexual and intellectual relationships. In this respect, they dramatize the conflict between mind and body that Beckett subsequently evokes more sparingly in terms of couples like Vladimir and Estragon, or in terms of tormented individuals such as Krapp.

The Alba confesses to finding her intellectual friends to be particularly complicated souls: 'I cannot have a simple relation with the cerebral type . . . I have to make it a mess and a knot and a tangle . . . So what's the good? It's too difficult to untie' (146). Exemplifying precisely this kind of 'cerebral type', Belacqua discovers that analogous, and indeed still more intense, confusions arise from his alternating desire and disdain for sexual initmacy. On the one hand, Belacqua seems to be indifferent to the Alba's physical charms, 'shrinking away from contact with the frail dust of her body' (172), and cordially inviting her to 'take a loiny cavalier servente . . . and leave me in peace' (17). These strategies appear to restrict his relationship with the Alba to a relatively uncomplicated platonic level, enabling him to conceive of her in terms of a vague, asexual identity. But, on the other hand, Belacqua finds that he consistently imagines that he is with the Alba when frequenting the prostitutes of Paris.

As a result, he confuses his initial, asexual image of the Alba with a subsequent, contradictory, erotic image, somewhat as Marcel confuses his nautical and his sexual images of Albertine. Or in William Burroughs's terms, Belacqua makes the mistake of 'cutting' a disturbing 'sex image' into his habitual concept of reality.[12] Attempting to superimpose the Alba's innocence upon the Parisian prostitute, and to 'extract from the whore that which was not whorish' (36), Belacqua confuses their differing realities so successfully that they become indistinguishable in their own terms. In other words, like Marcel before the intermingled images of Balbec, Albertine and Vinteuil's daughter, he finds himself 'cursed by some displaced faculty of assimilation' (36),[13] and abandoned to 'an abominable confusion, a fragmentation of the realities of her and him, of the reality in which she and he were related' (37). Resurrecting one of the key adjectives in *Proust* the narrator specifies that these confusions are 'intolerable' (36). And just as *Proust* argues that Marcel attempts to eliminate his intolerable confusions by effecting the 'ablation of desire' (*PTD*, 18) and by 'obliterating the faculty of suffering' (*PTD*, 63), the narrator of *Dream of Fair to Middling Women* explains that Belacqua similarly strives to seek solace by entering into 'a Limbo purged of desire' (38) in which he may perfect the 'neutralisation of needs' (107).

Most of Beckett's critics tend to conflate such concepts as the 'ablation of desire' and the 'obliterating of the faculty of suffering' with his celebrated reference to the artist's gesture of withdrawing from the outside world in order to immerse himself in the internal, microcosmic reality that he evokes as 'the core of the eddy' (*PTD*, 65). According to this interpretation of Beckett's works, his characters shrink from the suffering and the desires peculiar to the 'big world' of the macrocosm, so as to attain more profound self-awareness in the 'little world' of the mind. This generous approach to his writings ignores the fact that the impulse to obliterate the faculty of suffering necessarily entails the obliteration of *all* modes of non-habitual and microcosmic awareness. Briefly, the faculty of suffering is part of 'the free play of every faculty' (*PTD*, 20) and can only be obliterated when every other non-habitual faculty is obliterated, and the 'suffering of being' (*PTD*, 20) is replaced by the 'boredom of living' (*PTD*, 19). Not surprisingly, Belacqua's attempts to effect the 'ablation of desire' and the 'obliteration of the faculty of suffering' culminate in his nihilistic ambition to retreat from both macrocosmic *and* microcosmic reality.

Some indication of this complex ambition is given by the Alba, who remarks upon Belacqua's wish to avoid all contact both with other people and with himself, in terms of his 'dread of leze-personality, at his own hands or another's' (173) — a phrase which Beckett echoes in a letter to Thomas MacGreevy when describing his own life as 'a crescendo of disengagement of others and myself'.[14] Elaborating his own variation of this 'crescendo of disengagement' in somewhat more hermetic terms, Belacqua determines:

I shall separate myself and the neighbour from the moon, and the lurid place that he is from the lurid place that I am; then I need not go to the trouble of hating the neighbour. I shall extinguish also, by banning the torchlight in the city that is I, the fatiguing lust for self-emotion. (21)

Belacqua's images are, admittedly, a trifle obscure, but there is no mistaking his wish to detach himself both from his 'neighbour' and from himself. Anticipating the Unnamable's avowal, 'I've shut my doors against them, I'm not at home to anything', (*The Unnamable*, 395), he craves 'to find himself alone in a room . . . And troglodyse himself . . . locking the door, extinguishing, and being at home to nobody' (114). That this concept of 'nobody' includes both other people and himself is made perfectly plain when the narrator specifies that Belacqua longs for 'the emancipation from identity, his own and his neighbour's' (108).

Few critics seem to have paid attention to the significance of these statements, and it is usually argued that the Beckettian hero, like the ideal Proustian artist discussed in *Proust*, 'is active, but negatively, shrinking from the nullity of extracircumferential phenomena' and from 'the centrifugal force of self-fear, self-negation' (*PTD*, 65–6). Put another way, both the Beckettian hero and the Beckettian *oeuvre* are usually associated with a centripetal impulse towards essential self-knowledge. But, as the following absolutely fundamental passage from *Dream of Fair to Middling Women* stipulates, Belacqua is no more satisfied by centripetal existence (or the life of the mind) than he is satisfied by centrifugal existence (or life in society). Rather, he would achieve their mutual negation. Were it possible, he would 'live' no life at all. Offering repeated examples of Belacqua's wish to transcend both macrocosmic and microcosmic modes of existence, and to enter into the existential 'immunity' of states of 'neither' and of 'not', the narrator expostulates:

At his simplest he was trine. Just think of that. A trine man! Centripetal, centrifugal and . . . not. Phoebus chasing Daphne, Narcissus flying from Echo and . . . neither. Is that neat or is it not? The chase to Vienna, the flight from Paris, the slouch to Fulda, the relapse into Dublin and . . . immunity like hell from journeys and cities. The hand to Lucien and Liebert and the Syra-Cusa tendered and withdrawn and again tendered and again withdrawn and . . . hands forgotten. (107)

Incapable of attaining this ideal immunity from others and from the self, Belacqua becomes an unwilling fly in the web of human relationships. Lacking friendship, he suffers 'profoundly', because 'never, never by any chance at any time, did he mean anything at all to his inferiors' (113). Unlike Beckett's subsequent characters, Belacqua initially desires everyday social intercourse. Yet, as the narrator observes:

It is not so very wide of the mark to say that day after day, year in and out, he could enter at the same hour the same store to make some triflingly indispensable purchase ... and never know his assiduity to be recognised by as much as smile or a kind word or the smallest additional attention ... He had no success with the people, and he suffered profoundly in consequence. (113)

Distressed by 'this boycott' (114), Belacqua rapidly develops the eccentric misanthropic traits of the mature Beckettian hero (or, indeed, of Joycean 'Dubliners' like Mr James Duffy), [15] and the reader learns:

Children he abominated and feared. Dogs, for their obviousness, he despised and rejected, and cats he disliked, but cats less than dogs and children.

Such general suffering seems inconsequential, however, in comparison with the 'gehenna of sweats and fiascos and tears and ... absence of all douceness' (16) that Belacqua associates with his various love affairs. To some extent, his experience is prefigured by Marcel's exposure to the 'Albertine tragedy'. Unlike Belacqua, however, Marcel might be defined as a fly in both the web of human relationships and the consoling ointment of human relationships, since his painful experience of the torments of passionate love are to some extent relieved by the benevolent love that he receives from his grandmother, and by the selfless friendship offered by Saint-Loup.

Unacquainted with such positive human relationships, Belacqua rejects friendship and love as utterly as he abandons any hope of ever composing an orderly novel. This wholesale rejection of human intercourse, with its concomitant commitment to the ideal of troglodysing the self and entering into a state of 'neither' and 'not', overlaps with his equally nihilistic response to his third main category of experience: the realm of intense modes of self-perception. This complicated aspect of Belacqua's existence is best introduced obliquely, with reference to Beckett's short story entitled 'Assumption' (1929). [16]

Somewhat as Beckett's *Proust* distinguishes between the relatively unthreatening 'boredom' of habitual 'living' (*PTD*, 19) and the extremely threatening, intolerable quality of non-habitual modes of 'being' (*PTD*, 20), the narrator of 'Assumption' very interestingly differentiates between habitual and non-habitual forms of art in terms of 'the pleasure of Prettiness' and 'the pain of Beauty' (269). Elaborating this distinction, he observes:

Before no supreme manifestation of Beauty do we proceed comfortably
up a staircase of sensation, and sit down mildly on the topmost stair to
digest our gratification: such is the pleasure of Prettiness. We are taken
up bodily and pitched breathless on the peak of a sheer crag: which is
the pain of Beauty. (269)

In other words, habitual perceptions are equated rather
derisively with 'pleasure', 'comfort', and the mildly disturbing
activity of climbing up a relatively orderly and relatively pretty
'staircase of sensation'; whereas non-habitual perceptions, or
the intensity of beauty, provoke the shock of 'pain'.

To some extent, this distinction finds certain counterparts in *A
la recherche du temps perdu*. For example, Marcel associates
creativity — or creative and authentic modes of perception —
with 'la pente abrupte de l'introspection' (the steep slope of
introspection), while he dismisses the less profound fancies of
the imagination in terms of 'la pente aisée de l'imagination'
(III.465) (the gentle slope of the imagination). Hereafter, all
resemblances between the Proustian vision and the Beckettian
vision abruptly terminate. For while Proust associates non-
habitual introspection with a beatific sense of revelation, Beckett
emphasizes the painful quality of such non-habitual insights.
Beckett's *Proust* refers to the 'intolerable brightness' (*PTD*, 70) of
the Proustian revelation; 'Assumption' emphasizes 'the pain' of
non-habitual beauty; and in much the same way, *Dream of Fair
to Middling Women* contrasts the discomforts of habitual,
'workaday glare' (170) with excruciating modes of 'inward glare'
(110).

This 'inward glare' accompanies four principal kinds of non-
habitual awareness or remembrance: those evoking doomed
love, those attending the creative impulse, those precipitated by
music, and those permitting authentic self-knowledge. Far from
welcoming such manifestations of 'the free play of every faculty'
(*PTD*, 20), Belacqua makes every attempt to curtail them as
rapidly as possible, and to retreat to the antithetical realm of
habitual experience. Better still, he would eliminate all
consciousness and savour what he variously defines as 'wombtomb' (39), as 'the slush of angels' (108), as 'the gift of blindness'
(162), and as 'the Dark Night of the Soul' (165).

Belacqua suffers 'from time to time' from painful memories of
the Smeraldina-Rima, an affliction diagnosed by the narrator's
cynical and clinical comment:

She continued to bother him as an infrequent jolt of sentimental heart-burn, nothing to write home about. Better, he thought, the odd belch than the permanent gripe. (97)

While Marcel experiences comparable memories of Albertine in *A la recherche du temps perdu*, he qualifies them as being both painful and pleasurable, experiencing 'les souvenirs de ses trahisons . . . en même temps que ceux de sa douceur' (III.535) (memories of her deceptions . . . along with those of her affection). Later Beckettian heroes, such as Krapp, also recollect positive and negative memories of love. But as a novel equating love and memories of love with 'an absence of all douceness' (16),[17] *Dream of Fair to Middling Women* treats such sentiments more simply, as symptoms of the undesirability of intense perceptions.

Belacqua's responses to the literary muse serve a similar function. Far from suggesting that Belacqua savours the 'ecstasy' (*PTD*, 76) that Beckett associates with Marcel's 'joies artistiques' (III.892) (artistic joys), the narrator of *Dream of Fair to Middling Women* implies that his creative impulses have more in common with the panic-stricken 'fizz of scampering birds' (137) contem-plated by the Alba. Apparently operating as a force destroying tranquillity, 'the mind achieving creation' is characterized in terms of the deplorable transition from the placidity of the 'mind . . . entombed' to its frenzy when 'active in an anger and a rhapsody of energy, in a scurrying and plunging towards exitus' (14). And whereas Marcel values inspiration precisely because it portends artistic immortality and resurrection, and thereby rescues the artist from the obscurity of the tomb, Belacqua desires nothing so much as to be mentally 'entombed'. Accordingly, he deplores all modes of mental resurrection, just as his chum 'the Polar Bear' deplores physical resurrection and rails against the 'megalomaniacal impertinence' of Christ's 'interference in the affairs of his friend Lazarus' (187).

It is scarcely surprising, then, that Belacqua has little regard for the evocative power of music. Whereas Marcel experiences 'une joie ineffable qui semblait venir du paradis' (III.260) (an ineffable joy that seemed to come from paradise) before Vinteuil's 'céleste phrase' (III.258) (celestial phrase), Belacqua suffers from unforgettable musical morsels in much the same way that he suffers from 'sentimental heartburn' (97), finding one particular phrase to be 'moaning in his memory' and 'coming now to a head in . . . a stress of remembrance' (204). By accident or design, the narrator of *Dream of Fair to Middling Women* additionally

derides the Modernist writer's characteristic reverence for music
by repeatedly making mocking references to 'grace-notes' (a
concept which Joyce's *A Portrait of the Artist as a Young Man* and
Beckett's *Proust* both employ as an index of artistic value)[18] in
terms of 'the shakes and grace-note strangulations' of Chopin (12
and 61). If music affords a salutary 'catalytic element' (*PTD*, 92)
in the work of Proust, it merely serves to increase Belacqua's
perceptual torments in *Dream of Fair to Middling Women*.

As one might expect, Proustian values are once again reversed
in those passages describing Belacqua's experience of the
'inward glare' of intense, non-habitual self-awareness. This
process becomes particularly clear if one traces the ways in which
Beckett's presentation of Belacqua's sufferings redeploy a
number of Proustian images, such as the 'fish', 'tunnel' and
'light' images that are used in the contexts of the perceptual
illusions and delusions of Charlus and Marcel. While these
images are not usually considered by Proust's critics, they are
consistently underlined and annotated in Beckett's copies of *A la
recherche du temps perdu*.

Proust's most memorable 'fish' image probably appears in the
following passage, in which Marcel meditates upon the
disadvantages of Charlus's eccentric perceptual categories, and
compares him with:

le poisson qui croit que l'eau où il nage s'étend au delà du verre de son
aquarium qui lui en présente le reflet, tandis qu'il ne voit pas à côté de
lui, dans l'ombre ... le pisciculteur tout-puissant qui, au moment
imprévu et fatal ... le tirera sans pitié du mileu où il aimait vivre pour
le rejeter dans un autre. (II.1049)
(the fish that thinks that the water in which it is swimming extends
beyond the reflecting glass walls of its aquarium, while failing to notice,
right beside it, in the shadow ... the all-powerful pisciculturist, who, at
some unforseen and fatal moment ... will mercilessly pluck it from its
happy habitat in order to cast it into another one.)

Specifying that 'le pisciculteur, à Paris, sera Mme Verdurin'
(II.1049) (the pisciculturist, in Paris, was to be Mme Verdurin),
Marcel hints that Charlus might have protected himself from the
machinations of this dreadful schemer, had he interpreted
Parisian society more objectively, rather than naively living in
the world of his own megalomaniacal fantasies. Put another
way, Proust's Baron de Charlus, like Sir Walter Scott's Baron
Bradwardine,[19] is guilty of living in the past — and in a highly
fanciful and idiosyncratic version of the past at that — rather than

coming to terms with the hazards of the present, in which a sadistic social climber like Mme Verdurin can make mincemeat of egotistical aristocrats who tend to misinterpret everything 'au point de vue de l'art' (II.1106) (from an artistic point of view).

This passage must have impressed Beckett considerably. He not only annotated these lines with the comment 'Frequent image',[20] but also subsequently elaborated his own variant of it in *Dream of Fair to Middling Women*, in conjunction with his variants of the 'tunnel' and 'light' imagery that Marcel employs when describing his despair after the flight of Albertine. Marcel equates his despair with the darkness of a tunnel, and evokes his occasional relief from this misery in terms of moments when:

le noir tunnel sous lequel ma pensée rêvassait ... s'interrompait brusquement d'un intervalle de soleil ... et comme une fleur qui s'entr'ouvre, j'éprouvais la fraîcheur rajeunissante d'une exfoliation. (III.534)
(the black tunnel in which my thoughts drifted ... was suddenly punctuated by a burst of sunshine ... and like a flower unfolding its leaves, I felt the refreshing relief of an exfoliation.)

Belacqua's devotion to the comforting torpor of the mind 'enwombed and entombed' (4) makes him particularly intolerant of such 'brèves illuminations' (III.534) (brief illuminations).

As the narrator of *Dream of Fair to Middling Women* explains, Belacqua is happiest of all when he finds 'the glare of understanding switched off', and is able to take refuge from all kinds of consciousness 'in the umbra, the tunnel, when the mind went wombtomb' (39). Far from welcoming the kind of sunny interval that Marcel finds so refreshing in *his* tunnel, Belacqua contentedly reflects that for most of the time his tunnel protects him from 'the glare of living', and that 'punctuation from the alien shaft was infrequent and then, thanks to his ramparts, mild' (40). These 'ramparts' are 'a string or earthworks' that Belacqua builds 'to break ... the ebb of him to people and things' (38), an edifice which begs a number of comparisons between Proust's and Beckett's values.

Firstly, whereas Marcel deplores the way in which Charlus complacently hides from exterior reality within the walls of his 'aquarium', the narrator of *Dream of Fair to Middling Women* freely commiserates with Belacqua's impulse to sustain a state of perceptual indolence within the 'umbra' of his 'tunnel'. Secondly, as the narrator explains in the course of elaborating a crustacean variation of Marcel's 'fish' image, the 'diver' (*PTD*,

32) of involuntary memory seems not so much the positive force
that Beckett's essay on Proust associates with the 'salvage' (*PTD*,
32) of 'the essence of ourselves, the best of the many of our
selves' (*PTD*, 31), as the deplorable source of 'pestilential
consciousness' (149). As the reader discovers, Belacqua's
involuntary memories are derisively described in terms of
'furious divers' (108) that 'used to drive him crazy, the way a crab
would be that was hauled out of its dim pool into the pestiferous
sunlight . . . and set to fry in the sun' (40).

Like Marcel's tante Léonie, Belacqua becomes the victim of
nightmarish self-awareness. Having once savoured his own
peculiar paradise within his own peculiar tunnel, he suddenly
discovers unwelcome gleams of non-habitual introspection, and
never fully recovers the kind of comfortable gloom that tante
Léonie rather similarly enjoys in her initial 'absolute inertia'
(I.50). In the narrator's elegiac formulae, 'He remembers the
pleasant gracious bountiful tunnel, and cannot get back' (110).

These words require slight qualification. On one occasion,
towards the end of the novel, Belacqua briefly rediscovers
something approximating to the pleasures of his tunnel, when
blessed by a 'whale of a miracle' with the curious 'gift of
blindness' (162). As the narrator explains, this 'miracle' offers a
singularly Beckettian 'mystical experience', insofar as it leaves
Belacqua 'vacated' (162) rather than filled with a more conventional mystical plenitude. Apprehending 'A void place and a
spacious nothing', he attains 'the apex of ecstasy . . . furnished
by . . . the Dark Night of the Soul' (165). As one might suspect,
and as the narrator of *Dream of Fair to Middling Women* carefully
explains, this nihilistic ecstasy offers the very antithesis of the
'radiant . . . bright . . . luminous . . . mystical experience' (*PTD*,
70, 71 and 75) that Beckett associates with the Proustian miracle
of involuntary memory.

Blessed by the gift of something approximating to authorial
omnipotence, the narrator makes so bold as to draw the reader's
attention to 'a red-letter term in the statement of Belaqua':

a phrase he let fall on the way back to the city after a disastrous day on
the course, a phrase that we propose now to the reader as a red-letter
term in the statement of Belacqua and a notable arc of his circumscription. "Behold, Mr Beckett" he said, whitely, "a dud mystic."
(165–6)

On this occasion, the narrator's estimate of his own analytical
capacities is surely over-modest. This notorious 'red-letter term

in the statement of Belacqua' is not simply 'a notable arc of his circumscription', but rather a notable circumscription of Belacqua, and indeed of almost every one of Beckett's brigade of dud mystics. Like Belacqua, Beckett's successive heroes — or anti-heroes — invariably exemplify the plights of the doubly 'dud' mystic. Firstly, their finest visions are 'dud', insofar as they reveal 'nothing'; and secondly, their mysticism proves 'dud', insofar as it proves incapable of duplicating this comfortingly vacuous 'vision'.

Like almost all of Beckett's subsequent characters, Belacqua responds to the frustrations of this 'dud mysticism' by vainly attempting to realize two wildly paradoxical alternatives to 'pestilential consciousness' (149). Firstly, he tries to consciously contemplate unconsciousness, by somehow or other keeping 'his mind a blank' with 'all the candles quenched but one' (76). Over and over again, Beckett's characters rephrase this ambition. The narrator of *How It Is* rapturously refers to 'brief blanks good moments brief blacks',[21] while Moran, one of the narrators in *Molloy*, somewhat more explicitly longs to be 'incapable of motion ... mute ... deaf ... blind ... your memory a blank! And just enough brain intact to allow you to exult' (*Molloy*, 140–141). As recently as 1983, the highly abstract cogitations of the narrator of *Worstward Ho* have reiterated similar sentiments:

Remains of mind then still. Enough still. Somewhose somewhere somehow enough still. No mind and words? Even such words. So enough still. Just enough still to joy. Joy! Just enough still to joy that only they. Only! (*WH*, 29)

And in much the same way, the narrator of *Ill seen ill said* (1981) concludes his narrative by pleading for 'One moment more. One last. Grace to know that void. Know happiness' (*Isis*, 59).

Secondly, Belacqua endeavours to attain this conscious unconsciousness by means of the equally paradoxical process of willfully abolishing the will, an ambition that he recognizes to be the 'worse than stupid' desire to 'mechanise what was a dispensation' (110). As we have remarked, Marcel partly prefigures this second aspiration when he refers to the way in which 'l'intelligence ... abdique par raisonnement' (III.423) (the intelligence ... abdicates rationally), so as to make way for more profound, extra-rational modes of self-realization, after first eliminating lesser, habitual distractions. This concept obviously envisages the existence of a positive variant of the intelligence permitting mankind certain modes of self-determination; a possibility quite at odds with Beckett's suggestion that Proust's fictional cosmos is grotesquely 'predetermined' (*PTD*, 89). Insisting that Belacqua is equally incapable of voluntary self-determination, the narrator explains:

> But the wretched Belacqua was not free and therefore . . . could not will and gain his enlargement from the gin-palace of willing . . . It was impossible to switch off the inward glare, wilfully to suppress the bureaucratic mind. It was stupid to imagine that he could be organised as Limbo and wombtomb, worse than stupid . . . How could the will be abolished in its own tension? . . . The will and nill cannot suicide, they are not free to suicide. (109–10)

Belacqua 'leaves the rails' (110) precisely because he is 'Convinced like a fool' that it *is* possible 'to induce at pleasure a state so desirable' (109). He has not yet learned the crucial Beckettian dictum that there is 'nothing to be done' (although the narrator is certainly no stranger to this maxim, and freely confesses that 'we cannot do anything for him' (110)).

Over and over again, Beckett's successive heroes are subjected to the unpredictable, incomprehensible and uncontrollable alternating currents of habitual torpor and non-habitual torment. As they rapidly discover, there is quite literally nothing to be done. They cannot consciously contemplate unconsciousness, and cannot wilfully nullify their will. At best, they may simply resign themselves to the fate that Belacqua's friend Lucien defines as 'le calme plat ponctué . . . de vertigineuses éjaculations . . . de clarté' (19) (calm stretches punctuated . . . by vertiginous ejaculations . . . of clarity). In much the same way, Molloy's respective French and English narratives evoke existence as 'une torpeur miséricordieuse traversée de brefs et abominables éclairs' (*Molloy* 81), and as 'a deep and merciful torpor shot through with brief abominable gleams' (*Molloy*, 54).

Nevertheless, despite the failure of their attempts to consciously and wilfully extirpate their consciousness and will, Beckett's heroes take recourse to one other survival strategy: the attempt to inhibit intense non-habitual introspection by distracting themselves with habitual routines. These routines are usually both mental and physical in quality, and range from the peculiarly symmetrical structure of their stories, songs and jokes, to the peculiarly symmetrical movements with which they 'come and go'. In many respects these verbal and physical routines find their prefiguration in the invariable 'traintrain' (I.110) of tante Léonie's nihilistic lifestyle. [22]

While Belacqua never really emulates tante Léonie's capacity to generate endless stories in 'un perpétuel monologue' (I.50) (a perpetual monologue), his thoughts certainly approximate to tante Léonie's repetitive mental routines when he reduces them to the 'boomerangs of ... fantasy' (38). These mental 'boomerangs' appear to be comfortingly uncomplicated concepts which he releases 'unanxiously', and which, meeting no opposition or contradiction, 'return with the trophy of an echo' (38).

Considered in the context of 'Dante ... Bruno. Vico .. Joyce', Belacqua's 'boomerangs' have the dubious distinction of being superficially 'soothing, like the contemplation of a carefully folded ham-sandwich'. [23] It is to precisely this kind of 'carefully folded' pastime that Beckett's heroes invariable turn in their vain efforts to relieve their condition. Thus in *More Pricks Than Kicks* (1934), Belacqua's namesake entertains himself with a kind of boomerang shuffle, opting for the 'simplest form of ... exercise ... boomerang, out and back' (*MPTK*, 40). Somewhat later, the narrator-heroes of Beckett's trilogy perfect the boomerang hypotheses that Molloy dubs 'dutiful confusions' (*Molloy*, 15), or else devote themselves to the boomeranging symmetries of the mathematical problems that 'the arty Countess of Parabimbi' condemns in *Dream of Fair to Middling Women* as being 'so infernally finical and nice ... like working out how many pebbles in Tom Thumb's pocket' (192).

Belacqua and the narrator of *Dream of Fair to Middling Women* are probably the least 'finical' of Beckett's fictional progeny. Neither of them shares their mature counterparts' passion for manic mathematical calculations, and neither of them really experiences the kind of excruciating verbal crisis that drives the later narrator-heroes to the distraction of 'carefully folded' narratives. Indeed, on occasion they contemplate symptoms of 'Words and images run riot' (*Malone Dies*, 198) with considerable good humour.

For example, when witnessing the Smeraldina-Rima's 'ropes and ropes of logorrhoea streaming out in a gush', the narrator pronounces this spectacle 'extremely amusing' (11–12), rather than raising his hands to the heavens in ever-decreasing despair, like the 'auditor' in *Not I*. And even though he is often at a loss for words, the narrator frequently glosses over this dilemma by making such light-hearted comments as: 'flying, there is no other word for it, about their business' (206). On other occasions, the narrator even goes so far as to applaud his own polysyllabic formulations, punctuating his narrative with such triumphant parentheses as, 'crucible of volatilisation (bravo!)' (103), and 'tumultuous coenaesthesis (bravo!)' (28). Belacqua, too, seems sensitive to verbal felicity, and pauses to remark that the phrase 'Black diamond of pessimism' is 'a nice example, in the domain of words, of the little sparkle hid in ashen' (42).

All things considered, the narrator and Belacqua appear to become most disenchanted before language when they look beyond such concise verbal niceties, and ponder upon the difficulties of writing novels. Belacqua's gravest doubts on this score lead him to speculate that:

The experience of my reader shall be between the phrases, in the silence, communicated by the intervals, not the terms, of the statement . . . his experience shall be the menace, the miracle, the memory of an unspeakable trajectory. (123)

Despite its somewhat threatening allusion to a sense of 'menace', this recipe for the 'miracle' of an 'unspeakable' fiction seems surprisingly compatible with confidence in the act of writing. Proust, for example, praised Gérard de Nerval precisely because his works reveal 'l'inexprimable' (the inexpressible), not so much in verbal terms as 'entre les mots' (*CSB*, 242) (between his words), thereby approximating to the kind of art of 'intervals' that Beckett has in mind; and he similarly celebrated the solemnity which emerges 'Entre les phrases' (Between the sentences), and 'dans l'intervalle qui les sépare' (*CSB*, 193) (in the interval between them), in certain ancient and biblical writings.

Beckett, in turn, applauds the fragmentary quality of Proust's narrative in 'Proust in Pieces' (1934), suggesting that its originality resides in 'the perturbations and dislocations of the text'.[24] Writing to Axel Kaun three years later, Beckett once again advocates an art of silences and pauses:

Gibt es irgendeinen Grund, warum jene fürchterlich willkürliche Materialität der Wortfläche nicht aufgelöst werden sollte, wie z.B. die von grossen schwarzen Pausen gefressene Tonfläche in der siebten Symphonie von Beethoven, so dass wir sie ganze Seiten durch nicht anders wahrnehmen können als etwa einen schwindelnden unergründliche Schlünde von Stillschweigen verknüpfenden Pfad von Lauten? (Is there any reason why that terrible materiality of the word surface should not be capable of being dissolved, like for example the sound surface, torn by enormous pauses, of Beethoven's seventh symphony, so that through whole pages we can perceive nothing but a path of sounds suspended in giddy heights, linking unfathomable abysses of silences?)[25]

It should be clear, then, that the general tone of *Dream of Fair to Middling Women* is remarkably optimistic. In between its more specific delineations of Belacqua's various crises this novel generates an almost Joycean enthusiasm for the rich potential of language. Thus, when a Leipzig prostitute proffers the exclamatory tongue-twister, 'Himmisacrakrüzidirkenjesusmariaundjosefundblütigeskreuz!', the narrator turns a blind eye — or deaf ear — to the Beckettian conviction that 'There is no communication' (*PTD*, 64) and approvingly ejaculates: 'All in one word! The things people come out with sometimes!' (213).

At this point, some comment must be made regarding the form and the content of Beckett's work. Although it is very tempting to suggest that Beckett, like Joyce, creates works in which 'form is content' and 'content is form',[26] it is extremely misleading to equate form and content in his work. Sometimes this *seems* to be the case, insofar as both the form and content of his writing might lend themselves to some general definition, such as 'minimal art'.[27] *Waiting for Godot*, for example, encloses a minimum of action within an extremely simple binary structure. When examined more rigorously, however, the inimitable impact of Beckett's work appears to derive not so much from a coincidence between form and content, as from the dynamic tension between different kinds of form and content.

Thus while Beckett's works undoubtedly evince a continual formal optimism, insofar as they continually explore unusual formal conventions within the fictional, dramatic, poetic and cinematic arts, single-minded emphasis upon this formal trait tends to distract the reader from the peculiarly Beckettian vision expressed by his writings. In the case of *Dream of Fair to Middling Women*, this kind of 'formal' reading might misleadingly lead one to assume that this novel is a predominantly playful, and therefore predominantly optimistic, piece of early Post-Modern fiction. At one level, it *is* a formally playful, optimistic novel. But at another level, it is peculiarly pessimistic. The crucial tension between the formal vivacity and the thematic misanthropy of *Dream of Fair to Middling Women* can best be illustrated by examining its curious conclusion.

Although Belacqua's adventures come to their conclusion

when a voice, 'slightly more in sorrow than in anger', enjoins
him to move on, 'which, the pain being so much better, he was
only happy to do' (214b), the most haunting image in these last
few paragraphs appears just before his final 'panic of discomfort'
(214), as the narrator muses:

But the wind had fallen, as it so often does with us after midnight . . .
and the rain fell in a uniform untroubled manner. It fell upon the bay,
the champaign-land and the mountains, and notably upon the central
bog it fell with a rather desolate uniformity. (213)

Considered in terms of general, rhetorical conventions, this
description seems most notable for its onomatopoeic quality. The
repetition of soft sounds such as 'fallen' and 'fell' clearly
corresponds in tone with their evocation of 'uniform untroubled'
rain.

Viewed within a more precise, comparative context, this
passage becomes definable as an imitation of the equally
onomatopoeic paragraph in which James Joyce evokes softly
falling snow at the end of his story 'The Dead':

A few light taps upon the pane made him turn to the window. It had
begun to snow again. He watched sleepily the flakes, silver and dark,
falling obliquely against the lamplight. The time had come for him to set
out on his journey westward. Yes, the newpapers were right: snow was
general all over Ireland. It was falling on the dark central plain, on the
treeless hills, falling softly upon the Bog of Allen and, farther westward,
softly falling into the dark mutinous Shannon waves. It was falling, too,
upon every part of the lonely churchyard on the hill where Michael
Furey lay buried. It lay thickly drifted on the crooked crosses and
headstones, on the spears of the little gate, on the barren thorns. His
soul swooned slowly as he heard the snow falling faintly through the
universe and faintly falling, like the descent of their last end, upon all
the living and the dead. [28]

However, as William Burroughs has conveniently remarked,
this passage seems likely to have influenced any number of
writers, insofar as 'everyone, every writer, has passages like
that'.[29] Burroughs's point is that certain passages in the work of
great Modernist writers such as Joyce invariably resound in some
way or another in Post-Modern writing. In this respect, it does
not help very much to simply state that Beckett's evocation of
'untroubled' rain exhibits formal parallels with Joyce's elegiac
prose. The same observation might equally well be made with
reference to Burroughs's fiction. In other words, any discussion

of the implications of Beckett's work necessitates analysis of the way in which its content differs from formally similar texts by predecessors such as Joyce or by contemporaries such as Burroughs.

As one might expect, Burroughs's variations on the ending of 'The Dead' tend to evoke hallucinatory images of urban disorder, such as the following description from *Dead Fingers Talk*:

He listened for a moment then stepped quickly down the stairs — In the doorway he stumbled over a pile of rags that smelled of urine and pulque — Empty streets and from radios in empty houses a twanging sound of sirens that rose and fell vibrating the windows — The air was full of luminous grey flakes falling softly on crumpled cloth bodies — The street led to an open square — He could see people running now suddenly collapse on to a heap of clothes — The grey flakes were falling heavier, falling through all the buildings of the city — [30]

Becoming more and more abstract, and intermingling cryptic allusions to Burroughs's preoccupations with 'image' and 'old film sets' among such Joycean adjectives and images as 'silver', 'flakes' and the process of 'raining down', this episode concludes:

Panic through streets of image — Dead nitrous streets of an old film set — Paper moon and muslin trees in the black silver sky great rents as the cover of the world rained down in luminous film flakes. (172)

As we have remarked, Burroughs perceptively contrasts the 'inward' quality of Beckett's writing with the 'outward' concerns of his own writing. [31] The predominantly 'outward' register of Burroughs's oneiric vision of cosmic destruction, as 'the cover of the world rained down in luminous film flakes', typifies the apocalyptic impulse in Post-Modern fiction, and, more particularly, the ways in which Burroughs's use of urban and cinematic imagery have transformed Joyce's optimistic blend of symbolism and pantheism into a curiously poetic vision of global chaos. At the same time, Burroughs's distinction points to the ways in which Beckett's work typifies the solipsistic impulse in Post-Modern fiction by transforming the harmonious unity of the Joycean epiphany into the 'inward' chaos of the narrator-hero's tormented consciousness.

The ending of 'The Dead' emphasizes the way in which the soothing spectacle of snow gently falling upon 'all the living and the dead' offers the protagonist a certain insight into his existence, as 'His soul swooned slowly', and helps to free him from the 'paralysis'[32] that Joyce associated with Dublin by prompting him 'to set out on his journey westward'. But the ending of *Dream of Fair to Middling Women* reveals that the prospect of 'uniform untroubled' rain provokes quite antithetical consequences in Beckettian Dublin. Voyaging neither north-wards, southwards, eastwards or westwards, Belacqua finds himself immobilized by physical discomfort, and he remains convinced that he has 'no choice but to sit down on the streaming pavement' (214), until that point at the end of the novel when he is enjoined to move on, and accepts to do so. Far from suggesting that Belacqua's meditations before falling rain afford the kind of solace and self-knowledge that Joyce's Dubliner attains before the prospect of falling snow, the narrator of *Dream of Fair to Middling Women* intimates that this kind of cloudy spectacle merely exacerbates perceptual confusion.

While the first lines of the narrator's description of 'untroubled rain' might be interpreted as a reverent imitation of Joyce's visionary evocation of 'snow . . . all over Ireland', the remainder of the narrator's description remorselessly trivializes its precursor. Having set the scene in a Joycean manner, the narrator systematically 'unsets' it in the Beckettian manner, interjecting:

What would Ireland be, though, without this rain of hers. Rain is part of her charm. The impression one enjoys before landscape in Ireland, even on the clearest of days, of seeing it through a veil of tears . . . to what source can this benefit be ascribed if not to our incontinent skies? (213)

Arguably, this speculation merely mocks the pantheistic impulse of Modernists like Joyce and Proust. It acknowledges that nature has charms, but insists upon belittling nature in terms of its 'incontinent skies'. By contrast, the next section of this commentary strikes a more serious blow at the metaphorical poetics of Modernism. Suggesting that clouds are clouds, and that hills are hills, the narrator argues that only those suffering from acute nostalgia could possibly derive satisfaction from confusions between cloud formations and hill formations. In the narrator's terms:

Standing on the Big Sugarloaf, it may be objected . . . the Welsh Hills are frequently plainly to be discerned. Don't cod yourselves. Those are clouds that you see, or your own nostalgia. (213)

This cryptic observation appears to refer to the claim that 'the Welsh Hills' may sometimes be discerned from Ireland: a possibility that the narrator of *Watt* might dismiss as 'so much Irish' (*Watt*, 167), and which the narrator of *Dream of Fair to Middling Women* attributes to the impact of clouds upon the nostalgic imagination. In much the same way, the narrator of *Company* alludes to a similar vision: 'East beyond the sea the faint shape of high mountain. Seventy miles away according to your Longman' (*Company*, 33). He adds that his listeners ridiculed his first account of this vision on the grounds that he was confusing land with sky. In this narrator's terms: 'You told them and were derided. All you had seen was cloud' (*Company*, 33). For the Beckettian protagonist, clouds have no silver lining, but merely compound the difficulties of interpreting and communicating reality.

By contrast, Modernist narrator-heroes like Proust's Marcel take particular delight in 'ces illusions optiques dont notre vision première est faite' (I.838) (those optical illusions which make up our first impressions), and, at the drop of a hat, make ecstatic metaphorical mileage out of this kind of ambiguity. Indeed, Proust's early essay entitled 'Les nuages' (Clouds) (of 1885–86) positively boils over with enthusiasm as its author ardently exclaims:

O beaux nuages, merci de toutes les consolations que vous avez données aux malheureux. Car votre approache les a remplis de cette mélancolie rêveuse, de cette tristesse poétique qui seule peut adoucir les douleurs qu'on ne peut pas calmer. (*CSB*, 329)
(Oh beautiful clouds, thank you for all the comfort that you have given to those who are unhappy. For your approach fills them with that melancholy reverie, with that poetic sadness which alone may palliate our uncalmable sufferings.)

As *Dream of Fair to Middling Women* suggests, Beckett's fiction depicts a world in which 'uncalmable sufferings' find little palliation. At best, Belacqua unexpectedly 'troglodyses' both his body and his mind, transcends both macrocosmic and microcosmic reality, and enters the 'transcendental gloom' (5) which forms the perfect antidote to his more frequent exposure to the equally non-habitual gleams of 'pestilential consciousness' (149). At worst, Belacqua realizes that he can do nothing to attain this nihilistic idyll, and helplessly hovers between the habitual world of mental and physical 'boomerang' exercises and the non-habitual world of intolerable self-awareness.

Failing to find a publisher for *Dream of Fair to Middling Women*, Beckett revised, refined and expanded its grim fictional cosmos in the short stories collected as *More Pricks Than Kicks* (1934) and in his first published novel *Murphy* (1938). Like *Dream of Fair to Middling Women*, these two subsequent volumes evince the fascinating tension between the playful formal qualities of Beckett's fiction, and the unswervingly misanthropic content deriving from his conviction that there is 'nothing to be done'.

10

THE EVOLUTION OF BECKETT'S EARLY FICTIONAL VISION IN *MORE PRICKS THAN KICKS* AND *MURPHY*

The ten short stories collected in *More Pricks Than Kicks* were published in 1934, two years after Beckett began *Dream of Fair to Middling Women*, and three years after the publication of Beckett's *Proust*.[1] These stories duplicate some of the lighter episodes from *Dream of Fair to Middling Women*, and likewise, present an indolent hero named Belacqua, who 'must be left strictly alone' and who 'must be left in absolute tranquillity' until 'his mind got . . . still' (10). At the same time, *More Pricks Than Kicks* complements its portrayal of Belacqua's mental misadventures with innumerable allusions to the fiasco of physical existence, along with hints that the torments of the mind survive the demise of the body. Like 'Echo's Bones', an unpublished short story that Beckett wrote some time between 1934 and 1935, *More Pricks Than Kicks* intimates that 'The Dead die hard'.[2]

These themes become particularly explicit in 'Dante and the Lobster', the first of the stories in *More Pricks Than Kicks*, in which Belacqua's sympathy for his supper distracts him from the Dantesque quality of his own mental existence. This story begins by describing Belacqua's vulnerability to the 'inward glare' (*Dream*, 110) of poetic ambiguity. Reading Dante's *Divine Comedy*, Belacqua finds himself compulsively 'running his brain against (an) impenetrable passage' which leaves him 'so bogged that he could move neither backward nor forward' (9). Next, as the story's second paragraph reveals, Belacqua responds to the 'workaday glare' (*Dream*, 170) of the macrocosmic world, when the 'midday strike' (9) provokes an almost Pavlovian response to 'Three large obligations . . . First lunch, then the lobster, then the Italian lesson' (10). From this point on, he becomes more and more aware of the differences between the physical and mental poles of his existence.

As he prepares burned toast for his midday cheese sandwich,

Belacqua unfolds 'an old Herald' and chances upon an article
announcing the imminent execution of 'McCabe the assassin'
(10). Further symptoms of mortality and corruption accompany
his peregrinations. Upon entering a grocery shop to purchase
cheese, he carefully orders 'a good green stenching rotten lump
of Gorgonzola' (14), and upon approaching his aunt's garden,
after his Italian lesson, his eyes espy 'whatever flowers die at that
time of year' (20. The story ends as he learns to his horror that the
lobster that he has collected for his aunt has 'about thirty seconds
to live' before 'going alive into scalding water' (21).

At this point, Belacqua appears to attain painful intimations of
mortality. Rapt in an almost Joycean epiphany, he piously
thinks: 'Well ... it's a quick death, God help us all' — an
alarmingly optimistic speculation which immediately incites the
narrator to intervene and exercise authorial veto by adding: 'It is
not' (21). As the remainder of the stories indicate, the body may
well degenerate, but the mind encounters neither a quick death,
nor a long, lingering death like some 'stenching rotten lump of
Gorgonzola' (14). Rather, the mind seems permanently 'bogged'
(9) in existence. Or, put another way, the mind's excruciating
essence exceeds the body's existence. When physical existence
ends, another reincarnated physical existence, or else a ghostly
variant of reincarnation within the realm of the dead, continues
to nurture the essential 'inward glare' of the mind.

In 'What a Misfortune' Belacqua attains intimations of
precisely this kind of mental immortality. Transfixed by 'an overwhelming sense that all this would happen to him again, in a
dream or subsequent existence' (159), he discovers the
inescapable, Dantesque quality of his fate. Not surprisingly, his
world-weary teacher, 'the Ottolenghi', tires of guiding him
through *The Divine Comedy*, and pounces upon the innocently
owlish question 'Where were we?' (19) with the impatient
rejoinder 'Where are we ever? ... where we were, as we were'
(20). For such 'microcosmopolitans' (*Murphy*, 163), there is no
such thing as 'a quick death' and no possibility of varying one's
condition. Essential, mental existence simply endures, while
inessential, physical existence quite naturally declines.
Accordingly, the primary problem in life becomes the effort to
palliate existence in the mind, which, in Belacqua's opinion, is
'the last ditch when all was said and done' (174).

The immediate consequence of this evocation of existence is
that Beckett's characters, incidents and images all become
extremely predictable, and alarmingly like the 'clockwork

cabbages' (*Dream*, 106) that he ridicules in *Dream of Fair to Middling Women*. For example, when Belacqua and Lucy, his betrothed, visit the countryside in 'Walking Out', the narrator lovingly alludes to 'dead lambs' and other such 'emblems of the spring of the year' (117), before recounting the way in which a Daimler, turning a bend with clockwork punctuality, crashes into the horse upon which Lucy is riding. Lucy's horse, like the aforementioned lambs, dutifully expires 'there and then', whereas Lucy is 'not so fortunate, being crippled for life . . . her beauty dreadfully marred' (118). As the following story, 'What a Misfortune', relates, Lucy dies only 'after two years of great physical suffering' (125).

On the one hand, this emphasis upon physical deterioration transforms Beckettian fiction into the kind of phantasmagoric vision of 'Time made flesh' (*PTD*, 76) that Marcel witnesses at the Guermantes' matinée, as aristocratic geriatric after aristocratic geriatric files past him towards their grave. As critics such as Georg Lukács have observed, this kind of fiction seems to reduce reality to 'an image of the utmost human degradation'.[3] On the other hand, however, it can be argued that Beckett's impatience with physical reality, and his preoccupation with the 'ideal core' (*PTD*, 29) of mental reality, led him to maximize the 'mental' content of his fiction by minimizing its 'physical' content; in the event, by describing characters whose age, illnesses or death give them mental rather than physical presence.

If Lukács's criticism remains particularly pertinent, this is surely because the strategy of reducing fictional reality to the kind of minimal physical level evoked by Beckett need not entail the further reduction of this subject-matter to the chronic impotence of Beckett's characters. It seems odd, to say the least, that the 'ideal core' of the Beckettian 'onion' should always turn out rotten. Belacqua's Dublin appears to have more than its fair share of cripples, corpses and senile delinquents (such as the 'two grotesques' (147) — a 'powerfully built nymphomaniac panting in black and mauve between shipped crutches' and 'an aged cretin' (148) — who haunt Belacqua's wedding), and less than its fair share of benign, comforting characters, such as Saint-Loup and Marcel's grandmother.

Upon inspection, however, it is not really surprising that Belacqua's circle should lack such comforting characters. For although the narrator hints that the labourer who sets down his pick, or the dandy who pauses to remove his hands from his pockets, may effortlessly offer passing funeral processions 'a

gesture of more value than a ton of lilies' (144), Belacqua, like
Molloy, has little time for 'the charitable gesture' (*Molloy*, 24). So
far as Belacqua is concerned, such gestures, though worthy of a
ton of lilies, are still little more than 'conversational nuisance'
(13), or an intrusion from the macrocosmic into the microcosmic
world. Accordingly, Belacqua prepares 'a hot reception' for all
'little acts of kindness' (173).

Like his namesake in *Dream of Fair to Middling Women*, Belacqua
aspires above all to enter a nihilistic state of 'wombtomb' (*Dream*,
39) far away from his neighbour and from himself, explaining: 'I
want very much to be back in the caul, on my back in the dark for
ever' (31). Standing in front of a pier-glass, he revealingly
comments: 'what I am on the look out for . . . is nowhere as far
as I can see'; and, upon making out his own reflection on the lens
of the pier-glass, he equally tellingly '(turns) away from the
blurred image of himself' (146). The difficulties attending
Belacqua's attempts to return to 'the caul', to look out upon
'nowhere' and to avoid all traces of his own 'blurred image'
become particularly acute in the penultimate short story entitled
'Yellow'. Here, Beckett once again adumbrates his own fictional
ideals by subverting a number of central images from Proust's *A
la recherche du temps perdu*.

At first sight, 'Yellow' appears to confirm the widespread
theory that Beckett's fiction depicts a heroic search for self-
knowledge *within* the 'last ditch' (174) of the mind. According to
the narrator, Belacqua 'bragged of how he furnished his mind
and lived there' (174). Moreover, just as his namesake in *Dream
of Fair to Middling Women* builds 'ramparts' around the 'tunnel' of
his mind (*Dream*, 40), he constructs similar fortifications in order
to guarantee his inviolability from unwelcome ideas. As the
narrator explains, he is either 'content to barricade his mind
against the idea' (174), or else turns to more desperate measures,
in order to eliminate these intrusions once and for all. On such
occasions,

His plan . . . was not to refuse admission to the idea, but to keep it at bay
until his mind was ready to receive it. Then let it in and pulverise it.
Obliterate the bastard . . . Flitter the fucker. (175)

But, like most of the Beckettian hero's recipes for mental
tranquillity, this plan is appallingly impractical, and it abruptly
grinds to a halt as Belacqua reflects: 'So far so good. But by what
means' (175). To his considerable chagrin, Belacqua finds that he

has no means of 'flittering' this kind of 'fucker'. Quite simply, he can no more 'obliterate' his most disturbing insights than he can 'barricade' himself against them, just as his namesake can no more wilfully abolish the will than he can consciously attain unconsciousness.

Accordingly, just as the earlier Belacqua decides to forsake both the macrocosmic realm of the outside world *and* the microcosmic realm of the mind, in order to enter into the 'immunity' of 'neither' and of 'not' (*Dream*, 107), he determines in his turn to retreat from both the external word and from the internal 'last ditch': 'His mind might cave in for all he cared, he was tired of the old bastardo' (172). Craving the same kind of 'blessedly sunless depths' in which the earlier Belacqua enjoys 'the slush of angels' until he is disturbed by 'the furious divers that hauled him out to fry in the sun' (*Dream*, 108), he resolves to dive into unconsciousness in the manner of 'that Delian diver who, after the third or fourth submersion, returns no more to the surface' (176).

Belacqua's final mortal kicks against the pricks of unwanted introspection take place within a hospital, as he ineffectively tries to evade both the outer 'yellow' of sunlight, and the inner 'glare' of his mind, before submitting to an operation to remove the tumour the size of a brick that he had on the back of his neck' (176).[4] As the ending to this story reveals, he dies on the operating table because of an unfortunate oversight — 'They had clean forgot to auscalate him!' (186). In a sense, this oversight is the least of the ironies in this story. Although Belacqua's surgeons blunder, they offer him a reasonable chance of attaining relief from physical distress. By contrast, he appears to have no chance at all of relieving the mental distress precipitated by the luminous prospect of the hospital's 'grand old yaller wall' and its overlying 'pillar of higher tone, representing the sun' (180).

This reference to the 'yaller wall' of the hospital almost certainly makes a somewhat oblique parodic allusion to the passage in *A la recherche du temps perdu* describing the way in which the dying writer, Bergotte, drags himself from his deathbed in order to ponder one last time upon the rare beauty of the 'petit pan de mur jaune' (III.186) (little patch of yellow wall) in Vermeer's painting 'View of Delft'. Persuaded that this detail in Vermeer's painting reveals 'une beauté qui se suffirait à elle-même' (III.187) (a self-sufficient beauty), and might in its own right be valued as 'une précieuse oeuvre d'art chinoise'

(III.186–7) (a precious work of Chinese art), the dying Bergotte —
like Proust himself one year before his death — makes his way to
an exhibition of Dutch Masters.[5]

Enfin il fut devant le Ver Meer ... où, grâce à l'article du critique, il
remarqua pour la première fois ... la précieuse matière du tout petit pan
de mur jaune. Ses étourdissements augmentaient; il attachait son
regard, comme un enfant à un papillon jaune qu'il veut saisir, au
précieux pan de mur. 'C'est ainsi que j'aurais du écrire, disait-il. Mes
derniers livres sont trop secs, il aurait fallu passer plusieurs couches de
couleur, rendre ma phrase en elle-même précieuse, comme ce petit pan
de mur jaune.' (III.187)
      (At last he stood before the Vermeer ... where, thanks to the critic's
article, he became aware for the first time of ... the precious substance
of the tiny little patch of yellow wall. His vertigo increased; he
concentrated, like a child about to pounce upon a yellow butterfly, on
the precious patch of wall. 'I should have written like that, he told
himself. My last books are too arid, I should have used several layers of
colour, so as to make my words precious in themselves, like this little
patch of yellow wall.')

These passages abound with references to Proustian values.
Like the flowers and the trees described in Proust's early
writings,[6] Vermeer's most sublime patch of yellow is utterly
'self-sufficient'. Like the metaphorical insights advocated by
Marcel (III.889), it combines 'several layers' of substance. And
like the novel that Marcel proposes to write for the benefit of his
readers (III.1033), it offers valuable, if belated, illumination, by
showing Bergotte how he 'should have written'. By contrast,
Belacqua perceives few virtues in his sunny vision. Far from
passionately lisping 'petit pan de mur jaune ... petit pan de mur
jaune' (III.187) — or 'yaller wall ... yaller wall' — he determines
to 'draw the blinds, both blinds' (180) as rapidly as possible; a
plan that is prevented by the unexpected arrival of a matron.
      'Yellow' makes no specific reference to Bergotte's beatific
meditations upon Vermeer's 'View of Delft', but Beckett almost
certainly had this incident in mind, just as he has it in mind in
Murphy, where an inconsequential reference to Miss Carridge's
'big room' specifies that 'The lemon of the walls whined like
Vermeer's' (*Murphy*, 155). Ultimately, of course, the question of
what Beckett may or may not have had in mind becomes of
secondary importance; more significant is the function of this or
that image in his writing. By accident or design, Beckett's
'Yellow' utterly reverses the highly positive function that

Bergotte attributes to Vermeer's yellow wall. Belacqua's repugnance for the 'pillar of higher tone, representing the sun' (180) similarly subverts the Proustian protagonist's characteristic enthusiasm for rays of sunshine.

Throughout Proust's writings, his narrators and heroes respond with particular reverence to sunlight. As the narrator of an early version of *Contre Sainte-Beuve* remarks, when celebrating the pleasures of sunlit mornings, 'le poète est comme la statue de Memnon: il suffit d'un rayon de soleil pour le faire chanter' (the poet is like the statue of Memnon: a ray of morning sunshine suffices to make him sing).[7] By contrast, Belacqua dislikes rays of morning sunshine: 'Daybreak, with its suggestion of a nasty birth, he could not bear' (172). Although Beckett sometimes compares the posture of his heroes with that of Memnon, they seldom celebrate sunshine or sunrise. On the contrary, they dislike such light, '(rail) at the source of all life' (*Isis*, 7), and might well be considered as anti-Memnons, sitting, waiting, for the sun to set.

Like so many of the Beckettian hero's impulses, Belacqua's antipathy to sunlight has its prototype among the Proustian hero's more nihilistic responses. For example, during his prolonged grief after Albertine's death, Marcel similarly attempts to retreat from the light of day and from the light of consciousness, relating that on one typical occasion during this grief-stricken period, 'Je disais à Françoise de refermer les rideaux pour ne plus voir ce rayon de soleil' (III.479) (I asked Françoise to draw the curtains in order to shut out the sun's rays). Like Belacqua, however, Marcel finds that this sunlight 'continuait à filtrer, aussi corrosif, dans ma mémoire' (III.479) (continued to filter, as corrosively as ever, into my memory).

Marcel finally escapes the thrall of such torturous memories when he rediscovers the superior domain of positive involuntary memory at the end of his adventures. But unlike Marcel, Belacqua seems permanently 'bogged' (9) in the realm of painfully 'corrosive' experiences, be these mental or physical, habitual or non-habitual, or of this world or its successor. Beckett does not describe Belacqua's afterlife in *More Pricks Than Kicks* (though he rather sketchily traces an episode from his existence in 'the beyond' in the unpublished short story, 'Echo's Bones'), but Belacqua very significantly fears that 'all this would happen again' (159). Confirming the worst, the narrator of 'Draff' (the story which immediately follows the account of Belacqua's accidental death in 'Yellow') admits that he 'was not wholly dead' (200). Belacqua discovers as much in 'Echo's Bones', in which his surprisingly conscious existence in 'the beyond' makes him ponder 'if on the whole he had not been a great deal deader before rather than after his formal departure, so to speak' (*EB*, 1), and leads him to wonder 'whether death is not the greatest swindle of modern times' (*EB*, 21).

Like *More Pricks Than Kicks*, Beckett's first published novel *Murphy* (1938), traces the ways in which mental anguish seems doomed to 'happen again' and again and again. Written some time between 1934 and 1937,[8] *Murphy* commences with one of its many evocations of the invariably cyclical quality of existence:

The sun shone, having no alternative, on the nothing new. Murphy sat out of it, as though he were free, in a mew in West Brompton. (5)

Nothing could be less like Proustian narration, or, indeed, more quintessentially Beckettian in tone. Far from announcing a new day, the sun shines on 'the nothing new', 'having no alternative'. And far from breaking into sunlit song, Murphy sits 'out of it' 'as though he were free'. But as Beckett intimates in his pun upon 'mew', Murphy is far from free. On the one hand, this idiosyncratic term indicates that Murphy inhabits a singular variant of a 'mews' (or street) and, on the other, it toys with the obscurer meaning of 'mew' (cage for hawks), suggesting that Murphy, like the sun, has no alternative but to remain a prisoner of existence.

Lest the 'gentle skimmer' (60) should overlook the implications of this pun, Beckett's narrator carefully spells them out for the duration of the opening paragraph. The narrator gradually establishes the prevalence of mortality and isolation in a world in which even the mews are 'condemned', and in which Murphy will soon be exposed to 'alien' surroundings. He additionally suggests the strangely symmetrical quality of Murphy's 'closed system' (45) by presenting these observations within an antithetical analysis which perfectly enacts the way in which Murphy's habitual world resembles 'a well with two buckets .... one going down to be filled, the other coming up to be emptied' (44). Having been introduced to Murphy's room, we discover that:

Here for what might have been six months he had eaten, drunk, slept, and put his clothes on and off, in a medium-sized cage of north-western aspect commanding an unbroken view of medium-sized cages of south-eastern aspect. Soon he would have to make other arrangements, for the mew had been condemned. Soon he would have to buckle to and start eating, drinking, sleeping, and putting his clothes on and off, in quite alien surroundings. (5)

With quite startling economy, the content and the structure of this opening paragraph introduce the reader to the peculiarly repetitive dynamics of Murphy's habitual universe. Viewed very summarily, the remainder of *Murphy* might be said to elaborate the dichotomy between its hero's habitual responses to this condition, and his alternative responses to the more unusual, non-habitual stimuli of 'pestilential consciousness' (*Dream*, 149). Like all of Beckett's heroes, Murphy finds himself vacillating between the monotony of habitual existence and habitual awareness, and the shock of non-habitual consciousness.

Predictably enough, Murphy's monotonous, cyclical world is devoid of all traces of moral value and existential progress. His mind, for example, functions independently of the 'ethical yoyo' (76), and 'could not be disposed according to a principle of worth' (77). In much the same way, almost all human relations in *Murphy* exist independently of the 'ethical yoyo', and exhibit an amoral 'yoyo' pattern, or 'The old endless chain of love, tolerance, indifference, aversion and disgust' (174). At best, life simply exhibits a grim status quo. According to Wylie, 'For every symptom that is eased, another is made worse', so that

while one may not look forward to things getting any better, at least one need not fear their getting any worse. (43)

On such occasions, it is tempting to detect a certain defiant strength in the Beckettian character's attempt to counter the monotonous symmetry of his existence with wittily symmetrical rhetoric. Neary, for example, resigns himself to the 'yoyo', 'chain', 'swings' and 'roundabouts' of abortive love by formulating the 'Very prettily put' (44) reflection: 'What I make on the swings of Miss Counihan . . . . I lose on the roundabouts of the non-Miss Counihan' (43). In much the same way, Belacqua amuses himself with 'Very prettily put' sayings, such as 'Hungry dogs eat dirty puddings' (*EB*,17).

Sometimes characters in *Murphy* employ alternative methods in order to alleviate their condition, such as the 'alcoholic depressant' (41) favoured by Cooper; the 'dingy stingy repose' (21) savoured by Mr Kelly; or Neary's short-lived ability to 'stop his heart more or less whenever he liked and keep it stopped, within reasonable limits, for as long as he liked' (6). But more often than not, Murphy and his fellow sufferers prefer to distract and dull their senses by perfecting the kind of symmetrical verbal and physical gestures anticipated by the 'boomerang' exercises of the early Belacqua (*Dream*, 38) and his later namesake (*MPTK*, 40).

Neary typifies this strategy by killing time in Mooney's bar, where he is seen to 'move slowly round the ring of counters, first in one direction, then in the other' (42), describing what one might think of as centrifugal, peripheral arcs and circles in order to avoid descent into the painful 'core' (*PTD*, 65) of his existence. From the very first pages of this novel, Murphy similarly strives to distract himself in order to be 'quiet' and 'free' (10). Initially, he rocks himself to and fro in his rocking-chair, just as 'V' sits in her rocking-chair 'saying to the rocker/ rock her off/ stop her eyes' (*Rockaby*, 26). On subsequent occasions, Murphy distracts himself by walking 'round and round Pentonville prison', and 'round and round cathedrals that it was too late to enter' (54), until, surpassing himself in the service of the Magdalen Mental Mercyseat, or M.M.M., he even spends time *between* his 'rounds' 'walking round and round' (161).

Celia, Murphy's sometime sweetheart, similarly walks 'clockwise' (105) around the Round Pond in London, and produces the 'footfalls' of her 'soft swaggering to and fro' (155), as she disconsolately waits for Murphy during his absence. In this respect, Celia both anticipates the footfalls of May, in *Footfalls*, and duplicates the 'soft padding to and fro' of the 'old boy': a fellow lodger who is 'Never still' (50), until he kills time more definitively with his 'cut-throat razor' (94). Such successful suicide offers an exception to the general pattern of Beckett's writings. Dead or alive, his characters invariably 'revisit the vomit' (*EB*, 1).

On other occasions, Murphy and his fellow characters similarly take refuge in verbal and numerical 'boomerang' exercises, such as Neary's 'swings' and 'roundabouts' wordplay. Sometimes this wordplay resembles the 'inner elemental vitality' that Beckett's early criticism enthusiastically detected in Joyce's 'endless verbal germination, maturation, putrefaction',[9] and seems little more than an innocent flexing of the rhetorical muscles. Elegantly compressing paradoxes and puns, the narrator generates such splendid lines as '"My poor child," said the virgin Miss Carridge' (94), just as the narrator of 'Echo's Bones' wittily bounces utterance against nomenclature in lines like '"Though you hedge" said Belacqua, "Miss Privet ... "'

(*EB*, 5). Murphy, in his turn, takes considerable pleasure in the semantic ambiguities of his 'barmaid champagne' joke (97), a pleasantry which he 'always found ... most funny, more than most funny' (98) and which surfaces somewhat earlier in 'Echo's Bones', in the following even more ritualistic question and answer routine:

"Why did the barmaid sham pain?" demanded Belacqua.
"Because the stout porter bit her" answered Lord Gall quite correctly. (*EB*, 12)

The key words here seem to be 'always' and 'quite correctly', two qualifications which emphasize the formulaic and cere-monial qualities of the Beckettian pun. Arguably, these favourite refrains, like the Beckettian character's physical 'boomerang' exercises, provide rituals which may be repeated 'quite correctly', and which therefore afford superficial consolation before 'the big blooming buzzing confusion' (7). In other words, while the narrator's puns and paradoxes may simply evince innocent exhuberance, the self-consciously 'carefully folded'[10] wordplay of Murphy and his fellow characters seems to constitute a deliberate retreat into the unthreatening realm of 'line and surface' and 'penny-a-line vulgarity' (*PTD*, 76). Such play, then, is not so much defiant as compliant. Rather than confronting 'deep' reality, it enables Beckett's characters to retreat to soothingly superficial structural symmetries.

Mathematical games offer Murphy similar consolation. Although he notionally spurns the superficiality of 'sums with the petty cash of current facts' (123), he repeatedly turns to such 'sums' for distraction. While Marcel contemplates the 'beauty' of harmonious involuntary introspection in all of its 'infallible proportion' (*PTD*, 72–3), Murphy resigns himself to rather more mundane manifestations of proportion, such as the 'total permutability' (68) of five biscuits, or the 'perfectly balanced' proportion of a meal costing him 'Twopence the tea, twopence the biscuits' (58). At his most ambitious, he habitually defrauds a tea-room by exploiting his 'egg and scorpion voice' (59), against which 'No waitress could hold out', in order to obtain '1.83 cups approximately' (60) while only paying for one cup of tea.

This comforting calculation could scarcely be confused with the Proustian ideal of 'fertile research' (*PTD*, 65). But it does at least derive from one of the few successful verbal exchanges in this novel. More often than not, Murphy's words and gestures

abundantly justify Beckett's suggestion that 'There is no communication, because there are no vehicles of communication'
(64); indeed, *Murphy*, more than any other of Beckett's works,
offers a monument to the fallibility of gestural communication.

Compared with the rich and varied 'ballet of gestures'[11] in
Proust's *A la recherche du temps perdu*, Beckett's fiction describes
a continual comedy of errors, or theatre of mistakes. For
example, far from functioning as windows to the soul, Beckettian
eyes close, glaze and consistently thwart all attempts at
communication. When Murphy forcibly engages Celia's
attention by taking her 'angrily by the shoulders', and
commands, 'Look at me', he finds that 'She looked through him.
Or back off him' (96). Briefly, Celia seems neither willing nor able
to emulate the way in which Odette communes with Swann
during her transfiguration, as 'some purely human thought,
some generous impulse such as everyone feels ... flashed from
her eyes like a golden ray' (I.314).

Similarly, when Murphy attempts to communicate with Mr
Endon, a 'very superior' (133) inmate of the M.M.M., and 'took
Mr Endon's head in his hands and brought the eyes to bear on
his, or rather his on them' (170), he utterly fails to make contact
with his mentor. He merely meets his own unwelcome image,
'seeing himself stigmatized in those eyes that did not see him'
(170–71). Horrified by this involuntary instant of self-
perception, Murphy retreats from Mr Endon 'without reluctance
and without relief' (171). In much the same way, Celia regrets
'her reflection' in Miss Carridge's linoleum, just as aged 'high-
class whores with faces lately lifted' regret their reflection in the
glass framing such works as 'Claude's Narcissus' (155). It seems
to be precisely this kind of vulnerability to painful self-perception
which drives Murphy to the soothing superficiality of his carefully permutated biscuits and his '1.83' cups of tea.

At this point, it seems possible to distinguish two distinct
formal aspects in Beckett's work. At their thematic level, novels
such as *Murphy* and plays such as *Footfalls* vividly evoke the ways
in which protagonists impose superficial rituals and repetitive
gesture upon 'the mess' in order to alleviate the pain of
introspection. As *Murphy* and *Footfalls* indicate, these 'boomerang' gestures are not very effective. For all their pacing, the
characters of these two works continue to suffer from 'It all' and
continue 'revolving it all' in their 'poor mind' (*F*, 10)

Yet while these 'boomerang' gestures offer symptoms of 'self-
fear' and 'self-negation' (*PTD*, 66) at the thematic level, they also

afford considerable formal satisfaction at the aesthetic level. There is a pleasing symmetry in the way in which Murphy brings Mr Endon's eyes 'to bear on his, or rather his on them' (170), just as there is a pleasing symmetry in the almost identical process by which a ghostly 'she' lifts a bowl towards her lips, or rather, inclines her lips towards a bowl, in the more recent *Ill seen ill said*, when:

At last in a twin movement full of grace she slowly raises the bowl toward her lips while at the same time with equal slowness bowing her head to join it (*Isis*, 35)

In much the same way, May, the heroine or anti-heroine of *Footfalls*, moves with considerable grace as she paces up and down and provokes her mother's comment: 'Let us watch her move .... Watch how feat she wheels' (*F*, 11). Arguably, it is in passages such as these that Beckett discovers a 'shape' to contain 'the mess'. But for all their structural felicity, these passages are patently evocations of impotence, isolation and despair. Murphy fails to communicate with Mr Endon; the anonymous narrator of *Ill seen ill said* abandons his attempt to 'see her again' (*Isis*, 51), and yearns instead to 'say farewell ... to ... her tenacious trace' (*Isis*, 59); and 'V', the mother of 'May', seems haunted by her physical distance from her daughter, while at the same time her presence seems to haunt May, just as May's sufferings haunt her dead mother's 'deep sleep' (*F*, 9). Whether they be living or dead, or something in between, and whether their actions be formulated within the beautiful symmetry of the lines above from *Ill seen ill said*, or within the more incoherent prose of *The Unnamable*, Beckett's characters invariably discover that there is 'nothing to be done' to alleviate their condition.

Of all Beckett's characters, Mr Endon is perhaps the only one to enjoy immunity to the gestures of the eye and to have the 'good fortune not to be at the mercy of the hand, whether another's or his own' (169–70). Unlike Mr Endon, Murphy and Celia are continually at the mercy of their hands, and continually reveal their anguish, impotence and isolation with gestures of the hand, evincing the kind of helplessness that the early Belacqua associates with 'The hand .... tendered and withdrawn and again tendered and withdrawn' (*Dream*, 107).

For example, upon learning that Murphy has left her in order to work in the 'M.M.M.', Celia sadly ascends the staircase to her room as the odorous Miss Carridge watches her hand on the banister, 'gripping, then sliding a little, gripping again, then sliding a little more' (108). In her turn, Celia is transfixed by the way in which Murphy's hands drift to and from a railing as he leaves her, and later,

she continued to see, at the most unexpected times, whether she would or no, the hand clutching the spike of the railing, the fingers loosening and tightening. (100).

The very trees in *Murphy* make this plaintive kind of gesture, and the narrator carefully describes a yew which exhibits:

the hopeless harbour-mouth look, the arms of two that can reach no farther, or of one in supplication, the patient impotence of charity or prayer. (177)

These evocative words summon a number of Proustian and Beckettian parallels to mind. First of all, the gestures of this disconsolate yew tree seem to express the same 'regret impuissant' (impotent regret) that Marcel discerns in the 'gesticulation naïve et passionnée' (I.719) (naive and passionate gestures) of the Hudimesnil trees. Secondly, both this Beckettian yew and the Proustian Hudimesnil trees foreshadow the ways in which Beckettian protagonists evince equally impotent regret in plays such as *Eleuthéria* and *Not I*. Both plays employ 'the pathos of .... dangling arms' (*Isis*, 47) in order to depict the pitiful 'impotence of charity' and affection.

Charting the misadventures of its hero, the ironically named Victor, *Eleuthéria* (1947) specifies that Victor's servant, Jacques, is particularly fond of his master. Stage directions stipulate: 'On sent qu'il pense à son maître dont il touche doucement le fauteuil à plusieurs reprises' (*Eleuthéria*, 3) (He is clearly thinking of his master and gently touches his armchair a number of times). Unfortunately, this affection appears to defy adequate communication, and Jacques finally conveys his dilemma as '(il) lève les bras et les laisse retomber ... regarde Victor avec tristesse. Lève les bras, sort' (*Eleuthéria*, 108–9) ((he) lifts his arms and lets them fall ... looks sadly at Victor. Lifts his arms, exits).

Identical gestures recur in *Not I*, some quarter century later, when the arms of the mysterious 'Auditor' offer 'Mouth' the equally fallible consolation of 'a gesture of helpless compassion' which 'lessens at each recurrence till scarely perceptible at third' (*Not I*, 16). As this gesture occurs four times, it seems to have reached vanishing point by the end of the play. After excluding the Auditor from his 1976 production of the play because of lighting problems, Beckett introduced a revised ending for his 1978 production, 'with the Auditor placing his hands over his ears at the end of the play, unable, it would appear, to bear any longer Mouth's confession'. [12]

Murphy likewise attempts to exclude all painful perceptions (rather than descending to their 'core') and, like the various Belacquas, he expects to find some sort of sanctuary within his mind; a realm that he naively supposes to be a source of 'unique delights' (123) and 'a closed system, subject to no change but its own, self-sufficient and impermeable to the vicissitudes of the body' (77). While Murphy's mind is reasonably 'bodytight', it offers no defence against the 'inward glare' (*Dream*, 110).

Judged in its own terms (or in the narrator's summary of its own terms), Murphy's mind falls into three zones. The first of these affords a state of 'light' in which Murphy enjoys 'the pleasure of reversing the physical experience' (78). Next comes a zone of 'half-light' which transcends both the physical experience and its reverse, in which 'the pleasure was contemplation' (79). Finally, the third zone grants access to a state of 'dark' in which the two preceding zones are reduced to 'pure forms of commotion' and 'absolute freedom' (79). Here, Murphy seems to attain the Beckettian idyll of 'immunity' (*Dream*, 107) from *all* kinds of experience.

Somewhat like the 'void place . . . and spacious nothing' that the early Belacqua considers to be 'the apex of ecstasy' (*Dream*, 165), and the state of 'nowhere' (*MPTK*, 146) sought by the later Belacqua, Murphy's third zone appears to grant him

nothing, that colourlessness which is such a rare postnatal treat . . . the positive peace that comes when the somethings give way, or perhaps simply add up, to . . . Nothing. (168)

Murphy's dilemma is, of course, that he is powerless to attain or retain this delectable condition. His various 'boomerang' exercises may 'sway the issue in the desired direction, but not clinch it' (124). In other words, just as the later Belacqua wonders 'by what means' he may 'flitter' (*MPTK*, 175) disturbing ideas and preserve peace of mind, Murphy gradually realizes that 'it was not enough to want nothing' when 'The means of clinching it were lacking' (124).

Worse still, Murphy's mind remains vulnerable to two kinds of disturbance. Firstly, he still seems susceptible to physical, macrocosmic temptations, such as 'Celia, ginger, and so on'

(124). Secondly, and more seriously, he finds that those 'immured in the mind' (125) do not simply have 'a glorious time' (124) luxuriating in its 'unique delights' (123), but also experience 'pain, rage, despair and in fact all the usual' (124), when exposed to the kind of intense involuntary memories that he associates with 'inner voices' (116) and the contents of 'the mental belch' (158): two torments which reveal 'a fly somewhere in the ointment of Microcosmos' (124). It is precisely this 'fly' which drives Murphy to abandon 'the little world' (125).

That Murphy's projected return to 'the big world' should be thwarted by the extravagant *deus ex machina* of an exploding W.C. is of middling significance compared with his traumatic discovery of the 'inner voices' (116) — or inner visions — which precipitate his decision to depart from the microcosmic haven of the 'M.M.M.'. He makes this decision at the end of chapter eleven, upon discovering the peculiar process by which a succession of fragmentary memories ominously annunciate the prospect of intolerably 'deep' introspection. On the brink of descending 'to the core of the eddy' (*PTD*, 65–6), he determines to halt this process as rapidly as possible. Describing the way in which Murphy contemplates a positively Burroughsian vista, as 'Scraps of bodies, of landscapes, hands, eyes, lines and colours evoking nothing' rise before his eyes, 'as though reeled upward off a spool level with his throat', the narrator adds the crucial coda:

It was his experience that this should be stopped, whenever possible, before the deeper coils were reached. (172)

It is difficult to exaggerate the importance of this statement. For, while most of Beckett's critics would concur with Raymond Federman's hypothesis that Murphy aspires to the 'classical mystical experience that all Beckett's French heroes seek in the depth of their consciousness',[13] this specification makes it evident that Murphy entertains quite antithetical aspirations. Far from voluntarily exploring the 'deeper coils' of his being, Murphy recoils towards the macrocosm in order to minimize the risk of confronting the depths of his consciousness. Some seven years after the publication of *Murphy*, Beckett once again depicted similar responses to the 'deeper coils' of consciousness when composing *Watt*, the third and the last of his English novels.

11

WATT AND THE PROBLEM OF INTELLIGIBILITY

Watt is one of Beckett's most difficult novels. When excerpts from it appeared in the Paris-based little magazine *Merlin*, in 1952, even the readers of this radical review protested.[1] Richard Seaver, a former editor of *Merlin*, amusingly reports:

We received several angry letters and cancellation of five per cent of our subscriptions (i.e., five cancellations). Avant-garde all right, the letters said, but let's draw the line at total absurdity. We knew we were on the right track.[2]

Later, when the *Merlin* collective persuaded Maurice Girodias to publish *Watt* among the predominantly pornographic titles issued by the Olympia Press's 'Traveller's Companion' series,[3] Seaver remained less than sanguine about the future of *Watt*, and in an early review of this novel predicted that:

Watt will probably either be placed on the shelf reserved for those books to be read and re-read, or tossed angrily into the wastepaper basket.[4]

At the same time, Seaver also commented: 'It is difficult to imagine anyone reacting passively to Beckett's work'.[5] As Seaver suggests, *Watt* seems the kind of novel that either elicits baffled wonder or impatient indignation. Yet, ironically enough, most of Beckett's critics offer exceptions to this rule. Taking their hint from Beckett himself, the majority of them have passively accepted that *Watt* is simply an elaborate literary joke rather than anything more consequential.

Beckett relates that he wrote *Watt* while 'on the run' in occupied and unoccupied France between 1943 and 1945, explaining that he composed it 'in dribs and drabs' as 'a way to keep (his) hand in',[6] and dismisses *Watt* as 'an unsatisfactory book', 'a joke' and 'only a game'.[7] Countless critics have taken him at his word, and have treated the novel with undue levity, as if it

233

were a literary puzzle awaiting scholarly solution and nothing
more. Pounced upon as one of the illustrious corpses of early
Post-Modernity, *Watt* has been endlessly disinterred, dis-
embowelled, dissected, desiccated, diagrammatized, decoded
and generally deconstructed, in order to serve the polemics of
two distinctive dynasties of literary criticism. Firstly, *Watt*
frequently functions as a favourite exhibit in the argument of
those critics, usually writing in the sixties and seventies, who
found Beckett's work to typify the supposed 'death of the novel'.
More recently, and, admittedly, rather less frequently, *Watt* has
again been taken up as a key exhibit by those structuralist and
post-structuralist critics preoccupied with the supposed 'death of
the author'.[8]

For many of Beckett's early critics, *Watt* epitomized the 'death'
of the novel. Incarnating, so it seemed, the impossibility of
fiction, it appeared most significant in terms of its wit and its
formal intricacy. For example, Melvin Friedman concluded that
Watt 'carries the plotless novel to new lengths', while John
Spurling praised its ' "senseless" but beautiful patterns', and
Hugh Kenner postulated that it generates 'the great calm of some
computation' as 'fact dissolves into symmetry'.[9] Elaborating this
thesis, Jean-Jacques Mayoux concluded that *Watt* replaces
'materiality' with 'organization', anticipating the 'pure formal-
ism' of Beckett's later prose; while Lawrence Harvey found it to
be a novel in which the 'serious aspect of art' was 'muted in
favour of the amusing, the pleasing . . . and symmetries of
form'.[10]

Watt certainly lends itself to this kind of interpretation, in as
much as it chronicles the confusions of a character named Watt,
who enters service in the house of a perplexing Mr Knott, where
he witnesses events full of formal symmetry and yet signifying
'nothing'. Watt repeatedly finds that 'nothing had happened, a
thing that was nothing had happened, with the utmost formal
distinctness' (73), and Beckett's early critics repeatedly assert
that 'nothing' happens with the 'utmost formal distinctness' in
Watt, anticipating Vivian Mercier's famous oxymoron that
Waiting for Godot is 'a play in which nothing happens, twice'.[11]

At this point, the hypothesis that *Watt* is simply about the
impossibility or 'death' of the novel, overlaps with the alternative assumptions of those structuralist and post-structuralist
theorists who postulate that texts make best sense in terms of
recurrent patterns and conventions, rather than in terms of
authorial anxiety, or apocalyptic generalizations about the 'death

of the novel'. Or put more plainly, by converts such as Jonathan Culler, 'meaning is to be explained in terms of systems of signs', rather than in terms of the authorial anxiety or ecstasy of some 'biographically defined individual'.[12] Accordingly, literary studies become a 'pursuit of signs' (xi) in the most general sense of this phrase, rather than the attempt to analyse texts as 'independent objects' (25) created by independent, original authors.

The preoccupations of structuralist and post-structuralist thought, and the limitations of these theories, appear remarkably similar to those of Beckett's Watt. Indeed, in retrospect, Watt might best be understood as a manic structuralist *avant la lettre*. Watt's misadventures offer uncanny premonitions of the contradictions within structuralist literary theory, just as the preoccupations of structuralist theorists like Roland Barthes, and of structuralist apologists like Jonathan Culler, point to the peculiar contemporaneity of Beckett's fiction, and help to define the quality of Watt's perceptual dilemma.

Perhaps the most important concept in Culler's writings is that of 'intelligibility'. According to Culler, the critic should examine those laws which make a text intelligible, and focus upon 'banalities', or those 'meanings already known or attested within a culture', in order to explicate 'the conventions that members of that culture are following' (99). Culler defines his purpose as the wish to introduce 'methodical clarity ... into literary studies' (48) by undertaking 'the attempt to grasp, master, formulate (and) define' the conventions of language without surrendering to 'the temptations of interpretation' (98). For, according to Culler, the impulse to interpret a text becomes redundant once the reader emphasizes the general conditions and conventions of intelligibility. There is no point in attempting to interpret the individual vision, message, or sense of an author, since 'the self is dissolved' once 'its various functions are ascribed to impersonal systems' (33).

Culler's theories derive from the hypotheses of pioneer, and somewhat more perspicacious, theorists, such as Roland Barthes. Best known, perhaps, for his highly influential essay entitled 'The Death of the Author', Barthes follows the familiar French convention of introducing relatively new ideas by boldly announcing the so-called 'death', or obsolescence, of that with which one disagrees. An archetypal exercise in polemical overkill, Barthes's thesis condemns literary studies which focus upon the author and authorial meaning by declaring this convention, along with the very concept of 'the author', to be 'undermined', 'removed' and 'buried' by an alternative poetics which insists 'everything is to be disentangled, nothing deciphered'.[13] Rather than relating texts to biographical or authorial meaning, he argues that the writer is 'never original'; that he may only 'mix writings'; and that writing is therefore nothing more than 'words only explainable through other words'.[14] It seems to follow, then, that 'the text is henceforth made and read in such a way that at all its levels the author is absent'.[15] Accordingly, texts may be 'disentangled' in terms of general conventions, but may not be 'deciphered' in terms of some sort of original, authorial meaning.

Strange and surprising as it may seem, Watt's endeavours to make the most general sense of Mr Knott's world have much in common with the structuralist enterprise. Just as Barthes would 'disentangle' reality, and just as Culler would 'grasp, master, formulate (and) define' (xi) the conventions of language, Watt attempts 'to weigh, to measure and to count with the utmost exactness' (84) the minutiae of Mr Knott's abode. And just as Barthes and Culler assiduously avoid all reference to precise, individual modes of meaning, and focus upon what Culler terms 'banalities' (99), Watt similarly attempts to reduce his own highly idiosyncratic perceptions to comfortingly general 'banalities' in order to render them 'innocuous' (75).

As the narrator stipulates, Watt's analyses of his surroundings enquire 'not into what they really meant, his character was not so peculiar as all that, but into what they might be induced to mean, with the help of a little patience, a little ingenuity' (72). In other words, Watt attempts to undertake a 'pursuit of meaning', while retaining 'indifference to meaning' (72). At most, he hopes to reduce disturbing perceptions to the banality of 'a manner of paradigm' or 'a term of a series' (129), or, still more modestly, to the kind of general formulation that the narrator evokes as 'a pillow of old words, for his head' (115).

Watt's dilemma derives from the fact that he cannot transform his most disturbing perceptions into 'old words', or the kind of conventional and impersonal language that Barthes defines as 'words ... explainable through other words'.[16] Defined in Proustian terms, Watt's most vivid perceptions are 'en partie subjective et incommunicable' (III.885) (partially subjective and incommunicable). As such, they are irreducible either to 'other words' or to *any* words. However, although Barthes's early essays argue that all texts are 'explainable through other words', and that all texts are therefore 'already read',[17] Barthes's later essays, particularly those published in *Camera Lucida*, very interestingly qualify this early assertion, and suggest that language and perception fall into two distinct categories: the realm of '*studium*' and the realm of '*punctum*'.[18]

Barthes defines the realm of '*studium*' as something 'average' and 'culturally' defined, resulting from 'a certain training' (26). According to Barthes, examples of '*studium*' always exemplify some kind of 'structural rule' (23), and are always explicable or 'coded' (51). For example, he suggests that a photograph depicting two soldiers and two nuns in a ruined street in Nicaragua briefly catches his attention, but does not substantially 'intrigue' him, because it evokes the recognizable asymmetry that he associates with the 'structural role' of 'duality' (23). He explains:

I understood at once that its existence . . . derived from the co-presence of two discontinuous elements, heterogeneous in that they did not belong to the same world . . . the soldiers and the nuns. I foresaw a structural rule . . . and I immediately tried to verify it by inspecting other photographs by the same reporter . . . many of them attracted me because they included this kind of duality. (23)

The key terms here are 'I understood', 'I foresaw' and 'I tried to verify'. In all three instances, Barthes exemplifies the way in which his general, cultural training allows him to understand general, cultural conventions without reference to the subjectivity of either the reporter or himself. In Watt's terms, such jargon as 'the co-presence of two discontinuous elements' provides 'a pillow of old words' for Barthes's head, and renders this photograph 'innocuous'. As we have suggested, Watt's experience *chez* Mr Knott is somewhat more knotty, and cannot be 'disentangled' in this way.

Despite the fact that Watt has lived in the realm of '*studium*' — or what the narrator terms 'face values' (70) — his entry into the house of 'not' or 'knot' forces him to ask 'what?' before a whole series of incidents which cannot be understood or verified. Perhaps the most traumatic of these is the 'incident of the Galls father and son', whose visit is characterized by 'great formal brilliance and indeterminable purport' (71). Despite its apparent 'formal brilliance', the visit of these two piano-tuners resists any definition in 'face values' and, worse still, haunts Watt's memory in a quite unpredictable and uncomfortable way.

Incapable of asserting that 'something' had happened, Watt is compelled to confess that:

nothing had happened, that a thing that was nothing had happened, with the utmost formal distinctness, and that it continued to happen, in his mind ... inexorably to unroll its phases ... at the most unexpected moments, and the most inopportune. (75)

Watt's dilemma is that this experience transcends the habitual categories of 'studium', and worse still, that it will not go away. As the narrator observes:

Watt could not accept ... that nothing had happened, with all the clarity and solidity of something, and that it revisited him in such a way that he was forced to submit to it all over again, to hear the same sounds, see the same lights, touch the same surfaces, and so on, as when they had first involved him in all their unintelligible intricacies. (75)

This kind of haunting, non-habitual experience is, of course, the staple diet of the Proustian and Beckettian hero. As we have remarked, Marcel's involuntary memories constantly resurrect the past in all of its 'unintelligible intricacies', revealing the kinds of experience that he eulogizes as:

ces mystères qui n'ont probablement leur explications que dans d'autres mondes et dont le pressentiment est ce qui nous émeut le plus dans la vie et dans l'art. (III. 1032–3)
(those mysteries which probably cannot be explained save in terms of other worlds, and whose signs move us more profoundly than anything else in life and art.)

As we have also seen, Beckett's heroes constantly find themselves profoundly moved by the *unwelcome* non-habitual memories which Krapp, one of his later protagonists, associates with the horrors of having to 'Be again' (*KLT*, 19).

Barthes's early writings make no provision for either the Proustian or the Beckettian variants of such 'mysteries'. Rather, Barthes blithely speculates that there are no 'mysteries', and that everything may be rendered intelligible in terms of the kind of general conventions that he subsequently defines as 'studium'. In this respect, *Camera Lucida* very interestingly qualifies his earlier hypotheses by identifying the mysterious realm of '*punctum*': a concept which seems to denote precisely the kind of inexplicable and non-habitual experiences that Proust and Beckett commemorate in their different ways.

According to Barthes, the realm of *'punctum'* consists of perceptions which are at once 'certain' but 'unlocatable' (51). Barthes finds that certain details in photographs manifest something which: 'holds me, though I cannot say why' (51). Put another way, this kind of detail 'overwhelms' (49) his habitual categories, and seems to 'disturb the *studium*' (27). Barthes exemplifies 'punctum' with reference to a number of photographs in which 'off-center detail' reveals his 'incapacity to name' (51), and in which the discovery of unlocatable and unnameable detail: 'pricks me (but also bruises me, is poignant to me)' (27). Like Watt, then, he appears to discover something that is 'nothing' (because it cannot be located or named as a codifiable 'something') and, more disturbing still, a 'nothing' which 'holds' him and which he is 'forced to submit to . . . all over again'.

Barthes confides that his most cherished experience of 'punctum' derives from a photograph of his mother which seems to radiate precisely the kind of indefinable benevolence that Marcel perceives in what we may now call the 'punctum' of his grandmother's voice. When his grandmother telephones him at Doncières, Marcel marvels before the miraculous process by which the tone of her voice reveals 'sa douceur même' (II.135) (her very affection). In a surprisingly similar way, Barthes specifies that this photograph of his mother mysteriously evinces a rare quality of 'kindness which had formed her being immediately and forever, without her having inherited it' (69). As Barthes stipulates, this kindness seems utterly personal, utterly original, and 'belonged to no system' (69). Accordingly, he refuses to publish this photograph among the other photographs in *Camera Lucida*, explaining:

It exists only for me. For you it would be nothing but an indifferent picture, one of the thousand manifestations of the "ordinary" . . . at most it would interest your *studium*: period, clothes, photogeny; but in it, for you, no wound. (73)

There is obviously something extremely Proustian about this evocation of the 'partially subjective and incommunicable' (III.885) qualities of Barthes's response to this photograph, and he concedes at one point that his experience resembles 'remembrance, just as Proust experienced it' (70). Moreover, despite the fact that he seems to echo Beckett's reservations about the pleasures of non-habitual insights, and refers to the ways in which the discovery of 'punctum' tends to 'prick' and 'wound' him, Barthes finally shares Proust's enthusiasm for the 'Enchantments' (*PTD*, 22) of non-habitual reality, and he suggests that 'punctum' 'utopically' (71) transport him beyond the 'usual blah-blah' (55) of conventional categories and reveal 'essential' (71) reality in works which he praises as 'the loveliest photographs in the world' (70).

The striking originality of Beckett's work resides in its paradoxical critique of both 'studium' and 'punctum'. While Proust and Barthes both derive consolation and comfort from the realm of 'punctum', Beckettian characters such as Watt find that the transition from the habitual to the non-habitual, or from 'studium' to 'punctum', merely demarcates the decline from bad to worse. For the Beckettian hero there are no such things as 'the loveliest photographs in the world'. Rather, evocative photographs are dreaded as a source of intolerable suffering, and are usually destroyed in order to eliminate their painful 'punctum'. The hero of Beckett's *Film*, for example, accomplishes the 'destruction of photographs', while the hero of *A Piece of Monologue* contemplates the remnants of this ritual, surveying, or at least, recollecting: [19]

Pictures of ... he all but said of loved ones. Unframed. Unglazed. Pinned to wall with drawing-pins. All shapes and sizes. Down one after another. Gone. Torn to shreds and scattered. Strewn all over the floor.

As 'O', the hero of *Film*, discovers, and as the 'Speaker' in *A Piece of Monologue* demonstrates, the destruction of photographs provides no safeguard against introspection. 'O' finally falls victim to the 'anguish of perceivedness' (*Film*, 11), while the 'Speaker' continually finds himself on the point of naming — and resurrecting — the anguishing images of 'loved ones'. Watt's exhaustive descriptions similarly function as flawed strategies for keeping 'punctum' at bay. While the early Belacqua tries to evade introspection by toying with the 'boomerangs of ... fantasy' (*Dream*, 38), and while the later Belacqua and Murphy derive distraction from the circular perambulations that the narrator of *More Pricks Than Kicks* describes as 'boomerang, out and back' (*MPTK*, 40), Watt consoles himself him with what one might think of as the 'boomerangs' of permutated '*studium*'.

For example, upon perceiving an ambiguous ecclesiastical figure, Watt neither understands, forsees and verifies the kind of 'structural rule' that Barthes discerns when contemplating a photograph of soldiers and nuns in *Camera Lucida* (23), nor

attains the kind of rapturous, transcendental inspiration that
Modernist heroes like Joyce's Stephen Dedalus receive when
glimpsing mysterious figures from afar. Rather, as the following
passage painstakingly demonstrates, Watt methodically works
his way through four sets of self-defeating hypotheses,
permutating 'studium', in order to evade the 'old error' of
pondering upon 'punctum'.

Offering the reader a splendid example of Beckett's concept of
'the comedy of an exhaustive enumeration' (*PTD*, 92), Watt
wonders:

how should he know, if it were a man, that it was not a woman, or a
priest, or a nun, dressed up as a man? Or, if it was a woman, that it was
not a man, or a priest, or a nun, dressed up as a woman? Or, if it were
a priest, that it was not a man, or a woman, or a nun, dressed up as a
priest? Or, if it was a nun, that it was not a man, or a woman, or a priest,
dressed up as a nun? (266)

Over and over again, Watt wades through series after series of
more or less complete sets of hypotheses, which, as structuralist
critics like Dina Scherzer have remarked, follow 'very precise
combining models' and 'identifiable rules'.[20] It is probably more
accurate to observe that Watt *parodies* various rules and models.
For instance, John J. Mood has shown that while certain passages
in *Watt*, such as that cited above, present all the variations of the
permutational 'rule' of '4 possibilities, figured as 2^2', other
passages travesty these rules and may only be defined in terms of
such formulae as: '14 possibilities, figured as $5+4+3+2$' with '1
missing'.[21]

In retrospect, *Watt* makes much more sense in a more specific
comparative context. For passages like the lines above not only
present a very general parody of the kind of systematic
objectivity that Mood and Scherzer submit to mathematical
analysis, but also offer devastating alternatives to the Modernist
writer's images of triumphant subjectivity. This distinction is
best exemplified by comparing the above passage with the lines
below from Joyce's *A Portrait of the Artist as a Young Man*. While
Watt confusingly counts the ways in which a man, a woman, a
priest and a nun might all be confused with one another,
Stephen Dedalus's vision of a distant figure, 'alone and still,
gazing out to sea', prompts his reverent permutation of his first
impressions of someone 'soft and slight, slight and soft', and his
subsequent impression of 'swooning into some new world' as he
realizes that[22]

Her image had passed into his soul for ever and no word had broken the holy silence of his ecstasy. Her eyes had called him and his soul had leaped at the call. To live, to err, to fall, to triumph, to recreate life out of life! A wild angel had appeared to him ... an envoy from the fair courts of life, to throw open before him in an instant of ecstasy the gates of all the ways of error and glory.

Modernist fiction abounds in such visions of plenitude and enlightenment: one has only to think of the final paragraphs of Virginia Woolf's *To the Lighthouse*, Thomas Mann's *Death in Venice*, or Proust's *A la recherche du temps perdu*. It is precisely Watt's failure to derive comfort and inspiration from non-habitual perceptions which makes *Watt* such an archetypal Post-Modern novel. Nevertheless, it is by no means 'plotless', nor indeed is *Watt* simply a compendium of amusingly permutated hypotheses. In a sense, Watt, like Stephen Dedalus, finds himself 'swooning into some new world', though, unlike Joyce's hero, he finds this process to be the very reverse of 'holy' or ecstatic.

Preoccupation with the intricate ways in which he attempts to distract himself from this 'new world' seems to have distracted most of Beckett's critics from the crucial perceptual crisis which transports Watt beyond the habitual world of 'face values' (70), into the non-habitual world of 'punctum', in which he finds himself 'lacerated with curiosity' (226) and 'obliged to think, and speak' (76). This crisis is best introduced in terms of Beckett's elaboration of the various 'stairs' and 'ladders' images with which he characterizes habitual and non-habitual existence in *Watt*.

Watt's plot might be summarized as the process by which its hero, like various other characters before him, 'falls' from the realm of habitual existence outside Mr Knott's house, and enters a new, non-habitual realm in Mr Knott's house, in which he learns how to distract himself by constantly permutating 'face values' or the banalities of 'studium'. Habitual existence in *Watt* is usually evoked in terms of those who spend their days going up and down different kinds of stairs or ladders, such as the newsagent whose life appears neatly sandwiched between the evening ritual of carrying his bicycle 'down the winding stone stairs' before cycling home, and the morning ritual of cycling to work and then carrying his bicycle 'up the stairs again' (24).

According to Arsene (the servant who welcomes Watt to Mr Knott's house), this habitual ritual admits of superficial numerical analysis, insofar as it may be likened to the process of 'screwing' oneself up a staircase, 'counting the steps' (38). But, as Watt discovers, non-habitual existence consists of a state in which reality resists enumeration and definition. Once working in Mr Knott's house, he finds himself baffled by 'the stairs which were never the same and of which even the number of steps seemed to vary from day to day' (80), and which, to his dismay, also 'never seemed the same stairs, from one night to another', and 'now were steep, and now shallow, and now long, and now short, and now broad, and now narrow, and now dangerous, and now safe' (113).

In terms of this metaphor, Watt falls off the steps and stairs of habitual reality. Or, rephrased in terms of one of the key images in Beckett's short story 'Assumption' (1929), he is no longer able to 'proceed comfortably up a staircase of sensation, and sit down mildly on the topmost stair' in order to 'digest ... the pleasure of Prettiness', but is 'taken up bodily and pitched breathless on the peak of a sheer crag'.[23] Beckett rather optimistically defines this non-habitual 'sheer crag' as 'the pain of Beauty'.[24] Barthes in his turn refers to this domain as the 'wound' (73) of 'punctum'. But in *Watt*, this entry into the realm of intense non-habitual perceptions is associated neither with 'Beauty' nor with the bitter-sweet revelations that Barthes associates with 'punctum', but with the perceptual torments that Arsene describes to Watt as 'that fire in your mind that shall never be snuffed, or only with the utmost difficulty' (61). Henceforth, Watt becomes the victim of

events that resisted all Watt's efforts to saddle them with meaning, and a formula, so that he could neither think of them, nor speak of them, but only suffer them, when they recurred. (75–6)

This mental 'fall' has its physical counterpart in the contorted shape of the first substantial character in *Watt*: the quaintly named 'Hunchy Hackett'. Hunchy hints that his hunchback dates back to that time when, at the tender age of one, he 'fell off the ladder' (13). While Hunchy quite literally falls off the ladder of habitual physical existence, Arsene and Watt fall from the more figurative 'ladder' of habitual mental existence. As they discover, this fall has two distinct phases.

First of all, they leave the habitual macrocosm of the world outside Mr Knott's house in order to work within this non-habitual, microcosmic domain. Initially, Mr Knott's house seems to afford the same kind of security that the early Belacqua finds in the microcosm of his 'tunnel', and that Murphy finds among the 'microcosmopolitans' (*Murphy*, 163) in the Magdalen Mental Mercyseat. Overcome by what he describes as 'premonitions ... of imminent harmony', Arsene feels 'in his midst at last, after so many tedious years spent clinging to the perimeter' (39), and prepares to enjoy the utopian inactivity of 'a situation where to do nothing exclusively would be an act of the highest value and significance' (39).

Had Arsene enjoyed the improbable advantage of reading Beckett's *Dream of Fair to Middling Women* and *Murphy*, then his initial exaltation in the house of Mr Knott might have been more reserved. Arsene would have been aware that Belacqua similarly cherishes the hope that his 'tunnel' will grant him 'immunity' (*Dream*, 107) from all the 'somethings', before he succumbs to 'pestilential consciousness' (*Dream*, 149); and he would doubtless recollect that while Murphy initially feels 'in his midst at last' among 'the race or people he had long despaired of finding' (*Murphy*, 117), and hopes to join them in 'doing nothing' (*Murphy*, 116), he too finally succumbs to the 'deeper coils' (*Murphy* 172) of non-habitual consciousness. But not having read either of these works, Arsene is quite unprepared for the way in which the relatively idyllic early phase of his non-habitual existence in Mr Knott's house is fated to give way to 'The change' (41).

Like the final cogitations of Belacqua in 'Yellow', this traumatic process takes place before a sunlit wall, and seems to offer yet another Beckettian reversal of Bergotte's bliss before his 'little patch of yellow wall' (III.187) in *A la recherche du temps perdu*. Hesitantly describing this 'change' to Watt, Arsene explains:

Something slipped. There I was, warm and bright ... watching the warm bright wall, when suddenly somewhere some little thing slipped, some tiny little thing. ... The sun on the wall ... underwent an instantaneous and I venture to say radical change of appearance. It was the same sun and the same wall ... but so changed that I felt I had been transported, without my having remarked it, to some quite different yard, and to some quite different season, in an unfamiliar country. (41–2)

This 'change' is the key event in Arsene's and Watt's misadventures. It is at this point that they 'slip' from the idyllic non-habitual tranquillity that the narrator of 'Echo's Bones' defines as 'a beatitude of sloth' (*EB*, 2), and fall into the perceptual inferno which Arsene associates with 'that fire in your mind that shall never be snuffed' (61). As Arsene emphasizes: 'What was changed was existence off the ladder' (42). Having savoured non-habitual inactivity, Arsene and Watt 'slip' into a state of frantic, non-habitual mental *activity*. While the comedy and the formal symmetry of *Watt* arise from Watt's manic attempts to translate his newly discovered 'unspeakable' (82) confusion into 'old words' (115), its tragic (or, at least, its pathetic) dimension derives from Arsene's and Watt's complete inability to retain the tranquillity of 'existence off the ladder' before 'the change'.

Arsene and Watt can quite literally do nothing to restore the 'positive peace' which they, like Murphy, associate with 'Nothing' (*Murphy*, 168). At best they merely reduce the pangs of 'punctum' by contorting non-habitual experience into the habitual, 'rung'-like paradigms of 'studium', and 'so descend, so mount, rung by rung' (43). But, as Watt realizes, such exercises afford only 'a comparative peace of mind' (114–15). Accordingly, his final philosphy is one of nihilism and despair. For example, having pondered upon the advantages of shutting a door, sitting down and setting down his bags in a whole series of different ways, he finally decides to do none of these things despite his discomfort and fatigue. As the narrator explains:

the conclusion of Watt's reflexions was this, that if one of these things was worth doing, all were worth doing, but that none was worth doing, no, not one, but that all were unadvisable, without exception. (220)

Like Beckett's *Waiting for Godot*, *Watt* is something of a 'tragi-comedy'.[25] For, as the lines above indicate, the general tone of *Watt* fluctuates from the heights of highly stylized comedy to the depths of despair. On other occasions, the transition works in reverse, when statements of despair suddenly contradict themselves by displaying dazzling instances of wordplay. On the one hand, the following statement by Arsene seems to confirm Beckett's gloomy thesis that 'to be an artist is to fail, as no other dare fail' (*PTD*, 125), since:

what we know partakes in no small measure of the nature of what has so happily been called the unutterable or ineffable, so that any attempt to utter or eff it is doomed to fail, doomed, doomed to fail. (61)

On the other hand, however, these lines temper their cloudy message with the joke arising from Beckett's mischievous derivation of the verb 'to eff' from the adjective 'ineffable'. This seemingly innocent sonorous wordplay assumes rather less

innocent overtones when one harkens back to the passage in
Dream of Fair to Middling Women in which Beckett similarly
deploys the adjective 'effing' in order to censor, abbreviate, or
perhaps, insinuate, the expletive 'fucking', as he muses: 'No
effing smoking in the effing Folterzimmer' (*Dream*, 64). Watt
likewise savours the silver lining of vulgar wordplay as Mr
Graves's Irish accent inadvertently transforms the words 'third
and fourth' into 'Turd and fart' (142). He is also 'exceeding fond'
of such 'meaningless sounds' as the 'wild dim chatter' (208) of
Mr Knott and the almost Oriental harmonies of 'the rain on the
bamboos, or even rushes' (209).

Such amusing and harmonious formulae and sounds only
offer Watt the most fleeting relief from what Estragon might term
'the horror of his situation' (*WFG*, 15). As one of the poems in the
addenda to *Watt* suggests, his 'situation' is one which 'Watt will
not abate one jot' (250). Ultimately, all the puns, all the jokes, all
the meaningless sounds, and all the fearful symmetry of Watt's
models, rules and systems, will not sweeten his situation.
Despite his hunger for such 'semantic succour' (79), and, one
might add, for 'structuralist succour', his confidence in these
remedies appears appallingly ill-founded. Not surprisingly, the
narrator comments: 'One wonders sometimes where Watt
thought he was. In a culture-park?' (73).

It is for this reason that any analysis of *Watt* must look beyond
the cultural conventions delineated by those critics establishing
the 'death of the novel' or the 'death of the author'. The novel is
obviously a treasure-trove of examples for those attempting to
'weigh', 'mete' and 'assess' such conventions. But, as the first of
the poems in the addenda intimates, it also concerns something
beyond the parameters of the 'culture-park' of 'studium'; a
'something' that Beckett is hard put to define, save with the
questions:

who may tell the tale
of the old man?
weigh absence in a scale?
the sum assess
of the world's woes?
nothingness
in words enclose? (247)

Despite his seductive insistence upon the inevitability of
failure, and despite his claims to be working with 'impotence,
ignorance',[26] Beckett's *Watt*, like all his previous and subsequent

writings, evokes a particularly Beckettian world view which
necessitates definition in its own terms and, more specifically,
within its own most forceful terms, or 'punctum', rather than in
terms of more general systems, rules and conventions. Were this
not the case, there would be little difference between *Watt* and
the many other Post-Modern works employing permutations
and other systematic modes of composition, such as the texts of
Brion Gysin, John Cage, Edwin Morgan and Ernst Jandl, to name
but a few contemporaries working in analogous compositional
fields. Gysin, for example, permutates phrases such as 'junk is
no good baby' in order to 'make words sing' in such stanzas as:

> JUNK IS NO GOOD BABY
> JUNK IS GOOD — NO BABY
> JUNK IS BABY — NO GOOD
> JUNK IS NO BABY — GOOD
> JUNK IS GOOD BABY — NO
> JUNK IS BABY GOOD — NO[27]

The American composer John Cage has redeployed Joyce's
Finnegans Wake by following the 'rule' of selecting 'the first words
on each page that presents him with the letters to spell out
Joyce's name, thus creating a new text' founded upon both this
system and its chance materials.[28] Cage's 'Writing for the Third
Time Through *Finnegans Wake*' commences:

> wroth with twone nathand Joe
> A
> Malt
> jh Em
> Shen[29]

The Scottish poet Edwin Morgan has, in turn, subjected Cage
to poetic justice in 'Opening the Cage', a poem which elaborates
'14 variations' on Cage's dictum 'I have nothing to say and I am
saying it and that is poetry'. This playful tribute to Cage begins:

> I have to say poetry and is that nothing and am I saying it
> I am and I have poetry to say and is that nothing saying it
> I am nothing and I have poetry to say and that is saying it
> I that am saying poetry have nothing and it is I and to say[30]

Finally, in a still more abstract vein, appealing as much to the
appearance of words upon the page as to their sound or

meaning, the Austrian poet Ernst Jandl has permutated the
letters that make up the word 'film' in order to create a semiotic
'film', depicting 'two actors, i and l', who appear, change
position, displace one another, and then reappear in the poem's
'happy ending'. Jandl's 'film' begins:

        film
        film
        film
        film
        fi m
        f im
        fi m
        f im
        f m[31]

It should be obvious by now that Post-Modern literature
contains a wide variety of permutational and systematic
compositions. If *Watt* deserves attention, then this is not simply
because it exemplifies this or that compositional system.
Innumerable works fulfil this function. Few permutational or
systematic compositions, however, generate an inimitable world
view in the manner of *Watt*, and it is to this quintessentially
Beckettian prospect that we must now return. As we shall see,
the existential priorities of *Watt*, like those of Beckett's earlier
fiction, may be both disentangled and deciphered in terms of the
more wayward, anti-Proustian postulations in Beckett's *Proust*.

Like Proust's vision, Beckett's is peculiarly romantic, insofar as
it doggedly pursues one particular concept of utopia, and
doggedly derides all others. For example, like Proust, he has little
time for the utopian objectivity of those who would reduce
reality to realist and naturalist fiction, or to what one might term
the banalities of 'studium'. Beckett's esssay approvingly paraphrases Proust's contempt for 'the prejudices of the intelligence'
(*PTD*, 71) and the 'piteous acceptance of face values' (*PTD*, 63),
and *Watt* suggests in turn that reality can be reduced neither to
'series of hypotheses' (75) nor to the miserable 'face values' (70)
from which Watt falls upon entering the house of Mr Knott.
Clearly, then, Beckett and Proust share the same 'anti-
intellectual tendency' (*PTD*, 81).

But, as we have seen, Beckett not only rejects utopian
objectivity, but also the utopian subjectivity that Proust
associates with the 'Enchantments' (*PTD*, 22) of non-habitual
reality. While Proust's utopia consists of 'rememoration, in its

highest sense' (*PTD*, 31), Watt's most dystopian experiences are those which threaten his habitual 'peace of mind' (75), and which revisit his mind in all their 'unintelligible intricacies' at 'the most unexpected moments, and the most inopportune' (73).

Accordingly, whereas Proust advocates the utopian lucidity that Beckett's essay perspicaciously qualifies as 'the free play of every faculty' (*PTD*, 20), Watt dreads such lucidity. For him, as for all of Beckett's heroes, involuntary lucidity is synonymous with involuntary anguish and the 'suffering of being' (*PTD*, 20). Quite predictably, Beckett defines his variant of utopia as the 'ablation' (*PTD*, 18) and the 'obliterating' (*PTD*, 63) of every faculty, or that state which Arsene and Watt briefly enjoy upon arriving in the house of Mr Knott, when they 'do nothing exclusively' (39).

Having attributed his own pessimistic wisdom to *A la recherche du temps perdu*, Beckett proceeds to discuss it as if it really did depict a world in which the only utopia was an unattainable state of 'Nothing', and in which all relationships, and indeed existence as a whole, represented 'a grotesque predetermined activity, within the narrow limits of an impure world' (*PTD*, 89). While this phrase utterly misrepresents Proust's existential vision, it prophetically summarizes the peculiarly disturbing representations of friendship, love and the general human (or inhuman) condition in *Watt*.

Beckett's essay caricatures Proust's presentation of friendship as 'a simian vulgarity', as something 'horribly comic' and as 'a social expedient' (*PTD*, 63). These phrases, combined with Beckett's aforementioned concept of the grotesquely 'predetermined', foreshadow the way in which Beckettian characters, such as Estragon and Vladimir, Pozzo and Lucky, and at another level, Estragon, Vladimir and Godot, are all tied to one another by grotesquely predetermined variants of friendship, companionship or interdependence. While Watt's relationship with Mr Knott is not exactly one of friendship, it is certainly very much a kind of 'social expedient, like . . . the distribution of garbage buckets' (*PTD*, 63).

Watt seems compelled to set himself 'turning about Mr Knott in tireless love' (61), like some garbage bucket distributor, and Mr Knott seems to be similarly dependent upon Watt and his other servants to distribute his 'garbage'. Although Mr Knott would prefer to have 'no one about him at all', he is 'obliged to have someone at all about him, to look after him, being quite incapable of looking after himself' (57). Worse still, although Mr

Knott patently desires the Beckettian utopia of 'the neutralisation of needs' (*Dream*, 107), he finds himself trapped within the paradoxical bind of 'needing nothing if not, one, not to need, and two, a witness to his not needing' (202). In this respect, *Watt* prefigures the disquieting interdependency between victims and oppressors which Beckett increasingly depicts in his mature fiction, and in such nightmarish scenarios as *Play*, in which the source of light interrogating three of the living dead 'begins to emerge as no less a victim of his inquiry than they'.[32]

Watt also prefigures Beckett's increasing emphasis upon grotesque and sadistic variants of love and of human relationships and existence as a whole: a development which also harkens back to his misreadings in *Proust*. According to this essay, Proust considered love to be a 'tragedy', whose 'failure is preordained' (*PTD*, 18), and which at best 'may have the nobility of that which is tragic' (*PTD*, 63). Suffice it to remark that this conclusion both travesties the complexity of Proust's representation of the human condition, and anticipates the inhuman condition represented in Beckettian variations of love.

Unlike *Watt*, Beckett's earlier fiction, particularly *Murphy*, describes love in terms which waver between the 'tragic' and the 'grotesquely predetermined'. Celia's devotion to Murphy is depicted with considerable poignancy, while the narrator rather more frivolously admits of 'Neary's love for Miss Dyer, who loved a Flight-Lieutenant Elliman, who loved a Miss Faren of Ringaskiddy, who loved a Father Fitt of Ballinclashet, who in all sincerity was bound to acknowledge a certain vocation for a Mrs West of Passage, who loved Neary' (*Murphy*, 7). But the narrator of *Watt* takes pains to deprecate the least sign of genuine affection.

For example, having described the way in which Mrs Case responds with particular 'satisfaction' to the sound of her husband's footfalls, the narrator abruptly concludes: 'She was a strange woman' (233). By contrast, he patiently elaborates grotesquely graphic accounts of Watt's embraces with Mrs Gorman, an admittedly strange woman 'of an advanced age and by nature also denied those properties that attract men to women' (137), whose solitary breast comforts Watt 'for as long as ten minutes, or a quarter of an hour' (138), while Watt kisses her in 'a despairing manner ... on or about the mouth, before crumpling back into his post-crucified position' (139).

Such sacrilegious jokes and allusions as this reference to Watt's 'post-crucified position' abound in this novel and in Beckett's subsequent writings. At their best, they precipitate splendidly pithy ironies. When Hunchy Hackett belatedly reports the indecent behaviour of a couple to a passing policeman, and piously protests 'Officer . . . as God is my witness, he had his hand upon it', the narrator memorably chimes in: 'God is a witness that cannot be sworn' (6). At worst, they culminate in Sam's sinister confession that he and Watt 'agreed . . . that we came nearest to God', when, having encouraged rats to 'glide up our trouserlegs and hang upon our breasts', they nourish these 'particular friends' by 'seizing suddenly a plump young rat, resting in our bosom after its repast', so as to 'feed it to its mother, or its father, or its brother, or its sister, or to some less fortunate relative' (153). By way of prelude to this confidence, Sam similarly specifies:

Robins, in particular, thanks to their confidingness, we destroyed in great numbers. And larks' nests, laden with eggs still warm from the mothers' breast, we ground into fragments, under our feet, with particular satisfaction. (153)

Passages like these suddenly confront the reader with symptoms of the peculiarly powerful and peculiarly unnerving impact of Beckett's most horrific writing.[33] Roland Barthes might describe this quality as its 'punctum'. Proust might describe it as Beckett's 'accent' (I.553). Beckett himself would probably describe it as 'the power of the text to claw'.[34]

With the discovery of this disturbing 'power', Beckett's writing attains its maturity. For all his insistence upon the way in which 'all writing, qua writing, is bound to fail',[35] his subsequent novels evoke the horrors of 'The change' (41) with ever increasing intensity. As we have suggested, Watt offers a deceptively restrained and a deceptively light-hearted account of its hero's desperate attempts to escape 'pestilential consciousness' (Dream, 149) and to attain the utopian 'immunity' (Dream, 107) of that 'neutral point' (Dream, 24) where 'the somethings give way . . . to Nothing' (Murphy, 168), and 'where to do nothing exclusively would be an act of the highest value and significance' (39).

Watt fails to attain this 'immunity', just as all inhabitants of Beckett's 'grotesque predetermined' (PTD, 89) fictional cosmos fail to attain, or retain, it. The following chapter will consider the ways in which Beckett compulsively redefines this irremediable dilemma, and patiently perfects and refines his 'power to claw', both in and after the 'wordy-gurdy' of Molloy, Malone Dies and The Unnamable.

12
BECKETT'S MATURE FICTION —
FROM 'SHIT' TO 'SHADES'

Beckett's mature fiction falls into three general phases. The first of these encompasses the years from 1946 to 1960, when, upon returning to Paris after the second world war, his French trilogy, *Molloy*, *Malone Meurt* and *L'Innommable*, along with his *Textes pour rien* and *Comment c'est*, described the perceptual crises of narrator-heroes whose most singular characteristic seems to be their penchant for plunging 'headlong into the shit'.[1] During the next decade, his work entered a second phase, as he turned his attention to infernal cylindrical environments plagued by 'intractable complexities'.[2] More recently, ever since the early seventies to the present day, the third phase of his mature writing has elaborated haunting visions from the realm of 'Shades'[3] — an image which Beckett himself selected to describe his latest works, and which nicely annunciates both the penumbral and spectral quality of their eerie evocations of the peculiar parity between the torments afflicting the living, the dying, and the dead.

Beckett returned to Paris in the winter of 1945, having spent the two preceding years in unoccupied France writing *Watt*, and in the following years, as he entered his forties, he wrote his three most famous novels in French, composing *Molloy*, *Malone Meurt* and *L'Innommable* in rapid succession between 1947 and 1949. Beckett wrote their immediate successor, *Textes pour rien*, in 1950, and their final companion piece, *Comment c'est*, in 1960. By 1956 he already had sufficient sense of this first phase of his mature writing to comment:

I wrote all my work very fast — between 1946 and 1950. Since then I haven't written anything. Or nothing that has seemed to me valid. The French work brought me to the point where I felt I was saying the same thing over and over again.[4]

There is no reason to doubt the validity of Beckett's final comments. *Molloy, Malone Dies, The Unnamable* and *How It Is* are very much the evocation of 'the same thing over and over again'. In this respect, it makes very little sense to discuss these anti-fictions in terms of such conventional fictional categories as 'character' and 'plot'. For as the American novelist William Burroughs has remarked in one of his splendidly provocative overstatements, 'Beckett . . . has only one character',[5] and, one might add, 'only one plot'.

Occasionally, of course, the trilogy's narratives throw up vague hints that its protagonists are veiled portraits of their author, such as the seemingly 'uncanny resemblance' between the 'gull's eyes' (193) of 'Sapo' and of Beckett.[6] But, as Beckett remarks, such resemblances appear accidental, and the consequence of instances when his fiction 'got a bit out of hand'.[7] Usually, Beckett's fiction is kept so firmly 'in hand' that his characters bear little resemblance to anything 'rightly human'.[8] Speculating that there may well be grounds for arguing that 'there are no characters and no sets' in Beckett's mature fiction, William Burroughs belligerently ruminates:

What do the characters, if they could be called so in Beckett, even look like, beside being awkward and not young? And the sets? What sets? His writing can be taking place anywhere . . . If the role of the novelist is to create characters and sets in which his characters live and breathe, then Beckett is not a novelist at all.[9]

Despite the obvious objections and exceptions to Burroughs's argument, it offers a salutary reminder that Beckett creates a fiction of abstract situation which could take place 'anywhere', rather than a fiction of concrete character and location. In this respect, he creates ever more 'clawing' representations of the same paradigmatic dilemma, rather than adding to any gallery of characters with significant, individual names. Indeed, in *What Where*, a 'puppet' play of 1983, names merely differentiate successive protagonists slightly in time and space, somewhat as the seasons subdivide the cyclical action of the play, while the 'last five', Bam, Bom, Bim, Bem (and 'Bum' presumably), successively interrogate one another while Bam dispassionately announces:

I am alone. It is spring. Time passes . . .
I am alone. It is summer. Time passes . . .
I am alone. It is autumn. Time passes . . .

I am alone ... It is winter ... Time passes ...
Make sense who may. [10]

Like the 'sense' of Beckett's trilogy and of all of his writings,
the 'sense' of *What Where* is primarily paradigmatic. His
protagonists invariably discover that their existence consists of
endless perceptual crises, which come and go, one after the
other. The most significant difference between his mature
protagonists resides in the way in which the narrator-heroes of
the trilogy hysterically personify the cause of 'Self-perception
... the most frightening of human observations', [11] in terms of
abstract 'Throes' (179) or the series of interrogators and
interrogated that the narrator of *How It Is* envisages 'glued two by
two together' (121), whereas the 'Shades' in the most recent
fictions tend to proffer rather calmer indications of the way in
which the 'throes' of self-perception affect those abiding both
before and beyond the grave.

It is, of course, extremely easy to overlook these cyclical
perceptual crises, and to typecast Beckett's mature fiction in
terms of the literary and creative crises that he repeatedly
discusses in the various critical and theoretical writings that he
wrote upon his return to Paris after the war, when he first began
to write in French. While these texts give voice to Beckett's
poetics, his existential vision emerges somewhat more furtively,
in and between the lines of the novels, plays and poems, in
which, like Moran, he remains 'content with paradigms' (173)
and delineates 'Just the main themes' (153).

While Beckett's critical writings in the early thirties testify to
his gradual dissatisfaction with the mysticism of Proust and
Thomas MacGreevy, his post-war writings introduce an all-
encompassing dissatisfaction with any kind of utterance at all. To
be sure, *Watt* similarly depicts a state which resists formulation,
but it also good-naturedly records that Mr Knott's 'wild dim
chatter, meaningless to Watt's ailing ears' becomes 'a noise of
which Watt grew exceedingly fond' (*Watt*, 208). Beckett's post-
war criticism makes no provision for such gratification. For
example, his article on 'La peinture des Van Velde' (1946)
characteristically insists that its contents are not only babble, but
unpleasant babble: 'un bavardage désagréable et confus' (disagreeable and confused chatter). [12]

Two years later, the 'dialogues' with Georges Duthuit still
more pessimistically postulated that 'to be an artist is to fail, as no
other dare fail' (*PTD*, 125), and that the artist's 'situation' is 'that

of him who is helpless, cannot act' (*PTD*, 119), since, in Beckett's beautifully expressed formulae:

there is nothing to express, nothing with which to express, nothing from which to express, no power to express, no desire to express, together with the obligation to express. (*PTD*, 103)

For those critics preoccupied with the 'death' of the novel, the post-war fiction, such as *Molloy* (1950), must have seemed like the answer to a prayer. For here, the narrator-hero not only bewails the limitations of language, when carefully folding such antitheses as 'there could be no things but nameless things, no names but thingless names' (31), but also appears to echo both the intonation and the implications of the passage above:

Not to want to say, not to know what you want to say, not to be able to say what you think you want to say, and never to stop saying, or hardly ever, that is the thing to keep in mind, even in the heat of composition. (28)

Molloy once again deploys such rhetoric when he muses:

For to know nothing is nothing, not to want to know anything likewise, but to be beyond knowing anything, to know you are beyond knowing anything, that is when peace enters in, to the soul of the incurious seeker. (64)

Arguably, though, there is a crucial difference between these negative refrains from the Duthuit dialogues and from *Molloy*. Whereas the dialogues focus upon the aesthetic problem of satisfying 'the obligation to express' in the absence of something 'to express', Molloy's meditations emphasize the desirability of having nothing to express, nothing to say, and best of all, nothing to know. Despite their hesitation before 'the common anxiety to express as much as possible, or as truly as possible, or as finely as possible', the Duthuit dialogues take the artist's 'expressive possibilities' (*PTD*, 120) sufficiently seriously to argue that the artist should avoid 'puny exploits' (*PTD*, 103), if only by transforming art into 'an expressive act . . . of itself, of its impossibility, of its obligation' (*PTD*, 125). According to this argument, the artist answers the creative obligation by boldly exhibiting incompetence.

At first sight, the narrator-heroes of Beckett's trilogy appear to evince the same intolerance towards 'puny exploits', as they scrupulously admit to their 'distortion of the truth' (209), and resolutely determine never 'to give way to literature' (152). But, as Malone observes, 'theory is one thing and reality another' (247). For all their theoretical hostility to 'literature', the narrator-heroes are in practice, or in 'reality', concerned not so much with their expressive possibilities as with their repressive and suppressive capabilities. Rather than responding to perceptual and expressive obligations with 'I can not', Beckett's heroes reply with variants of 'I shall not', 'I will not' or 'I am not', and distract themselves with 'puny exploit' after 'puny exploit' in order to nullify the 'Throes' (179) of introspection. Malone, for example, proposes to remain 'neutral and inert' (179) by recounting neutral and inert 'gibberish' (207) as he lies dying (and dies lying):

While waiting I shall tell myself stories, if I can. . . . They will be neither beautiful nor ugly, they will be calm, there will be no ugliness or beauty or fever in them any more, they will be almost lifeless, like the teller. (180)

Malone's problem, like that of all of Beckett's protagonists, is that he cannot remain 'neutral and inert', and cannot inhabit the Beckettian Shangri-La 'above the deluge' in that 'quiet zone above the nightmare' (*Dream*, 23) which Belacqua associates with 'tranquil living at the neutral point' (*Dream*, 24). Ugliness, beauty and the whole 'nightmare' of their personal history continually erupt within the consciousness of 'the incurious seeker' (64), as 'suddenly all begins to rage and roar again' and 'you begin to wonder if you have not died without knowing and gone to hell or been reborn again into an even worse place than before' (227).

If Molloy, Malone and the Unnamable, and all of their subsequent incarnations and reincarnations continue to 'go on' (418), this seems to be because their various stories and hypotheses offer them the only alternative that they know to the horrors of introspection. In the course of these stories and hypotheses, they distract themselves (and their readers) with innumerable pithy references to writers, philosophers, academic reviews and so on, along with occasional and variously veiled allusions to Beckett's personal experience. Yet far more significant, perhaps, than the ambiguous implications of the majority of these digressions is the fact that they are deliberately vague and inconsequential. Put another way, they typify the 'puny exploits' which Molloy defines as 'dutiful confusions' (15), and which Malone associates with the process of 'incurious wondering' (181).

As Malone helpfully stipulates, the stories and hypotheses in the trilogy follow the pattern 'supposer, nier, affirmer, nier' (65), or 'suppose, deny, affirm, drown' (210). And as the Unnamable specifies in his turn, these 'affirmations and negations invalidated as uttered' (393) serve 'to put off the hour when I must speak of me' (306). Somewhat as Watt's attempts to turn his disturbances into words afford him 'comparative peace of mind' (*Watt*, 114–15), Molloy and his fellow narrators find that their various narratives similarly provide a certain 'precarious calm' (49) and 'comparative peace of mind' (73), until 'the anguish of return' (42), when they once more find themselves exposed to 'all the horrors of it all all over again' (49), as though they were continually re-experiencing the agonies of Mr Kurtz at the end of Conrad's *Heart of Darkness*.

As we have seen, Molloy characterizes this dialectic between comparative peace of mind and intolerable self-awareness in fairly abstract 'light' and 'dark' imagery, describing his experience in terms of 'a deep and merciful torpor shot with brief abominable gleams' (54). Malone rather differently personifies his perceptual obligations by alluding to a mysterious third party who visits and interrupts him in the middle of his stories, and places him 'back in the shit' (270). Malone's English narrative explains:

I have had a visit. Things were going too well. I had forgotten myself, lost myself . . . I was elsewhere. Another was suffering. Then I had the visit. To bring me back to dying. (269)

Its French counterpart still more ominously observes:

On est venu. Ça allait trop bien. Je m'étais oublié, perdu . . . J'étais ailleurs. Un autre souffrait. Alors on est venu. Pour me rappeler à l'agonie. (178)

Taking this anonymous personification one step further, and elaborating Watt's passing reference to 'the meticulous phantoms that beset him' (*Watt*, 74), the Unnamable complains of his involuntary perceptual obligations in terms of 'the voices and thoughts of the devils who beset me' (350), and imagines that these 'devils' are similarly beset by yet another series of 'devils' towards whom they must turn 'to sue for their freedom' (387). In much the same way, *Rough for Radio II*, composed in the early

1960s, some fifteen years after *The Unnamable*, dramatizes the way in which an interrogating 'animator' and his tearful stenographer 'beset' the strangely named 'Fox', before finally revealing that they too appear answerable to some other 'devils' whose unwelcome authority prompts the 'animator' to conclude: 'Don't cry, Miss ... Tomorrow, who knows, we may be free'.[13] Beckett's *Play*, which also dates from the earlier sixties, similarly elaborates this motif by depicting a situation in which an 'inquirer (light)' emerges as the 'victim of his inquiry ... and as needing to be free'.[14]

As in *The Unnamable*, the interrogators in *Rough for Radio II* inhabit a mysterious situation in which only the most basic imperatives are clear. The Unnamable's interrogator confides: 'you don't understand, neither do I' (381); and the 'animator' similarly admits: 'It does not lie entirely with us, we know' (*R*, 121). All that is 'known' is that the Unnamable has somehow or other evaded or avoided his 'identity', just as 'Fox' has somehow or other refused to treat some crucial 'subject'. Accordingly, the Unnamable is implored to accept the identity depicted, as it were, in a photograph, by voices which plead:

But my dear man, come, be reasonable, look, this is you, look at this photograph ... make an effort, at your age, to have no identity, it's a scandal. (380)

'Fox' is similarly informed:

Be reasonable, Fox ... stop jibbing. It's hard on you, we know ... But this much is sure: the more you say the greater your chances. .... Don't ramble! Treat the subject whatever it is! (*R*, 121)

Like 'Fox', however, the Unnamable endlessly 'jibs' and 'rambles', generating incessant 'wordy-gurdy' (403) about 'Mahood', 'Worm' and other 'delegates' (299) in order to prolong 'the alleviations of flight from self' (371). Viewed in Proustian terms, the Unnamable, like Molloy, Malone and all of Beckett's subsequent narrators, discovers that 'nous avons le don d'inventer des contes pour bercer notre douleur' (III.464) (we have the gift of inventing stories to soothe our sufferings), and thereafter determines to 'go on' (418), endlessly, in order to obscure 'the mad need to speak, to think, to know' (349). Needless to say, the Unnamable's interminable stories are supremely 'puny' and inconsequential, since:

The essential is never to arrive anywhere, never to be anywhere, neither where Mahood is, nor where Worm is, nor where I am . . . The essential is to go on squirming forever at the end of the line. (341)

Considered in terms of post-Structuralist theory, such as the writings of Jean Baudrillard, the Unnamable and his fellow narrators seem to aspire to the 'weightless' vacuity that Baudrillard rather nihilistically discerns throughout contemporary culture. Having pondered upon the ways in which the mass media become 'murderers of the real' by 'substituting signs of the real for the real itself', Baudrillard concludes:

the whole system becomes weightless, it is no longer anything but a gigantic simulacrum — not unreal, but a simulacrum, never again exchanging for what is real, but exchanging in itself, in an uninterrupted circuit without reference or circumference. [15]

In a sense, the Unnamable and company similarly generate fictional modes of 'uninterrupted circuit without reference or circumference', or endlessly self-negating and self-perpetuating narratives which never 'arrive anywhere' (341). Indeed, in *How It Is* (1964), the narrator-hero quite literally depicts an 'uninter-rupted circuit' of tormenting and tormented 'delegates', describing 'a procession without end or beginning languidly wending from left to right' (139). He carefully specifies:

let us be numbered 1 to 1000000 then number 1000000 on leaving his tormentor number 999999 instead of launching forth into the wilderness towards an inexistent victim proceeds towards number 1

and number 1 forsaken by his victim number 2 does not remain eternally bereft of tormentor since this latter as we have seen in the person of number 1000000 is approaching with all the speed he can muster right leg right arm push pull ten yards fifteen yards (127)

Significantly, though, the Unnamable and the narrator of *How It Is* both suffer from moments of interruption when their 'weightless' fantasies give way to instants of substantial intro-spection. Discovering the presence of 'something there' (119), the narrator of *How It Is* admits that he is periodically vulnerable to visions of 'an old tale my old life' in between his encounters with his fellow victims and tormentors, 'each time Pim leaves me till Bom finds me' (145). On these rare occasions, he imagines the way in which equally tormented tribes of witnesses and scribes hover over his every word:

Kram who listens Krim who notes or Kram alone one is enough Kram
alone witness and scribe his lamps their light upon me Kram with me
bending over me till the age-limit then his son and his son's son so on
(145)

In much the same way, the Unnamable admits that his stories,
and the voices of his interrogators, sometimes falter during 'little
silences' (351) which initially offer a certain relief, and then
threateningly elicit precisely the kind of confessional statement
that he wishes to avoid. Like the house of Mr Knott and the
M.M.M., these instants reveal, or threaten to reveal, the way in
which blissfully neutral modes of non-habitual existence may
suddenly mutate into non-habitual revelations of 'all the usual'.
Pondering upon the ambiguous potential of these 'silences', the
Unnamable disconcertedly muses:

That's why there are all these little silences, to try and make me break
them. . . . It's true I dread these gulfs they all bend over, straining their
ears for the murmur of a man. It isn't silence, it's pitfalls, into which
nothing would please me better than to fall . . . and vanish for good and
all, having squeaked. (351)

The Unnamable's final comments are, of course, facetious.
Ultimately, he has no intention of 'squeaking' about himself,
although like all of Beckett's characters, he has every intention of
vanishing 'for good and all', were this only possible. But as all of
them discover in one way or another, they cannot vanish for
good and all.

Alive or dead, dead or alive, they invariably perceive the
'something there' (119) espied by the narrator of *How It Is*, as
some fragment from some 'old life' (145) zooms back into focus,
and demonstrates that their world is 'not yet bare'. Beckett's
most striking summary of this process appears in 'Something
There', a poem of 1974, in which a strangely disembodied voice
relates:

> something there
> where
> out there
> out where
> outside
> what
> the head what else
> something there somewhere outside
> the head

at the faint sound so brief
it is gone and the whole globe
not yet bare
the eye
opens wide
wide
till in the end
nothing more
shutters it again

so the odd time
out there
somewhere out there
like as if
as if
something
not life
necessarily[16]

The restrained, contemplative tone with which 'Something There' traces 'something/ not life/ necessarily' typifies the strangely resigned register of Beckett's recent fiction. By contrast, *Molloy*, *Malone Dies*, *The Unnamable* and *How It Is* continually testify to his power 'to claw', as his narrator-heroes 'shit stories' (383) in order to obscure revelations of 'something there'. While 'Something There' soothes the ear with resonant lines such as 'somewhere out there', the 'terror-stricken babble' (357) of these narrators 'claws' the reader with savage excremental rhetoric and systematically anti-Proustian imagery.

Molloy, for example, defines birth as the 'First taste of the shit' (16); defines himself as 'rather inclined to plunge headlong into the shit' (32); and conveys his contempt for humanity in the confession: 'Now they all give me the shits, the ripe, the unripe and the rotting from the bough' (83). Moran likewise describes his condition as 'the turd waiting for the flush' (163) and, in his French narrative, confides that he lives at 'Shit' (207); while Malone derides the head as 'the seat of all the shit and misery' (269); and the Unnamable speaks for all his fellow narrators when he announces: 'it's like shit, there we have it at last, the right word' (368). Confirming this hypothesis, the narrator of *How It Is* grimly envisages humanity as 'billions of us crawling and shitting in their shit' (58).

Considered more or less literally, this monotonous rhetoric emphasizes the physical degradation of Beckett's fictional cosmos, and the Beckettian protagonist's consistent 'horror of

the body and its functions' (118). Considered more metaphorically, the state of being 'back in the shit' (270) obviously
refers to the Beckettian hero's perennial vulnerability to the
'deeper coils' and 'devils' (250) of rememoration. In their turn,
these crises precipitate such 'clawing' images as Malone's
description of Lemuel, who, 'when not rooted to the spot in a
daze',

was to seen, with heavy, furious, reeling tread, stamping up and down
for hours on end, gesticulating and ejaculating unintelligible words.
(268)

Explaining that Lemuel is 'Flayed alive by memory ... not
daring to dream or think and powerless not to', Malone chillingly
describes the way in which Lemuel seeks solace by hammering
his head, adding the afterthought, 'it's only human' (268–9).

Lemuel's distractions are, of course, patently inhuman,
though not quite so horrific as the literally 'clawing' manner by
which the narrator of *How It Is* elicits distracting discourse from
his fellow travellers. Teaching a certain 'Pim' to sing, the narrator
of *How It Is* relates:

first lesson theme song I dig my nails into his armpit right hand right pit
he cries I withdraw them thump with fist on skull his face sinks in the
mud his cries cease end of first lesson (69)

This musical divertissement clearly elaborates Molloy's slightly
gentler system of communicating with his aged mother 'by
knocking her on the skull', and by 'replacing the four knocks of
my index knuckle by one or more ... thumps of the fist' (18). In
addition, each of these incidents also subverts Marcel's cherished description of the way in which his 'three little taps' (I.669)
allow him to communicate with his grandmother at Balbec.

Somewhat later in his narrative, Marcel once again eulogizes
these 'three little taps':

Et je ne demandais rien de plus à Dieu, s'il existe un paradis, que d'y
pouvoir frapper contre cette cloison des trois petits coups que ma
grand'mère reconnaitrait entre mille, et auxquels elle répondrait par ces
autres coups qui voulaient dire: "Ne t'agite pas, petite souris". (II.763)

(And I would not ask any more from God, if there really is a paradise,
than to be able, once again, to drum against that partition with the three
little taps which my grandmother could pick out from a thousand
others, and to which she would reply with those other taps which meant
"Don't worry, little mouse".)

In his turn, Molloy once again claws at Proust's values. Reducing Marcel's paean to triumphant gestural communication to the banality of his infantile enthusiasm for the sound of his bicycle-horn, Molloy garrulously confides:

if I were obliged to record, in a roll of honour, those activities which in the course of my interminable existence have given me only a mild pain in the balls, the blowing of a rubber horn — toot! — would figure among the first. (16)

The volumes of Beckett's trilogy, and *Molloy* in particular, abound with this kind of more or less self-conscious derision of Proustian ideals. Whereas Marcel innocently celebrates the beauty of hawthorns (I.145), the splendour of Françoise's cuisine (I.121), the originality of Vinteuil's music (III.258) and the charm of cathedrals (I.100), Molloy cynically comments: 'unfortunately I don't like the smell of hawthorn' (27) and 'Unfortunately I don't much care for good things to eat' (37), while Moran pauses to make such jaded asides as: 'If there is one thing gets on my nerves it is music' (105) and 'Passing the church, something made me stop. I looked at the door, baroque, very fine. I found it hideous' (100).

Beckett's twofold 'power to claw' surfaces once again in *The Unnamable*, in which this unspeakable narrator mercilessly festoons his stories with such repulsive details as 'my skull, covered with pustules and bluebottles' (330), and mirthlessly lampoons Marcel by formulating yet another counter-version of the miracle of the 'three little taps' at Balbec. Marcel commemorates the way in which the partition between him and his grandmother resonates with affection and appears to be 'pénétrée de tendresse et de joie' (I.670) (penetrated with tenderness and joy). Reversing this response, the Unnamable appropriates Marcel's vocabulary by comparing himself with a partition,[17] and then extolls the way in which his mind enjoys a state of vacuous stasis, before reverberating with the 'fear and fury' (390) of unwanted consciousness. Lovingly mulling over this short-lived anti-Proustian idyll, the Unnamable blissfully muses:

an outside and an inside and me in the middle, perhaps that's what I am, the thing that divides the world in two, on the one side the outside, on the other inside ... I'm neither one side nor the other, I'm in the middle, I'm the partition, I've two surfaces and no thickness ... on the one hand the mind, on the other the world, I don't belong to either. (386)

Once again a Beckettian character temporarily enjoys non-habitual tranquillity 'in the middle', between the microcosm of 'the mind' and the macrocosm of 'the world'. Considered in early Beckettian terms, the Unnamable discovers the kind of 'immunity' from both 'centripetal' and 'centrifugal' reality that Belacqua defines as his ideal 'neutral point' (*Dream*, 107 and 24). Or viewed in the Unnamable's terms, his condition approximates to his dream of a realm 'between' speech and thought, and therefore 'bereft of speech, bereft of thought', in which he may 'feel nothing, hear nothing, know nothing, say nothing' (390).

For an instant the Unnamable seems on the brink of uttering the triumphant chuckle that the narrator of *Texts for Nothing* defines as 'the long silent guffaw of the knowing non-exister' (*TFN*, 59). But this is not to be. Having had 'no thickness', and having virtually evaded speech and thought, the Unnamable falls back into the thick of introspection and utterance, finding 'words ... everywhere, inside me outside me', and confesses: 'I'm in words, made of words, others' words ... all words' (390).

The emphasis upon 'others' words' typifies the way in which the Unnamable's outbursts deny his 'true situation, revolting word' (311). Like the narrator of *Texts for Nothing*, who vehemently protests, 'It's not me, it's not true, it's not me, I'm far' (*TFN*, 18), and like 'Mouth', who still more frantically disgorges 'mad stuff', such as 'what? ... who? ... no! ... she! ... SHE!' (*Not I*, 15) in order to deny her identity, the Unnamable concludes his narrative with an avalanche of uneasy denials and negations: 'it won't be I ... it will never be I ... it was never I ... It's not I ... it can't be I ... I am far' (416–17). As William Burroughs remarks, when pondering upon the declining circumstances of the Beckettian narrator-hero in *The Unnamable* and *How It Is*, 'First he was in the bottle and now he is in the mud'.[18] Burrough's epigrammatic conclusion economically emphasizes the way in which Beckett's mature fiction rapidly becomes increasingly hermetic, abstract and private; and he probably speaks for the majority of Beckett's admirers when he describes the novels from *Murphy* to *Malone Dies* as 'terrific books', but expresses reservations about *The Unnamable*. While Burroughs sympathetically alludes to the perceptual conflicts, or 'differences', at the heart of this novel, he suggests that *The Unnamable* carries the fiction of physical immobility too far:

When I came to *The Unnamable* I just couldn't follow him somehow, he just couldn't hold my attention. I know what he's talking about, that when you get in far enough there are different organisms, different interests, in the same body. But he wound up much too static.[19]

This disconcerting sense of stasis becomes even more intense in the second, 'environmental', phase of Beckett's mature fiction, in which he tends to depict aged, anonymous and virtually fossilized figures encased within the kind of clinical structures that both the Unnamable and the narrator of *How It Is* occasionally prefigure when their rare architectural fantasies transport them beyond 'the bottle' and 'the mud' to more abstract modes of 'Closed Space'.

The Unnamable, for example, determines to distract himself with some sort of 'miserable statement of line and surface' (*PTD*, 76), on the grounds that he is 'so good at describing places, walls, ceilings, floors' and he prophetically muses:

if only I could put myself in a room, that would be the end of the wordy-gurdy . . . doorless, windowless, nothing but the four surfaces, the six surfaces, if I could shut myself up, it would be mine, it could be black dark, I could be motionless and fixed. (403)

It is precisely such 'doorless, windowless' conglomerations of 'surfaces' that Beckett's 'delegates' inhabit and depict throughout the second phase of his mature fiction, in the 'residua' of the sixties. *All Strange Away* (written between 1963 and 1964), its immediate successor, *Imagination Dead Imagine*, *The Lost Ones* (written in 1966), its companion-piece, *Ping*, and the aptly titled *Closed Space* (begun in 1968 and finished in 1975), all describe variants of the stark environment that the narrator of *All Strange Away* impassively identifies as 'A place . . . Five foot square, six high, no way in, none out'.[20]

Unlike the Unnamable's ideal room, however, these 'places' are neither 'motionless and fixed', nor proof against 'the wordy-gurdy'. On the contrary, they continually oscillate between the extremes of darkness and light, silence and sound, and immobility and mobility. Anticipating precisely this kind of inferno, the narrator of *How It Is* imagines a realm wherein the ear and eye perceive

the voice quaqua on all sides then within in the little vault empty closed bone-white if there were a light a tiny flame all would be white ten words fifteen words like a fume of sighs when the panting stops then the storm the breath token of life (140)

For much of the time, the narrators of these works offer excruciatingly detailed descriptions of their protagonists' environments, such as the reference in *Imagination Dead Imagine* to a 'rotunda' in which 'Two diameters at right angles AB CD divide the whole ground into two semicircles ACB BDA',[21] and *The Lost Ones's* vista of 'a flattened cylinder fifty meters round and eighteen high for the sake of harmony' (*TLO*, 7). As Beckett admits, this preoccupation with geometrical detail seems something of a false start (or false ending), and led to work being 'abandoned because of its complexity getting beyond control', and 'abandoned because of its intractable complexities'.[22]

At their most interesting, the environmental fictions of Beckett's 'residua' complement the relatively tempestuous perceptual crises of Molloy, Malone, the Unnamable and the narrator of *How It Is* with accounts of rather more subtle sufferings. For example, the figures described in *All Strange Away* and *The Lost Ones* almost imperceptibly offer some 'tremor of sorrow at faint memory' (*ASA*, 44), or else 'after a pause impossible to time' resignedly bow their head, as if 'in some unthinkable past for the first time' (*TLO*, 62–3). In this respect, the protagonists of this phase bear the same relation to the trilogy heroes, that the actions of figure 'A' in *Act without Words II* bear to those of figure 'B'. In both cases the former are 'slow', 'awkward' and brooding, whereas the latter offer 'brisk', 'rapid' and vigorous responses to the same general dilemma.[23]

At the same time, this second, relatively transitional phase in the mature fiction also very significantly testifies to Beckett's renewed interest in the theme of 'loved ones' (*APM*, 70). The narrator of *All Strange Away* makes passing references to 'evenings with Emma' (*ASA*, 14), while *The Lost Ones*, as its very title suggests, refers both to those who are 'lost' in the cylinder described in this work, and to those in this cylinder who find their world bereft of meaning in the absence of some 'lost' loved one. As Beckett explains, the original title, *Le Dépeupleur*, 'is meant to refer . . . to Lamartine's famous line: ''Un seul être vous manque et tout est dépeuplé'' ' (Lose but one person and the whole world becomes bare).[24] Or defined in terms of its opening sentence, the cylinder is an 'Abode where lost bodies roam each searching for its lost one' (7).

On the one hand, *The Lost Ones* seems to describe a very general environment in which long stretches of 'restlessness' are 'suddenly stilled like panting at the last', until a few seconds later 'all begins again' (7). At best, the lost ones enjoy 'brief losses of consciousness' (10). Usually they vainly search for one another in a 'gloom' in which 'Man and wife are strangers two paces apart to mention only this most intimate of bonds' (36). But, at worst, as the narrator indicates with references to the solitary figure described at the end of his narrative, individual lost ones find that their world is not yet bare, as they suddenly remember 'some unthinkable past' (63).

The third and most recent phase of Beckett's mature fiction describes individual figures in the throes of this kind of 'unthinkable past', as memories of specific locations and of relatively specific 'loved ones' drift to and fro in their consciousness. Usually sitting still in some sort of room, lying dead 'in the dark', or somehow or other watching the late departed sitting and walking in their 'dark', these 'shades' are not so much the prisoner of some elaborate, Dantesque 'rotunda' or 'cylinder', as the inhabitants of the 'madhouse of the skull' (*Isis*, 20). Like the speaker in the poem 'Something There', they suddenly become aware of 'something there somewhere outside the head', as they simultaneously enter both their own 'unthinkable past' and the equally 'unthinkable' ghostly pasts of their lost loved ones.

This is, of course, the self-same domain as that described in such recent plays as *Footfalls*, in which 'voice' (V)', the seemingly departed mother of the seemingly living 'May', explains how she still hears, sees or registers her daughter's sufferings from the realm of 'deep sleep'. 'V' solemnly intones:

Deep asleep ... I heard you in my deep sleep ... There is no sleep so deep that I would not hear you there. (F, 9)

As the American poet, Robert Lax, has suggested, the unusually haunting impact of these words appears to derive from the way in which their 'music' accords perfectly with their strange, other-worldly subject-matter. Meditating upon V's 'deep sleep', Lax memorably concludes:

It is down there in deep sleep that Beckett lives, and where all of us live, but few in our time have been so expert in visiting that region, in staying there and in bringing back a living report. It isn't just a matter of visiting — one needs a specially made, specially trimmed vocabulary to bring back true reports. One must understand the rhythms of the realm. One must bring back words and images, its particular music too. [25]

The remaining pages of this book will consider the ways in which *Still, Company, Ill seen ill said* and *Worstward Ho* 'bring back true reports' from the domain of 'deep sleep' and 'shades' in the third and most recent phase of Beckett's mature fiction.

CONCLUSION

"NOT LIFE/NECESSARILY" — BECKETT'S 'SHADES'

While Robert Lax proposes that Beckett's most recent writings be considered in terms of the mysterious rhythms, words, images and music of the realm of deep sleep,[1] the narrator of Beckett's *Company* suggests that they may be characterized by three slightly more tangible 'traits'.[2]

Firstly, like the narrator of *Company*, almost all of Beckett's recent 'delegates' exhibit a certain 'repetitiousness', as they relate 'the same bygone' 'Repeatedly with only minor variants' (20). Secondly, they all seem to employ the same solemn register, narrating without 'life' or lilt:

Same flat tone at all times. For its affirmations. For its negations. For its interrogations. For its exclamations. For its imperations. Same flat tone. (26)

Thirdly, as 'minor variants' of the same paradigmatic plight, their narratives all drift freely to and fro between the realm of the living and the dying, lifelessly suggesting that neither the quick nor the dead ever attain immunity to the invasions of 'intolerable' introspection. Living or dead, their minds remain 'Unstillable' (30), as the 'deeper coils' of their memories continually surface, 'now from one quarter and now from another' (19).

The seductive solemnity of these soliloquies has tempted some of Beckett's critics to conflate the superficially placid rhetoric of these recent works with their content. *Still*, for example, has been hailed as being as 'serene as little else in this author's work', as a work replete with 'quietude', and as the work in which Beckett finally 'found the calm he has spent a lifetime searching for'.[3] At first glance, the style and subject-matter of this 'fizzle' of 1973 certainly do appear surprisingly serene. It begins:

Bright at last close of a dark day the sun shines out at last and goes down. Sitting quite still at valley window normally turn head now and see it the sun low in the southwest sinking. Even get up certain moods and go stand by western window quite still watching it sink and then the afterglow. Always quite still some reason. (19)[4]

Upon inspection, however, it seems evident that this picture of 'calm' depicts nothing more substantial than the temporary calm before a perceptual 'storm', and that the figure is 'not still at all but trembling all over' (20). Indeed, as the narrator also specifies, this figure resembles the legendary Memnon, or 'that old statue some old god twanged at sunrise and again at sunset' (20), and therefore appears liable to 'twang' with unwanted consciousness when activated by sunlight, or by some other minor variant of the 'throes'.

Confirming this hypothesis, the final lines of 'Still' stipulate that the figure is 'quite still head in hand listening for a sound' (21). Considered in terms of Beckett's previous works, this 'sound' seems likely to be yet another variant of the 'buzzing' which demonstrates that 'Mouth' is 'not exactly . . . insentient' (*Not I*, 7), the 'Ping' which hints that the protagonist of *Ping* is 'perhaps not alone',[5] or the 'faint sound so brief' which shows that the globe is 'not yet bare' in 'Something There'. But, as the conclusion to Beckett's *Sounds* suggests, this kind of 'sound' testifies both to the process of renewed perceptual stimulation and to a relatively new concern in the final phase of Beckett's writing: the possibility of sighting some sort of 'shades' or 'ghosts'. Recapitulating and elaborating the conclusion to *Still*, the final sentence of its companion piece, *Sounds*, concludes by describing its protagonist:

quite still head in hand as shown listening trying listening for a sound or dreamt away try dreamt away where no such thing no more than ghosts make nothing to listen for no such thing as a sound.[6]

Company (1980), *Ill seen ill said* (1981), and *Worstward Ho* (1983), all describe the ways in which narrator-heroes fail to 'dream away' to a realm where there are no sounds and no ghosts. Like the narrating consciousness in *A Piece of Monologue*, they drift hither and thither from their present sufferings to the realm of 'Ghost light. Ghost nights. Ghost rooms. Ghost graves. Ghost . . . loved ones' (*APM*, 15).

Company records the monologues of a protagonist 'haunted' by the 'twangs' of memory, who 'dreams', or daydreams, 'of himself as of another' (34) in order to escape the visitations of old memories. While aware that he may have 'imagined ill' (44), and that he 'reasons ill' (14), this narrator attempts, nevertheless, to 'Imagine warily ' (65) and to 'Imagine . . . within reason' (43), in order to evade the depths of the 'Rashly' (71) and the 'too hastily' (74) imagined. In Proustian terms, the narrator of *Company* dreams up carefully censored stories with his 'reason-ridden' (45) imagination in order to prevent himself from falling down 'la pente abrupte de l'introspection' (III.465) (the steep slope of introspection). While he concedes that 'he must display a certain mental activity' (15) in order to invent imaginary 'company . . . In which to escape from his own' (77), he tellingly concludes: 'But it need not be of a high order. Indeed, it might be argued the lower the better. Up to a point' (15).

For much of the time, the narrator of *Company* succeeds in imagining 'warily', 'within reason' and 'Up to a point'. As he reiterates the refrain, 'What an addition to company that would be!', he invents such unthreatening, imaginary 'company' as 'a voice in the first person singular' (21), the ability 'to utter' (27), 'A dead rat' (36), 'A live fly' (38), 'An unscratchable itch' (78), and the presence of 'Yet another' (84). But, on two occasions, these 'entertaining' (60) and 'diverting' (68) inventions fail to provide protection from memories that the narrator admits that he has 'never forgotten'. On each of these occasions, he offers only the most oblique account of his 'deeper' memories, refusing to be 'drawn in to the core' (*PTD*, 65) of such unwelcome exceptions to his safe, familiar 'bygones'.

The first of these incidents offers a slightly more veiled and slightly more personal variation of the curious incident in Beckett's early short story, 'La Fin' (1945), in which, to quote Beckett's English translation,

A small boy, stretching out his hands and looking up at the blue sky, asked his mother how such a thing was possible. Fuck off, she said. [7]

Describing the similar way in which he once paused to ask his mother why the sky appeared both 'more distant' and 'less distant' than 'in reality it is', the narrator of *Company* cautiously concludes:

For some reason you could never fathom this question must have angered her exceedingly. For she shook off your little hand and made you a cutting retort you have never forgotten. (13)

These brief sentences are not particularly enlightening. Like the narrator, the reader is left very much 'in the dark', with little more information other than the facts that the mother curtails her son's affectionate proximity by shaking off his 'little hand', and adds verbal insult of some kind to this gestural injury by making a 'cutting retort'. 'The End' appears to offer a fictional substitute for this retort. Rather than revealing its precise 'cutting' content, the narrator transmutes it into the banality of 'Fuck off'.

Similarly in *Company*, all of the narrator's imaginary modes of company transmute 'deep' reality into consoling superficiality. His meditations upon a purely imaginary smell — 'Such as might have once emitted a rat long dead. Or some other carrion. Yet to be imagined' (72) — afford unthreatening fictional relief from the second memory that he has 'never forgotten'; that of 'The stench' of a hedgehog which he attempted to nurture 'in an old hatbox ... in a disused hutch' (38), and which for some reason he temporarily abandoned. Explaining that 'weeks passed before you could bring yourself to return to the hutch', the narrator nervously terminates this anecdote with the abrupt confession:

You have never forgotten what you found then. You are on your back in the dark and have never forgotten what you found then. The mush. The stench. (41)

In retrospect, life in the Beckettian 'dark' offers precisely the same pattern as that which Beckett's *Proust* imputes to *A la recherche du temps perdu*: the movement of a 'pendulum' which 'oscillates between ... two terms ... Suffering ... and Boredom' (*PTD*, 28). Either the narrator of *Company* 'suffers' from memories which he has 'never forgotten', or else 'bores' himself with imaginary company, or with the 'Simple sums' (54) and 'figures' (55) that he finds to be 'a help', 'A haven' (54) and 'a comfort' (55). Like the narrators of Beckett's 'residua', the narrator of *Company* intermittently entertains such geometrical fancies as 'A rustic hexahedron. Entirely of logs' (53), or the 'seemingly endless parallel rotation round and round the dial' (83) of a watch's second hand.

These tedious 'variables and constants' (83) offer the last substantial trace of the 'intractable complexities' traced in Beckett's 'residua'. To one's considerable relief, his most recent works turn their attention from fearful architectural symmetries, to the kind of poignant physical symmetry that the narrator of *Company* portrays when describing the peculiarly peaceful intimacy that he once enjoyed with a mysterious 'She'. Recollecting a particularly idyllic interlude, when life approximated to the Proustian felicity that Beckett begrudgingly defined as 'Enchantments of Reality' (*PTD*, 22), the narrator muses:

Your eyes opened and closed have looked in hers looking in yours. In your dark you look in them again. Still. You feel on your face the fringe of her long black hair stirring in the still air. Within the tent of hair your faces are hidden from view. She murmurs, Listen to the leaves. Eyes in each other's eyes you listen to the leaves. In their trembling shade. (66–7)

The complicated wordplay and antitheses of this passage typifies the concerns of Beckett's subsequent fiction. On the one hand, the passage evokes the stasis of 'still air'. On the other, it evokes memories which the narrator can 'Still' see, even from the ghostly realm of 'his dark'. In this respect, it combines and contrasts terrestial shadows or 'shade' with the spectral quality of the narrator's 'dark' and, by implication, with the whole spectral realm of 'Shades'. Offering yet another contrast between the 'still' and its antithesis, the passage juxtaposes the immobility of the 'still air' with the subtle mobility of 'stirring' hair and of the leaves' 'trembling shade'.[8] Finally, of course, it offers a rare Beckettian evocation of eyes which actually meet and 'look in' at one another — rather than looking 'through' or 'off' their object, like those of Celia (*Murphy*, 96); and more significantly still, the eyes meet with a certain formal symmetry, mirroring each other from within a 'tent of hair'.

Collectively, these symmetrical and antithetical references foreshadow the way in which Beckett's subsequent ghostly narrators delineate visions of trembling, shadowy figures and objects, which, somewhat like the snowflakes described at the end of Joyce's 'The Dead', activate memory and revelation as they hover, ambiguously, between the realms of 'all the living and the dead'. But, whereas Joyce appears to celebrate the way in which his characters are united, as 'One by one, they were all becoming shades',[9] the narrators of *Ill seen ill said* and *Worstward Ho* seem torn between their sensitivity to past 'shades' and their compulsion to 'finish with it all at last' (*Isis*, 51).

Occasionally, these tormented souls pause to admire rare, elegiac images of human affection and grace, such as the unexpected evocation in *Ill seen ill said* of the 'twin movement full of grace' with which another mysterious 'she' drinks from a bowl, as she 'slowly raises the bowl towards her lips while at the same time bowing her head to join it' (*Isis*, 35).

In a sense, 'she' offers this bowl precisely the kind of careful, intimate attention that the aforementioned 'mother' denies the narrator of *Company*, when 'she shook off (his) little hand' (13), just as an 'old man' described by the narrator of *Worstward Ho* offers a child the same kind of comfort as they walk with 'equal plod', presenting another 'twin movement full of grace'. Writing from 'the dim void', the narrator of this ghostly tale relates:

Hand in hand with equal plod they go ... Backs turned both bowed with equal plod they go. The child hand raised to reach the holding hand. Hold the old holding hand. Hold and be held. Plod on and never recede. Slowly with never a pause plod on and never recede. Backs turned. Both bowed. Joined by held holding hands. Plod on as one. One shade. Another shade. (*WH*, 13)

It is in passages such as this that Beckett seems to perfect his 'true reports' from the realm of 'deep sleep', as he generates a peculiarly repetitive and alliterative prose poetry in such sentences as 'Hold the old holding hand. Hold and be held'. In keeping with his subject-matter, Beckett 'plods on' with 'equal plod' by carefully reiterating all or part of a preceding statement, as he qualifies it in its successor. 'Plod on and never recede' almost inevitably precipitates the variation: 'Slowly with never a pause plod on and never recede'.

Try as one may, it is impossible not to compare this diction with the poetry and prose of Gertrude Stein, with its equally hesitant, overlapping refrains. Anticipating the tone of much of Beckett's most recent writing, sections four and five of Gertrude Stein's poem 'They may be said to be ready' characteristically recount:

They were waiting. For them.
They were ready when. They were waiting. Then. For them.

More often than not they were ready.
With them.
Especially. With them. [10]

The rhythms of Gertrude Stein, or, more accurately, rhythms remarkably akin to the rhythms of Gertrude Stein, unobtrusively animate almost all of Beckett's 'reports' from the realm of 'Shades'. Arguably, his very words have 'shades'. Each utterance awaits its echo, somewhat as the 'Mother' in May's

story, in *Footfalls*, echoes and re echoes her every statement as
she asks her daughter, Amy, why she too continually echoes, or
'revolves', 'it all':

Amy ... Amy ... Will you never have done? ... Will you never have
done ... revolving it all? ... It? ... It all ... In your poor mind ... It all
... It all. (*F*, 13)

The same ghostly rhythms appear in poems such as Beckett's
'recent croak' entitled 'PSS' (1981), a work which cryptically
evokes and enacts the difficulties of telling, retelling and
untelling until all is 'unsaid' and 'done'. Composed in three
short sections, 'PSS' seems to compare the paradoxical way in
which the urge to 'retell' continually frustrates the wish to leave
'all ... unsaid' with the way in which the wish 'not to be at the
mercy of the hand' (*Murphy*, 170), and to 'unclasp', gives way to
the lonely imperative, 'hold me':

> there
> the life late led
> down there
> all done unsaid
>
> again gone
> with what to tell
> on again
> retell
>
> head oh hands
> hold me
> unclasp
> hold me[11]

In a sense, 'PSS' synthesizes both the form and the themes of
Ill seen ill said. Considered from a formal point of view, Beckett's
most recent 'ghost prose' is forever emulating the faltering
'ghost poetry' of 'PSS'.[12] For example, the preceding quotation
from *Worstward Ho* might well be retranscribed as the 'poem':

> Hand in hand
> with equal plod
> they go.
> Backs turned
> both bowed
> with equal plod
> they go.

The child
hand raised
to reach the
holding hand.
Hold the old
holding hand.
Hold and
be held.

Considered in terms of its content, 'PSS' typifies the crucial uncertainties and contradictions of *Ill seen ill said*.[13] Just as the speaker in 'PSS' appears to doubt his capacity to 'unsay' and 'unclasp' 'it all', the protagonist of *Ill seen ill said* inhabits an uncertain and contradictory realm in which imminent death sometimes appears to offer the long-awaited relief of 'perfect dark' (59), but on other occasions seems likely to inaugurate existence within the ghostly realm in which a mysterious 'she' helplessly suffers from precisely the same perceptual anguish that the narrator experiences on his side of the grave.

Ill seen ill said relates two overlapping stories. It begins by introducing 'she', a shadowy figure 'already dead' (41), who sits in a 'rigid Memnon pose' (35), the victim of 'helplessness . . . she cannot help', and who 'rails at the source of all life' (7). Like 'Mouth', 'she' is afflicted by perceptual obligations even when she no longer shares 'the misfortune to be of this world' (42).[14] By contrast, *Ill seen ill said* ends as its dying narrator paints a rather more favourable picture of the next world, by suggesting that death affords the 'happiness' sought by all previous Beckettian heroes: the paradoxical, and seemingly unattainable 'knowledge' of the 'knowing non-exister' (*TFN*, 59). Desiring only sufficient faculties to be aware of his demise, this narrator savours his 'First last moment' (or deliriously imagines as much) as he naively prays:

Grant only enough remain to devour all. Moment by glutton moment. Sky earth the whole kit and boodle. Not another crumb of carrion left. Lick chops and basta. No. One moment more. One last. Grace to breathe that void. Know happiness. (59)

Since *Ill seen ill said* ends with these words, it is not possible to confirm or deny their validity empirically by alluding to subsequent developments. Nevertheless, when considered paradigmatically, in terms of the post-mortem sufferings of 'she', *Ill seen ill said* seems to suggest that the narrator's 'happiness' is preordained to give way to visions of the same kind of 'ancient horror' (28–9) which persistently haunts 'she' in the realm of the dead. In this respect, the narrator's suggestion that the more serene expressions of 'she' are 'Worthy those worn by certain newly dead' (25) does not merely toy with the more familiar concept of the 'newly born', but quite literally suggests that sustained serenity is only fleetingly enjoyed by the 'newly dead' in Beckett's fictional cosmos. When no longer 'newly dead', Beckett's 'Shades', like his lunatics in the M.M.M., seem exposed once again to the ravages of 'all the usual' (*Murphy*, 124).

As we have already indicated, 'she' suffers from sunlight, and 'rails at the source of all life' (7). In addition to this general Beckettian complaint, 'she' also appears haunted by some specific 'loved one', and is both compulsively 'drawn to a certain spot' (11) within a graveyard, and held 'in thrall' by the photographs within her 'shadowy album' (14). In his turn, the narrator compulsively follows every movement of 'she', longing to 'be by her' as she examines her photographs, and to discover and share the 'scenes' that 'draw the head down lower still and hold it in thrall' (14). At this point, a whole series of haunted 'delegates' looms into focus. The narrator sits spell-bound before 'she', who sits spell-bound before some photograph of a third person, who, for all one knows, is depicted sitting spell-bound before a photograph of another, fourth person, and so on *ad infinitum*.

While *Ill seen ill said* never spells out this kind of infinitely regressive vision in the way that *How It Is* does, when surveying its suffering 'billions', its narrator notes that 'she' is also observed by 'The twelve' (15), a group of ghostly figures 'she' approaches and almost acknowledges, before turning away at the last moment. Describing this strange process, the narrator explains:

The others are there. All about. The twelve. Afar. Still or receding. She raises her eyes and sees one. Turns away and sees another. Again she stops dead. Now the moment or never. But something forbids. (15)

Pondering upon the reasons for her refusal to acknowledge the 'twelve', who all seem to be dead or 'her own', the narrator concludes that, logically speaking, she should have no 'need' of anybody once she is dead:

What is it defends her? Even from her own. Averts the intent gaze . . . What but life ending. Hers. The other's . . . She needs nothing. Nothing utterable . . . How need in the end? (16)

Nevertheless, despite the narrator's conviction that one cannot 'need' after death, the gestures of 'she' suggest that in death, as in life, Beckett's characters invariably both experience 'need' of others and, at the same time, repudiate and deny others, in order to maintain relative peace of mind. Or in terms of the poem 'PSS', they simultaneously wish to 'unclasp' their hands and to have hands 'hold me'.

Exemplifying this pattern in his turn, the narrator restlessly oscillates between his compulsion to 'be by her' (14) and to 'see her again' (51), and his antithetical desire to 'Let her vanish . . . For good' (31), and to 'say farewell. If only to the face. Of her tenacious trace' (59).

Predictably, the narrator of *Ill seen ill said* cannot eradicate his memories of 'her tenacious trace'. While he longs to obscure her 'trace' by transforming it into the imaginary reality that he calls 'figments', wishing that 'she could be pure figment' and that 'all could be pure figment' (20), he seems fated to endure these 'Unspeakable' and 'Unbearable' (57) onslaughts of 'Remembrance! When all worse there than when first ill seen' (52–3). In the same way, the sorrows of 'she' find no relief. She remains 'Within as sadly as before . . . at first sight ill seen' (50). As the narrator of *Worstward Ho* suggests, the sorrows of Beckett's fictional progeny are 'Unnullable' (*WH*, 32), 'Unlessenable' and 'Unstillable' (*WH*, 36).

This 'Unstillable' quality becomes most explicit when the bodies and objects in *Ill seen ill said* follow the example of the figure described in the misleadingly titled *Still*, and begin 'trembling all over' (*S*, 20), as their 'deep sleep' is violated by deep awakenings.[15] For example, a 'buttonhook' once used by 'she' prompts the comment: 'It trembles faintly without cease. As if here without cease the earth faintly quaked' (18), an 'old key' similarly starts 'trembling' (25), and a suspended greatcoat likewise evinces the 'Same infinitesimal quaver' (47).

'She', too, eventually 'vacillates' (47). While she initially appears to incarnate 'Voidlike calm' as she sits 'dead still' amidst 'motionless' grass in the 'still air' (29), she finally becomes 'alive as she alone knows how' (50), when the grass 'shivers' 'With faintest shiver from its innermost' (29) and she too becomes 'ashiver from head to foot' (30). Briefly, there seems no such thing as 'Voidlike calm' in *Ill seen ill said*. Or, if there is, then this 'Void' is far more threatening than the narrator assumes it to be, when praying to 'breathe that void' (59).

Worstward Ho[16] Beckett's most recent substantial 'report' from the realm of 'shades' suggests, yet again, that the Beckettian protagonist may never attain the perfect peace that the narrator of *Ill seen ill said* fondly anticipates within 'that void'. Although the narrating consciousness of *Worstward Ho* longs to 'Know no more. See no more. Say no more' (18), and desires 'No mind and words' save those sufficient to contemplate his freedom from mind and words, he finally judges his 'void' to be 'Unnullable'. It may 'Never to naught be brought. Never by naught be nulled' (32). For like all of Beckett's fictional progeny, this narrator is fated to be pursued, forever, by 'Something there' (38).

Confirming William Burroughs's thesis that Beckett's fiction is finally devoid of 'characters' and 'sets', *Worstward Ho* recounts the 'Remains of mind' (9) of an anonymous 'Him', 'one' or 'It', narrating from his own 'narrow field' (24), 'narrow vast' or 'narrow void' (28) from within a wider, more nebulous, general 'field' or 'void'. This 'narrow void' is not so much a perfect, as an imperfect void, 'Rife with shades' (24). Indeed, somewhat as the narrator of *Company* self-consciously alludes to his 'reason-ridden' (45) imagination, the narrator of *Worstward Ho* locates himself within a 'Shade-ridden void' (25), alive, as it were, with the dead. Far from affording happiness or joy, this domain precipitates the same kind of anguished introspection that the protagonist of *Film* manifests with 'that look' (*Film*, 44), as the narrator of *Worstward Ho* succumbs to 'that stare' (22), when he peers 'Into the hell of all. Out from the hell of all' (44).

Worstward Ho presents its vision of the 'so-said void' (24) in a series of monosyllabic references to such motifs as 'the void', 'the dim', 'the shades', 'the one', 'the twain', 'the skull' and 'the stare'. Inhabiting a microcosmic, 'narrow void', within the macrocosmic, wider void, the narrator sporadically finds this realm activated and illuminated by 'The dim' (16), a source of stimulation which he tries to 'dimmer' (35) with 'worsening words' (27), somewhat as Watt 'little by little' turns 'a disturbance into words' (*Watt*,115). Predictably, these words and the stories or images that they describe are studiously superficial. Like Moran's heroes, they are merely fictional cannon fodder, created in order to be negated and brought, as it were, to 'naught'.

Introducing his recipe for this kind of instant 'void', Moran explains:

Yes, I let them spring within me and grow in strength, brighten and charm me with a thousand fancies, and then I swept them away, with a great disinterested sweep of all my being, I swept myself clean of them and surveyed with satisfaction the void they had polluted. (162)

With much the same intent, the narrator of *Worstward Ho* admits that he has been 'Preying' on such 'remains' (17) as his partially remembered, and, it seems, partially invented, images of two sorts of 'shades': 'the one' and 'the twain' (14). The 'one' is a woman 'Stooped . . . in that graveyard', somewhat as 'old grave-stones stoop', with 'loving memory' (45). The 'twain' are the aforementioned old man and child, walking with 'equal plod' (13) until the narrator's imagination decimates them and separates them, envisaging them as 'Topless baseless hind-trunks' (43), 'Vast void apart' (44).

Ideally, the narrator of *Worstward Ho* would eliminate all trace of 'the one' and the 'twain' from the 'narrow void' of his 'skull'. But, as he discovers, his memories persistently return before his 'staring eyes'. Just when everything seems safe, and all his memories are 'sudden gone', they reappear to his dismay: 'sudden back . . . All back in the skull'. Mulling over this disturbing process, he disconsolately meditates:

Say all gone. So on. In the skull all gone. All? No. All cannot go. Till dim go. Say then but the two gone. In the skull one and two gone. From the void. From the stare. In the skull all save the skull gone. The stare. Alone in the dim void. Alone to be seen. Dimly seen . . . By the staring eyes. The others gone. Long sudden gone. Then sudden back. Unchanged. Say now unchanged. First one. Then two. Or first two. Then one. Or together. Then all again together . . . All back in the skull together. Unchanged. Stare clamped to all. In the dim void. (25–6)

As the following equally revealing passage indicates, the narrator's words can only temporarily 'dim' his surroundings and his memories. Eventually 'less' turns back into more, and the dim becomes 'undimmed', as the narrator watches his verbal smoke-screen come and go, and comments:

Less. Less seen. Less seeing. Less seen and seeing when with words than when not . . . Stare by words dimmed. Shades dimmed. Void dimmed. Dim dimmed . . . all dimmed. Till blank again . . . Then all undimmed. Stare undimmed. That words had dimmed. (39)

'Gnawing to be gone' (41), the narrator of *Worstward Ho* eventually abandons this aspiration for mere 'lessness', and like the narrator of *Ill seen ill said*, who finds 'Absence supreme good' (58), argues: 'Less no good. Worse no good. Only one good.

Gone' (41-2). But as the narrator of *Worstward Ho* is well aware, 'All cannot go' (25). At most he can merely lessen or worsen his images of existence as his words advance 'Lessward' or 'Worstward'.

Finally, this narrator 'lessens' himself still further, from a staring skull to some kind of ghastly Cyclops with 'One dim black hole mid-foreskull' (44), and from this Cyclops figure to a diminutive 'pinhole' staring at 'pins' of life at the bounds of a 'boundless void' (46–7). Ultimately, then, however much his image of his unfortunate condition may change, his dilemma remains the same. At the end as at the beginning, the narrator of *Worstward Ho* is exposed to 'the hell' (44) of his 'narrow void', as he once again sees 'All at once as once ... The whole narrow void. No blurs. All clear' (45). He then watches this 'All' recede, reduced to 'pins' towards the very periphery of his vision, before 'All' resurges once again, presumably, in some other ghostly form, in some other ghostly fiction.

Worstward Ho, like *Ill seen ill said* and *Company*, is as intransigently anti-Proustian as all of Beckett's earlier fictions. Though speaking from the realm of 'shades' rather than from some intractably mathematical inferno, or some unsavoury blend of excrement and mud, the narrating consciousness of *Worstward Ho*, like the narrating consciousness portrayed in all of Beckett's mature fiction, is a voluntary exile from the 'deeper coils' of memory and introspection. Like the narrator of the early short story 'The Expelled', the narrator of *Worstward Ho* might well avow:

Memories are killing. So you must not think of certain things, of those that are dear to you, or rather you must think of them, for if you don't there is the danger of finding them, in your mind, little by little. That is to say, you must think of them for a while, a good while, every day several times a day, until they sink forever in the mud.[17]

Proust's heroes, by contrast, consider such memories and moments of luminous introspection to be their greatest treasure. According to his early notes on 'the mysterious world of Gustave Moreau',[18]

tous ceux qui ont une âme intérieure dans laquelle ils peuvent quelquefois pénétrer ... sont avertis par une joie secrète que les seuls véritables moments sont ceux qu'ils y passent. Le reste de leur vie est une espèce d'exil ... Car ils sont des exilés intellectuels: dès qu'ils sont exilés, ils ont perdu du même coup le souvenir de leur patrie et savent

seulement qu'ils en ont une, qu'il est plus doux d'y vivre, mais ne savent comment y revenir. (*CSB*, 672)
(all those who have an innermost soul which they occasionally penetrate . . . are made aware by a secret joy that the only true moments are those which are spent there. The rest of their life is a kind of exile. . . . For they are intellectual exiles: once exiled, they simultaneously lose the memory of their homeland, and know only that they have one, that it is more pleasant to live there, but that they have no way of returning there.)

It is, of course, unfair to equate the complexity of Proust's mature vision with this kind of early fragment. Nevertheless, these lines nicely illustrate the basic differences between the Proustian and Beckettian responses to memory and to the undesirability or the desirability of 'exile' from introspection, even if they limit their discussion to the plight of the 'intellectual' exile, rather than that of the 'sentimental' exile haunted by memories of 'those that are dear to you'.

The most surprising aspect of Beckett's most recent fiction resides in the way in which it reverses, or at least revises, his youthful contempt for the 'tragedy of the human relationship' (*PTD*, 18), and explores the ways in which remnants of affection interlink 'all the living and the dead'. For all his early insistence upon the 'intellectual' problem of writing, and for all his early narrators' emphasis upon the difficulties of telling stories, Beckett's work has always been primarily concerned with the rather more personal problem of anguished introspection, a concern which reaches its climax in works such as *Not I*, and which subsequently extends into the realm of ghostly inter-personal relationships in such recent writings as *Company*, *Ill seen ill said*, *Worstward Ho*, *Footfalls*, *A Piece of Monologue*, *Ohio Impromptu* and *Nacht und Träume*.

The unashamedly elegiac tone of Beckett's most recent writing probably becomes most explicit in *Nacht und Träume* (*Night and Dream*), a ten-minute television play first broadcast in 1983. Somewhat as *Worstward Ho* evokes the solidarity between an old man and a child 'joined by held holding hands' (*WH*, 13), *Nacht und Träume* commemorates the consolation offered by what Beckett himself defines as the 'compassionate hand'.[19] More specifically, this play depicts the comforting presence of two ghostly hands which 'gently' emerge from a 'kinder light' than the domain of the 'minimally lit' dreamer, 'A', and which 'gently' wipe the brow of his dreamt self, 'B'. Finally, they 'gently' rest upon the dreamt self's hands, as he gazes at a cherished 'invisible face'.[20]

Beckett's other writings of the late seventies and eighties rather more poignantly interweave moments of anguished introspection, anguished 'loving memory' (*WH*, 45) and evanescent compassion, as characters remember one another, listen to one another, look at one another, hold one another, and stoop over one another's graves with solicitous attention. As a ghostly messenger relates in *Ohio Impromptu*, another 'dear face' informs a surviving 'Reader' that 'my shade will comfort you', as he vainly searches for 'some measure of relief' (*OI*, 30). While these fictions and plays nearly all suggest that the 'human relationship' is 'doomed, doomed to fail', and might at first sight be condemned as wholesale negations of Proust's studies of 'l'espace et le temps rendus sensibles au coeur' (III.385), the subtlety and the intensity of their visions of lingering lost love, and their astonishing capacity to counterpoint and complement Proust's terrestial visions of 'Time and Space made perceptible to the heart' (*PTD*, 58), with equally poignant ghostly variations of 'loving memory', suggest that Beckett, like Proust, is every inch a master of the mysterious art of tracing 'l'interpénétration des âmes' (III.386) (the interpenetration of souls).

Beckett's remarkable 'reports' from the realm of 'Shades', like all of his fictional, dramatical, poetical and critical writings, offer the perfect foil to Proust's magnificent evocations of 'dualism in multiplicity', just as Proust's fictional and critical *oeuvre* offers the ideal counterpoint to Beckett's 'clawing' images of 'the mess'. As Beckett himself suggested long ago in his article on the paintings of the brothers Van Velde, and as the pages of this book have attempted to demonstrate, the analysis of the 'divergence' between two such masters as Beckett and Proust may help, perhaps, to 'situate', or indeed resituate, their rare achievements, 'one in terms of the other'[21] as 'the incomparable' illuminates 'the incomparable', and lends itself to comparison.

NOTES

Preface

1. Virginia Woolf, 'Modern Fiction', *The Common Reader*, (1925; rpt. London: Hogarth Press, 1968), pp.184–95, p.189.
2. *Ibid.*
3. Samuel Beckett, *Proust*, in *Proust and Three Dialogues with Georges Duthuit* (1931; rpt. London: John Calder, 1965), p.76. Henceforth abbreviated as *PTD*.
4. Marcel Proust, *A la recherche du temps perdu*, ed. Pierre Clarac and André Ferré (Paris: Gallimard, Bibliothèque de la Pléiade, 1968 and 1969), 3, p.885. My translations throughout. All subsequent references are to Clarac and Ferrés three-volume edition, unless otherwise indicated. Henceforth abbreviated as I, II and III.
5. For further discussion of these chronologies, see my article 'Beyond Beckett: Reckless Writing and the Concept of the Avant-Garde within Post-Modern Literature', *Yearbook of Comparative and General Literature*, no.30 (1981), 37–56.
6. See for example the endings of Joyce's *A Portrait of the Artist as a Young Man*; Lawrence's *Sons and Lovers*; Mann's *Death in Venice*; Musil's *Young Torless*; and Woolf's *To the Lighthouse*.
7. As Leslie Fiedler has convincingly argued, it seems possible to distinguish the relatively morbid, self-reflexive quality of European Post-Modernists, such as Beckett and Robbe-Grillet, from the more playful, imaginative quality of such North and South American Post-Modernists as Kesey, Heller and Marquez. My remarks concerning Post-Modernism are more typical of European writing than American writing. See Fiedler's essay 'Cross the Border — Close the Gap' in *The Collected Essays of Leslie Fiedler*, 2 (New York: Stein and Day, 1971), pp.454–85.
8. Samuel Beckett, letter to Alan Schneider of 29 December 1957, in Samuel Beckett and Alan Schneider, 'Beckett's Letters on *Endgame*', *Village Voice*, 19 March 1958, 15. Beckett comments: 'My work is a matter of fundamental sounds . . . made as fully as possible, and I accept responsibility for nothing else. If people want to have headaches among the overtones, let them. And provide their own aspirin.'
9. Samuel Beckett, quoted by Israel Shenker, in Israel Shenker, 'Moody Man of Letters', *New York Times*, 6 May 1956, Section 2, 3.
10. See for example John Fletcher and John Spurling, *Beckett: A Study of His Plays* (London: Eyre Methuen, 1972), p.28. Spurling argues that Beckett's *Proust* affords 'a table of the law for any student of either Proust, or Beckett'.
11. Samuel Beckett, 'Dante . . . Bruno. Vico . . Joyce', *transition*, no.16–17 (June 1929), 242.
12. Samuel Beckett, 'Papini's Dante', review of Giovanni Papini's *Dante Vivo*, *The Bookman*, LXXXVII (Christmas 1934), 14.
13. Samuel Beckett, 'La peinture des Van Velde ou le monde et la pantalon', *Les cahiers d'art* (1945–1946), 349–56, 354. My translation, as are all subsequent translations, unless otherwise indicated.
14. Samuel Beckett, *Ohio Impromptu*, collected in Samuel Beckett, *Three*

Occasional Pieces (London: Faber and Faber, 1982), p.32. Henceforth abbreviated as *OI*.

15. While this book argues that Beckett's fiction systematically subverts Proustian values, and establishes a distinctively 'anti-Proustian', or 'Beckettian', perspective, it would not wish to suggest that Beckett's work, or indeed, that of any writer, makes sense solely in terms of a *single* precursor. This book would simply introduce the considerable advantages of considering — or reconsidering — Beckett's vision in the context of Proust's vision, and reciprocally, the considerable advantages of reconsidering the Proustian vision with reference to that of Beckett.

16. Samuel Beckett, quoted by S.E. Gontarski, in *The Intent of Undoing in Samuel Beckett's Dramatic Texts* (Bloomington: Indiana University Press, 1985), p.xvii. Beckett refers to the problem of establishing the chronology of his manuscripts. Here, as elsewhere, he implicitly advocates the comparative approach employed in this book.

17. Samuel Beckett, *Watt* (1953; rpt. London: John Calder, 1963), p.62.

1. Proust and Critical Perspectives

1. See Roland Barthes, 'The Death of the Author', in *Image-Music-Text*, essays selected and translated by Stephen Heath (Glasgow: Fontana, 1977), pp.142–48; and Michel Foucault, 'What is an Author?', in *Language, Counter-Memory, Practice*, edited with an Introduction by Donald F. Bouchard; translated by Donald F. Bouchard and Sherry Simon (Ithaca, New York: Cornell University Press, 1977), pp.113–38. No further reference will be made to Foucault.

2. Wayne C. Booth defines and discusses the concept of the 'implied author' and the 'implied vision' in *The Rhetoric of Fiction* (Chicago: University of Chicago Press, 1961).

3. Marcel Proust, in *Marcel Proust et Jacques Rivière: Correspondance (1914–1922)*, ed. Philip Kolb (Paris: Plon, 1955), p.2. Rivière attributes this undated letter to 7 February 1914.

4. Marcel Proust, *Jean Santeuil*, in *Jean Santeuil précédé de Les Plaisirs et les jours*, ed. Pierre Clarac and Yves Sandre (Paris: Gallimard, Bibliothèque de la Pléiade, 1971), p.489. Henceforth abbreviated as *JS* and *PJ*.

5. Marcel Proust, 'La Personne d'Alphonse Daudet "Oeuvre d'Art" ', in *Contre Sainte-Beuve précédé de Pastiches et Melanges et suivi de Essais et articles*, ed. Pierre Clarac and Yves Sandre (Paris: Gallimard, Bibliothèque de la Pléiade, 1971), pp.399–402. Henceforth abbreviated as *CSB*.

6. Michel Raimond, *Le Roman depuis la Révolution* (Paris: Armand Colin, 1967), p.158; Georges Cattui, *Marcel Proust* (Paris: Juilliard, 1953), p.59; Leo Bersani, *Marcel Proust: The Fictions of Life and of Art* (New York: Oxford University Press, 1965), p.199; George Stambolian, *Marcel Proust and the Creative Encounter* (Chicago: University of Chicago Press, 1972), p.119.

7. Jean Pommier, *Le Mystique de Marcel Proust* (Paris: Droz, 1939), p.32; Germaine Brée, *Marcel Proust and Deliverance from Time*, with an introduction by Angus Wilson (London: Chatto and Windus, 1956), p.224; E.F.N. Jephcott, *Proust and Rilke: The Literature of Expanded Consciousness* (London: Chatto and Windus, 1972), p.261.

8. Roger Shattuck, *Proust's Binoculars: A Study of Memory, Time and Recognition in À la recherche du temps perdu* (London: Chatto and Windus, 1964), p.38; Henri Peyre, *Marcel Proust* (New York: Columbia University Press), p.21; Jean Rousset, *Forme et Signification* (Paris: Corti, 1962), p.150.

9. Roger Shattuck, *Proust* (Glasgow: Fontana, 1974), p.9.
10. Ernst Robert Curtius, *Marcel Proust*, translated from the German by Armand Pierhal (Paris: Éditions de la Revue Nouvelle, 1929), pp.45–6.
11. *Ibid.*, p.149.
12. Harry Levin, *The Gates of Horn: A Study of Five French Realists* (New York: Oxford University Press, 1963), p.442.
13. Angus Wilson, Introduction to Germaine Brée, *Marcel Proust and Deliverance from Time*, p.x.
14. Edmund Wilson, *Axel's Castle: A study in the Imaginative Literature of 1870–1930* (1931; rpt. New York: Charles Scribner's Sons, 1969), p.145.
15. *Ibid.*, p.164.
16. *Ibid.*, p.162.
17. André Maurois, *A la recherche de Marcel Proust* (Paris: Hachette, 1949), p.311; Harold March, *The Two Worlds of Marcel Proust* (Philadelphia: University of Pennsylvania Press, 1948), p.206.
18. Gilles Deleuze, *Proust et les signes* (1964; rpt. Paris: Presses Universitaires de la France, 1964), p.54; George Stambolian, *Marcel Proust and the Creative Encounter*, p.113.
19. Samuel Beckett, *Molloy, Malone Dies, The Unnamable* (London: John Calder, 1959), p.30. Subsequent references to the English version of *Molloy, Malone Dies* and *The Unnamable* are to this edition of Beckett's trilogy.

2. Positive Modes of Existence in *A la recherche du temps perdu*

1. Samuel Beckett, 'Proust in Pieces', *The Spectator*, 22 June 1934, 976. This reference to the 'indeterminate' quality of Proust's characters contrasts somewhat with Beckett's assertion three years earlier in *Proust* that his characters are 'active with a grotesque *predetermined* activity' (*PTD*, 89; my italics). Beckett's own fiction might well be defined as an elaboration of such 'stupefying antics . . . of indeterminates'.
2. For the sake of simplicity, this diagram does not indicate the 'nihilistic' actions of Proust's characters. Inhabiting the lowest point in Proust's sphere of existential possibilities, these actions will be analysed in Chapter 4.
3. Using much the same rhetoric, Swann derides the Verdurin salon as: 'ce qu'il y a de plus bas dans l'échelle sociale, le dernier cercle de Dante' (III.287) (the very lowest point on the social scale, the last of Dante's circles).
4. Henri Peyre, *Marcel Proust*, p.33; Germaine Brée, *Marcel Proust and Deliverance from Time*, pp.244 and 42.
5. Howard Moss, *The Magic Lantern of Marcel Proust* (London: Faber and Faber, 1963), p.85; Gaëton Picon, *Lecture de Proust* (Paris: Mercure de France, 1963), p.70; E.F.N. Jephcott, *Proust and Rilke*, p.285; Adele King, *Proust* (Edinburgh: Oliver and Boyd, 1968), p.58.
6. Albert Feuillerat, *Comment Proust a composé son roman* (New Haven: Yale University Press, 1934), p.155.
7. F.C. Green, *The Mind of Proust* (Cambridge: Cambridge University Press, 1949), p.159.
8. *Ibid.*
9. Roger Shattuck, *Proust*, p.163.
10. Germaine Brée, *Marcel Proust and Deliverance from Time*, p.111.
11. *Ibid.*, p.42.

12. Samuel Beckett, *Dream of Fair to Middling Women*, (c.1932), 212-page unpublished typescript, p.110. Photocopy in the Reading University Library Beckett Collection, MS 1227/7/16/18. Henceforth abbreviated as *Dream*.
13. Samuel Beckett, *Eleuthéria*, (c.1947), 133-page unpublished typescript, p.116. Copy in the archives of Les Éditions de Minuit, Paris.
14. Roland Barthes employs the same concept of the *accent* to evoke the original quality of such contemporary creativity as the cinematic works of Sergei Eisenstein, defining this kind of accent as the symptom of a radically 'Nouvelle pratique . . . affirmée contre une pratique majoritaire' (New practice . . . affirmed against a majority practice), in 'Le troisième sens', *Cahiers du cinéma*, 222 (July 1970), 17. Translated by Stephen Heath as 'the Third Meaning', in Roland Barthes, *Image-Music-Text*, pp.52–68, p.62. In this general sense of the term, all of Proust's exemplary characters evince their individuality *via* the artistic or gestural 'accent' of their finest actions.
15. Samuel Beckett, *Mercier et Camier* (Paris: Les Éditions de Minuit, 1970), p.155. My translation: Beckett's own translation of this novel omits this exchange.
16. Samuel Beckett, *Mercier and Camier* (London: Calder and Boyars, 1974), p.118; *Rockaby*, in Samuel Beckett, *Three Occasional Pieces*, p.26.
17. Gilles Deleuze, *Proust et les signes*, p.51.

3. Negative Modes of Existence in
A la recherche du temps perdu

1. Burroughs introduces the notion of addiction to images, and the concept of the 'image fix', in *Nova Express* (New York: Grove Press, 1964). A 'death dwarf' confides: 'Images — millions of images — that's what I eat' (p.53); and cryptically confesses: 'If I don't get the image fix I'm in the ovens' (p.54). Burroughs subsequently employs this concept in an interview of 1974, collected by Victor Bockris in *With William Burroughs: A report from the Bunker* (New York: Seaver Books, 1982), p.66. For further discussion of Proust's and Burroughs's theories of the image see my article 'Beckett, Proust, Burroughs, and the perils of Image Warfare', in Pierre Astier, Morris Beja and S.E. Gontarski, eds., *Samuel Beckett: Humanistic Perspectives* (Ohio: University of Ohio Press, 1982), pp.172–87.
2. 'Literary and critical notes' is a subtitle invented by Pierre Clarac and Yves Sandre in their edition of Proust's *Contre Sainte-Beuve précédé de Pastiches et mélanges et suivi de Essais et articles* in order to denote those essays in Proust's notebooks which address issues analogous to his concerns in *Contre Sainte-Beuve*.
3. Alain Robbe-Grillet, *La Maison de rendez-vous* (Paris: Les Éditions de Minuit, 1965), p.11.
4. William Burroughs, interview with Lawrence Collinson and Roger Baker (1973), in Winston Leyland ed., *Gay Sunshine Interviews*, volume one (San Francisco: Gay Sunshine Press, 1978), p.15. Burroughs elaborates his theories concerning the subversive potential of conflicting images in *Electronic Revolution* (1971), collected in *Ah Pook Is Here and Other Texts* (London: John Calder, 1979), pp.123–57.
5. Marcel subsequently reiterates the fact that 'Swann . . . s'était trompé en . . . assimilant (ce bonheur proposé par la petite phrase de la sonate) au plaisir de l'amour' (III.877) [Swann . . . erred by equating . . . (this pleasure offered by the little phrase of the sonata) with the pleasure of love].

6. Roland Barthes, *Mythologies*, selected and translated from the French by Annette Lavers (New York: Hill and Wang, 1972), pp.84–7.
7. Edmund Wilson, *Axel's Castle*, p.147.
8. Samuel Beckett, *Texts for Nothing* (London: Calder and Boyars, 1974), p.46. Henceforth abbreviated as *TFN*.
9. Samuel Beckett, *Play* (London: Faber and Faber, 1964), p.17. 'Man' asks: 'All this, when will all this have been … just play?'. Ruby Cohn takes this concept as title and theme for her book *Just Play: Beckett's theater* (Princeton, N.J.: Princeton University Press, 1980).
10. Céleste Albaret, *Monsieur Proust: Souvenirs receuillis par Georges Belemont* (Paris: Robert Laffont, 1973), p.65.
11. Marcel offers two conflicting accounts of Saniette's death. The first (III.265–66) suggests that he dies in a coma shortly after being harangued by M. Verdurin; the second (III.326–27) recounts that he dies of a heart attack, and receives financial support from the Verdurins during the final months of his life.
12. Walter Pater, *The Renaissance: Studies in Art and Poetry* (1873; rpt. New York: Johnson Reprint Corporation, 1967), p.235.
13. Alain Robbe-Grillet, *La Maison de rendez-vous*, p.9
14. Samuel Beckett, *Waiting for Godot: A tragicomedy in two acts* (1956; rpt. London: Faber and Faber, 1977), pp.60 and 14. Henceforth abbreviated as *WFG*.
15. Walter Pater, *The Renaissance*, pp.236–37.

4. Nihilistic Modes of Existence in *A la recherche du temps perdu*

1. Samuel Beckett, 'Proust in Pieces', 976.
2. Edmund Wilson, *Axel's Castle*, p.163.
3. Samuel Beckett, *Murphy* (1983; rpt. London: Calder and Boyars, 1970), p.30.
4. Beckett has donated his copies of Proust's *A la recherche du temps perdu* (1917–27; rpt. Paris: Gallimard, Éditions de la Nouvelle Revue Française, 1926–29), to the Reading University Library Samuel Beckett Collection. The annotated copies of this 'abominable edition' (*PTD*, 9) consist of: *Du Côté de chez Swann*, volume one (107e édition, 1928); *Du Côté de chez Swann*, volume two (107e édition, 1928); *A l'ombre des jeunes filles en fleurs*, volume two (119e édition, 1929); *A l'ombre des jeunes filles en fleurs*, volume three (119e édition, 1929); *Le Côté de Guermantes*, volume one (73e édition, no date); *Le Côté de Guermantes*, volume two (54e édition, 1927); *Sodome et Gomorrhe*, volume one (71e édition, 1927); *Sodome et Gomorrhe*, volume two (71e édition, 1927); *Sodome et Gomorrhe*, volume three (71e édition, 1927); *La Prisonnière*, volume one (46e édition, 1927); *La Prisonnière*, volume two (46e édition, 1927); *Albertine Disparue*, volume one (45e édition, 1926); *Albertine Disparue*, volume two (45e édition, 1926); *Le Temps Retrouvé*, volume one (36e édition, 1929); *Le Temps Retrouvé*, volume two (36e édition, 1929). One volume, *A l'ombre des jeunes filles en fleurs*, volume one (presumably, 119e édition, 1929), is missing. Beckett's annotations include verbal comments, cross-references, underlinings and one or more vertical lines opposite passages that caught his interest.
5. Beckett annotates these lines from *La Prisonnière*, volume one (Paris, 1927), p.117 (III.87) with several bold vertical lines.

6. Samuel Beckett, *Company* (London: John Calder, 1980), p.36.
7. Samuel Beckett, *Footfalls* (London, Faber and Faber, 1976), p.9. Henceforth abbreviated as *F*.
8. Samuel Beckett, *Le Dépeupleur* (Paris: Les Éditions de Minuit, 1970), p.13; translated by Beckett as *The Lost Ones* (London: Calder and Boyars, 1972), p.14. Henceforth abbreviated as *TLO*.
9. Jeffrey Mehlman, *A Structural Study of Autobiography: Proust, Leiris, Sartre, Levi-Strauss* (Ithaca: Cornell University Press, 1974), p.28.
10. Mehlman adapts Lacan's terminology here; *ibid.*, p.31.
11. *Ibid.*
12. Marcel's concept of the 'wisdom of hope' nicely negates Beckett's suggestion that Proust's 'wisdom' would merely ablate desire (*PTD*, 18).
13. Samuel Beckett, *Mal vu mal dit* (Paris: Les Éditions de Minuit, 1981), pp.75–6; translated by Beckett as *Ill seen ill said* (London: John Calder, 1982), p.59. Henceforth abbreviated as *Mvmd* and *Isis*.
14. Samuel Beckett, *Ill seen ill said*, p.47; *From an Abandoned Work* (London: Faber and Faber, 1958), p.10; *Not I* (London: Faber and Faber, 1973), p.16.
15. Samuel Beckett, quoted by John Pilling in John Pilling, 'Beckett's *Proust*', *Journal of Beckett Studies*, No.1 (Winter 1976), 24.

5. Beckett's Prousts — the Singular and the Multiple

1. Anna Balakian, 'Influence and Literary Fortune: The Equivocal Junction of Two Methods', *Yearbook of Comparative and General Literature*, XI (1962), 29.
2. Deirdre Bair's *Samuel Beckett: a biography* (New York: Harcourt Brace Jovanovich, 1978) reports that Beckett wrote *Proust* in 1930 (p.109). It was published in 1931 in London by Chatto and Windus as a 'Dolphin Book'. All references to this essay are to the reprint edition, in Beckett's *Proust and Three Dialogues with Georges Duthuit* (London: John Calder, 1965). Throughout the following three chapters, all unidentified page references are to Beckett's *Proust*.
3. Frank Kermode, 'Beckett, Snow and Pure Poverty', *Encounter*, XV, No.82 (July 1960), 73. Two other articles deserve mention. John Fletcher's 'Beckett et Proust', *Caliban: Annales Publieés par la Faculté des Lettres de Toulouse*, 1 (January 1964), 89–100, itemizes a number of minor inconsistencies and borrowings in *Proust*, but indulgently concludes that 'Beckett est en général très fidèle à la pensée proustienne' (98) (Beckett is usually very faithful to Proust's thought); and James Acheson's 'Beckett, Proust, and Schopenhauer', *Contemporary Literature*, XIX, No.2 (Spring 1978), 165–79, argues that *Proust* is often 'obscurely worded and seriously underargued' (165), but gives more attention to the obscurities of Beckett's references to Schopenhauer than to the inadequacies of his reading of *A la recherche du temps perdu*.
4. Steven J. Rosen, *Samuel Beckett and the Pessimistic Tradition* (New Brunswick, New Jersey: Rutgers University Press, 1976), p.137.
5. John Pilling, 'Beckett's *Proust*', 16.
6. Deirdre Bair, *Samuel Beckett: a biography*, p.109.
7. *Ibid.*, p.108.
8. Deirdre Bair, letter of 3 May 1978. I am very grateful to Deirdre Bair for this information, taken from notes made while examining this annotated first edition of Beckett's *Proust* with its owner, Mr Thomas Wall, of Dublin.

9. Deirdre Bair reports the following pagination: 'Dog vomit' (p.8); 'terrible jargon' (p.4); ' "too abstract" indeed . . . the argument' (p.7).
10. John Pilling, 'Beckett's *Proust*', 16.
11. Samuel Beckett, lecture on naturalism at Trinity College, Dublin, 1931, quoted by S.E. Gontarski from notes taken by Rachel Burrows, in his *The Intent of Undoing in Samuel Beckett's Dramatic Texts*, p.11.
12. Samuel Beckett, 'Proust in Pieces', 976.
13. Vladimir Nabokov, *Lolita* (1955; rpt. New York: G.P. Putnam's Sons, 1958), p.255. Nabokov's Humbert Humbert amusingly regrets: 'I have reached the part which (had I not been forestalled by another internal combustion martyr) might be called "Dolorés Disparue" '.
14. Marcel Proust, *Marcel Proust et Jacques Rivière, Correspondance (1914–1922)*, p.2.
15. Colin Duckworth's introduction to his edition of Beckett's *En attandant Godot* (London: Harrap, 1966), p.xlv, reports that Beckett wrote this play between 9 October 1948 and 29 January 1949. First published in Paris by Les Éditions de Minuit in 1952, the play appeared in English translation as *Waiting for Godot* (New York: Grove Press, 1954; London: Faber and Faber, 1956).
16. Samuel Beckett, 'Proust in Pieces', 976.
17. John Pilling, 'Beckett's *Proust*', 16.
18. 'V', the mother of 'May', is especially attentive to the sound of both her daughter's voice and her daughter's footfalls, telling May: 'There is no sleep so deep I would not hear you there' (*Footfalls*, p.9) — a statement not unlike Marcel's grandmother's assuring affirmation that she could not possibly confuse his tappings with other sounds, and that 'entre mille sa grand'mère les reconnaîtrait!' (I.669) (his grandmother could pick them out from among a thousand others!).
19. Beckett underlines the word 'cloison' in Marcel's reference to the way in which he despairingly turns his head to the wall immediately after his 'poisoned' memory of his grandmother, and recalls: 'ce cloison . . . servait jadis entre nous deux de messager matinal' (II.762) (that partition once served the two of us as an early morning messenger), in *Sodome et Gomorrhe*, volume one (Paris, 1927), p.186. He annotates Marcel's subsequent reference to the way in which this partition separates him from Albertine (II.1118) with the comment '2 aspects of cloison', in *Sodome et Gomorrhe*, volume three (Paris: 1927), p.219.
20. Samuel Beckett, *Dream*, p.187; *More Pricks Than Kicks* (1934; rpt. London: Calder and Boyars, 1970), p.61; *Murphy*, p.125. Henceforth, *More Pricks Than Kicks* is abbreviated as *MPTK*.
21. These references to Albertine occur on II.390 and III.1118.
22. 'Proust in Pieces', 976.
23. James Joyce, *A Portrait of the Artist as a Young Man* (1916; rpt. Harmondsworth: Penguin, 1972), p.89.
24. *Dream*, p.61. Minor spelling variations occur on pp.12–13.
25. This quotation from *Dream of Fair to Middling Women* is, admittedly, taken from an evocation of Belacqua's love-life and is not an explicit reference to the human condition. But whereas Marcel's amorous misfortunes are entirely atypical of existence as a whole in *A la recherche du temps perdu*, Belacqua's unhappy relationship with the 'Smeraldina-Rima' is absolutely typical of the prevailing 'absence of douceness' (or absence of 'enchantment') pervading the Beckettian fictional universe.

6. Beckett's Interpretation of the 'Albertine Tragedy'

1. Samuel Beckett, 'Proust in Pieces', 976.
2. Samuel Beckett, 'Dante . . . Bruno. Vico . . Joyce', 242.
3. See Chapter 3, p.53.
4. Just as Burroughs employs the slang of drug addiction as a metaphor for perceptual needs, he appropriates medical terminology to define the subversive potential of words and images as a 'virus' in the section of *Nova Express* entitled 'Technical Deposition of the Virus Power'. 'Mr. Winkhorst' explains: 'We first took our image and put it into code. A technical code developed by the information theorists. The code was written at the molecular level to save space, when it was found that the image material was not dead matter, but exhibited the same life cycle as the virus. This virus released upon the world would infect the entire population' (*Nova Express*, p.57). Burroughs's terminology overlaps with Beckett's notion of perceptual 'infection'.
5. Charles Baudelaire, 'Correspondances', *Les Fleurs du Mal*, in *Oeuvres complètes*, ed. Marcel A. Ruff (1857; rpt. Paris: Les Éditions du Seuil, 1968), p.46.
6. William Burroughs, *Nova Express*, p.75.
7. *Ibid.*, p.70.
8. William Burroughs, 'The Art of Fiction XXXVI', interview with Conrad Knickerbocker, *Paris Review*, No.35 (Autumn, 1965), 21.
9. *Ibid.*, p.23.
10. *A l'ombre des jeunes filles en fleurs*, volume three (Paris, 1929), p.194 (I.907).
11. *A l'ombre des jeunes filles en fleurs* volume two (Paris, 1929), p.19 (I.612).
12. Walter Pater, *The Renaissance*, p.235.
13. *Ibid.*, pp.236–7.
14. *Le Temps Retrouvé*, volume two (Paris, 1929), p.240 (III.1033).
15. As James Acheson remarks in 'Beckett, Proust, and Schopenhauer', 179, Marcel also associates friendship with the 'warmth' of companionship. Acheson refers to Marcel's suggestion that friendship may generate 'la chaleur que nous ne pouvons pas trouver en nous-même' (II.395) (the warmth that we cannot draw from ourselves).

7. Beckett and the 'Paradox' of the 'Mystical Experience'

1. John Fletcher, *Samuel Beckett's Art* (London: Chatto and Windus, 1971), p.19.
2. Samuel Beckett, untitled review of *Poems* by Rainer Maria Rilke, *The Criterion*, XIII, No.LIII (July 1934), 705–6, 706.
3. Samuel Beckett, 'Casket of Pralinen for a Daughter of a Dissipated Mandarin', *European Caravan*, eds. Samuel Putnam, Madia Castelhun Darnton, George Reavey and Jacob Bronowski, Part I (France, Spain, England and Ireland) (New York: Brewer, Warren, and Putnam, 1931). Reprinted in Lawrence E. Harvey, *Samuel Beckett, Poet and Critic* (Princeton, N.J.: Princeton University Press, 1970), pp.378–83, p.281.
4. Samuel Beckett, letter of 1946 to anonymous recipient, quoted by Deirdre Bair in *Samuel Beckett: a biography*, p.352.
5. Marcel cryptically explains that 'beaucoup d'années passèrent' (III.854) (many years were to pass) during his post-war sojourns in successive sanatoriums.

6. Samuel Beckett, *Molloy* (Paris: Les Éditions de Minuit, 1951), p.268.

7. *Albertine Disparue*, volume one (Paris, 1926), p.14.

8. *Le Temps Retrouvé*, volume two (Paris, 1929), p.16.

9. Samuel Beckett, 'Dante . . . Bruno. Vico . . Joyce', 242.

10. Beckett coins the phrase 'chartered recountant' in 'An Imaginative Work!', review of Jack B. Yeats's *The Amaranthers*, *The Dublin Magazine*, XI, No.3 (July – September 1934), 80. His allusion to literary 'book-keeping' appears in 'Dante . . . Bruno. Vico . . Joyce', 242.

11. The narrator of *Company* twice refers, very fleetingly, to memories 'you have never forgotten' (13) and which 'You have never forgotten' (41). Evading such deep, autobiographical 'company', he invents superficial, imaginary 'company'.

12. Roland Barthes, 'Littérature Objective', *Essais Critiques* (Paris: Les Éditions du Seuil, 1964), p.30. Translated by Richard Howard as 'Objective Literature', in Roland Barthes, *Critical Essays* (Evanston: Northwestern University Press, 1972), p.14.

13. *Ibid.*

14. Roland Barthes, 'Littérature Littérale', *Essais Critiques*, p.67. 'Literal Literature', *Critical Essays*, p.55.

15. 'Littérature Objective', p.33. 'Objective Literature', p.17. Robbe-Grillet has tellingly criticized Barthes's analysis as 'a simplification'. See 'Confessions of Voyeur', Robbe-Grillet, interviewed by Roland Caputo, *Tension* (Victoria), (September–October, 1986), 10–11.

16. Roland Barthes, 'Il n'a pas d'école Robbe-Grillet', *Essais Critiques*, p.102. 'There is no Robbe-Grillet School', *Critical Essays*, p.92.

17. 'Littérature Objective', p.32. 'Objective Literature', p.16.

18. William Burroughs, *Nova Express*, p.54. Harold Pinter offers this hypothesis somewhat idiosyncratic confirmation: 'the more he grinds my nose in the shit the more I am grateful to him'. Pinter quotes from a letter of 1954 in 'Beckett', his contribution to *Beckett at 60: A Festschrift*, ed. John Calder (London: Calder and Boyars, 1967), p.86.

19. Other examples include Marcel's discussion of Swann's timidity (I.233), which employs three successive clauses commencing with 'soit', and his comments upon the way in which his mother avoids looking directly at his dying grandmother (II.319), which lists four explanations beginning with 'peut-être'. Beckett annotates Marcel's successive analyses of Swann's artistic taste, which employ the word 'peut-être' three times (I.223), with the comment 'Finical pure logic' in his copy of *Du Côté de Chez Swann*, volume two (Paris, 1928), p.14. He also annotates Marcel's prolonged explanations of Albertine's nasal intonation (I.877) as 'Timid pure logic' in *A l'ombre des jeunes filles en fleurs*, volume three (Paris, 1929), p.155; and locates another example of 'Timid logic' in *Sodome et Gomorrhe*, volume two (Paris, 1927), p. 178, where Marcel's relativism attains its apotheosis in an explanation reiterating the word 'soit' on five successive occasions (II.919-20).

20. Samuel Beckett, *Worstward Ho* (London: John Calder, 1983). Henceforth abbreviated as *WH*.

21. Ernst Robert Curtius, *Marcel Proust*, p.134. All subsequent references to Curtius's book in this chapter appear in the text.

22. F.S. Flint, untitled review of Samuel Beckett's *Proust*, *The Criterion*, X, No. XLI (July 1931), 792. This six-line review is aptly gathered among 'Shorter Notices'.

23. Bonamy Dobrée, untitled review of Edmund Wilson's *Axel's Castle* and Samuel Beckett's *Proust*, *The Spectator*, 18 April 1931, 641–2.

24. F.S. Flint, 'The History of Imagism', *The Egoist*, 1 May 1915, 71.

25. Beckett writes this annotation in the upper margin of his copy of *A l'ombre des jeunes filles en fleurs*, volume three (Paris, 1929), p.151.
26. Samuel Beckett, 'Proust in Pieces', 976.
27. James Acheson, 'Beckett, Proust and Schopenhauer', 176.
28. Arthur Schopenhauer, *The World as Will and Idea*, translated by R.B. Haldane and J. Kemp (London: Kegan Paul, Trübner and Co., 1909), volume one, p.176.
29. Samuel Beckett, 'Proust in Pieces', 976.
30. James Acheson, 'Beckett, Proust and Schopenhauer', 169.
31. Samuel Beckett, letter of 22 April 1958 to Aidan Higgins (concerning the manuscript of Higgins's story 'Killachter Meadow'), *The Review of Contemporary Fiction*, III, No.1 (September 1983), 157.
32. Samuel Beckett, letter of 1946 to anonymous recipient, quoted by Deirdre Bair, in *Samuel Beckett: a biography*, p.352.
33. Samuel Beckett, conversations of 1977 and 1975, quoted by Charles Juliet in *Rencontre avec Samuel Beckett* (Montpellier: Fata Morgana, 1986), pp.51 and 38.
34. Samuel Beckett, *Krapp's Last Tape* (1959; rpt. London: Faber and Faber, 1968), p.18. Henceforth abbreviated as *KLT*.

8. Beckett and Critical Perspectives

1. Tom F. Driver, 'Beckett by the Madeleine', *Columbia University Forum*, IV (Summer 1961), 23.
2. Samuel Beckett, untitled review of Rilke's *Poems*, 706; and 'Schwabenstreich', review of Eduard Moerike's *Mozart On The Way To Prague*, *The Spectator*, 23 March 1934, 472.
3. Samuel Beckett and Georges Duthuit, *Three Dialogues*, transition '49, No.5 (December 1949), 97–103; reprinted in Samuel Beckett, *Proust and Three Dialogues with Georges Duthuit* (London: John Calder, 1965), pp.95–126, p.103. Henceforth abbreviated as *PTD*.
4. Samuel Beckett, 'Ex Cathezra', review of Ezra Pound's *Make It New*, *The Bookman* (Christmas 1934), 10.
5. Samuel Beckett, 'MacGreevy on Yeats', review of Thomas MacGreevy's *Jack B. Yeats, An Appreciation and an Interpretation*, *The Irish Times*, 4 August 1945, 2.
6. *Ibid*.
7. *Ibid*.
8. Samuel Beckett, letter to Thomas MacGreevy of 1 March 1954; and letter to H.O. White of 15 April 1957. Both letters cited by Deirdre Bair, in *Samuel Beckett: a biography*, pp.444 and 483.
9. John Pilling, in James Knowlson and John Pilling, *Frescoes of the Skull, The Later Prose and Drama of Samuel Beckett* (New York: Grove Press, 1980), p.254. Pilling refers to the light/dark dichotomy in Beckett's 'Hommage à Jack B. Yeats', *Les Lettres Nouvelles*, II (April 1954), 619–20, predicating his conclusions upon the inaccuracies in Ruby Cohn's translation of this text as 'Homage to Jack B. Yeats', in *Jack B. Yeats: A Centenary Gathering*, ed. Roger McHugh (Dublin: The Dolmen Press, 1971), pp.75–6. Beckett's original text praises Yeats's work for 'son insistance à renvoyer au plus secret de l'esprit qui la soulève et à ne se laisser éclairer qu'au jour de celui-ci' (619) (its insistence upon withdrawing to the most secret parts of the spirit which animates it and upon accepting illumination only from this source). Ruby

Cohn rather confusingly renders this as: 'its insistence upon sending us back to the darkest part of the spirit that created it and upon permitting illuminations only through that darkness' (75).

10. *Ibid.*
11. Samuel Beckett, 'Papini's Dante', 14.
12. Hans Arp, Samuel Beckett, Carl Einstein, Eugene Jolas, Thomas MacGreevy, Georges Pelorson, Theo Rutra, James J. Sweeney, Ronald Symond, 'Poetry Is Vertical', *transition*, No.21 (March 1931), 148. This manifesto concludes by aspiring to 'the illumination of a collective reality and a totalistic universe' (149).
13. Quoted by Deirdre Bair from a conversation of 13 April 1972, in *Samuel Beckett: a biography*, p.141.
14. Jolas employs this term in 'Poetry is Vertical' (148), and in innumerable other statements regarding 'the revolution of the word' in *transition*.
15. *Ibid.*
16. John Spurling, in John Fletcher and John Spurling, *Beckett: A Study of His Plays*, p.28.
17. William Burroughs, interview with Nicholas Zurbrugg, Lawrence, Kansas, 22 November 1983.
18. William Burroughs, notes for a lecture on 'Proust and Beckett', given at the University of Kansas in 1983. Page two of an unpaginated six-page typescript.
19. Samuel Beckett, 'An Imaginative Work!', 80 and 81.
20. *Ibid.*, 81.
21. Samuel Beckett, 'Dante ... Bruno. Vico .. Joyce', 242.
22. Samuel Beckett, 'Schwabenstreich', 472.
23. *Ibid.*
24. Samuel Beckett, 'The Essential and the Incidental', review of Sean O'Casey's *Windfalls*, *The Bookman* (Christmas 1934), 111.
25. *Ibid.*
26. Samuel Beckett, 'Proust in Pieces', 976.
27. *Ibid.*
28. *Ibid.*
29. *Ibid.*
30. Quoted by Tom F. Driver, in 'Beckett by the Madeleine', 23.
31. Samuel Beckett, 'An Imaginative Work!', 81; 'The Essential and the Incidental', 111; 'Proust in Pieces', 975 and 976.
32. Andrew Belis (Samuel Beckett), 'Recent Irish Poetry', *The Bookman* (August 1934), 235. All subsequent references appear in the text.
33. Roland Barthes discusses the 'caractère ... purement fonctionnel' (purely functional character) of Robbe-Grillet's descriptions in 'Littérature Objective', 29; 'Objective Literature', 13.
34. Samuel Beckett, 'Humanistic Quietism', review of Thomas MacGreevy's *Poems*, *Dublin Magazine*, IX, No.3 (July—September 1934), 79–80, 79. All subsequent references appear in the text.
35. Friedrich Marcus Huebner, 'The Road through the Word', translated by Eugene Jolas, *transition*, No.22 (February 1933), 110–113, 110 and 112. All subsequent references appear in the text.
36. The phrase 'not on misanthropy but on hope' is Thomas MacGreevy's.
37. Samuel Beckett, 'Dante ... Vico. Bruno .. Joyce', 249.
38. *Ibid.*, 247.
39. Samuel Beckett, 'Denis Devlin', review of Denis Devlin's *Intercessions*,

transition, No.27 (April–May 1938), 289–94, 293.
40. Quoted by Tom F. Driver, in 'Beckett by the Madeleine', 23.
41. Raymond Federman, 'Fiction Today or The Pursuit of Non-Knowledge', *The Journal of Art, Performance and Manufacture*, No.1 (April 1977), 9–16, 10.
42. *Ibid.*, 12 and 14.
43. Quoted by Israel Shenker, in 'Moody Man of Letters', 1 and 3.
44. *Ibid.*, 3.
45. R.C. Kenedy, letter of 8 August 1979, in ' "Advances" and the Contemporary Avant-Garde', *Stereo Headphones*, No.8-9-10 (1982), 69–79, 70.
46. See for example, Raymond Federman's *Take It or Leave It* (New York: Fiction Collective, 1976); an 'exaggerated second-hand tale to be read aloud either standing or sitting', which mixes ribald stream of consciousness in the manner of Henry Miller and Jack Kerouac with such asides as: 'I want to tell a story that cancels itself as it goes', and: 'nothing is cancelled nothing is erased (or else everything is cancelled erased lost)'. Unpaginated.
47. Richard Sheppard, 'The Crisis of Language', in *Modernism: 1890–1930*, ed. Malcolm Bradbury and James McFarlane (Harmondsworth: Penguin, 1976), pp.323–36, p.324. Sheppard offers a lucid overview of this 'crisis'.
48. John Pilling, *Samuel Beckett* (London: Routledge and Kegan Paul, 1976), p.26; Lawrence E. Harvey, *Samuel Beckett, Poet and Critic*, p.250.
49. Samuel Beckett, note to Nicholas Zurbrugg of 18 April 1981, published in *Stereo Headphones*, No.8-9-10 (1982), 80. Beckett refers to the recorded work of the French sound poets Henri Chopin and Bernard Heidsieck. For further discussion of the relationship between Beckett's work and that of the contemporary avant-garde, see my article 'Beyond Beckett: Reckless Writing and the Concept of the Avant-Garde within Post-Modern Literature', *Yearbook of Comparative and General Literature*, No.30 (1981), 37–56.
50. Alan Rodway, 'There's a Hole in Your Beckett', *Encounter*, XLII, No.2 (February 1974), 49–53, 52; Vivian Mercier, *Beckett/Beckett* (New York: Oxford University Press, 1979). p.175.
51. John Fletcher, *Samuel Beckett's Art*, pp.95 and 140.
52. *Ibid.*, pp.22 and 145.
53. Hannah Case Copeland, *Art and the Artist in the Works of Samuel Beckett* (The Hague: Mouton, 1975), p.11; Francis Doherty, *Samuel Beckett* (London: Hutchinson, 1971), p.20.
54. John Fletcher, *The Novels of Samuel Beckett* (London: Chatto and Windus, 1964), p.149.
55. Ruby Cohn, *Samuel Beckett: the comic gamut* (New Brunswick, New Jersey: Rutgers University Press, 1962), p.145; Richard N. Coe, 'God and Samuel Beckett', *Meanjin Quarterly*, XXIV, No.1 (March 1965), 73; Rosette Lamont, 'Beckett's Metaphysics of Choiceless Awareness', in *Samuel Beckett Now*, ed. Melvin J. Friedman (Chicago: The University of Chicago Press, 1970), p.205.
56. J.D. O'Hara, 'Introduction', *Twentieth Century Interpretations of 'Molloy', 'Malone Dies' and 'The Unnamable'*, ed. J.D. O'Hara (Englewood Cliffs, New Jersey: Prentice-Hall, 1970), p.14; Northrop Frye, 'The Nightmare Life in Death', review of Samuel Beckett's *Molloy, Malone Dies, and The Unnamable*, *The Hudson Review*, XIII, No.3 (Autumn 1960), 448.
57. Melvin J. Friedman, 'The Novels of Samuel Beckett: An Amalgam of Joyce and Proust', *Comparative Literature*, XII, No.1 (Winter 1960), 57.
58. Josephine Jacobsen and William R. Mueller, *The Testament of Samuel Beckett* (New York: Hill and Wang, 1964), p.148.

59. Martin Esslin, 'Worth the "Wait" ', review of Samuel Beckett's *Texts for Nothing, Books and Bookmen*, 19, No.9 (June 1974), 91.
60. Robert Currie, *Genius, An Ideology in Literature* (London: Chatto and Windus, 1974), pp.183 and 188; Theodor W. Adorno, 'Towards an Understanding of *Endgame*', in *Twentieth Century Interpretations of 'Endgame'*, ed. Bell Gale Chevigny (Englewood Cliffs, New Jersey: Prentice-Hall, 1969), p.94. Translated by Samuel M. Weber, from 'Versuch das *Endspiel* zu versehen', from *Noten zur Literatur*, II (Frankfurt am Main: Suhrkamp Verlag, 1961).
61. Samuel Beckett, 'Dante ... Bruno. Vico .. Joyce', 253.
62. *Ibid.*

9. Beckett, Proust and *Dream of Fair to Middling Women*

1.   All references to *Dream of Fair to Middling Women* in this chapter appear as unidentified page references to the photocopy of Beckett's corrected typescript in the Reading University Library Samuel Beckett Collection, MS 1227/7/16/8.
2.   John Pilling, in James Knowlson and John Pilling, *Frescoes of the Skull*, p.5; John Fletcher, *The Novels of Samuel Beckett*, p.36; Lawrence E. Harvey, *Samuel Beckett, Poet and Critic*, p.320.
3.   Tzvetan Todorov introduces his theory of 'basic predicates' in 'Les catégories du récit littéraire', *Communications*, No.VIII (1966), 125–51. Todorov's ideas are in turn usefully analysed by Seymour Chatman, in 'New Ways of Analyzing Narrative Structure, With an Example from Joyce's *Dubliners*', *Language and Style*, II, No.1 (Winter 1969), 3–36.
4.   John Pilling, 'Beckett's *Proust*', 14. Pilling rather derisively concedes: 'Beckett remains sufficiently wide-awake to catch Proust repeating a whole sentence verbatim'.
5.   Beckett makes his reference to 'the mess' of existence in his interviews with Tom F. Driver in 'Beckett by the Madeline', 21.
6.   Lawrence E. Harvey, *Samuel Beckett, Poet and Critic*, p.340.
7.   Quoted by Israel Shenker in 'Moody Man of Letters', 3.
8.   Alluding to Joyce, Beckett comments: 'He's tending towards omniscience and omnipotence as an artist. I'm working with impotence, ignorance', 'Moody Man of Letters', 3.
9.   Samuel Beckett, 'Proust in Pieces', 976.
10. My translation. Beckett's English version of *Molloy* transforms 'poliment perplexe' into 'dutiful confusions' (*Molloy*, 15).
11. The final lines of *Dream of Fair to Middling Women* are unpaginated and handwritten, on the reverse of page 214. Henceforth notated as (214b).
12. Burroughs discusses the subversive and disorientating potential of 'sex images' in *Electronic Revolution*, pp.134–41, speculating upon the possibility of creating a 'sex virus', itself 'created by very small units of sound and image', which 'so inflames the sex centers in the back brain that the host is driven mad from sexuality, all other consideration (being) blacked out' (p.139).
13. The concept of the 'displaced faculty of assimilation' perfectly defines the perceptual plight of many Post-Modern heroes. Instead of assimilating reality metaphorically or metonymically, they find reality runs riot, resisting 'assimilation'.
14. Samuel Beckett, letter of 10 March 1935, quoted by Deirdre Bair, in *Samuel Beckett: a biography*, p.198.

15. See James Joyce, 'A Painful Case', *Dubliners* (1914; rpt. Harmondsworth: Penguin, 1971), pp.105–15.
16. Samuel Beckett, 'Assumption', *transition*, No.16–17 (June 1929), 268–71. All subsequent references appear in the text.
17. The word 'douceness' is Beckett's invention.
18. James Joyce, *A Portrait of the Artist as a Young Man*, p.89; Samuel Beckett, *Proust*, p.35.
19. See Sir Walter Scott, *Waverley* (1814; rpt. Harmondsworth: Penguin, 1982). Scott's Baron Bradwardine, a cousin in pomposity to Proust's Baron de Charlus, is affectionately chided as 'the most absurd orginal that exists north of the Tweed!' (p.346).
20. Beckett writes 'Frequent image' opposite Marcel's comparison of Charlus with 'the fish . . . ' (II.1049), in *Sodome et Gomorrhe*, volume three (Paris, 1927), p.126.
21. Samuel Beckett, *How It Is* (London: John Calder, 1964), p.111.
22. Beckett uses precisely this formula in an early draft of *Endgame*, entitled 'Avant *Fin de Partie*' (Reading University Library Samuel Beckett Collection, MS 1227/7/16/7). On the first page of this 21 page typescript, a character identified as 'X' comments: 'Comme c'est bon, mediter à haute voix, surtout le matin, avant que se dechaîne le train-train quotidien' (How pleasant it is to think out loud, above all in the morning, before starting the daily routine). My translation.
23. Samuel Beckett, 'Dante . . . Bruno. Vico . . Joyce', 242.
24. Samuel Beckett, 'Proust in Pieces', 976.
25. Samuel Beckett, letter of 9 July 1937, collected as 'German Letter of 1937', in Samuel Beckett, *Disjecta: Miscellaneous Writings and a Dramatic Fragment*, ed. with a foreword by Ruby Cohn (London: John Calder, 1983), p.53. English translation by Martin Esslin, p.172.
26. Samuel Beckett, 'Dante . . . Bruno. Vico . . Joyce', 248.
27. 'Minimal art' is of course used here as a very general concept; usually it pertains to the fine arts.
28. James Joyce, 'The Dead', *Dubliners*, pp.173–220, p.220.
29. William Burroughs, interview with Nicholas Zurbrugg, Minneapolis, 6 October 1983. Burroughs refers to the ending of Joyce's 'The Dead' and to the ending of Scott Fitzgerald's *The Great Gatsby*. I am very grateful to James Grauerholz for arranging this interview.
30. William Burroughs, 'combat troops in the area', *Dead Fingers Talk* (London: John Calder, 1963), p.169.
31. William Burroughs, 'The Art of Fiction XXXVI', *Paris Review*, No.35, interview with Conrad Knickerbocker, 23.
32. James Joyce, letter to Grant Richards of 5 May 1906. In *James Joyce: 'Dubliners' and 'A Portrait of the Artist as A Young Man'*, ed. Moris Beja (London: Macmillan, 1973), p.38. Joyce writes: 'I chose Dublin for the scene because that city seemed to me the centre of paralysis'.

10. The Evolution of Beckett's Early Fiction Vision in *More Pricks Than Kicks* and *Murphy*

1. All references in this chapter to *More Pricks Than Kicks* and to *Murphy* appear as unidentified page numbers.
2. Samuel Beckett, 'Echo's Bones', p.1. All references to this unpublished 28-page short story, dated '34? 35?' in Beckett's handwriting, refer to the

typescript in the Baker Library of Dartmouth College. Quoted by kind permission of Samuel Beckett. Henceforth abbreviated as *EB*.

3. Georg Lukács, *The Meaning of Contemporary Realism*, translated from the German by John and Necke Mander (1963; rpt. London: Merlin Press, 1972), p.31.
4. Belacqua's ailment is not entirely fictional. As Deirdre Bair indicates, Beckett suffered from similar 'persistent boils', *Samuel Beckett: a biography*, p.125.
5. Proust seems to have based his description of Bergotte's visit to Vermeer's *View of Delft* upon his own visit to an exhibition of Dutch painting at the Jeu de Paume in 1921.
6. See Marcel Proust, *Jean Santeuil*, p.471.
7. Marcel Proust, *Contre Sainte-Beuve*, ed. Bernard de Fallois (Paris: Éditions Gallimard, Collection Idées, 1954), p.83.
8. See Deirdre Bair, *Samuel Beckett: a biography*, p.219.
9. Samuel Beckett, 'Dante ... Bruno. Vico .. Joyce, 250.
10. *Ibid.*, 242.
11. Jean-François Revel, *Sur Proust* (Paris: Juilliard, 1960), p.15. Revel's concept of Proust's 'ballet' of gestures and his complex array of manual gestures is nicely exemplified in Marcel's account of his grandmother's last hours. Marcel analyses almost everybody at his grandmother's bedside in terms of their hands, successively identifying the professional courtesy of a doctor who 'tendit gracieusement la main' (II.318) (graciously offered his hand); the ostentatious posturing of the duc de Guermantes who studiously embarks upon 'la cérémonie complète du salut' (II.338) (the entirety of the greeting ceremony); the compulsive sadism of 'les mains cruelles de Françoise' (II.333) (Françoise's cruel hands); the hypocritical voyeurism of a monk who pretends to pray, while spying through the 'abri de ses mains' (II.339) (shelter of his hands); and last, but not least, the dying tremors of his grandmother's hands, which, as Marcel triumphantly testifies, 's'agitèrent' (II.344) (began to flutter) in response to his last embrace.
12. James Knowlson, '*Pas* and *Pas Moi* at the Théâtre d'Orsay, Paris, 11 April 1978', *Journal of Beckett Studies*, No.4 (Spring 1979), 72.
13. Raymond Federman, *Journey to Chaos: Samuel Beckett's Early Fiction* (Berkeley: University of California Press, 1965), p.71.

11. *Watt* and the Problem of Intelligibility

1. All references in this chapter to *Watt* appear as unidentified page numbers. Excerpts from *Watt* first appeared in *Merlin*, No.1 (Winter 1952−3), 118−26.
2. Richard Seaver discusses the publishing history of *Watt* in an untitled text in *The Olympia Reader: Selections from the 'Traveller's Companion' Series*, ed. Maurice Girodias (New York: Grove, 1965), pp.221−25, p.223.
3. *Watt* was first published in Paris in 1953 by the Olympia Press. Maurice Girodias discusses the activities of this press in 'Advance through Obscenity?', *The Times Literary Supplement*, August 6 1964, 708−9.
4. Richard Seaver, untitled review of *Watt*, *Nimbus* (Autumn 1953), 61−2; collected in *Samuel Beckett: The Critical Heritage*, eds. Lawrence Graver and Raymond Federman (London: Routledge and Kegal Paul, 1979), p.124.
5. *Ibid.*, p.122.
6. Beckett explains that he wrote *Watt* 'on the run' and in 'dribs and drabs', in a letter to George Reavey of 14 May 1947, quoted by Deirdre Bair in *Samuel Beckett: a biography*, p.364. Lawrence E. Harvey records Beckett's suggestion that he wrote *Watt* to 'keep my hand in', in *Samuel Beckett, Poet and Critic*, p.222.

7. Beckett describes *Watt* as an 'unsatisfactory book' in the same letter to George Reavey as above, *ibid*. Lawrence E. Harvey records Beckett's suggestion that *Watt* is a 'joke' and a 'game' in *Samuel Beckett, Poet and Critic*, pp.381 and 222.
8. Catherine Belsey's *Critical Practice* (London: Methuen, 1980) exemplifies the position of those critics who have responded enthusiastically, and perhaps over-literally, to the notion of 'the death of the author'.
9. Melvin J. Friedman, 'The Novels of Samuel Beckett: An Amalgam of Joyce and Proust', 52; John Spurling, in John Fletcher and John Spurling, *Beckett: A Study of His Plays*, p.35; and Hugh Kenner, *Samuel Beckett: A Critical Study* (London: John Calder, 1962), pp.114 and 101.
10. Jean-Jacques Mayoux, *Samuel Beckett* (London: Longman, 1974), p.22; Lawrence E. Harvey, *Samuel Beckett, Poet and Critic*, p.382.
11. Vivian Mercier, 'The Mathematical Limit', *The Nation*, CLXXXVIII (14 February 1959), 144–5.
12. Jonathan Culler, *The Pursuit of Signs: Semiotics, Literature, Deconstruction* (Ithaca: Cornell University Press, 1981), pp.33 and 38. All subsequent references in this chapter to *The Pursuit of Signs* appear in the text.
13. Roland Barthes, 'The Death of the Author', pp.147, 146 and 147.
14. *Ibid.*, p.146
15. *Ibid.*, p.145
16. *Ibid.*, p.146
17. Roland Barthes, 'From Work to Text', *Image-Music-Text*, p.160. Barthes speculates that 'the citations which go to make up a text are anonymous, untraceable, and yet already read'.
18. Roland Barthes, *Camera Lucida: Reflections on Photography*, translated by Richard Howard (New York: Hill and Wang, 1981). All subsequent references in this chapter to *Camera Lucida* appear in the text. Barthes italicizes '*studium*' and '*punctum*' throughout.
19. Samuel Beckett, *Film* (London: Faber and Faber, 1972), p.36; Samuel Beckett, *A Piece of Monologue*, in *Three Occasional Pieces*, pp. 11–15, 12. Henceforth abbreviated as *APM*..
20. Dina Sherzer, *Structure de la trilogie de Beckett: Molloy, Malone Meurt, L'Innommable* (The Hague: Mouton, 1976), p.11.
21. John J. Mood, ' ''The Personal System'' — Samuel Beckett's *Watt*', *PMLA*, 86, No.2 (March 1971), 262 and 261.
22. James Joyce, *A Portrait of the Artist as a Young Man*, pp.172 and 173.
23. Samuel Beckett, 'Assumption', 269.
24. *Ibid.*
25. *Waiting For Godot* is subtitled 'A tragicomedy in two acts'.
26. Quoted by Israel Shenker, 'Moody Man of Letters', 3. See Preface, p. 3.
27. Brion Gysin discusses his permutated poems in 'Cut-Ups Self-Explained', in William Burroughs and Brion Gysin, *The Third Mind* (London: John Calder, 1979), p.34. A computerized version of 'Junk is no good baby' appears in the same volume, p.80.
28. Charles Russell, 'Literary Disruption as the Basis of Creation', in *The Avant-Garde Today: An International Anthology*, ed. Charles Russell (Urbana: University of Illinois Press, 1981), p.121.
29. John Cage, 'Writing for the Third Time through *Finnegans Wake*', *ibid.*, pp.131–41, p.131.
30. Edwin Morgan, 'Opening the Cage', in *British Poetry Since 1945*, ed. Edward Lucie-Smith (Harmondsworth: Penguin, 1980), p.319.

31. Ernst Jandl's 'film', and his comments upon this poem, are collected in *An Anthology of Concrete Poetry*, ed. Emmett Williams (New York: Something Else Press, 1967), unpaginated.
32. Samuel Beckett, letter to George Devine, discussing *Play*, of 9 March 1964. Typescript reproduced in *New Theatre Magazine*, XI, No.3, 16–17.
33. It would probably be erroneous to equate the sadism of 'Sam' and Watt with Beckett's own past or present values. Discussing Beckett's affection for birds and animals, Agnès Vaquin-Janvier observes: 'Il les aime tous' (He loves them all), Ludovic Janvier and Agnès Vaquin-Janvier, 'Traduire avec Beckett: *Watt*', *Revue d'Esthétique* (1986), Beckett issue, 57–64, 63.
34. Samuel Beckett, letter to Alan Schneider of 11 June 1956, in 'Beckett's Letters on *Endgame*', 8. Beckett writes: 'Have at last written another, one act, hour and a quarter I fancy. Rather difficult and elliptic, mostly depending on the power of the text to claw'.
35. Samuel Beckett, 'Schwabenstreich', 472.

12. Beckett's Mature Fiction — From 'Shit' to 'Shades'

1. Samuel Beckett, *Molloy, Malone Dies, The Unnamable* (London: Calder and Boyars, 1959), p.32. All subsequent page references to these three novels appear as unidentified page numbers, as do references to the French editions of *Molloy* (Paris: Les Éditions de Minuit, 1951); *Malone Meurt* (Paris: Les Éditions de Minuit, 1951); and *L'Innomable* (Paris: Les Éditions de Minuit, 1953); and references to Beckett's *How It Is* (London: John Calder, 1964).
2. Beckett alludes to the 'intractable complexities' of *Le Dépeupleur* in a note attached to the drafts of *Bing*, reproduced in facsimile by Richard L. Admussen, in *The Samuel Beckett Manuscripts: a study* (Boston, Mass.: G.K. Hall, 1979), p.22.
3. Beckett gave the title 'Shades' to the BBC television screening of *Not I, Ghost Trio* and ... *but the clouds* ..., of 17 April 1977. This term becomes increasingly prevalent in his later fiction.
4. Quoted by Israel Shenker, 'Moody Man of Letters', 1.
5. William Burroughs, interview with Nicholas Zurbrugg, Lawrence, Kansas, 22 November 1983.
6. See Deirdre Bair, *Samuel Beckett, a biography*, p.376.
7. *Ibid.* Deirdre Bair quotes Beckett's suggestion, to John Fletcher, that Sapo 'got a bit out of hand'.
8. The concept of the 'rightly human' appears in Beckett's *Murphy*, p.56.
9. William Burroughs, 'Beckett and Proust', pp.2 and 5.
10. Samuel Beckett, *What Where, Collected Shorter Plays* (London: Faber and Faber, 1984), pp.310, 312, 314 and 316. Beckett described *What Where* as 'puppet theatre' in conversation with Nicholas Zurbrugg, Paris, 28 January 1985. S. E. Gontarski cites a similar statement about this play in *The Intent of Undoing in Samuel Beckett's Dramatic Texts*, p.214.
11. Samuel Beckett, quoted by John Gruen, in 'Samuel Beckett talks about Samuel Beckett', *Vogue* (February 1970), 108.
12. Samuel Beckett, 'La peinture des Van Velde', 349.
13. Samuel Beckett, *Rough for Radio II* (ca.1962), *Collected Shorter Plays*, p.124. Henceforth abbreviated as *R*.
14. Samuel Beckett, letter to George Devine, discussing *Play*, of 9 March 1964, *New Theatre Magazine*, XI, No.3, 16–17.

15. Jean Baudrillard, *Simulations*, translated by Paul Foss, Paul Patton and Philip Beitchman (New York: Semiotext(e), Foreign Agents Series, 1983), pp.10-11.
16. Samuel Beckett, 'Something There', *Collected Poems in English and French* (London: John Calder, 1977), p.63.
17. The Unnamable declares 'je suis la cloison' (196) (I'm the partition), appropriating Marcel's key term: 'la cloison'; a word which Beckett underlined in his copy of *Sodome et Gomorrhe*, 2, volume one (Paris: 1927), p.186 (II.762).
18. William Burroughs, 'The Art of Fiction XXXVI', *Paris Review*, No.35, 23.
19. William Burroughs, interview with Nicholas Zurbrugg, Lawrence, Kansas, 22 November 1983.
20. Samuel Beckett, *All Strange Away* (London: John Calder, 1979), p.7. Henceforth abbreviated as *ASA*. Beckett explains that *All Strange Away*, *Imagination Dead Imagine*, *The Lost Ones* and *Ping* are all 'residual', '(1) Severally, even when that does not appear of which each is all that remains and (2) In relation to the whole body of previous work'. Quoted by Brian H. Finney, in *Since How It Is: A Study of Beckett's Later Fiction* (London: Covent Garden Press, 1972), p.10.
21. Samuel Beckett, *Imagination Dead Imagine* (1956), *No's Knife: Collected Shorter Prose 1945–1966* (London: Calder and Boyars, 1967), pp.161–64, p.161.
22. Samuel Beckett, quoted by Brian H. Finney, in *Since How It Is*, p.9; and by Richard L. Admussen, in *The Samuel Beckett Manuscripts*, p.22.
23. Samuel Beckett, *Act Without Words II* (1959), *Collected Shorter Plays*, p.49.
24. Samuel Beckett, quoted by Brian H. Finney, in *Since How It Is*, p.11.
25. Robert Lax, letter to Nicholas Zurbrugg of 16 September 1984.

Conclusion:
"not life/necessarily" — Beckett's 'Shades'

1. Robert Lax, letter to Nicholas Zurbrugg of 16 September 1984.
2. The narrator of *Company* self-consciously refers to 'Another trait' and 'Another trait', *Company*, p.20. Henceforth, all subsequent page references to *Company* appear as unidentified page numbers.
3. Publisher's blurb on the back cover of *Signature Anthology*, No.20 (London: Calder and Boyars, 1975); Vivian Mercier, *Beckett/Beckett* (New York: Oxford University Press, 1979), p.232; John Pilling, 'The Significance of Beckett's *Still*', *Essays in Criticism*, XXVIII, No.2 (April 1978), 153.
4. All page references to Beckett's *Still* appear as unidentified page numbers.
5. Samuel Beckett, *Ping*, in *No's Knife, Collected Shorter Prose 1945–1966* (London: Calder and Boyars, 1967), p.167.
6. Samuel Beckett, *Sounds*, a text of May 1973, *Essays in Criticism*, XXVIII, No.2 (April 1978), p.156.
7. Samuel Beckett, 'The End', *No's Knife, Collected Shorter Prose 1945–1966* (London: Calder and Boyars, 1967), pp.43–67, p.46. Andrew Walker draws attention to this correspondence in a letter to the editor, *Times Literary Supplement*, No.4035, 25 July 1980, 845. Another variant of this incident occurs in *Malone Dies*, when Malone relates: 'One day we walking along the road ... I said, The sky is further away than you think, is it not, mama? I was without malice, I was simply thinking of all the leagues that separated me from it. She replied, to me her son, It is precisely as far away as it appears to be. She was right. But at the time I was aghast.' (*Malone Dies*, 269–70).

8. Linda Ben-Zvi offers a slightly different interpretation of this 'trembling shade', in 'Fritz Mauthner for Company', *Journal of Beckett Studies*, No.9 (1983), 65-88, suggesting that the word 'trembling' indicates 'the impossibility of totally capturing the desired state of objectivity' (87) in which memories will no longer be painful.
9. James Joyce, *Dubliners*, p.219.
10. Gertrude Stein, 'They may be said to be ready', collected in Gertrude Stein, *Stanzas in meditation and other poems*, with a preface by Donald Sutherland (New Haven: Yale University Press, 1956), pp.236–37, p.237.
11. Samuel Beckett, 'PSS', a three-poem sequence accompanied by a note to Michael Horovitz from Beckett dated '17.9.81', describing these lines as 'recent croaks', in *New Departures*, No.14 (1982), 64.
12. Marjorie Perloff discusses similar aspects of the 'prose-verse ambiguity' of *Ill seen ill said* in 'Between Verse and Prose: Beckett and the New Poetry', *Critical Enquiry*, 9 (December 1982), 415–33, 416. A comprehensive analysis of the linguistic features of Beckett's 'prose-verse' appears in Wanda Avila's 'The Poem Within the Play in Beckett's *Embers*', *Language and Style*, 17, No.3 (Summer 1984), 193–205.
13. All subsequent references to *Ill seen ill said* appear as unidentified page references.
14. David Read, 'Beckett's Search for Unseeable and Unmakeable: *Company* and *Ill Seen Ill Said*, *Modern Fiction Studies*, 29, No.1 (Spring 1983), 111–25, 113, and Marjorie Perloff, 'Between Verse and Prose', 419. Both assume that 'she' is still alive. On the contrary, as the narrator specifies, 'she' is no longer 'of this world' (42).
15. David Read, 'Beckett's Search for Unseeable and Unmakeable', discusses the trembling objects in *Ill seen ill said* somewhat more literally, in terms of their analogies with 'the tremulous quality' (115) in the work of Beckett's friend, the artist Avigdor Arikha.
16. Save where inappropriate, all subsequent page references to *Worstward Ho* appear as unidentified page references.
17. Samuel Beckett, 'The Expelled', collected in Samuel Beckett, *No's Knife*, pp.9–24, p.9.
18. Clarac and Sandre date these notes from some time after 1898 (*CSB*, 968). Proust subsequently extends the notion of 'penetrating' one's own soul into the concept of the 'interpenetration of souls' (III.386).
19. Samuel Beckett made reference to the workings of the 'compassionate hand' in *Nacht und Träume* in conversation with Nicholas Zurbrugg, Paris, 17 January 1987.
20. Samuel Beckett, *Nacht und Träume*, in *Collected Shorter Plays*, pp.305–306.
21. Samuel Beckett, 'La Peinture des Van Velde', 354.

SELECT BIBLIOGRAPHY

The following books and articles should prove helpful as introductions to the work of Samuel Beckett and Marcel Proust.

Anon (ed.), *As no other dare fail: for Samuel Beckett on his Eightieth Birthday* (London: John Calder, 1986)

James Acheson, 'Beckett, Proust and Schopenhauer', *Contemporary Literature*, XIX, No. 2 (Spring 1978), 165–79.

James Acheson and Kateryna Arthur (eds.), *Beckett's Later Fiction and Drama: Texts for Company* (London: Macmillan, 1987)

Céleste Albaret, *Monsieur Proust: Souvenirs receuillis par Georges Belemont* (Paris: Robert Laffont, 1973)

Deirdre Bair, *Samuel Beckett: A biography* (New York: Harcourt Brace Jovanovich, 1978)

Roland Barthes, *Camera Lucida: Reflections on Photography*, translated by Richard Howard (New York: Hill and Wang, 1981)

Linda Ben-Zvi, 'Fritz Mauthner for Company', *Journal of Beckett Studies*, No. 9 (1983), 65–88.

Jacques Bersani, *Les critiques de notre temps et Proust* (Paris: Garnier, 1971)

Leo Bersani, *Marcel Proust: The Fictions of Life and of Art* (New York: Oxford University Press, 1972)

Pierre Chabert (ed.), Beckett issue of *Revue d'Esthétique* (hors série: Paris, 1986)

Richard N. Coe, *Beckett* (Edinburgh: Oliver and Boyd, 1964)

Ernst Robert Curtius, *Marcel Proust*, translated into French from the German by Armand Pierhal (Paris: Editions de la Revue Nouvelle, 1929)

Gilles Deleuze, *Proust et les signes* (Paris: Presses Universitaires de la France, 1964)

Raymond Federman and John Fletcher, *Samuel Beckett: His Works and his Critics* (Berkeley and Los Angeles: University of California Press, 1970)

Beryl S. Fletcher, John Fletcher, Barry Smith and Walter Bachem, *A Student's Guide to the Plays of Samuel Beckett* (London: Faber and Faber, 1978

John Fletcher, *The Novels of Samuel Beckett* (London: Chatto and Windus, 1964)

Melvin J. Friedman (ed.), *Samuel Beckett Now* (Chicago: University of Chicago Press, 1970)

Melvin J. Friedman, 'The Novels of Samuel Beckett: An Amalgam of Joyce and Proust', *Comparative Literature*, XII, No. 1 (Winter 1960), 47–58

S.E. Gontarski, *The Intent of Undoing in Samuel Beckett's Dramatic Texts* (Bloomington: Indiana University Press, 1985)

Lawrence Graver and Raymond Federman (eds.), *Samuel Beckett: The Critical Heritage* (London: Routledge and Kegan Paul, 1979)

Lawrence E. Harvey, *Samuel Beckett, Poet and Critic* (Princeton, N.J.: Princeton University Press, 1970)

E.F.N. Jephcott, *Proust and Rilke: The Literature of Expanded Consciousness* (London: Chatto and Windus, 1972)

Charles Juliet, *Recontre avec Beckett* (Montpellier: Editions Fata Morgana, 1986)

Frank Kermode, 'Beckett, Snow and Pure Poverty', *Encounter*, XV, No.82 (July 1960), 73–7

Harry Levin, *The Gates of Horn: A Study of Five French Realists* (New York: Oxford University Press, 1963)

Charles R. Lyons, *Samuel Beckett* (London: Macmillan, 1983)

Jeffrey Mehlman, *A Structural Study of Autobiography: Proust, Leiris, Sartre, Levi-Strauss* (Ithaca: Cornell University Press, 1974)

Marjorie Perloff, 'Between Verse and Prose: Beckett and the New Poetry', *Critical Enquiry*, 9 (December 1982), 415–33.

John Pilling, 'Beckett's *Proust*', *Journal of Beckett Studies*, No. 1 (Winter 1976), 8–29.

Jean-François Revel, *Sur Proust* (Paris: Juilliard, 1960)

Alan Rodway, 'There's a Hole in Your Beckett', *Encounter*, XLII, No. 2 (February 1974), 49–53

Steven J. Rosen, *Samuel Beckett and the Pessimistic Tradition* (New Brunswick, N.J.: Rutgers University Press, 1976)

Roger Shattuck, *Proust* (Glasgow: Fontana, 1974)

George Stambolian, *Marcel Proust and the Creative Encounter* (Chicago: University of Chicago Press, 1972)

Clas Zilliacus, *Beckett and Broadcasting: A Study of the Works of Samuel Beckett for and in Radio and Television* (Abo: Abo Akademi, 1976)

Nicholas Zurbrugg, 'Beyond Beckett: Reckless Writing and the Concept of the Avant-Garde within Post-Modern Literature', *Yearbook of Comparative and General Literature*, No. 30 (1981), 37–56.

Nicholas Zurbrugg, 'Beckett, Proust, Burroughs, and the perils of Image Warfare', in Pierre Astier, Morris Beja and S.E. Gontarski (eds), *Samuel Beckett: Humanistic Perspectives* (Ohio: University of Ohio Press, 1982), pp. 172–87.

Nicholas Zurbrugg (ed.), Beckett issue of *The Review of Contemporary Fiction*, Vol. 7, No. 2 (Summer 1987).

INDEX

INDEX

Index Section Two: References to Beckett's writings by title

INDEX